DATE DUE

Our Fritz

EMPEROR FREDERICK III AND
THE POLITICAL CULTURE OF IMPERIAL GERMANY

FRANK LORENZ MÜLLER

HARVARD UNIVERSITY PRESS
Cambridge, Massachusetts, and London, England   2011

Library of Congress Cataloging-in-Publication Data

Müller, Frank Lorenz, 1970–
  Our Fritz : Emperor Frederick III and the political culture of imperial
Germany / Frank Lorenz Müller.
    p. cm.
  Includes bibliographical references and index.
  ISBN 978-0-674-04838-6 (alk. paper)
  1. Frederick III, German Emperor, 1831–1888. 2. Frederick III, German
Emperor, 1831–1888—Public opinion. 3. Germany—Kings and rulers—
Biography. 4. Emperors—Germany—Biography. 5. Princes—Germany—
Biography. 6. Prussia (Germany)—Kings and rulers—Biography. 7. Political
culture—Germany—History. 8. Memorialization—Germany—History.
9. Germany—Politics and government—1871–1918. 10. Germany—History—
Frederick III, 1888. I. Title.
  DD224.M79 2011
  943.08'4092—dc22
  [B]   2011000049

für Hugo und Nicholas

Contents

The Hohenzollern Monarchs (1640–1918)

Frederick William I ("The Great Elector"), 1620–1688
Elector of Brandenburg, 1640–1688
∞ Louise Henrietta of Nassau

|

Frederick III/I, 1657–1713
Elector of Brandenburg, 1688–1713; King in Prussia, 1701–1713
∞ Sophie Charlotte of Hanover

|

Frederick William I, 1688–1740
King in Prussia, 1713–1740
∞ Sophie Dorothea of Great Britain

Frederick II ("the Great"), 1712–1786
King of Prussia, 1740–1786
∞ Elisabeth of Brunswick-Wolfenbüttel

Prince August William, 1722–1758
∞ Louise of Brunswick-Wolfenbüttel

|

Frederick William II, 1744–1797
King of Prussia, 1786–1797
∞ Friederike of Hessen-Darmstadt

|

Frederick William III, 1770–1840
King of Prussia, 1797–1840
∞ Louise of Mecklenburg-Strelitz

Frederick William IV, 1795–1861
King of Prussia, 1840–1861
∞ Elisabeth of Bavaria

William I, 1797–1888
Prince-Regent, 1858–1861; King of Prussia,
1861–1888; German Emperor, 1871–1888
∞ Augusta of Saxe-Weimar

|

Frederick III, 1831–1888
King of Prussia and German Emperor, 1888
∞ Victoria of Great Britain

|

William II, 1859–1941
King of Prussia and German Emperor,
1888–1918
∞ Auguste of Schleswig-Holstein

Our Fritz

Introduction

On 15 June 1888, a mere ninety-nine days after he had ascended the throne, Frederick III, king of Prussia and German emperor, succumbed to throat cancer. He was in his fifty-seventh year and had already been a dying man when he succeeded his nonagenarian father, Emperor William I, on 9 March. Ever since the spring of 1887, when it became known that the heir to the throne was suffering from a mysterious illness, the tragic story of the doomed crown prince who turned into a moribund emperor had held the public spellbound. Both in Germany and abroad, people were gripped by the tale of a cruel fate nobly borne by a much-loved public figure. For more than two decades, the crown prince had been a celebrated national hero. He had enjoyed almost unparalleled popularity, not just in Prussia but across the whole of Germany and beyond. For some, the thought of his agony and impending death was simply unbearable. It was reported that a number of grief-stricken individuals were prepared to sacrifice themselves, offering their own healthy larynxes as potential transplants for the ailing emperor.[1]

Frederick's misery attracted attention not only as a human tragedy but also because of its enormous political importance. By the time of his death, the German Reich had established itself as the single most powerful state on the European continent. Even those unaffected by Frederick's personal plight could not, therefore, afford to ignore the question of who was holding the reins of this powerful newcomer. With the benefit of hindsight, the events of 1888 have acquired an even more momentous appearance. They have "left behind a myth that endures to this day"; as a recent master narrative of German history explains, there is "the widespread opinion that Emperor Frederick, had he lived and ruled longer, would have given a different course to German history—a liberal turn on the domestic front, and externally an understanding with England."[2] Instead of achieving these desirable outcomes during the reign of a peaceful, liberal monarch closely in touch with the political and social developments of the West, the argument goes, Germany embarked on a disastrous journey. The Golden Legend of the enlightened Emperor Frederick and the idyllic future he would have delivered is contrasted with the Black Legend of Emperor William II, Frederick III's illiberal, militaristic, and aggressive son, and of a Reich whose baneful tendencies he allegedly epitomized and reinforced. A direct line is thus drawn, which connects the early demise of the purportedly liberal emperor with the First World War and the even greater catastrophes that followed. The present work confronts some of the legends underpinning this narrative with a more realistic appraisal. It explores both the roots of these myths and the reasons for their prominence and longevity.

The strength of the Prusso-German Reich, which Frederick had helped to found in 1870–1871, was a novelty in international affairs. Previously, there had always been something precarious about Prussia's status as one of Europe's great powers. Before the middle of the eighteenth century, the lands of the Prussian king had been a collection of heterogeneous territories scattered across much of Northern Europe and lacking defendable borders. The kingdom was sparsely populated and almost devoid of natural resources. Its sudden rise under King Frederick II, known as Frederick the Great (1740–1786), who emerged bloodied but unbowed from a series of wars against varying combinations of great powers, struck contemporaries as nothing short of miraculous. A mere two decades after Frederick II's death, though, Prussia stood at the verge of total destruction. Having suffered a devastating defeat at the hands of Napoleon in 1806, the country limped on as a truncated and occupied satellite of the French emperor. Seven years later, however, Prussia had revitalized itself by committing to a process of modernizing reforms. As remnants of France's defeated Grande Armée were retreating from Russia in 1813, the kingdom joined the anti-Napoleonic coalition and played a crucial part in securing the allies' eventual victory in 1814–1815.

The campaigns of 1813–1815 and the European settlement nego-tiated at the Congress of Vienna did not only confirm Prussia's return to great power status; these years also changed the relationship be-tween Prussia and Germany. During the fight against Napoleon, lead-ing Prussian statesmen, soldiers, and even King Frederick William III (1797–1840) had used the vocabulary and arguments of German nationalism to rally the people. In so doing, they helped to turn the national idea into a powerful political force that resonated strongly amongst the growing middle classes. Moreover, the territorial changes agreed to at Vienna turned parts of the Rhineland, Westphalia, and a large portion of Saxony into Prussian provinces. The kingdom's geopolitical centre of gravity was now unquestionably German. As a further result of these developments, Prussia soon found itself locked into a Janus-faced relationship with the other German great power, the Austrian Empire. On the one hand, the two states were competi-tors who vied for predominance within the German Confederation, a league of more than thirty states that was founded in 1815. On the other hand, Prussia and Austria were partners in a political project dedicated to suppressing revolutionary unrest through the robust application of the principles of monarchical government.

By committing to this authoritarian policy and terminating its pro-gramme of internal reforms, the Prussian government frustrated those whose zeal for liberal change and a more closely united Germany had been fired up during the wars against Napoleonic France. Neither King Frederick William III, who never honoured his promises to grant a constitution, nor his son, King Frederick William IV (1840–1861), succeeded in squaring the circle of the kingdom's political dilemma: even though Austria was a bitter rival within the German arena, the conservatism of Prussia's monarchical forces pushed the country to-ward a close relationship with the Habsburgs' reactionary empire. This also made it hard for decision makers in Berlin to accommodate, let alone utilize, the growing forces of political opposition. At the Prussian level, liberals were calling for the kingdom to be transformed into a constitutional monarchy with guaranteed civil liberties and an elected legislature. For Germany as a whole, the national move-ment demanded greater unity and a forceful pursuit of the nation's interests.

The revolution of 1848–1849 eventually dragged Prussia into the constitutional age. The settlement conceded in December 1848 lim-ited the king's power by establishing a parliament to pass legislation and authorise state expenditure. Royal control of the executive and especially the military remained almost undiminished, though, and the attempt to use Austria's temporary paralysis to establish Prussia's hegemony in Germany failed. After the counterrevolutionary victory, King Frederick William IV withdrew into a shell of authoritarian rigidity at home and indecisive obsequiousness toward Russia and Austria abroad.

Soon Prussia was once again perceived as slipping from its marginal position as a great power. As a neutral country of seemingly little consequence, it was effectively excluded from the Congress of Paris, where the settlement to end the Crimean War was thrashed out in 1856. The result of the policy pursued in Berlin, the London *Times* observed in October 1855, "has been twofold; it has completely degraded Prussia from the rank of a first-rate power, making her presence in the councils of Europe a mere fraud. . . . The second effect is, unless we be much mistaken, to establish a wide and impassable breach between the court and people of Prussia." This, the paper suggested, made it probable that the current illiberal system would soon be swept away by revolution.[3]

London's venerable daily decided to lay into Prussia's royal family, the Hohenzollerns, at news of the engagement between the heir to the Prussian throne and Queen Victoria's eldest daughter. Prince Frederick William, the *Times* insisted, was simply unworthy of Princess Victoria. Weak, despotic, and doomed, Prussia could only become an embarrassing entanglement for Britain and its royal family. Thirty-three years later, the man who had been scoffed at as a Prussian prince in 1855 died as the German emperor Frederick III. A remarkable transformation had taken place by then. To mark the sad occasion, William Henry Smith, the Leader of the House, rose in the British parliament in June 1888 and proposed that a message of condolence be conveyed. "It was scarcely a year ago," Smith recalled, "that the Crown Prince of Germany received the cordial and hearty welcome of this country, as the son-in-law of the Queen, and the heir to the throne of a great and friendly empire."[4] The very different tenor of Smith's speech reflected the extent to which the political complexion of Europe had been revolutionized since the 1850s.

Between 1862 and 1871, a combination of Otto von Bismarck's brilliant statecraft and military victories over Denmark, Austria, and France had brought about the foundation of the German Reich. Presided over by the Prussian king in his new capacity as German emperor, this constitutional federal state comprised all of non-Austrian

Germany. A series of carefully crafted compromises reconciled the dominant power of the kingdom of Prussia with the other member states' demands for diversity, local autonomy, and respect for their own traditions. A similar balance was struck by limiting the power of the Reichstag—the all-German parliament elected on the basis of universal, equal male franchise—vis-à-vis the Prussian tradition of strong monarchical government. Although crucial for passing legislation and approving the budget, the Reichstag had no control over the imperial chancellor, whose exercise of governmental power depended solely on the emperor. A way had thus been found to reconcile the demands of German nationalism and even liberalism with the interests of the Prussian crown. The latter had harnessed the energy of these ideologies in pursuit of the political and military conquest of German unity under its own leadership.

As would be expected from the heir to the Prussian throne, Frederick William's entire life was woven into this story. He was born in 1831, in the thirty-fourth year of the reign of his grandfather. King Frederick William III had long since ended the progressive dynamism of Prussia's reform era and was now presiding over the kingdom's integration into the conservative camp. Prussia's political alignment was symbolized by the readiness of the emperors of Russia and Austria to stand as the young prince's highest-ranking godfathers. As an adolescent, Prince Frederick William was exposed to the conservatism of the Prussian court and its military culture; he also encountered—mainly through his mother—the ideas of a moderate liberalism. Together with his boyhood friends, the prince sang the patriotic songs through which the national movement disseminated its ideas. As a seventeen-year-old, he witnessed Berlin's revolutionary events of 1848 firsthand. He heard bullets whizzing past as he watched troops attacking the revolutionaries whose actions struck him as traitorous. Frederick William nevertheless endorsed the principle of constitutional government. A firm supporter of the liberal thaw that accompanied the beginning of his father's regency in 1858, Crown Prince Frederick William was thrown into a quandary when the new king abruptly changed course. Faced with a parliament whose majority opposed his plans for military reform, King William I decided to impose his will by adopting a policy of authoritarian and extraconstitutional measures.

By the end of 1862, all the key individuals and forces were in play that would eventually deliver Prussia's mastery in Germany and dominate Frederick William's political life: King William I, his father, who remained committed to strengthening Prussia's military might and safeguarding the monarch's prerogatives; Otto von Bismarck, his father's chief minister, who shared the king's monarchical outlook but was prepared to cooperate with the forces of liberalism and nationalism when it suited Prussia's interests; and a confident liberal-national movement whose opposition to King William and Bismarck was somewhat qualified by its hope that Prussia might successfully place itself at the helm of the quest for national unity. For the crown prince, who also subscribed to constitutional beliefs while yearning for Prussian aggrandizement and German unity, this tension was heightened by a duty of obedience to his father and the determined liberalism of his English wife.

Having received a sharp rebuke for his only public criticism of the king's government, though, Frederick William withdrew into a sullen passivity from which he was only roused when summoned to join the campaigns during the Wars of German Unification in 1864, 1866, and 1870–1871, which brought Prussia victories over Denmark, Austria, and France. Celebrated as a military hero and full of enthusiasm for the newly founded German Reich, the crown prince returned from the field to a life of enforced inaction. Since his father and Chancellor Bismarck doubted the crown prince's political reliability and denied him any real power, Frederick William was to spend another seventeen increasingly depressing years waiting for the throne. At the time, biology appeared to be on his side. William I was almost seventy-four years old when the Reich was founded in 1871 and his son's reign seemed imminent. Planning for the future intensified after the emperor entered his ninth decade in 1877. A great opportunity to effect liberal change for some, a hazardous crisis for others, Frederick William's succession became a pivotal issue in the politics of the Reich. The tragic circumstances under which the long-anticipated event finally occurred in March 1888 were not only cruelly ironic but also contributed significantly to turning the story of Emperor Frederick III's life and death into the stuff of legend.

This is a book about Frederick and the roles he played within the state, politics, and society of Prussia and the Reich. It is, above all, a biographical study that seeks to tell the story of a man who lived an extraordinary life through extraordinary times and surrounded by extraordinary people. As such, it is interested in Frederick as a human being and in his relationships as a son, fiancé, husband, son-in-law, and father. It explores what shaped him and how he affected others. It wants to convey an impression of Frederick's strengths and weaknesses, joys and sorrows, fears and desires. The boy born on 18 October 1831 was not a private individual, though. He was born a future monarch, and this inevitably made him a figure of great political significance with a highly public profile. Because of this and in order to probe the claim that his reign would have made a dramatic difference, his political beliefs and aspirations require careful investigation. Frederick's life coincided with the emergence of mass politics and the early development of the modern media system. Attention must therefore be paid to the ways in which the crown prince and emperor was portrayed, as well as to his perception by both contemporary and later audiences. As heir to a crown endowed with real power, Frederick embodied the hopes and fears that others projected onto his future reign. These expectations and the political manoeuvres that resulted from them—as well as those triggered by his desperate weakness on the throne—are also analysed. Finally, this book examines Frederick's political life after death: the ways in which his name and life story were remembered, commemorated, fashioned into myth, and utilized.

The present work pursues two concentric aims. Besides its biographical remit, it also hopes to add to our understanding of the Hohenzollern monarchy within the politics and society of nineteenth-century Prussia and Germany. Using the life lived, roles played, and images generated by Crown Prince Frederick William and Emperor Frederick III as a prism, it seeks to throw light on issues central to the operation of the Hohenzollerns' monarchical system. These include the manner in which the dynasty was presented to the various relevant publics with their different political and cultural tastes, as well as the various media employed to do this; succession as a recurring constellation generating political instability; memory, myth-making, and a dynastic narrative adding up to a monarchical politics of memory—that is, to a conscious political effort to control the accepted version of the past; and the contingent factors determining the power balance between monarchical figures and their environment.

In addressing these topics, this study wants to explore more than a narrowly defined political sphere. Looking beyond the court, the government, and the state proper, it also intends to illuminate facets of Germany's wider "political culture." This involves an appreciation not only of the "system of empirical beliefs, expressive symbols, and values, which defines the situation in which political action takes place," but also of the institutions and individual agents that sustained and communicated this system in nineteenth-century Prussia and Germany.[5] The background against which all of this unfolded was the process of a fundamental political mobilization of Germany's society that took place within the existing authoritarian state. This transition from a politics of the notables to mass politics was driven and shaped but also hampered by a combination of forces. The emergence of a political mass market within which a number of actors had to compete was facilitated by growing literacy and the formation of modern political parties and pressure groups, as well as by the increasing reach and power of the print media. Some of the crucial developments that brought about the transformation of Prussia-Germany's political culture were implemented from above and proved the general applicability of the law of unintended consequences. Basing the parliament of the German Reich on universal and equal male suffrage, for instance, had been part of Bismarck's plan for defeating the liberal challenge. Rather than overcoming his adversaries in tightly managed elections and with the help of a strong popular conservatism, however, this step accelerated and amplified the politicization of German society. Ultimately, the authoritarian state proved unequal to the task of mastering and harnessing the vibrancy and mobilization of Germany's politicized society.[6]

This failure was not caused by a want of trying, though, and the state's resources were formidable. Together, the crown and the government controlled the civil service, the police, and the military. The chancellor could effectively dissolve parliament at a time of his choosing and schedule elections to coincide with international or domestic crises carefully whipped up to serve his own purposes. More often than not this was helped by Bismarck's ability to bully, cajole, and bribe sections of the press. Even though they were not directly managed from above, a number of wider cultural and political phenomena also strengthened the government's hand. The Wars of German Unification and the foundation of the Reich spawned a pervasive feeling of national pride and a sentiment of popular royalism. Since the aged emperor and the crown prince were widely venerated, opposition to William I's government could easily be attacked as unpatriotic. Such feelings dovetailed neatly with the high regard in which the armed forces were held and the militarization of many aspects of German life. Certain forms of public ceremonial—such as monarchical anniversaries and birthdays, the celebration and commemoration of battlefield victories and patriotic worthies, or military parades—further consolidated an authoritarian culture of politics.[7]

Impressive though it was, this panoply of the conservative state did not manage to defend the status quo against the dynamics of change. On the one hand, there was a slow but steady advance of the Reich at the expense of its federal components, the gradual emergence of an all-German national identity that first existed alongside the Germans' loyalty toward their particular home state—such as Bavaria, Prussia, or Saxony—but eventually assumed a dominant position. Just as Bismarck had planned, the Reich remained palpably federal, with the symbols of its central element—above all, the figure of the emperor—never eclipsing those of the separate German states, but flourishing alongside them. By the time of Emperor Frederick's death in 1888, the formation of the German nation-state was more or less complete and a process of further imperial centralization was firmly entrenched. On the other hand, this form of nation-state building was closely intertwined with the expansion and restructuring of Germany's political space. The active involvement of ever more Germans in the political process—through their membership in parties, associations, trade unions, and pressure groups; as consumers of an increasingly diverse, confident, and politicized press; and, above all, through their participation in elections—amounted to a sea change in Germany's political culture. Encompassing tendencies toward more pluralist, participatory, and nonexclusionary forms of politics, it marked the beginning of a trajectory aimed at a process of fundamental democratization.[8]

Where controlling electoral politics and securing the results of ballots were concerned, Margaret Anderson concluded, the German government, operating as it did within a constitutional framework and bound by the rule of law, resembled not the imperious Caesar but Gulliver—securely tied down by a mass of Lilliputians. This is powerfully illustrated by the woeful outcomes of the two major domestic campaigns waged by Bismarck: the attempts to thwart the political fortunes first of German Catholicism and then of the "Socialist Workers' Party." Both groupings firmed up their milieux under pressure. As mass organisations, they also seized the opportunity offered to them by Germany's wide franchise. They used their successful performances at the ballot box to defend themselves against being stigmatized as outsiders and to demonstrate their resilience.[9] Once the strength of liberalism at the level of communal politics and the conspicuous success of the German bourgeoisie in the cultural, economic, and scholarly spheres are taken into account, the peculiarly heterogeneous quality of the Reich's political culture and the unreconciled juxtaposition of some of its key features are thrown into sharp relief. Imperial Germany remained an authoritarian state, Thomas Nipperdey concluded, but alongside it a confident bourgeois society gradually established itself.[10]

This book seeks to show that Emperor Frederick embodied much of this curious juxtaposition at the heart of the Reich's political culture and played an active part in many of its elements. He was knowledgeable about and eager to utilize the power of the media, but often did so for purposes of monarchical display and elevating the dynasty. He participated with genuine commitment in the culture of bourgeois life, yet subscribed to an exalted notion of the majesty of his imperial office. A passionate advocate of further growth of the Reich in Germany, Frederick was also determined to defend the key prerogatives of the Prussian crown. His liberalism combined a constant commitment to constitutional government with scepticism about the Reich's wide franchise, a shrill hostility to the exponents of Political Catholicism and Socialism, and ultimately the readiness to cooperate with Bismarck.

In order to embed Frederick's personality and life more effectively in their different contexts and meet the challenge of engaging with a biography—considerable stretches of which were characterized by inaction—this book offers its findings through a combination of chronology and thematic concerns. The first chapter examines three personal relationships that shaped Frederick's life: first, his relationship with his father, King and Emperor William I; second, his relationship with his wife, Victoria; and, finally, his relationship with the political titan that was Otto von Bismarck. The second chapter explores Frederick's political ideas and convictions, especially the nature of his liberalism, his attitude toward German nationalism, and his notions of empire. The crown prince's public image and the popularity it generated are investigated in the third chapter. Chapter 4 is dedicated to the tactical moves and party political machinations that were triggered by the anticipation of his accession. Frederick's fatal illness and the events of his short reign are the topics of the fifth chapter. The sixth and final chapter analyses the struggle to define and control the emperor's posthumous myth.

The life of Emperor Frederick III was marked by uncommonly stark contrasts. An extremely popular and revered public figure, he commanded such affection that strangers offered their lives to save him, yet almost all of the people close to him—including his father and his eldest son—treated him with coldness and disregard. Expectations of the most momentous change were projected onto him for decades. But even though many anticipated his future rule either with confident hope or with dark foreboding, the heir to the throne never overcame his own vagueness and indecision to formulate a clear intention. As crown prince of Prussia and the German Reich and then as king and emperor, Frederick lived a life on the cusp of commanding extraordinary power, but it was weakness that emerged as the decisive feature of his existence. The attempt to account for these apparent contradictions leads to three recurring sets of factors: the personal qualities of the individuals involved; the legal and power-political framework that defined the position of the heir to the Prussian throne; and the wider political culture of nineteenth-century Germany. By being mindful of the interactions of these three factors, this book hopes to give an insight into the life and meaning of the man widely known as Our Fritz, as well as contribute to our understanding of the great adoration and harsh treatment he received both during his lifetime and beyond.

CHAPTER ONE

Shaping a Prince's Life

On 18 October 1831, a 101-gun salute thundered across Berlin to announce the good news to the inhabitants of the Prussian capital: Princess Augusta, the wife of Prince William of Prussia, had given birth to a healthy boy. The marriage of the crown prince, Prince William's elder brother, had remained childless for eight long years, but with the arrival of this infant, the future of the Hohenzollern dynasty once again seemed secure. The baby's grandfather, King Frederick William III of Prussia, immediately rushed to Potsdam's New Palace to welcome the boy who was destined to inherit his throne. That the kingdom's heir presumptive was born on such an auspicious day—the anniversary of the great victory over Napoleon at Leipzig in 1813—was widely noted and interpreted as a good omen. A few weeks later, in a grand ceremony, the young prince was christened Frederick William Nicholas Charles. The long list of his godparents—there were twenty-one sponsors that included the tsar of Russia, the emperor of Austria, the queen of the Netherlands, the Grand Duke of Saxe-Weimar, and the Grand Duke of Mecklenburg-Strelitz—illustrates how the lives of nineteenth-century royals were woven into networks of dynastic and political relationships far beyond their own personal concerns.

Every human life is shaped by the forces of nature and nurture, of individual will and happenstance. In addition to that, the personality and life of a man born to be the king of Prussia and German emperor was imprinted by other overlapping and intersecting influences:

dynasty, tradition, politics, and power. In the case of Prince Frederick William, these different forces were bundled together with particular intensity in three individuals whose relationships with him crucially shaped the life of the heir to the throne. The relationship with his father comprised all the emotional aspects of a close family link, but these were enveloped in and intensified by a context of dynastic hierarchy. Moreover, William's longevity, combined with the early incapacitation and death of his older brother, meant that for three decades Frederick William's father was also his sovereign. This added important elements of monarchical power and political disagreement to the relationship. In the end, the intrinsically problematic constellation of ruler and successor—whereby the son owes his prospects to his father's life, but their realisation to his death—emerged as a dominant factor in Frederick William's existence. His wife, Princess Victoria, and the couple's children gave the crown prince a rich and affectionate private life. This sanctuary was, however, a source of both solace and sorrow. Victoria's personality and reputation, as well as the nature of their marriage had a powerful political effect. It shaped Frederick William's own outlook and impacted on the role he played within the political process. The crown prince's relationship with Otto von Bismarck resembled that with his father in several ways, as periods of agreement and cooperation were mixed with conflict and ill-disguised resentment. Frederick William ultimately had to defer to the superior power commanded by Bismarck, who had been pivotal in creating the German Reich. The crown prince experienced the hurt Bismarck inflicted on him as different from that he associated with his father. It was not dulled by filial affection, by a sense of dynastic duty, or by the expectation that the antagonist would pass away in the foreseeable future.

Son and Heir: Frederick William and His Father

It appears to have been an unfortunate yet readily acknowledged tradition of the Hohenzollerns that the relationship between father and son—between the monarch and his successor—was fraught at best and borderline homicidal at worst. As King Frederick William I of Prussia slowly approached his death in 1740, power was palpably draining away from him and flooding toward his son, whose previous relationship with his father had been nothing short of disastrous. Contemplating the loss of dignity suffered by the dying monarch, the novelist Reinhold Schneider coined a bleak aphorism to capture this characteristic feature of the Prussian dynasty: "Kings are not fathers, and those who will be kings are not sons." When Emperor William II, the last Hohenzollern on the throne, read Schneider's novel in his Dutch exile, he agreed with the author's observation. His father also had been painfully aware of this phenomenon. "The unedifying tension between father and son, a tradition in the Prussian family, is now also established with us," Crown Prince Frederick William wrote to his wife in November 1883, after a bitter argument with his son.[1]

The weight of family tradition was certainly inauspicious. During the 1630s, Frederick William, the future Great Elector, had initially refused to return to his father's court from a stay in the Low Countries; when he finally arrived in Berlin, Elector George William treated him like a stranger, which fuelled the prince's fear that his father's ministers were planning to murder him. Once on the throne, Elector Frederick William in turn showed nothing but disrespect for his own son, who was so concerned about his safety at court that he relied on dubious potions to ward off the effects of a possible poisoning. Open conflict between Elector Frederick III—who succeeded his father in 1688 and elevated himself to the title King Frederick I in 1701—and his son Frederick William was only avoided by the father's conciliatory attitude toward his bloody-minded successor. The destructive and often hateful relationship between King Frederick William I and his son, the later King Frederick II, assumed the character of a Greek tragedy. The crown prince met his father's brutal authoritarianism with cynical subterfuge. His unsuccessful attempt to escape in 1730 triggered a crisis that saw him incarcerated, humiliated, and threatened with the death sentence. Eventually, Frederick was made to witness the execution of a close friend, as prison warders forced his face to the window overlooking the scaffold.[2]

Even though this atrocity marked the nadir of the desolate story of Prussia's royal fathers and sons, the Hohenzollerns' reputation as a dysfunctional family remained firmly in place. One hundred fifty years later, as the ninety-year-old emperor William I was failing while his son was dying of cancer and his grandson waited impatiently for his inheritance, the foreign office official and diarist Friedrich von Holstein could only shake his head at their behaviour. "Warmth of feeling is poorly developed in all three generations of the family," he noted on 12 February 1888.[3]

The relationship between Crown Prince Frederick William and his father did not reach the dramatic lows of fear and loathing that had been experienced by previous generations. There were even occasional expressions of mutual respect and affection. Yet these exceptions only proved the rule of the Hohenzollerns' unhappy tradition. Throughout his three decades at the helm of the Prussian kingdom and then of the German Reich, William I did not fully trust his son and doubted his abilities. The monarch actively sought to control the crown prince and curtailed his influence. Frederick William was acutely aware of his father's attitude, but he loyally accepted the inferiority of his own position as son and successor. His reluctance to challenge his father's authority prompted contemporaries to observe that he was "a better son than politician."[4] The crown prince did, however, grow increasingly bitter and resentful as his father's longevity was beginning to shade out his own prospects.

William I should have been well prepared to handle the relationship with his successor in a sensitive and constructive manner. After all, he had personally experienced the painful reality of what it could mean to occupy the junior position in a dynastic family. He was born in 1797, as the second son of Crown Prince Frederick William of Prussia and his wife, Louise. Less mentally agile than his older brother, Prince William demonstrated real talent for his predetermined military career. After the trauma of the Napoleonic wars and his mother's early death in 1810, he rapidly rose through the ranks. In 1820 he assumed command of the First Guards Division. Until this point, there was little to suggest that anything might seriously strain the prince's relationship with his father. That year, however, the king learned about his son's tender feelings for Princess Elisa Radziwill, a young Polish noblewoman. William considered Elisa "indispensable for [his] life's happiness," but her inadequate rank posed an insuperable obstacle to the union. The touching saga of "Wimpus," the lovestruck prince, and his lady fair dragged on for six agonising years. In 1826 the king eventually wrote to his son to forbid the relationship. The prince obeyed. "In pious humility and subordination I will bear a fate that the heavens impose on me," he replied. The cut was deep. Thirty years later, William still listed his first great love amongst the most important events of his life. He also complied with his father's wish that he should find a suitable spouse and, in 1829, he dutifully married Princess Augusta of Saxe-Weimar.[5]

Prince William proved less deferential in his capacity as heir to his childless brother's throne. After the death of his father in 1840, he assumed a far more powerful role, chairing the council of ministers and the council of state, as well as continuing to serve as the army's most senior general. Reluctant to support even the limited constitutional changes his brother was introducing in the 1840s, Prince William became increasingly unpopular. His palace was specifically attacked by the crowd in the course of Berlin's 1847 bread riot. During the revolution of 1848, William was reviled as the "Shrapnel Prince" because he was known to have advocated the ruthless use of military force. When Frederick William IV decided to pull back the troops from the capital rather than continue the fight against the revolutionaries, William reacted with an outburst. "Up until now I have known that you are a babbler," he screamed at the king, "but not that you are a coward. One cannot serve you with honour any more!" Fredrick William IV ordered his brother to leave the country for a while to avoid the fury of the crowd, and although William returned to lead the Prussian military in their defeat of the revolutionary forces in 1849, the relationship between the brothers remained strained. In the 1850s William, whose politics had meanwhile become more moderate, attacked the course of Prussia's right-wing government. When he learned in May 1854 that his confidant, Eduard von Bonin, had been removed from the position of minister of war, he sent the king an unusually brusque letter. William demanded Bonin's reinstatement and threatened his brother with a public gesture of protest. The king ignored his advisers' suggestion to take stern legal action against the rebellious heir and simply ordered him to take a four-week holiday. Slapped down and outmanoeuvred, William spent the remaining years until the beginning of his regency focused on his military duties.[6]

The first three decades of the relationship between Prince William and his son may have raised hopes that the Hohenzollern family's bleak tradition had been broken. There was nothing in these years to suggest that father and son would ever encounter serious disagreement. Frederick William was born just over two years after William and Augusta's wedding and, seven years later, the family was completed by the arrival of the couple's second child, Louise. Alongside the education Frederick William received from civilian tutors, he also underwent the military training considered crucial for a Prussian prince. He acquitted himself well. Many contemporary accounts describe Prince William's pride when, in March 1839, his seven-year-old son, wearing the uniform of the Stettin Guard Landwehr Regiment and standing correctly to attention, delighted his father with a full military report. Two years later, Frederick William was commissioned as a second lieutenant; in 1849 he was promoted to first lieutenant and began his active military service. When Prince William fled revolutionary Berlin in 1848, his son sent him letters full of warmth and affection. "I hope to God," the young man wrote on 24 March, "that he may give you a happy and safe journey and that we will see each other again after a short separation and in a happier mood. I have not stopped thinking of you." Four weeks later, Frederick William found it "almost impossible to convey to you all the proofs of attachment and love on the part of the officers, which I come across daily. Everyone asks after you and is so happy when I tell them about you."[7]

This untroubled relationship between father and son continued throughout Frederick William's early adulthood. William and Augusta's household at Koblenz became the political hub of the moderately liberal Wochenblatt Party, and their son, who was a student at nearby Bonn University from 1849 to 1852, often visited his parents. William and Augusta happily welcomed the idea of introducing the young prince to Princess Victoria, the eldest daughter of Queen Victoria and Prince Albert. With the engagement of Frederick William and Victoria in 1855, family bonds reinforced the dismay with which both sets of parents and the young couple viewed the ultra-conservative Russophile policy pursued by the king's government in Berlin. In January 1858, Prince William attended his son's wedding in London. Nine months later, after a lengthy struggle with the conservative clique controlling the Prussian government, William became prince regent and assumed the full monarchical powers which his gravely ill brother had been forced to relinquish.

Initially at least, the regency led to an even closer relationship between father and son. The prince regent's assumption of power and the dismissal of the conservative ministry headed by Otto von Manteuffel were perceived as heralding a "New Era" in Prussian politics. There were widespread and somewhat exaggerated hopes for more liberty in Prussia's domestic affairs and progress toward Germany's national unity. From the start, Prince Frederick William was actively involved in the regency. On 8 November 1858, William introduced his newly appointed ministry to his son and also invited him to attend the meetings of the council of ministers. Frederick William was delighted by the confidence the prince regent placed in him. "I experienced endless happiness in the great trust, with which my father inducted me into all the affairs during his preparation for the regency as well as ever since and without interruption," he wrote in January 1859.[8]

The intergenerational honeymoon lasted for more than a year, bolstered by the son's firm support of his father's key project, a programme of military reforms. For Frederick William, monarchical loyalty dictated that the regent's proposals should be accepted unaltered. He shared his father's annoyance at the Prussian parliament's reluctance to endorse them. In June 1860 William publicly rewarded his son's reliability by appointing him colonel-in-chief of the First Infantry Regiment. "What joy and honour," Frederick William noted in his diary. Unqualified support and devotion to his father were still the hallmarks of a letter in which the crown prince considered his father's reign half a year later. "Highly honoured and respected both at home and abroad he ascends the throne," he wrote to a former tutor in February 1861, a few weeks after the death of the ailing King Frederick William IV had ended the regency. The crown prince went on to praise his father's rebuilding of the Prussian army, as well as the new king's justice, honesty, and conscientiousness. "May God help me," he concluded, "to act as a son deserving of such a father and to let him find in me the support that I so long to be."[9]

In the absence of any real bones of contention before 1861, the early relationship between Frederick William and his parents had been dimmed only by emotional issues. The son seems to have found his parents somewhat distant. He was also painfully aware of the tensions between his father and mother. Headstrong, intelligent, and accustomed to the cultural richness of Weimar but with a penchant for courtly grandeur and more than a hint of haughtiness, Princess Augusta had not found it easy to settle into life in the austere environment that was the Prussian court. Prince William resented having to cope with his young wife's superior intellect and acute critical faculty. This often led to stormy scenes. "Unfortunately Mama has increasingly made it her habit to raise strong objections to many of my father's actions. This, along with her delicate state of health, has made my infrequent evenings alone with my parents very unpleasant," Frederick William confessed to his fiancée in December 1857. "Since I no longer have the desire to play the role of mediator between the two of them, I often find myself in the most embarrassing of situations." In 1861 Princess Victoria informed her mother that her husband had never really experienced the "confiding and fearless love of a child to a parent" and had never looked to his parents as his best friends. Indeed, in 1863 Frederick William was surprised that a letter he received from his father was written "in a fatherly affectionate way, as has rarely been his style."[10]

These underlying psychological fault lines in the relationship between father and son assumed a greatly amplified importance when the two men found themselves locked into political disagreement. The crisis that ended the halcyon days of the New Era and threw Prussia into a constitutional conflict acted as a powerful catalyst in the deterioration of their relationship. The king reacted with outrage when the liberal-dominated lower house of parliament stubbornly opposed his military reforms, and soon the monarch turned away from the moderate liberalism of the beginning of his regency. He accused all but the most conservative of his ministers of mishandling the issue and insisted dogmatically on the full implementation of his scheme, including the controversial three-year term of conscription.

Frederick William supported his father's plan to strengthen Prussia's military wholeheartedly and publicly. When the newly created regiments were ceremoniously presented with their colours in January 1861, the crown prince commanded the assembled troops and experienced the occasion as an "unforgettably beautiful celebration." He did, however, strongly disagree with the king's alarmist reading of the political situation. "You will know," Frederick William wrote to his father-in-law in April 1861, "that Papa can unfortunately not free himself from those black thoughts which see revolution everywhere and frequently ascribes levelling intentions to our ministers." Ahead of the elections in December 1861, the crown prince sent his father a long letter urging him not to replace the ministry with a more conservative one in order to avoid accusations that he was reverting to reactionary politics.[11]

The decisive liberal victory in these elections led to a marked escalation of the political crisis. The king now believed he had to prepare for the worst; on 16 January 1862, two days after the first meeting of the new parliament, he signed secret orders organising the deployment of troops in case of an uprising. His son was firmly opposed to this line of action. In a letter to his brother-in-law, Frederick William deplored his father's "baneful view that the forces of democracy command a monstrous power here." His preferred option was to meet with moderate liberals such as the deputy August von Saucken-Julienfelde, the Speaker of the lower house, Wilhelm Grabow, or Victor, the Duke of Ratibor, in order to find a political way out of the threatening impasse.[12] His efforts were overtaken by events. After the parliament had made it clear that it would not continue its provisional funding of the military reforms, the king dissolved it on 11 March 1862. Three days later, he dismissed the liberal members of the ministry and formed a new conservative government under the leadership of Adolf, prince of Hohenlohe-Ingelfingen.

As King William was patently stressed by these dramatic developments, his relationship with the crown prince took a turn for the worse. "I felt more sorry than ever for Papa, whom I found so internally collapsed and excited that he was quite incapable of accepting as correct any opinion other than his own," Frederick William wrote to his wife on 17 March 1862, after a meeting with his father. "I had to listen to a few things about my liberal views, too." During a conversation on the following day, the king lost his temper. In front of Minister Alexander von Schleinitz, he accused his son of "being in cahoots" with the sacked liberal ministers. After Schleinitz had left, William openly berated Frederick William for being disloyal; he told him that the democratic papers were portraying the crown prince as the king's opponent and as their friend. He also warned his son to be more careful with the company he was keeping. Frederick William was shaken when he left his parents, and informed his wife that she "would not believe how [he] cried and sobbed before going to sleep" that night.[13]

Supported by Victoria, Frederick William nevertheless continued to steer a middle course between his opposition to the radical German Progressive Party—the clear winner of the elections of 6 May 1862—and his refusal to endorse the line pursued by his father, who seemed prepared to ride roughshod over the parliamentary rights enshrined in the Prussian Constitution. Obeying the king's orders, the crown prince continued to attend meetings of the council of ministers, but he never spoke. Frederick William visited the dismissed ministers and their wives to bid them farewell, but he also used a long conversation with War Minister Albrecht von Roon, the king's most loyal adviser, to put on record his complete support in the military question.[14]

In September 1862, a possible resolution of the stalemate between the crown and parliament once again foundered on the rock of King William's rigid commitment to a three-year term of conscription. Since the parliament refused to pass the budgets for 1862 and 1863 without a reduction in the length of military service and the king felt poorly supported by his ministers, William no longer saw a way forward. Determined not to damage the fullness of the crown's power by making military concessions to a parliamentary majority, he considered abdicating in favour of his son. Frederick William, however, who had rushed to Berlin after receiving a telegram from the king, advised emphatically against taking a step so deeply damaging to the interests of the monarchy.[15]

Even though they parted on good terms, the two long conversations between father and son failed to heal the rift between them. Having spoken to the crown prince on 19 and 20 September and to Otto von Bismarck on 22 September, the king eventually decided against abdicating and called upon Bismarck to lead the Prussian government. The new minister-president had convinced William that it was his duty to continue the fight. Believing that Bismarck's reputation as an extreme reactionary would embitter the parliamentarians, Frederick William was shocked when he found out about this appointment. "Did it have to come to this," he sighed, "after the regency was established in November 1858 with such high hopes?" The crown prince still found himself in a dilemma: fearful of aggravating his father, he was now even more strongly opposed to the course steered by the king's new government. Having ducked the issue for two months by travelling through France, Italy, Malta, and North Africa, Frederick William returned to assume a pose of studied silent rigidity. "The crown prince does not talk about politics at all, not at all," one of Frederick William's confidants wrote in February 1863. "He sits in the council of ministers as a monument and as a memento mori. . . . On the one hand this silence is designed to prevent compromising him vis-à-vis the people, on the other hand to avoid a breach with the father."[16] The longer he maintained this passive role and the more fiercely the conflict between the crown and parliament raged, however, the more the crown prince found himself under pressure to show his true colours.

For several months, Frederick William had been aware of rumours that the government was planning to use the parliamentary recess in the summer of 1863 to clamp down on the opposition press. By the end of May, the plot was clearly thickening. Since the king refused to discuss the issue, the crown prince decided to write to his father to warn him against taking any unconstitutional steps. The tone of the letter—sent just hours before he left Berlin for a trip to East Prussia—reflected Frederick William's embarrassment: "You know, dear Papa, how I am attached to you with all my soul, that there is no-one on earth who is more devoted to you than I and that your wishes are always commands for me. As my father you will expect from me that I will always be frank and honest with you." Having reminded the king of his scrupulously maintained silence since their confrontation in March 1862, he begged for just one thing—that William would never approve a violation of the constitution, for such an act would threaten "your happiness, your reputation, your God-given position, which are one with the happiness of your country, your children and grandchildren." Having dispatched the letter, Frederick William recorded in his diary that he would have to give up his "neutral negative attitude" if unconstitutional steps were taken, and then "the long-dreaded moment when I will have to hurt my father's heart" will have arrived. "May God prevent it!"[17]

His prayer was not answered. The king's reply accused Frederick William of having failed to be sufficiently discreet about his political misgivings. William exhorted his son to speak out against the opposition and to support the conservatives. Moreover, on the same day, an order was issued that restricted the constitutionally guaranteed freedom of the press. The legal basis for this emergency decree was widely regarded as more than dubious. In the crown prince's opinion, the conditions that compelled him to take a public stand had now been met. On 4 June 1863, he wrote to his father to express his emphatic opposition to the press order. He finished by reassuring the king that it remained his "keenest endeavour to maintain your love to me." The following day, however, he used a public occasion at the city hall in Danzig to express his regret that a conflict had arisen between the government and the people, and declared that he had had no foreknowledge of the press order. His intention had been, he wrote in his diary that evening, "loudly to declare myself an opponent of Bismarck and of his theories." He had wanted to "make the government feel targeted," but knew that his father would consider himself personally attacked. Frederick William ended his speech by loyally referring to the king's "noble and fatherly intentions and magnanimous convictions," but the damage was done. King William sent his son a furious letter, rebuking him severely and warning him that any further statements along these lines would result in his being summoned to Berlin and possibly stripped of his commissions.[18]

The king's own chequered history of painful obedience to his father on the one hand and insolent opposition to his brother on the other did not appear to predispose William I to a lenient reaction. Some of his conservative advisers even talked of court-martialling and incarcerating the crown prince. Bismarck recalled that he still had to struggle on 10 June 1863 to dissuade the king from taking steps reminiscent of the treatment that King Frederick William I had meted out to his son in 1730. It took a curious combination of forces to convince William of the virtues of moderation: Queen Augusta, whose hatred of Bismarck burnt even more fiercely than her son's, and the minister-president himself, who did not want to see the crown prince turned into a liberal martyr. Frederick William had meanwhile replied to the king. He informed his father that—with a broken heart and after fervent prayer—he still felt compelled by his conscience not to abandon his position. He was prepared to suffer the consequences. He would not speak out again; he offered to resign from his military appointments and invited the king to allocate a place where he could live as a political exile. William ignored these dramatic suggestions. His letter of 10 June, written "with fatherly love, but with royal earnestness," merely repeated the strict rebuke and made the promise of forgiveness dependent on his son's future discretion. The crown prince's crime against "king, father and state" had been that he had placed himself "publicly and on purpose in opposition to the orders of the king." Rather than helping the monarch to consolidate "peace and harmony between the king and his people," Frederick William had seemed poised to force the country to choose between father and son.[19]

In this final accusation lies an explanation for the violence of the king's initial reaction and for the permanence of the damage the Danzig episode inflicted on the relationship between William I and Frederick William. Prussia's constitutional conflict had reached its height and many feared that a revolutionary outburst might be imminent. "The country cannot be expected to see with indifference," the British ambassador in Berlin reported in May 1863, "the complete nullification of its constitutional rights by almost the same process which was punished in France in 1830 by the expulsion of a dynasty." William, who often watched his minister-president's boldness with trepidation, felt vulnerable and in need of support. He had asked for his son's help in his letter of 1 June 1863, but instead the crown prince had publicly attacked the government. Nor had Frederick William complied with the renewed request for support implied in his father's letter of 10 June 1863. He may have honoured his promise not to criticise the government again in public, but his attitude was clear. "My views are illuminated by the words spoken in Danzig," he wrote to his confidant, Max Duncker, in July 1863, "I do not want to do or say any more, because I do not wish to become a leader of the opposition."[20]

Even though the crown prince found his father "gracious and affectionate" during two long conversations they had in August 1863, these meetings did not produce a rapprochement. Their differences flared up again the following month, when Frederick William requested to be excused from attending the council of ministers. The infuriated king ordered his son's presence so that he might learn directly what the government was trying to do instead of relying on others for information. Refusing to accept this ruling, the crown prince sent his father a somewhat laborious memorandum outlining his views of the rights and responsibilities of the heir to the throne and complaining about being identified—merely by dint of his presence at these meetings—with policies at odds with his own convictions. Frederick William once again repeated his urgent wish to be dispensed from attending. He threatened that he might otherwise feel compelled to dispel any misconceptions by sharing his views with selected outsiders. The crown prince persisted even after he had received another refusal from the king. In a letter written in Windsor Castle on 20 November 1863, he challenged his father's claim that the crown prince was obliged—rather than merely entitled—to be present at ministerial meetings. He once again explained his opposition to what he considered an unconstitutional government and declared himself unable to attend. As could be expected, the next clash was just a matter of time. In January 1864, Frederick William met his father to seek clarification as to why he had been instructed not to share governmental information with his wife anymore. The crown prince described the ensuing exchange as "painful" and "marked by vehement outbursts." His lack of trust in Frederick William was a consequence of the Danzig speech; the king had snapped at his son. The crown prince was a man of the opposition and one had to keep an eye on what he was doing.[21]

Father and son lived for almost another quarter of a century after this meeting, during which time they were at the centre of almost unimaginable change of momentous importance for their dynasty and country. In spite of this, William never really abandoned the basic concerns about his son that he had voiced in January 1864—that Frederick William opposed him and therefore could not be trusted. It is telling that, in moments of acute political stress, the king tended to portray the crown prince as aligned with his opponents. After the Prussian victory over Austria in 1866, King William and Bismarck were locked into a fierce battle of wills. The minister-president insisted on a quick and lenient peace, while the king demanded a triumphant and punitive settlement. Forced to yield, the embittered monarch wrote that since Bismarck had "deserted [him] in front of the enemy" and his son "had agreed with the minister-president's view [he] considered himself painfully compelled . . . to accept a shameful peace." The same pattern could be observed during the king's outburst on the day before his proclamation as German emperor in January 1871. Distraught by the idea of betraying Prussia's noble traditions, the old man was beside himself and shouted: "My son supports the new state of affairs with all his heart, whereas I don't give a fig for it and stick to nothing but Prussia."[22]

In the decades that followed their initial conflict, William was frequently indiscreet about the fundamental doubts and misgivings he entertained about his son. His immediate family was well aware of his feelings. In 1869 the king complained about Frederick William to his daughter. His son's opposition, he told Louise, "was not only excessive but crowded out every dutiful expression of filial reverence." During a heated conversation with his wife in March 1880, William called their son dangerous and a supporter of parties hostile to the state. "If he were not the crown prince," he reportedly said to Augusta, "he would be worth getting rid of."[23] The emperor did not keep his views within the family, though. Talking to the governor of Alsace-Lorraine and Bismarck's son, Herbert, in the autumn of 1886, he described Frederick William variously as under his wife's thumb, lacking in openness, disrespectful of the monarch's prerogatives, and overly suspicious. According to the court official Karl von Wilmowski, the emperor declared on more than one occasion in 1887 that he no longer had a son and that the crown prince was a stranger. When William spoke of "his son" during his final years, it was reported, he was almost always referring to his grandson, Prince William, rather than to the crown prince. Even a public snub was possible. In April 1864, during the unveiling of a monument commemorating the recent campaign against Denmark, William effusively thanked numerous individuals but completely ignored the crown prince, who was not only present but had played an important role alongside Field Marshal Wrangel and General Moltke.[24]

William's alienation from his son chiefly manifested itself in two ways. The emperor seemed determined to exclude the crown prince from matters of state and he exercised very close control over his son's domestic life. Frederick William and his wife were painfully aware of both these practices. In his memoirs, Wilmowski mentioned that the crown prince frequently complained that his father never discussed politics with him, leaving him entirely uninformed. Wilmowski's recollection appears well supported. In July 1864, Frederick William wrote to the king with more than a hint of bitterness that he had just started a letter to him to discuss a possible cease-fire in the Danish campaign when he learned that one had already been concluded. Similarly, never having received an official notification, the crown prince had to consult the newspapers to find out that the peace with France had been ratified in March 1871. Seven years later, William opposed Bismarck's plan to provide the crown prince with some experience of government by appointing him governor of Alsace-Lorraine. William cited fears that Frederick William's family might grow into foreigners if they lived in Strasbourg. The British ambassador to Berlin reported in 1881 that the emperor never discussed matters of state with the crown prince, who complained about this "in bitter terms." Friedrich von Holstein noted three years later how curiously the different generations of the royal family treated each other: "The emperor ignores the crown prince in everything, tells him nothing wherever possible." Things had not even changed by the time William entered his tenth decade. "I hear nothing," Frederick William told the governor of Alsace-Lorraine in March 1887. "I learn everything through the newspapers and that with the emperor being ninety years old."[25]

William's intrusive control of his son's family was even more upsetting and infantilizing for Frederick William than his own exclusion from the political sphere. "How can I tell my poor little wife all of this?" the crown prince wrote in his diary in October 1864. He had received a letter in which his father had determined a maximum duration of a planned family trip to Switzerland, forbidden that their children accompany them, and ordered that the newborn baby be given to a wet nurse. In October 1870, Princess Victoria complained to her mother about a "very unkind letter" that the king had sent her: she was "to go back to Berlin—and that he did not give his consent to [her] taking the children, the travelling was bad for their health and education, and that [she] did not understand [her] duty etc." So close was the emperor's supervision that Frederick William even felt it necessary to ask for his father's permission to alter the itinerary of the couple's return journey from a trip in 1873 so that his wife could see the Italian Lakes. "We are having very great difficulties with the emperor just now about the children and unpleasant scenes," Victoria wrote to her mother in 1876. "He is alas! very autocratic and tyrannical and very obstinate in these matters and Fritz takes it dreadfully to heart and it makes him very bitter and excites and distresses him very much." In the autumn of 1883, Frederick William begged his father to allow his son, Prince William, to accompany him on an official trip to Spain. His father's negative reply, the crown prince wrote to his wife, "could not be phrased more harshly. All my wishes are curtly turned down, like with a very young person, who depends on a superior; this hurts me, and I have no possible defence."[26]

Before 1871 the military sphere had mitigated the corrosive effect of these tensions on the relationship of father and son. Both men were devoted to the army and there had been mutual pleasure in a process whereby William formally recognised the crown prince's military achievements and Frederick William took delight in the honours he received. This had provided a much-needed tonic for their otherwise troubled relationship. During the campaign against Denmark in 1864, Frederick William congratulated his father on the fiftieth anniversary of the day he was decorated with the Iron Cross. In return, the king awarded his son the "Red Eagle with Swords" medal. The crown prince knew that he had done precious little to deserve this honour, but he appreciated his father's kindness. William, in turn, wrote that his "paternal heart and his soldierly nature" rejoiced because of his son's fine performance. After the crown prince had saved the day by leading his troops onto the battlefield at Königgrätz in July 1866, father and son embraced each other tearfully. The king then handed Frederick William his own "Pour le Mérite" medal, Prussia's highest decoration for valour. In September 1869, William inspected the second army corps commanded by his son and found it in such good order that he publicly expressed "his full recognition" to Frederick William, who had "confirmed afresh the trust [he] had always placed in [him]." According to Louis Schneider, the king's private secretary and reader, William was bursting with paternal pride as he rewarded his son's triumphs during the French campaign of 1870. The crown prince, in turn, gratefully appreciated the "touching, movingly beautiful, appreciative words" chosen by his father when he promoted him to the rank of field marshal.[27]

After 1871, however, the extraordinary days of military glory gave way to the routine of peacetime life, family squabbles, and unspoken political disagreement. There were increasingly fewer joyous moments to grease the grinding wheels of the Hohenzollern family machine. Paralysed by a combination of legal strictures and political constellations, his sense of filial duty, and an unwillingness to confront problems energetically, Frederick William endured his position with increasing frustration. He was painfully aware of his own age and noted his father's seemingly indestructible longevity with quiet exasperation. "His Majesty, 79 today, [is] physically more robust than for many years," Frederick William noted in his diary in 1876. "Every year he falls ill three times only to get healthier every time," he told his confidant, Albrecht von Stosch, in 1887. The old emperor even bounced back from the injuries he suffered when he was shot in 1878. William's "elastic agility and freshness" stunned everyone, Frederick William wrote to his wife in September 1879. "Papa is so fresh that he absolutely demanded yet another hunt in Letzlingen," the crown prince reported the following year without any enthusiasm. By the time he himself turned fifty, Frederick William's mood was one of profound resignation, if not depression. "Fifty years, life therefore behind me, idle observer in daily self-denial, discipline practised over a life-time, condemned passively to while away the final years," is how he described himself in his diary. Such feelings were not merely a passing cloud. In 1886 he wrote to his wife, deploring his parents' "geriatric peculiarities, which traditionally hurt children and descendants most," and declaring "bland resignation" as his "only option in this unbearable situation."[28]

Harsh though it may seem, for the son of the monarch, only bad news about his father was good news, and hope had to take flight on a vulture's wing. When opening parliament in 1882, the emperor struck his son as insecure, weak, and incoherent. In 1883 the inspection of two brigades and one battalion clearly proved too much for William, leaving him exhausted. Three years later, the crown prince informed his wife that the emperor had passed out during a dinner and suffered from bowel trouble afterward. Albrecht von Stosch noted in August 1886 that Frederick William spoke "without any reservation" about his father's expected death. The harsh reality of the dynastic principle was not lost on Emperor William, either. He was in no rush to put his son out of his misery and enjoyed the occasional cruel dig at the crown prince's expense. During the celebration of his ninetieth birthday in March 1887, the old emperor was reported to have quipped that he would not die since the crown prince was still alive. Even though William did not know then that within weeks his son would be diagnosed with a terminal disease and would only outlive him by ninety-nine days, the father's comment throws the essentially antagonistic nature of the relationship between the emperor and the crown prince into sharp relief. Its essence is powerfully illustrated by a story that diplomat Ludwig Raschdau recalled in his memoirs. When an artist once showed William a sketch that depicted his son's foot resting on a dais on which the emperor was standing, he grabbed a pencil and corrected the image by relegating the crown prince's foot to a lower level.[29]

Frederick William as Husband and Father

On 9 February 1888, Frederick William underwent a tracheotomy, which saved him from the immediate danger of suffocation but permanently deprived him of the use of his voice. For the rest of his life, he communicated by means of *Sprechzettel*—"talking slips" on which he scribbled questions, messages, and orders. The last of these, written only hours before his death on 15 June 1888, poignantly documents what really mattered to the dying emperor. The shaky, barely legible scrawl reads, "Victoria, I & the chil—," and then breaks off. Carefully labelled and dated by his widow, this moving relic illustrates the centrality of his marriage and family in Frederick William's life.

There can be no doubt that Frederick William and Victoria's relationship was a loving and fulfilling one and that both spouses cared deeply about their large family. Between 1859 and 1872, Victoria gave birth to eight children: William (born in 1859), Charlotte (1860), Henry (1862), Sigismund (1864), Viktoria (1866), Waldemar (1868), Sophie (1870), and Margaret (1872). Together Frederick William and Victoria experienced intensely the joy of parenthood, as well as the frustration and unspeakable pain it can bring. As the crown prince was slipping in and out of depression during the final decade of his life, it was his family that sustained him. "I acutely feel how I am ageing," he confided to his diary on his fiftieth birthday, "and if I had not wife and children as my all—I would long since have wished to be out of this world."[30]

The bedrock of Frederick William's domestic bliss was the success of his marriage to Victoria, from which he drew enormous comfort and strength. "Thirty years of happiness have passed," he noted in his diary on the day of their anniversary in January 1888. This deep, mutual, and openly expressed affection was a consistent feature of their marriage. The crown princess praised her husband's "kind, generous heart" and his "sweet amiable temper." She told her mother what a blessing it was "when besides one's deep love, one [could] give one's whole confidence and esteem." On Victoria's twenty-fourth birthday, Frederick William wrote in his diary, "May God bless my dear little wife, my life's only true joy, my other self." On the occasion of their twenty-second wedding anniversary, the crown prince assured Victoria that "I could not love you better, my dear, deeply beloved little wife. . . . If only God allows that you and I can stay together, then life in its drab form can be endured and with this hope in my heart I embrace you, little darling wife, with the entire fullness and strength of my love."[31]

Frederick William and Victoria's happiness was even more remarkable because their marriage was the result of a carefully prepared plan that mixed dynastic ambition with topical politics. At the beginning of the 1850s, the interests of the British royal family dovetailed neatly with those of Prince William's court at Koblenz. William and his wife advocated a policy of moderate domestic reform in Prussia and urged a rapprochement with the Western powers. Their criticism of what they saw as the government's overly Russophile and reactionary course was music to British ears. Moreover, Prince Albert was looking for a channel through which he could influence the country that he expected would one day lead a reformed and united Germany. The interest of the British court in a link between the two royal families was further fuelled by King Leopold of the Belgians, an uncle of both Victoria and Albert, who was eager to shore up his fragile new kingdom by strengthening its dynastic connections. Attracted by the idea of uniting two great Protestant monarchies, Baron Christian von Stockmar, Albert's trusted physician, private envoy, and political guru, reportedly had been in favour of this marriage for several years. A union between Frederick William and Princess Victoria, the eldest daughter of Queen Victoria and Prince Albert, would provide a perfect vehicle for all of these plans. The matchmaking was further facilitated by the fact that Albert, Victoria, William, and Augusta knew each other personally. Augusta had corresponded regularly with Queen Victoria ever since she had spent a happy week in London in 1846, and William had enjoyed Victoria and Albert's hospitality during the three months of his exile from Prussia in 1848. It was, therefore, not exclusively for the official purpose of marvelling at the wonder of the Great Exhibition that Prince William, his wife, and their two children travelled to London in 1851.[32]

The visit proved a great success and marked the beginning of Frederick William's lifelong connection with the British royal family. Queen Victoria and Prince Albert were favourably impressed by the young Prussian prince, and he in turn took an immediate liking to his future parents-in-law. Frederick William later recalled how "sweet" and "perfect" Princess Victoria had been in 1851, but it is unlikely that the ten-year-old princess would have appeared as anything more than a bright and engaging child to the nineteen-year-old prince. Frederick William did not mention her specifically in the grateful letter he sent to Prince Albert after his departure, choosing instead to add a collective greeting to all the "dear children." Queen Victoria, for her part, was looking further ahead. She informed King Leopold on 27 May 1851, that her daughter had formed "an amazing friendship" with the Prussian prince. "Might this one day lead to a union! God knows it would make us very happy, for I never saw a more amiable, unspoilt, and good young man than he is." The carefully planned match was not even abandoned when the political relations between Prussia and Britain hit rock bottom after 1854. The decision of the government in Berlin to pursue what was regarded as a pro-Russian policy of neutrality during the Crimean War earned Prussia the wrath of Britain's politicians and public opinion. The strained relationship also made it more difficult to secure King Frederick William IV's permission for the marriage.[33]

All these obstacles were overcome, though, and in January 1855, Queen Victoria sent Frederick William an invitation to visit the new "house" at Balmoral in the Scottish Highlands, along with an assurance that all the children had changed a great deal since he last saw them. After months of further careful planning, the prince's more or less secret trip began in the autumn of 1855. While officially sea bathing on the Belgian coast, he made his way to Scotland.[34]

It speaks volumes for the strength of the bond between Victoria and Frederick William that they managed to fall in love during this meeting. A more stressful personal situation could hardly be imagined. Since the plan was politically controversial, efforts were made to keep it hidden from public view. Amongst the matchmakers, however, politics were considered with considerable frankness. In her invitation to Frederick William, Queen Victoria had described Prussia's current political situation as painful. It was her view, though, that the "friendly, honest attitude" of the British government would help to improve matters, but only after the removal of the party currently in charge in Berlin. Moreover, both sets of parents were lacking in confidence about their offspring. Augusta wrote to Albert ahead of Frederick William's visit in order to lower expectations. A trifle disloyally, she conceded that her son's education had been deficient and referred to his "somewhat indolent and limp nature." Queen Victoria, however, fretted about whether her eldest daughter, whose precocious intelligence and sharp mind were beyond doubt, was actually pretty enough for the handsome young prince.[35]

None of this mattered when Frederick William, now almost twenty-four years old, met Victoria. Her fifteenth birthday was still a few weeks off, yet he saw her as a graceful young woman and she mesmerized him immediately. After almost a week of piano playing, card games, flirtatious conversation, and much "looking at each other," Frederick William gathered up his courage and asked her parents for the princess's hand. Queen Victoria and Prince Albert were overjoyed and gave their consent. The initial plan was to keep the princess ignorant of the agreement until her confirmation the following Easter, but after nine days of amorous torment, Frederick William expressed himself so clearly to his bride that she guessed the situation correctly. She happily accepted his gift of a sprig of white heather, as well as a first kiss. The young couple declared themselves to Victoria and Albert, who shared in their bliss. Frederick

William's departure two days later—his stay was kept short to avoid arousing public suspicion—occasioned great sadness and lovers' agony. "My Vicky is always in front of my mind's eye," Frederick William wrote to Queen Victoria on the same day, "every word, every gaze of hers are precious to me, and support me amid the dark realization, that many months will pass before we will see each other again."[36]

Even the investment of so much heartache proved not enough to put the public off the scent. A mere two days after Frederick William had left his weeping fiancée at Balmoral, the London *Times* printed a harsh reminder of the political context. A noticeably aggressive leader not only acquainted the public with the entire plan—from the first encounter in 1851 until the recent events in Scotland—but also spoke out brusquely against the match with a royal family "associated in the minds of the people with the notions of foreign subjection, national degradation, and the systematic sacrifice of Prussian interests to Russian influence." Believing the days of the Prussian monarchy to be numbered, the paper opposed a "union with the bankrupt dynasties that yet for a little while encumber the central thrones of Central Europe." It painted an ominous picture of the princess—now rushed into this marriage "with ill-omened haste"—being forced to return as a fugitive "stripped of the pomp and dignity with which she departed." The *Times* ended with the emphatic declaration that the people of England had "no wish to improve its acquaintance with any Prince of the house of Hohenzollern."[37]

The Prussian conservatives grimly reciprocated the feelings expressed by the English paper. Prince Charles, Frederick William's reactionary uncle, had already attacked the planned marriage a few times, the young fiancé informed Queen Victoria in October 1855, and Berlin's governing clique was "beside itself that the trip had taken place without its knowledge and permission." In the spring of 1856, Otto von Bismarck and his erstwhile mentor, the king's ultraconservative adjutant general Leopold von Gerlach, sceptically discussed the "English marriage." Bismarck opposed the influence Britain might gain in Prussia by using the princess as a political conduit. The marriage could only be beneficial if Victoria were to "leave the Englishwoman at home and [if she] became a Prussian."[38]

These reactions to the news of the engagement illustrate what was to become a permanent feature of Frederick William and

Victoria's marriage: it was seen as a political issue. Being married to the "Englishwoman" impacted on the way the crown prince was perceived and on the role he played within Prussian and German politics. As time went on, the quality of the relationship between Frederick William and Victoria, as well as the personality and beliefs of the crown princess emerged as the key factors driving this development. Initially, however, the political dimension of the marriage resulted purely from the symbolic power of a dynastic connection with what the liberal newspaper *Kölnische Zeitung* celebrated as "kindred England, the land of liberty and the rule of law."[39]

When the wedding day finally arrived, the mood in London had softened considerably since the attack in the *Times* in 1855. "The crowds that collected in the Park and the vicinity of the Palace were immense," the paper reported in January 1858. "It was a good and hearty popular feeling, and the unmistakable manner in which it was displayed must have been very gratifying." In Prussia, the couple received an enthusiastic welcome that involved weeks of pageants and celebrations. The festivities were not wholly innocent, though. "Very obvious that it was a political demonstration," the diarist Theodor von Bernhardi noted on 28 February 1858, "and the royal house has understood this well." The couple fully appreciated the political quality of their reception. "We look upon the great enthusiasm demonstrated on the occasion of our marriage and our entry here as the expression of the feelings of the people, which are at present those of hope," Victoria wrote to her father on 5 March 1858. "They think that now they have a chance of seeing Russian sympathies, the source of so much harm, lessened."[40]

That she described herself as embodying the people's hope for profound political change less than a month after she had arrived in her new country illustrates that the seventeen-year-old newlywed was not lacking in self-confidence. This was not only the result of Victoria's forceful personality but also of the knowledge that Prince Albert had carefully prepared her for her role in Prussia. The princess adored her father. She deemed his wisdom peerless and his guidance beyond question. Albert's admonitions did not cease when Victoria left England: "Your place is your husband's wife and your mother's daughter; you must not demand anything else," he wrote to her on 17 February 1858, "but you must not give up anything which you owe to your husband or your mother." The princess took all of this to heart. Proudly aware of her status as Britain's princess royal, she was nevertheless deeply committed to her husband. Paternal advice was thus another ingredient that strengthened the bond between Vicky and her Fritz. Their marriage was clearly based on a love that eludes historical analysis, but it was also sustained by steady communication, mutual respect, and agreement between the spouses. This combination was unusual for its time and context, and seems to have owed a fair deal to the model of Queen Victoria and Prince Albert. All of this also meant, however, that it proved easy to tar Victoria with the brush of Bismarck's apprehensions: that she was an English princess refusing to become Prussian and bent on influencing her husband.[41]

Anyone reading the surviving correspondence between Frederick William and Victoria will be struck not only by its volume—they would normally send each other a daily letter when they were separated, so their marriage is documented by thousands of letters—but also by the issues addressed in these letters and by their tone. Husband and wife wrote to each other with complete openness, sharing concerns, hopes, ideas, and information and seeking each other's opinion and advice. The most private and humdrum issues—such as annoyance over a wedding present—sit alongside international politics and the minutiae of the German legislative process. Frederick William and Victoria shared moments of great elation, like his appointment to the colonelcy of the oldest Prussian regiment; of curious speculation, like Bismarck's suggestion that the crown prince might become governor of Alsace-Lorraine; and of great frustration, like the many references to the perceived maltreatment at the hands of Emperor William.[42] Husband and wife cooperated closely on the most delicate issues. They sat up until one o'clock in the morning drafting the crown prince's answer to King William's sharp rebuke after the Danzig speech. When, in August 1885, proclamations for Frederick William's accession were secretly prepared in anticipation of Emperor William's death, the crown prince sent his wife the drafts and asked for her alterations to be incorporated.[43]

The exchanges between Frederick William and Victoria were informed by a self-evident mutual respect. The crown prince appreciated his wife's learning, intelligence, and energy and never baulked at bowing to her superior judgement or failed to express his admiration for her. In May 1879, he sent Victoria a draft letter to the Prussian minister of justice. "If you don't like it," he assured her, "I will make changes and only return the corrected version." A few days later, he thanked his wife for helping him with certain economic questions which she "already knew and understood . . . when [he] had not the faintest inkling of them." Though written in a playful and slightly tongue-in-cheek manner, a love letter Frederick William sent to his wife in March 1864 captured a characteristic aspect of their relationship. "I am a little fearful now and then," the crown prince wrote from the Prussian headquarters during the campaign against Denmark, "because I do not know yet, how a creature, as excellent and all-round talented as my little animal, can bear permanently being stuck with a creature as vastly inferior to her as her little man." Victoria's bossy tendencies, to which this letter teasingly alluded, lose much of their sting, though, because of the strong sense of agreement that permeates the correspondence between husband and wife. There is rarely a word of contradiction amid a general pattern of mutual reassurance and endorsement. "I could not agree more with everything you say about [our son] William," the crown prince wrote to his wife in September 1879. In November 1884, he assured her that "as you well know, I fully share your opinions as a matter of principle." Two years later, he wrote to his wife that it gave him particular joy "that we daily find each other thinking the same thoughts and taking the words right out of each other's mouths."[44]

Victoria repaid Frederick William's trust and respect by giving him her unstinting support and strengthening his resolve. In times of acute stress, this proved invaluable. "During these days of suffering Vicky has been like a kind angel to me," the crown prince wrote to his mother ten days after his speech at Danzig. "Indefatigably thinking, helping, writing; giving courage, never losing her head, I cannot emphasise enough what she is to me and what I have in her. She has thoughts that would distinguish a statesman." Over the years, a pattern emerged that demonstrated how Victoria's more energetic and upbeat personality mitigated Frederick William's increasing lethargy and resignation. The crown prince's letters were often full of dark pessimism and foreboding. "How can, under current circumstances, a free spirit emerge, true to its own convictions?" he asked in May 1879. By the time they might come to the throne, "old, used up and disgusted," so much would be spoilt, he continued, that he "would rather resign altogether." Given his age, it seemed barely thinkable, Frederick William told his wife in November 1884, that he would one day be able to make any lasting improvements.[45]

The tone of Victoria's letters, in contrast, was often more optimistic and encouraging. In May 1879, she sketched out a plan for a liberal party. "Would that not be a party," she wondered, "with which you could work later, on which you could lean, from which you could recruit ministers, with whom you would share one and the same programme and carry out reforms?" Things have not been easy, she conceded in January 1880, "yet I know as well as you, that, given the chance, I could be useful and that there are people, who would not let me down." Even after the 1884 Reichstag election, which had badly damaged the political fortunes of the left-liberal party she favoured, Victoria remained defiantly optimistic. "The sensible, solid Freisinn Party will make itself recognised," she wrote to her husband in November 1884, "its time will come."[46]

Frederick William admired his wife's strength of character. "May you be right in thinking that it is still possible to bring about some good one day," he let her know in May 1879. "One has to have such confidence, because it is one's fate to be heir to the throne." His doubts remained, though. Bismarck's regime had ruined German politics, the crown prince continued, and his own strength was shattered: "As you know, being unable to get to work during the best years of my life has utterly depressed me." The recent death of their son, Waldemar, had "completed this spiritual decline," Frederick William explained, "I feel neither interest nor do I consider it worth my while to busy myself with politics during the few years which I may still have; and I resign myself."[47]

This reference to Prince Waldemar was not an isolated comment. It points to a different aspect of Frederick William and Victoria's marriage, which assumed an increasingly prominent proportion in the course of the 1880s. Waldemar had been a much-loved, promising child, and when he succumbed to diphtheria in March 1879 at the age of eleven, both parents were devastated. Waldemar's birth in 1868 had helped Frederick William and Victoria cope with the earlier loss of their two-year-old son, Sigismund, who had died of meningitis in 1866. The bereavement they experienced in 1879 reopened this old wound. From 1879 on, both husband and wife were locked into a permanent, painful, and mutually reinforcing pattern of mourning for their lost sons. While it bonded Frederick William and

Victoria even closer together—sometimes at the expense of some of their surviving six children—this ritualized grieving also played an important role in causing the crown prince's periods of despair. When writing to her husband in September 1879, Victoria observed that he was likely to receive her letter "on our sweet Siggie's birthday. The dear treasure would be fifteen years old now! Oh God, why are we not allowed to have them any more those two dear boys, the most beautiful and vigorous and dearest heaven gave us?" Frederick William needed no reminding. "Tomorrow our unforgettable Siggie would have been fifteen years old," he wrote on 14 September, "I am so sad, my heart is so melancholy." Upon his return to Berlin two months later, the crown prince shared with his wife how hard he was finding it to enter their home and especially the children's rooms upstairs.[48]

During the year of Waldemar's death, Frederick William and Victoria settled into a rhythm of commemorating the anniversaries of their late sons' births and deaths. After a visit to the boys' graves in March 1880, Frederick William contemplated Victoria's "bleeding mother's heart" and found that their formerly much-loved country house at Bornstedt now offered only tears and memories. "How I have to think of the days two years ago, when dearest Waldie lay sick," Victoria wrote on 24 March 1881, and her husband replied on the anniversary of Waldemar's death, recalling the "unspeakable pain and bitter suffering that befell us two years ago." After he had seen schoolchildren walking past in September 1885, Frederick William informed Victoria that he had experienced what he always felt when encountering groups of children: "My heart wanted to break at the thought of the two dear boys who were taken from us." Writing to her husband on 15 September 1886, the crown princess noted that "the beloved child, the little blond angel who was torn from us" would have been twenty-two years old that day.[49]

The deaths of the boys and the subsequent mourning had a profound direct and indirect impact on the happiness of Frederick William and Victoria's family. The lost sons assumed a status of perfection that could never be equalled by the surviving children. William, Charlotte, and Henry, the three oldest children, appeared increasingly extraneous to the core family. Victoria's disappointment with what she saw as their various deficiencies of body, mind, and character became more pronounced. The fact that she had not breast-fed her oldest three children, who had therefore turned into "complete

Prussians," also appears to have carried much weight with the crown princess. Writing to her husband at the time of Sigismund's fifteenth birthday in September 1879, Victoria contrasted Waldemar's energy, sense of duty, and dedication with Henry's "insignificance (to put it mildly)." She would have been proud of all her four sons, she assured Frederick William, but "particularly of the two youngest ones who had been so beautifully endowed by nature and whom I fed myself." The younger children shed bitter tears for their brothers, the crown princess wrote on 18 September 1879, but "the three oldest ones cannot understand how we suffer, each one for a different reason." Even in a letter to her eldest son, William, Victoria mourned her "two darlings," while complaining about Henry's inability to write a decent letter and chiding William for neglecting his filial duties.[50]

Frederick William and Victoria's response to the loss of Waldemar and Sigismund thus contributed significantly to the breakdown of their relationship with their eldest son. Prince William had been a source of some disappointment to his parents for several years. After 1879 the situation grew markedly worse. Even though Victoria took a deep interest in her firstborn and lavished much care on him, their relationship had always been fraught. A difficult breech delivery had left William with a withered left arm, and Victoria had found it impossible to come to terms with this physical defect. William's intellectual development and emerging personality also suggested that the prince would never measure up to the sainted Prince Albert. From the late 1870s onward, William was beginning to repay his mother's overbearing attention and exacting intrusiveness with a mixture of disregard and heartless insolence. Mother and son inflicted a great deal of emotional pain on each other and soon they could barely stand being in each other's company.[51]

To his father, Prince William seemed cold and unfeeling. He had failed "to mention Waldie or to express his regret at not having seen me on 1 [January]," Frederick William wrote to his wife on 4 January 1880. The crown prince was also shocked that his son appeared unaffected by the death of Duke Frederick of Schleswig-Holstein, an old family friend and the father of William's fiancée. William's unsympathetic hardheadedness reminded his father of his reaction to Waldemar's death. After several painful conversations, Frederick William decided that his son was icy and self-seeking. He vowed to Victoria that he would deal with him accordingly.[52]

Over the remaining years of his life, however, Frederick William lost almost all control over his son. Prince William distanced himself from his parents, established close contacts with the Bismarck family, and successfully exploited the dysfunctionality within the Hohenzollern family in order to deny his parents any influence on him. Outgunned and outmanoeuvred, the crown prince reacted to his defeats with furious outbursts or deep despondency. It did not take Frederick William long to understand his son's modus operandi. William's cunning method of ingratiating himself with his grandfather was typical, the crown prince complained in 1880, but it "is very painful to me, since he is seeking to achieve ends in this manner, which I had already believed thwarted by having said 'No.' "[53]

The close relationship between Prince William and his grandfather, on top of William I's distrust of his own son, led to a series of blows for the crown prince. In the autumn of 1883, Prince William secretly persuaded the emperor to deny his father's urgent request to take his son with him on an official visit to Spain. Half a year later, Frederick William was confronted with the fait accompli that his father had chosen William to represent the emperor on a ceremonial visit to St. Petersburg. Writing to his mother in May 1884, the crown prince complained about having been left in the dark, and he expressed misgivings about William's lack of preparation. Frederick William certainly would have been even more dismayed if he had been aware of the secret correspondence with the tsar which William began during this trip. On 25 May 1884, he urged Alexander II to take no notice of his father, who was in love with the opposition and influenced by his wife, who saw everything from a British point of view.[54]

By 1885 the rift between the crown princely couple and their firstborn had become so bitter that hardly any effort was made to be discreet about it. At a regimental dinner in February 1885, Frederick William gave his son a public dressing-down, calling him immature and lacking in judgement. A similar scene occurred at the Berlin Opera a few weeks later, and by September 1885, General Waldersee noted in his diary that there were now "permanent clashes" between Prince William and his father. The crown prince's increasing pettiness—in May 1886, he triggered a row by ordering his son not to exhibit a picture the young prince had painted—must be seen in the context of the utter powerlessness that Frederick

William must have felt vis-à-vis Prince William. Favoured by the emperor and courted by Bismarck, the son ran rings around his father.[55]

In August 1886, William persuaded his grandfather and the chancellor to send him on yet another official trip to Russia and to authorise him to work in the German foreign office. Enraged at having been cut out of the deliberations once again, the crown prince tried everything to undo these decisions. He argued vehemently that William, who was recovering from a serious ear infection, should not be exposed to the strains of a long journey, offered to travel to Russia himself, wrote numerous urgent letters, and sought to enlist Bismarck's help. It was all to no avail. The chancellor, notwithstanding the good faith that the trusting Frederick William placed in him, played a duplicitous game; Emperor William openly dismissed the crown prince as politically immature and untrustworthy; and Prince William kept up the pressure. After his son had once again travelled to Russia and was sent to the foreign office, there was nothing left for the crown prince but apoplectic fury. Prince William told a friend that he had never seen his father so angry; the crown prince "had become greyish-white and threatened [him] with a clenched fist, saying: 'This is a trick that has been played upon me, and one which I shall never forget.'"[56]

All of this private misery contrasted starkly with the bliss of Frederick William and Victoria's early family life. Almost deliriously in love, they had happily applied themselves to bringing up their children and had treasured the time they spent together as a family. Each parent had brought a very different background to the task. Frederick William had experienced his childhood as loveless and his parents as distant, whereas Victoria had grown up with affectionate parents and amid a whole flock of siblings. In parenthood, as with their marriage, they followed the model of Victoria and Albert rather than the example set by Augusta and William. Their efforts did not go unnoticed. The American writer Poultney Bigelow, who was a childhood friend of Princes William and Henry during the 1860s, later recalled scenes of perfect harmony: "No parents could have shown more interest in their children than the Crown Prince and Princess. They were generally present during the simple evening meal. . . . They had a smile and a kind word for each of their little guests." The novelist Gustav zu Putlitz spent a fortnight with Victoria and Frederick William in 1864. His account of the family enjoying a summer morning also

paints an idyllic picture. Frederick William and Victoria were break-
fasting outside, happily chatting and waiting for their children.
"The whole upbringing appears to me to be entirely sensible and
success proves it right, for the children are entirely natural, obedient,
fresh and well-kept," Putlitz wrote to his wife. "It was really very lovely,
this unforced togetherness and the joy of a truly pleasing, happy
relationship."[57]

Viewed through the prism of later misfortune, those happy days
became a poignant memory for Frederick William. He also mourned
the loss of the protection his domestic refuge had offered him against
an outside world that he experienced as hostile. In May 1879, Frederick William reminded his wife of their wedding day and how they
had hoped for a life without cruel blows. "And now!? We have suffered every misfortune, have cried about the bitterest losses and
cannot find any more in the complete flock of our children the compensation for the external storms. Until now they could be borne
more easily because the closed door to our house kept them at bay.
One does not want to think back to the happiness of those bygone
days, for the present is too bitter, too joyless and the future cannot
repay us for the sacrifices we have been forced to make."[58]

Frederick William's metaphor was aptly chosen. The cruel winds
of political gossip did indeed rattle the door of the crown prince's
marriage and family life. The tone of this commentary justified Frederick William's distaste for the world beyond the domestic. All the
key aspects of his relationship with Victoria were freely and often
malevolently discussed by informed insiders concerned with the political dimension of the crown prince's existence. Whether they commented on Frederick William's state of mind, Victoria's personality,
the nature of the couple's marriage, or the connections with Britain,
everything attracted censure. A bitter irony lay in the fact that these
attacks were often fuelled by the very aspects of Frederick William's
marriage to Victoria that made it so successful and such a source
of strength to him: the vigour of Victoria's personality and the observation that her role in the marriage was neither passive nor
subordinate.

During the 1880s, even the trusted individuals to whom the crown
prince spoke openly bemoaned the impact of his depression on his
political future. "The crown prince's current mood is downright worrying," Frederick William's adjutant Karl von Normann wrote to the
novelist Gustav Freytag in January 1882. "He likes to indulge in

dark thoughts and pessimistic notions." General Albrecht von Stosch criticised at the same time that the "bitterness manifesting itself was turning into resignation rather than into resolve to act." In 1883 Heinrich Geffcken, an academic and writer who knew the crown prince since their student days at Bonn, found him "more pessimistic and more embittered than ever," and wrote to the former Badenese minister Baron Roggenbach that Frederick William "refused to clarify the situation with respect to his reign." Both Stosch and Roggenbach expressed fears for the future in view of Frederick William's "lack of energy" and "paralysing pessimism." The crude remedy that Stosch suggested indicated clearly whom he held responsible for Frederick William's incapacitation: "I believe there is only one way to bring the gentleman to his senses," he wrote in November 1883, "and that would be for his wife to be caught committing adultery in flagrante delicto."[59]

Stosch's comment was merely a particularly unpleasant note within a loud and sneering chorus. Amongst Prussia's political, governmental, and court circles, the crown princess was widely and heartily disliked. Frederick William's affection and the devotion of a small number of friends were beyond doubt, but it is striking how many people felt deeply alienated by her. Even though some of the invective against the crown princess must be ascribed to prejudice, malice, or pettiness, those who found it impossible to cooperate with her were by no means limited to family members, reactionaries, and the ill-intentioned. The liberal politician Wilhelm Wehrenpfennig accused Victoria of behaving like an "arrogant Englishwoman despising everything Prussian and German." Normann deemed it necessary to try to undermine her antinational influence on her husband. Stosch warned against Victoria's "unconditional rule" and called her "a real danger." Roggenbach, a lifelong adviser and trusted friend of the couple, described it as "a necessity that immediately after the succession she be removed for a few months." Even Victoria's close friend, Marie von Bunsen, could not help but criticise her for refusing to realise how ill-suited her behaviour was, and called the crown princess her own worst enemy.[60]

As Bunsen's comment suggests, Victoria's unpopularity was—to a significant extent—a self-inflicted wound. She was an intelligent and confident woman with great passion, considerable artistic talents, and infectious enthusiasm. Yet the crown princess also had, in the words of Lamar Cecil, "an uncurbable tendency, one that experience failed to alter, to do exactly as she pleased and to speak her mind with arresting bluntness, indifferent if not oblivious to the consequences of her behaviour." She relished a good argument and rarely doubted her ability to convince her interlocutors of the errors of their ways. Conflicts were often triggered by the irksome differences she perceived between life in Britain and the—usually inferior—situation she encountered in Prussia. Victoria had a sharp eye and rarely bit her tongue. Prussian silver plate was thin, she noted, and the palace china modest. The Rubens and Van Dyck paintings in the Prussian royal collection were all fakes. Ladies at court were poorly dressed and unattractive. Court culture was philistine and devoid of intellectual and artistic vibrancy. German feather duvets were "stultifying and unhealthy" and her children were to sleep covered by "fine, soft, beautiful English woollen blankets." Almost everywhere she looked, something painfully reminded her of the superior offerings of her homeland, the "country of white teeth and rosy children," as she called it in 1865.[61]

None of this helped to endear her to anyone, and as the people surrounding her became aware of her preferences, Victoria quickly found herself marginalised within a royal family that was not known for its warmth and tolerance at the best of times. In 1883 Emperor William commented on Victoria's "revulsion at having to be in Berlin" and noted sarcastically that she, "who is always cold when she is not in England," had recently decided to climb a Swiss mountain.[62]

For the crown princess, loyalty to the country of her birth and loving respect for her father meant more, however, than merely expressing her views on the limited refinement of Prussian comfort, society, and culture. These deeply felt emotions were inseparable from upholding and proselytizing the essentials of the British Constitution and Prince Albert's political teachings. Notwithstanding the annoyance caused by Victoria's carping about Prussia's many small shortcomings, it was this political dimension of her attachment to Britain that caused the real damage to her reputation.

Victoria's dogmatic commitment to the precepts of liberal, parliamentary government led to a reciprocal process of alienation. Victoria was puzzled and repulsed by the determination of many Prussians to adhere to a different, more strongly monarchical and authoritarian system, and they, in turn, rejected her views as dangerously left-wing and unpatriotic. Her father-in-law's refusal to concede parliamentary control over the Prussian government genuinely baffled Victoria. "For anyone that has had the privilege (one cannot be thankful enough for) of being born in England it is impossible to think otherwise," she wrote to her father in December 1860, "but even if one was not born there common sense, I think, would tell one which side to take in this question." Within the context of nineteenth-century German liberalism, Victoria's commitment to a parliamentary system along British lines located her very much to the left of the centre ground. Even though her views went well beyond the boundaries of her husband's cautious liberalism and earned her the hostility of both conservative and moderate politicians, Victoria stuck to her guns.[63]

The negative effect of her views was compounded by widely circulated stories illustrating that the crown princess not only had British preferences but also British loyalties. Victoria's reluctance to see art treasures transferred from Britain to Germany, for instance, was so well known that museum directors in Berlin asked the crown prince not to mention planned acquisitions to his wife, because she had previously tried to sabotage purchases. "She feels like an Englishwoman," Holstein noted in January 1884, and "supports the English side whenever there is a conflict between German and English interests." In November 1885, a German diplomat dining with Victoria was taken aback when he realised that she referred to Britain when using phrases such as "us" and "our interests." Such accusations were not without foundation. "I am not surprised that our British colonies are angry at this ridiculous hoisting of German flags in all sorts of places," the crown princess wrote to her mother in December 1884, after Germany had embarked on a course of colonial acquisition. "If Bismarck begins playing global empire," she continued, "I think it is time for us to let him know who we are."[64]

Victoria's reputation severely damaged her husband's political position. It gave a particularly sharp edge to the long-standing accusation that Frederick William was a craven weakling who meekly danced to his dominant wife's foreign tune. As early as 1862, the law professor Theodor Perthes, who had been one of Frederick William's university tutors, called him "merely a tool in a woman's hand." In 1868 Frederick William's brother-in-law, the Grand Duke of Baden, deplored "his dependence on female whims." By 1872 the grand duke found that Victoria had turned her husband into a "well-nigh spineless tool." Making full use of the liberty that came with its illegal status, the Socialist weekly *Der Sozialdemokrat* mocked the crown prince as "under the thumb of his English wife, who has varnished him with the liberal-conservative-parliamentary paint so common in England." General Waldersee believed that Frederick William was only allowed to have his wife's opinions. Frederick William's private secretary came to the same conclusion: "You only have to look at what she's made of him," he told Holstein in May 1885. "He has no thoughts of his own, if she does not approve them. He is nothing. 'Ask my wife' or 'Have you spoken to the crown princess?'—that says it all." For Stosch, the "future ruler [was] a rudderless ship towed by his wife and her whims." To make matters worse, the "informed public [was] fully aware of this." Many of these comments arose from a mixture of misogynist prejudice, outrage at the "position of nuptial equality" achieved by Victoria, and a desire to smear the crown princely couple. There was, however, a grain of truth in these accusations.[65]

It is fair to say that Frederick William's relationship with his wife occasionally reached a point where his deference to her wishes and concerns was tantamount to weakness. Victoria's maid of honour and close friend, Wally Hohenthal, considered the princess "a little tyrant" even in the early days of her marriage and believed that "with a less chivalrous and devoted husband there might have been difficulties." Naturally inclined to avoid conflict, Frederick William was usually happy to agree with his wife's wishes. He normally resolved disagreements by giving in, by prevarication, or with a white lie. Even in the rare cases where husband and wife differed on matters of importance—for instance, whether or not to retain Bismarck as chancellor after the succession—the crown prince preferred not to confront the issue. Torn between his own beliefs and his conviction that Victoria was intellectually superior, he tended to remain firmly, if unhappily, on the fence.[66]

Although this conciliatory approach was sensible in terms of maintaining domestic harmony, it raised doubts about his ability to steer an independent course. In October 1884, for instance, Frederick William, who chaired the meetings of the recently revived Prussian council of state, felt obliged to host a reception for its members. As Victoria was out of town, he prepared the event with some trepidation: "I have given specific orders that none of your things may be used or moved," he wrote to her, "so that you need not be concerned at all about this."

The crown prince's jumpiness attracted comment. Holstein gleefully recorded Frederick William's anxious requests that "no one is to use my wife's English silver or her china; that is not to be touched." This was proof enough for Holstein that "the crown prince's character was getting weaker by the year." In July 1885, Bismarck met Frederick William to explain his opposition to the crown princess's pet project, the marriage of her daughter Viktoria to Alexander von Battenberg, the prince of Bulgaria. After the meeting, the chancellor recalled the crown prince's tortured expression: "The poor devil agrees with me," Bismarck observed, "but does not dare to say it."[67]

Frederick William's vacillation between opposition to the Battenberg marriage and support for his wife touched a nerve because the match was not only perceived as the crown princess's personal obsession but also as a means of furthering Britain's foreign policy aims at the expense of cordial Russo-German relations. In a similar vein, Holstein disapproved of Frederick William's recent visit to the German foreign office, where the crown prince had asked questions "obviously at the behest of the queen of England to pursue English interests." There was a deeply entrenched damning notion that, where Britain was involved, the crown prince—led by his wife—could not be trusted to put his country first. The confrontation between Frederick William and his father on 11 January 1864 was triggered by the king's order not to share official papers with Victoria, who was known to brief her mother. In March 1871, Bismarck considered the British ambassador's alleged claim that Britain could influence German policy via the crown princess, and concluded that the delicate relationship between the crown prince's court and the British embassy in Berlin required adroit handling. In the autumn of 1883, the German government learned with consternation that Frederick William had passed on highly confidential information to Britain about his official trip to Spain. The steady flow of information from the crown prince to Queen Victoria via the crown princess still concerned Herbert von Bismarck in 1884; in his report to Emperor William II of 23 September 1888, the chancellor revealed that during the war of 1870–1871, King William I had not authorised him to share secrets with the crown prince in order to avoid indiscretions to the British court.[68]

If Frederick William was aware of the impact that his wife and their marriage had on his reputation, he certainly did not respond to it. It appears idle to speculate whether there is anything he could have done to change the nature of his relationship with Victoria or to induce sceptical observers to reconsider their views of him. His own concerns were diametrically opposed. "It pains me," he wrote to Stosch in October 1880, "that as rich a personality as my wife, whose spirit, intellect and talent are rarely equalled, is never offered an opportunity to develop them and has to hold back, maligned and misunderstood and must suffer loss upon loss." His very first monarchical act after his father's death was thus entirely in keeping with a lifelong conviction. Emperor Frederick III approached his wife, bowed reverentially, and with a tender gesture placed around her neck the order of the Black Eagle, Prussia's highest honour. He wrote a note thanking his doctors "for having let me live long enough to recompense the valiant courage of my wife."[69]

Remembering the crown prince a year after his death, the novelist Gustav Freytag described Frederick William's "dedication and subordination to his wife" as total. "In his life, this love was the highest and most sacred thing, which fulfilled him entirely. She was the mistress of his youth, the confidante of all his thoughts, his counsel wherever she deigned to offer advice. . . . He directed everything according to her personality."[70] Perhaps Frederick William was not only a better son than politician but also a better husband than both.

Frederick William and Otto von Bismarck

It proved a cruel twist of irony that Frederick William played an important role in launching Otto von Bismarck's twenty-eight-year career at the helm of Prussia and the German Reich. In September 1862, the crown prince had two long conversations with his father, in which he spoke emphatically against the king's intention to abdicate in his favour. Bismarck, who had carefully contrived to be on hand, met the king shortly afterward and offered him the somewhat dramatic assurance that he would fight for his monarch "like a Brandenburg vassal who sees his liege lord in danger." In light of this promise and his son's admonitions, William stepped back from the brink. Considering it his duty to soldier on, he called upon the battle-ready vassal to lead the Prussian government. Would Frederick William have advised his father differently if he had anticipated this next step? The crown prince certainly was not expecting any such nasty surprises when he departed: "Calm conversation with the king about abdication. Bismarck not true," he telegrammed his wife on 19 September. His own brief meeting with Bismarck on 20 September did not give him any cause for concern either. When news of the appointment reached Frederick William four days later, he reacted with astonishment and dismay: "Poor Papa will have to suffer many a hard hour because of this false character," he wrote in his diary.[71]

By the autumn of 1862, there was obviously nothing left of the friendliness that had characterised the first brief encounters between the teenage prince and the thirty-three-year-old counter-revolutionary hotspur in 1848. During their more recent meetings in April 1860, May 1862, and September 1862, Bismarck had clearly failed to impress Frederick William. Both the crown prince and his wife remained firmly opposed to tackling Prussia's escalating domestic crisis by appointing a politician with such reactionary credentials. In July 1862, Frederick William darkly reminded Victoria of "what would be coming our way if this man were to guide Prussia's fate sooner or later." In a letter to her mother, the crown princess described Bismarck as "such a wicked man that he does not care how many fibs he tells to serve his purposes." Once Bismarck was in office, the relationship with Frederick William went from bad to worse. Before embarking on a lengthy holiday in October 1862, the crown prince sent the minister-president a stern warning against using his absence to violate the constitution or circumvent the need for parliamentary authorisation of the budget. A long conversation with the minister-president in December 1862 confirmed the crown prince's low opinion of the politician, who had cracked tasteless jokes and openly considered the unilateral imposition of a budgetary law. Seeing in Bismarck the author of the unconstitutional press edict which had compelled Frederick William to declare his opposition publicly in June 1863, the crown prince subsequently lashed out against the minister-president. In a letter dated 30 June 1863, he openly doubted Bismarck's honesty, accused him of offending the people's sense of justice, warned him against triggering anarchy, and called him a danger to king and fatherland.[72]

While the opposition of many other early critics of the Prussian minister-president began to soften after the Prusso-Austrian victory over Denmark in 1864, Frederick William continued his implacable opposition to Bismarck's policies. In November 1864, the British diplomat Robert Morier, a trusted friend of the crown princely couple, reported that "the supposed brilliancy of Bismarck's successes during the last four months had altogether failed to produce any impression on them." Throughout 1865 and the first half of 1866, the crown prince persistently challenged the minister-president's key policies. A firm supporter of Prince Frederick of Augustenburg's claim to rule Schleswig-Holstein, Frederick William opposed the plan to annex the two duchies recently wrested from Danish control. He also argued passionately against Bismarck's manoeuvring toward war against Austria. General Moltke recalled that following a presentation by the minister-president at a meeting of the crown council in May 1865, the crown prince "turned fiercely against Bismarck and spoke of a 'civil war in Germany.' " "Bismarck's foolhardiness to start a war in Germany remains inexplicable to me," Frederick William wrote to the Duke of Coburg on 26 March 1866, "and I will try everything to meet this evil, to prevent, to warn and to avoid." He contacted his mother-in-law to ask for Britain's help in preserving the peace and begged his father repeatedly not to risk a war with Austria. "I cannot tell you often enough," he wrote to the king on 29 March 1866, "that it seems to me as if you were surrounded by something fatal which could easily be dispelled by your own wisdom and candour."[73]

Rather than inducing the king to dispel the fatal minister-president, however, the war of 1866 and its consequences removed the unequivocally hostile quality that had hitherto characterized the relationship between Frederick William and Bismarck. During the following two decades, both their attitudes toward each other and their expectations of their future relationship vacillated with bewildering frequency. The crown prince continued to express his old misgivings about Bismarck and added new grave failings to the list, but he also learned to appreciate the statesman's undeniable talent and achievements. After the defeat of Austria in 1866—and even more so after the victory over France and the foundation of the German Reich—Frederick William also recognised that he and Bismarck shared important political aims. Moreover, the crown prince came to accept that the chancellor's presence and power had become facts of Germany's political life relevant to his own future.

Bismarck reciprocated the realism of this appraisal. While never rating Frederick William's abilities very highly, he assessed the limits of the crown prince's liberalism more soberly than many others. He therefore regarded Frederick William's future reign as essentially compatible with his own continued government. Fully aware that his position was sustained by the trust and favour of a septuagenarian monarch, Bismarck understood the precariousness of his own political future within Prussia's emphatically monarchical system. As the dynastic principle also was a fact of political life, Bismarck's own mixture of Realpolitik and royalist sentiment compelled him to maintain some sort of modus vivendi with Frederick William. Nevertheless, the chancellor also mirrored Frederick William's continued if intermittent expressions of low regard and occasionally railed against the crown prince's alleged character flaws and political unreliability. Sometimes these opinions even led to statements indicating Bismarck's determination not to serve under the new monarch, but these were exceptions that proved the rule of the chancellor's firm belief in his own irreplaceability.

These occasional outbursts against the crown prince later in Bismarck's career stood in marked contrast to the self-discipline, calmness, and moderation he showed during his early years at the head of the Prussian government. Following his appointment in September 1862, he sent Frederick William several deferential letters in which he explained his policies and did his best to keep the travelling crown prince abreast of the government's plans. After the crisis triggered by Frederick William's Danzig speech, the minister-president did his best to mollify the incandescent king and ignored the crown prince's sharp attacks on his government and his personal integrity. During a meeting in September 1863, Bismarck tried to persuade Frederick William to adopt a less hostile position by pointing out that he would rule in the not-too-distant future and would do well to work for a smooth transition to the different principles he would then implement. In March 1864, the minister-president wrote to Lothar von Schweinitz, Frederick William's adjutant, to find out if his attempt to keep the crown prince informed by sending him copies of important state papers was welcome. If this were not the case, he would stop in order to avoid causing offence. A year later, Bismarck informed Schweinitz that he had decided to stay away from a regimental celebration attended by the crown prince. His presence, the minister-president feared, might annoy Frederick William.[74]

The tact Bismarck had shown during the previous years must have made it easier for Frederick William to come to the minister-president's aid at a critical juncture during the war against Austria in 1866. Worried about a possible French intervention, Bismarck urged the king to exploit Prussia's decisive defeat of the Austrian army and bring the war to a speedy conclusion. William and his military advisers, however, rejected the relatively moderate terms of the proposed preliminaries and insisted on imposing further losses on Austria. The deadlock was eventually resolved by the crown prince, whose support of the minister-president's position induced the king to give way. Frederick William recorded in his diary on 20 July 1866 that he had promised Bismarck to intervene "in order to consolidate and use the advantages of Prussia's position as leader of the common German fatherland." What a "strange contradiction," he wondered four days later. "I often have to be on Bismarck's side in order to defend what is really timely in his views against his majesty. The time is such, though, that consideration of party and individuals has to step back so that we can achieve great aims, so that strength and weal can come to the greatness and entirety of the fatherland." Both Bismarck and Frederick William richly embellished the story of their united effort: the minister-president recalled the crown prince's hand on his shoulder as he stood suicidally close to an open window; Frederick William described Bismarck sulking in a locked room or with tears flowing. More important than the drama of their cooperation was its motivation. As Frederick William's diary entries show, Bismarck's policies for a great and entire fatherland played a crucial role in winning him over. German soil became common ground.[75]

"Not the least of the successes these days have brought," Bismarck's secretary, Heinrich Abeken, wrote to his wife in August 1866, "is that [the crown prince] has come closer to Bismarck and is very much of one mind with him at least in matters of German and foreign policy."[76] Frederick William and the chancellor of the newly founded North German Confederation agreed that the unification of non-Austrian Germany constituted the key aim of Prussian statecraft. They both were also advocates of a compromise by which the conflict between Prussia's government and its parliament could be ended. This was achieved by means of an Indemnity Bill, in which the government admitted that its expenditure since 1862 had been nonconstitutional and was, in turn, granted retrospective authorisation. In September 1866, the Prussian parliament passed the bill by a large majority, thus ending the constitutional conflict without having established budgetary control over military expenditure.

The relationship between Frederick William and Bismarck underwent a gradual change. The traditional expressions of doubt and foreboding were now shot through with unprecedented signs of trust, optimism, and mutual regard. Frederick William told the liberal deputy Max von Forckenbeck in August 1866 that he had always been an enemy of Bismarck, "but now it was necessary to support him." Seven months later, the crown prince met a group of liberal parliamentarians to help ease the passage of the governmental proposal for the North German Constitution. When addressing the deputies, Frederick William freely admitted that Bismarck had agreed to the meeting. During a conversation with Schweinitz in April 1870, Frederick William spoke highly of the chancellor and indicated that he was not planning to dispense with his services. Talking to his press agent, Moritz Busch, in August 1870, Bismarck claimed that he and Frederick William were "quite good friends" and predicted that, once on the throne, the "entirely natural and honest" crown prince would behave perfectly reasonably.[77]

The Franco-Prussian War of 1870–1871 and the simultaneous foundation of the German Reich acted as a powerful fertilizer for these green shoots of mutual respect and cooperation. Along with Bismarck, the crown prince supported the candidacy of Leopold von Hohenzollern-Sigmaringen for the Spanish throne in the spring and summer of 1870. In spite of furious protests from Paris, he was convinced that the candidacy of a distant relative of the Prussian king was not inimical to France's interests and considered Prussia's position in the ensuing Franco-Prussian crisis unassailable. "If the French, in their limitless thirst for war, seek new pretences," he wrote to his father after Leopold had withdrawn his candidacy, "they are unmasked and certainly assured Europe's condemnation." As events were moving toward war, Frederick William commended Bismarck for the "great clarity and dignified seriousness," with which he explained the situation and acted on the chancellor's suggestion to travel to the capitals of the South German states whose troops he would command.[78]

The crown prince was swept along by a wave of patriotic excitement that he found "downright indescribable. . . . Everyone is hastening to the flag; everyone wants to join the fight." Less than a month later, after the first German victories had been won, Frederick William outlined to Bismarck how the "national enthusiasm," strengthened by these successes, should be used to bring about Germany's unification. Keen to "strike the German iron while it is hot," the crown prince raised the issue of a united German Reich in conversations with Bismarck and the king. The chancellor, who was engaged in secret negotiations with representatives of the southern German states about forming a united German Reich, appears to have been impressed by the crown prince. "He found infinitely much more and entirely different things in him than he had thought," Abeken informed his wife in October 1870. Bismarck also mentioned that Frederick William had spoken "openly and beautifully about their relationship."[79]

This is not to suggest that the crown prince and the chancellor passed those frantic months in complete harmony. Left in the dark about the progress of the delicate talks with Bavaria, Württemberg, Baden, and Hessen-Darmstadt, Frederick William grew increasingly impatient. Even in 1868, progress toward German unity had seemed unbearably slow to him and now he was worried that the process might be stalling again. To prevent this, he urged a very robust course indeed. During a heated exchange on 16 November 1870, the crown prince came close to suggesting that military force be used against the recalcitrant southerners to break the deadlock. "I, who represent the future, cannot observe such hesitation with indifference," he warned Bismarck. Concerned that Frederick William could easily ruin what had already been achieved, the chancellor reacted with outrage to this suggestion and suffered a bilious attack afterward. Undeterred, the crown prince continued to lobby for a speedy introduction of the office of emperor, opposed the concessions offered to the southern German states and pushed for a more centralised constitution.[80]

More than three years earlier, Bismarck had already gone to some lengths to convince Frederick William that disregarding the rights of the smaller German states was not the way to achieve German unity. In February 1867, after the crown prince had criticised Prussia's lenient treatment of Saxony, Bismarck sent him a memorandum explaining why all measures must be avoided "that could injure the feelings of the Saxons." Now that the same issue reemerged under much more precarious circumstances, the chancellor was more than a little annoyed. "One could almost despair," he told

Count Waldersee in December 1870 when complaining about Frederick William's shortsightedness and impatience. In conversation with his adviser, Ludwig Bamberger, three weeks earlier, Bismarck had been less guarded. "The crown prince," he had ranted, "is the most stupid and vainest human being and will, one day, die of his imperial delusions."[81]

Such vitriol notwithstanding, the desire to create a German Reich and the task of convincing a highly reluctant King William to play his part united rather than divided Bismarck and Frederick William. On 3 December 1870, the crown prince attended the briefing where Bismarck officially informed the king of a letter in which King Ludwig of Bavaria—speaking on behalf of all the German princes—invited the Prussian monarch to accept the imperial title. William's first reaction was to reject the entire scheme, which he considered a threat to Prussia's royal tradition. Frederick William recorded in his diary that he and Bismarck nevertheless shook hands after the meeting, "without much talking, since we felt that the decision had been made and that as of this day 'Emperor and Reich' had irrevocably been restored." In spite of his frustration with the halting pace of the entire process of founding the Reich and his subsequent carping about the halfheartedness of its constitution, the crown prince was deeply affected by what had been achieved.[82]

"Finally Emperor and Reich are an acknowledged fact proclaimed on the birthday of our Prussian monarchy," Frederick William wrote after the official proclamation of his father as German emperor in the palace of Versailles on 18 January 1871. He rejoiced in the observation that "the long-held hopes of our ancestors, the dreams of German poetry are fulfilled" and confidently welcomed the challenge ahead of him. The crown prince was particularly moved by the thought that "all the witnesses present in these rooms were not normal guests, but men who had for months risked their lives for the common cause of the fatherland, which was now consecrated before their very eyes. Germany had her emperor back."[83]

The new Reich now entered a so-called Liberal Era dedicated to the completion of a political edifice that had been founded not only heroically but also rather hastily. The National Liberal Party, which had grown out of the liberal majority which carried the 1866 Indemnity Bill, enjoyed electoral success and lent its parliamentary support to Bismarck's government. As Frederick William warmly endorsed many of the key initiatives—the building up of central Reich institutions, moderate legal and administrative reform, and the campaign against Political Catholicism—his relations with Bismarck improved significantly. Moreover, aware of Emperor William's advancing years, the chancellor made a special effort to woo the heir to the throne. In 1871 Bismarck agreed to include the crown prince, who still refused to attend ministerial meetings, in the regular circulation of cabinet papers. In 1872 and 1873, Frederick William's confidants Albrecht von Stosch and Heinrich Friedberg were appointed to ministerial positions. When addressing the council of ministers in May 1872, Bismarck declared it to be his duty to consider the heir to the throne's interests when making ministerial appointments. As the chancellor had no doubt anticipated, Stosch immediately passed the good news on to Frederick William.[84]

These efforts were not wasted and resulted in a marked shift in the crown prince's attitude toward his former nemesis. By September 1873, both the liberal-conservative deputy Chlodwig Hohenlohe-Schillingsfürst and Johann Heinrich Gelzer, a close adviser of the Grand Duke of Baden, believed that Frederick William would retain Bismarck after his accession. In April 1876, Frederick William noted in his diary that a long meeting with the chancellor had barely led to a discussion, "because we found ourselves agreeing on almost every question." It was Baron Roggenbach's opinion in April 1877 that the thought of Bismarck demitting office one day now positively frightened the crown prince. The account of Frederick William and Victoria's dinner with the Bismarck family in September 1877 sounded almost too cosy to be true. "Count Eulenburg was sent to receive him, Princess Bismarck, and their daughter at the station and red cloth was laid down and the Imperial waiting rooms opened for him, as if he were of Royal blood," the wife of the British ambassador reported to Queen Victoria. "The Crown Prince becomes daily more civil to the Chancellor and calls on him often at his own house and seeks to be on the best terms with him now . . . and this naturally pleases and flatters Prince Bismarck who says that if it continues he will consent to remain in office when the Emperor dies, and help the Crown Prince to govern Germany!"[85]

By expressing her surprise at the kind of fawning that seemed required to keep the chancellor happy, Lady Russell put her finger on an issue that was beginning to attract wider attention. Rather than acting like a humble "Brandenburg vassal," Bismarck now clearly considered himself indispensable and increasingly identified the state with his own tenure of office. If he were to leave the king, he told Bamberger in 1870, William would "entirely go to pieces." After the foundation of the Reich, the chancellor's hold on power became practically unchallengeable. On the few occasions when Emperor William disagreed with his minister, Bismarck called the monarch's bluff by threatening to resign and the old emperor eventually accepted his place. Even though he was quoted as grumbling that it was not easy "being emperor under Bismarck," he conceded that the chancellor was "more necessary" than himself. By 1879 Lothar von Schweinitz, who now served as Germany's ambassador to Russia, considered Bismarck's autocracy unparalleled, and six years later, Bismarck could openly boast to a foreign visitor that he was "master in Germany in all but name."[86]

Notwithstanding the warming of their relationship in the course of the 1870s, this aspect of Bismarck's government stuck in Frederick William's craw. With his highly developed sense of monarchical dignity, the crown prince resented the chancellor's position in relation to the dynasty he claimed to serve. In letters to Stosch in 1872, 1873, and 1877, he referred to this "almighty person," worried that "the Bismarckian Grand Vizier-Dom might . . . gain the upper hand at the expense of the crown" and criticised "the chancellor's omnipotence." This simmering resentment came to a boil in 1878. Following an assassination attempt against the emperor in June 1878, his son was asked to act as deputy during his father's convalescence. Furious that he had been denied the full powers of a regent, Frederick William berated the chancellor, whom he held responsible for this decision. When Bismarck stormed out, the crown prince asked him whose right it was to give orders. Bismarck's reply that he was merely an obedient servant was met with an instruction to stay for a full report. He obeyed—reportedly with tears of fury running down his cheeks.[87]

The appraisal of the chancellor, which Frederick William wrote when compiling a detailed account of his deputyship, conveys a similar flavour. "Because of the successes of his foreign and domestic policies and his despotic leadership he had become so omnipotent," the crown prince observed, "that the prestige of the king and emperor appeared pushed into the background." Looking back over the first decade of the new Reich in 1881, Frederick William noted that he would not have believed in 1871 that an almighty minister would place himself above his emperor. The nationwide celebrations marking Bismarck's seventieth birthday in 1885 were more than the crown prince could stomach. Holstein recorded that he was apoplectic about the honours showered on the chancellor: "A minister, what is a minister? Nothing but an official of the king's. But this is no minister, but a dictator. This is the demise of monarchy."[88]

By the time of this outburst, the relationship between Bismarck and the crown prince had almost completed another full circle since the happy days of 1877. Bismarck's decision to end his cooperation with the National Liberals in 1878–1879 by shifting the course of his domestic policies to the Right increased the tensions between him and the crown princely couple. The emergence in 1880 of the anti-Bismarck, left-liberal Secession Party, which reputedly enjoyed Frederick William's support, caused further aggravation, especially after the 1881 Reichstag elections had considerably strengthened the liberal opposition. In this context, the crown prince reacted with suspicion to the chancellor's idea of making him governor of Alsace-Lorraine. "Those in the know think Bismarck now wants to remove me from here so that he can more easily realize some plans he has kept hidden so far," Frederick William wrote to Victoria in February 1879. During the following months, he criticised the chancellor for having squandered trust in the government both at home and abroad, for suffocating a free spirit, for shattering the hopes for a real liberal party, and for destroying independent men. When Frederick William learned of the death of Frederick of Augustenburg, whose ancestral lands Bismarck had annexed after 1864, he wondered how heavily this would weigh on the chancellor's conscience, "if he has one." In October 1881, the crown prince bitterly resented having to stand by while "Bismarck's moods and arbitrariness . . . shake the power and prestige of the crown."[89]

In spite of the left-liberals' and Victoria's best efforts, however, the relationship between the chancellor and the crown prince did not break down completely and recovered remarkably quickly. Emperor William's increasing frailty and both protagonists' belief in each other's and their own inevitability forced them to find an acceptable form of coexistence. While Bismarck expressed apprehension about a left-liberal takeover under the next monarch in February and October 1882, these statements were not the whole picture. They should be seen alongside comments the chancellor made to the emperor in July 1879; to his press agent, Moritz Busch, in April 1880; during a dinner party in September 1880; and in a March 1883 conversation with Christoph Cremer, a conservative deputy in the Prussian parliament, in which he doubted the depth of Frederick William's liberalism and his commitment to the Secession.[90]

On this basis and notwithstanding Bismarck's occasional grumbles about the crown prince's "love of approbation," indolence, or lack of understanding, the smallest common denominator remained intact. After a meeting in May 1880, Frederick William praised Bismarck's assessment of British policy. In August 1881, he sent the chancellor a letter in which he felt confident to be "as open as I am during our private conservations in your room in Berlin." In a conversation with Holstein in December 1882, the diplomat Paul von Hatzfeldt, who had regular dealings with both the chancellor and the crown prince, confirmed that he could detect no animus against Bismarck in Frederick William.[91]

It is therefore not entirely surprising that in March 1883, the chancellor was almost a little baffled that Deputy Cremer had bothered to ask him what would happen after Emperor William's death. "I will tell you," he replied. "I will request to be relieved of my duties as chancellor and minister-president, and the following day I will be re-appointed as minister-president and chancellor." Throughout 1884, diarists like Holstein or Minister Robert Lucius commented on the good rapport between the crown prince and the chancellor. Frederick William wrote to Stosch in July 1884 that Bismarck was now making "every effort to account for my wishes and take me into consideration," and by August, even the leading left-liberal deputy Karl Schrader believed that the future emperor would have to retain Bismarck. The left-liberals' crushing defeat in the Reichstag elections later that year only accelerated and consolidated the preexisting development that pushed Bismarck and Frederick William toward closer cooperation.[92]

In 1885 the emperor's health appeared to be failing and then none other than Crown Princess Victoria also decided to seek a rapprochement with Bismarck. She sent a lengthy memorandum to Justice Minister Heinrich Friedberg in which she expressed confidence that "Prince Bismarck's strong hands will know how to build the bridge which will safely lead us from the old to the new, which will crown and complete his work." After an intermission of several years, the chancellor again accepted an invitation to lunch with Frederick William and Victoria in July 1885. Following another meeting in December, Frederick William declared that, as in 1866, he and Bismarck were agreed on every major issue and had taken the words out of each other's mouths. In March 1886, the crown prince asked Bismarck directly if he was prepared to stay on after Emperor William's death. Bismarck agreed—provided that Frederick William would pursue a German and not a foreign-inspired policy and would not introduce a parliamentary system of government. The crown prince agreed to both conditions. A political marriage had thus been entered long before the Reichstag elections in February 1887 further strengthened the chancellor's hand by returning a clear majority for the *Kartell* of Conservatives and National Liberals.[93]

This clearly was not a love match, but a marriage of political convenience or even dynastic necessity. In spite of the numerous protestations of mutual respect during these later years, resentment was simmering just below the surface. Bismarck's explicit demand—which he expressed on more than one occasion and did not treat as confidential—that the crown prince should pledge not to rule Germany as Britain's lackey was nothing short of insolent, and having to dignify it with a reply must have been painful for Frederick William. Nor did the chancellor pull his punches when considering the crown prince's personality. When talking to Deputy Cremer in 1883, he described Frederick William as a man "predisposed by nature to make the most comprehensive use of force," which would make it very strenuous one day to prevent him from taking extreme steps. In conversation with Minister Robert Lucius in December 1886, Bismarck complained about the crown prince's sensitivity, pretentiousness, ill-founded wishes, and distrust. Even in 1889, when Frederick William's suffering and death could have mellowed the chancellor's opinion, Bismarck still referred to his egotistical nature.[94]

Frederick William's bitterness had not gone away either. When asked to explain his hatred of the chancellor in June 1885, he replied that Bismarck had done things to him that could never be forgotten. Moreover, the crown prince still resented the royalty-like status assumed not just by the chancellor himself but also increasingly by his family. Herbert von Bismarck behaved as if he were of royal blood, Frederick William complained. Referring to the medieval court officials who eventually put themselves in the place of the ruling Merovingian dynasty, the crown princely couple frequently deplored Bismarck's majordomo-like status. A long, impulsive memorandum sketched on the flyleaves of his 1885 diary also illustrates Frederick William's anger about the "cult with which the nation surrounds B[ismarck]," who should be a minister but no more than that. He even drew up a political battle plan in case the chancellor refused to accept a reduced status and had to be dismissed. This was mere shadowboxing, though. After 1863, Frederick William never again dared to throw any punches against the real opponent. The public address to the chancellor that the crown prince agreed to in the summer of 1885 and published upon his accession in March 1888 had a very different ring: "As I begin my reign I feel the need to turn to you, the long-standing, tried and true first servant of my late father. You have been the loyal and brave counsellor who has given form to the aims of his policies and secured its successful realization. I am and my house remains gratefully indebted to you."[95]

At the end of the day, neither man had any choice. The dynastic principle tied Bismarck's hands. In his memoirs, he referred somewhat stiffly to "Emperor Frederick, the son of the monarch, who I designate *in specie* as my master." Given his own experience of working for an obedient master, "who felt elevated by the thought of having a highly regarded and mighty servant," and his successful management of the crown prince, the prospect was hardly a daunting one for the chancellor. Accepting Bismarck's continued presence was a much more painful process for Frederick William. According to the historian Hans Delbrück, who tutored Prince Waldemar and was for several years a member of Frederick William's household, this realisation "limited his sweet indulging in ideas about the art of governing in general" and pointed him to the "sober Realpolitik question" of how to position himself toward Bismarck.[96]

Having to cut his political coat according to the cloth provided by a disliked minister must have been a galling task for the proud heir to a royal and imperial title. He had no choice but to accept this outcome, though, because in terms of political power, he was no match for Bismarck. Lacking both alternative forms of support and the chancellor's Machiavellian toughness, Frederick William saw no viable alternative to retaining the services of this overmighty subject. This matter had been settled and the necessary concessions made long before the crown prince was struck down by illness.

Frederick William's relationship with the Iron Chancellor thus fit the pattern established by his equally important relationships with his father and his wife: a combination of contextual factors and

Frederick William's own tendency toward deference, compliance, and resignation made it impossible for him to play a coequal, let alone dominant, role vis-à-vis these powerful personalities. In different ways, for different reasons, and with different outcomes, they were all stronger than him.

CHAPTER TWO

Liberalism and Empire

Frederick William's political beliefs lie at the heart of the irresistible story of the handsome liberal prince who would one day be an emperor and change the course of his country's history. He was still in his teens when progressive sympathies were first ascribed to him; throughout the rest of Frederick William's life, conservatives scolded and liberals praised the heir to the throne—and even the dying monarch—for what they claimed were his political convictions. Conversing freely at a private dinner, Bismarck once growled that "people still ha[d] to realize that Emperor Frederick's liberalism sprang from his incredible political feeble-mindedness." As could be expected, the left-liberal journalist Arnold Perls offered a different perspective. "What was known about Frederick's action in matters of state," he declared in a pamphlet celebrating the late emperor, was enough to "justify the hopes the liberal part of the people had placed in his rule."[1] Even though the fairy tale of the liberal prince was cruelly robbed of its happily ever after when the protagonist died after ninety-nine days on the throne, the notion was not buried with him. To observers who looked back at Emperor Frederick III through the lens of his son's calamitous reign, the First World War, and eventually Nazism, the missing liberalism of a second Frederician era assumed a tragic and continuously relevant importance.

Once before, during the revolution of 1848–1849, Germany had, in the words of A. J. P. Taylor, "reached its turning point and failed to turn." It has been argued that Frederick III's early death, by removing the essential liberal pivot, again prevented Germany from turning away from militarism, authoritarianism, and reaction. Here was a central ingredient whose absence from the potion of political transformation made Germany the Mr. Hyde of the twentieth century, when Frederick III's benign rule could so easily have fashioned it into a kindly and civilised Dr. Jekyll. If Emperor Frederick III had lived until 1914, so Emil Ludwig's counterfactual musings predicted, he would have left behind a thoroughly peaceful Germany, "like England, a virtual republic" and "doubly attached to its hereditary reigning house, to whom it owed its liberty at home." Though with less imaginative licence, German liberal émigré historians Erich Eyck, Veit Valentin, and Hajo Holborn also considered "how different the course of German history would have been" if Frederick III had reigned. As a "believer in liberal and constitutional methods of government," he was expected to "translate his ideas into practice." Notwithstanding necessary caveats about exaggerating the extent of the change that Emperor Frederick was minded and able to bring about, the frisson of speculation has remained powerful. The world would not have been the same, a West German paper implied when contemplating the centenary of the emperor's death, "if the dawn of his accession had really turned into a new era of domestic liberalization."[2]

Obscured by such layers of wishful thinking, accusation, and imputation, as well as veiled by Frederick William's own tendency toward opacity, inconsistency, and resignation, the outlines of his political beliefs are not easy to discern. Because of its centrality to the claim that his reign would have changed the course of German history, the issue of the crown prince's liberalism—its origins, extent, and limitations—has dominated how he has been interpreted. This remains a central issue—not only because of its relevance to retrospective speculation but also because his relationship with liberalism, the most important political ideology of his age, locates him fully within the landscape of nineteenth-century Prussia, Germany, and Europe. Frederick William's political worldview and his participation in the politics of nineteenth-century Europe were not, however, one-dimensional. Alongside his liberalism, a second important agenda requires careful consideration: Frederick William's notions of Germany's *Kaisertum*, which encompassed his thoughts about the origins and traditions of the German Reich, as well as his views about its proper structure and the role he intended to play as emperor one day.

The Liberal Prince

In November 1849, only a few days after Frederick William had officially been declared of age, the obscure poet Max Waldau sent him a belated birthday present: fourteen stanzas of heartfelt doggerel begging the prince to intercede on behalf of Gottfried Kinkel, a renowned revolutionary democrat who had been arrested by Prussian troops a few months earlier. As Kinkel was beginning his life sentence at the Spandau fortress, associations sprang up all over Germany to organise collections for his wife and children. Waldau's poem—together with a note carefully identifying its original recipient—was published with all proceeds pledged to the good cause. There is no evidence to suggest that the eighteen-year-old prince acceded to this lyrical request, which was rendered superfluous anyway when Kinkel escaped from prison and fled to England. It is interesting to note, however, that Frederick William was considered a suitable recipient of this kind of public appeal. The same year witnessed a number of events which indicated that Frederick William's political views were perceived as less conservative than could be expected from a Prussian prince. During a regimental dinner in May 1849, General Leopold von Gerlach, one of the ultraconservatives advising King Frederick William IV, decried Prussia's recently introduced "absurd constitutionalism" and was brought up short when the young prince insisted that a representation of the people was necessary. On the occasion of Frederick William's eighteenth birthday, the liberal *Deutsche Zeitung* praised him as mild, sympathetic, eager to do good and bring peace, and, above all, as developing his preferences "more in harmony with those of his mother than with his father's."[3]

The reference to Frederick William's mother is telling. Augusta of Saxe-Weimar was clearly the initial driving force widening her son's educational, intellectual, and political horizons. Intelligent, highly strung, and a product of the liberal cultural context of Goethe's Weimar, Augusta struggled to accommodate herself to life at Prussia's conservative court at the side of her somewhat wooden and unimaginative husband. In spite of the many frustrations the young princess encountered after her marriage in 1829, she succeeded in leaving a powerful and innovative mark on her son's upbringing. "He belongs to the present and to the future," she explained her educational aims in 1848. "He must therefore incorporate new ideas and work them through so that he may gain a clear and lively awareness of his time and live in and with it, not outside it."[4] To this end, the young prince's traditional military training was complemented with a carefully planned curriculum informed by the ideals of a bourgeois neohumanism. Tutors like the theologian Frédéric Godet, the mathematician Karl Schellbach, and the classicist Ernst Curtius introduced Frederick William to the canon of nineteenth-century learning that ranged from classical antiquity to European literature, Enlightenment philosophy, and natural science. Augusta also made sure that there were always a good many commoners amongst the cadets and Berlin grammar school pupils selected to play with the prince. To round off his formal education, Frederick William eventually enrolled for four semesters at the University of Bonn in the relatively liberal Rhine Province—far from the royal court in Berlin. The first heir to the Prussian throne to attend a university, he mixed freely with other students and attended lectures by liberal-national luminaries like the historians Ernst Moritz Arndt and Friedrich Dahlmann.

Ever critical and prone to a somewhat uncharitable view of her son, Augusta was open about what she regarded as the deficiencies of Frederick William's education. These were caused principally by "the traditional and local influences from which, despite all my efforts, I have not been able to shield him," she explained to Prince Albert in 1855. Notwithstanding such admissions of partial failure, Augusta's role in the formation of her son's outlook was crucial and readily acknowledged. "I know well what we owe her," Queen Victoria observed. "Fritz never would have been what he is had she not watched over him and done her duty by him."[5]

The queen of England was more than a sympathetic onlooker. Frederick William's connection to the British royal family and, above all, to Prince Albert and Princess Victoria was a second significant source of his liberal thinking. Famously keen on mentoring and confident of Augusta's warm approval, Albert established a relationship with the young Prussian prince when Frederick William, his sister, and his parents visited London in 1851. "The treasure of excellent and instructive things you showed me and told me will remain my precious guide," Frederick William enthused after he had left England. In return, Albert eagerly promised "to give you my advice honestly and openly at all times and under every circumstance, should you seek it. My entire store of political experience and knowledge shall be at your disposal."[6] The 1850s brought numerous further meetings and countless letters which Albert sent either directly to Frederick William or to intermediaries such as Princess Victoria or Augusta. Albert's influence on Frederick William's political thinking became unrivalled and remained effective until long after his death in 1861.

The prince consort's guidance soon became a constant feature shaping Frederick William's entire political horizon. When the young prince deplored the Prussian government's manipulation of the elections in October 1855, Albert considered the duties of the next generations when confronted with such "sowing of dragon's teeth." The answer, he declared, was that "morality, conscience and patriotism must compel them not to witness the murder of a sworn constitution passively!" Three weeks later, Albert sent the Prussian prince two speeches—one by Gladstone, the other by Lord John Russell—that he thought would be of interest to him.[7] In April 1861, Frederick William received a gentle rebuke from his mentor. He had expressed a desire to see Prussia deliver "one hearty blow" in the field of foreign policy to rally the smaller German states behind it. In his reply, Albert explained that "Prussia must be the moral leader of Germany before it can raise its head in Europe." This could not be achieved through sudden decisions, but only through a "long, self-confident, logical, courageous, truly German and thoroughly liberal policy."[8] Frederick William could not always make sense of his father-in-law's involved cadences—his diary entry on 9 August 1861 contains the admission that he had failed to grasp how Prussia was to lead and merge into Germany at the same time—but Albert was still proud of his work. "Fritz has decidedly made a conscious advance in his mental and spiritual development," he reported to Augusta in August 1861, "and that pleased me."[9]

Within Queen Victoria's extended family, Prince Albert, who had been venerated during his life, achieved quasi sainthood after his early death. For Frederick William, his father-in-law's counsel became immortal. The invocation of his name featured regularly in his political discourse and Albert's absence was painfully felt. "I know that beloved Papa would have urged him this in the strongest manner," Queen Victoria insisted when recommending that Frederick William adopt a particular course of action in 1862. A year later, she implored him "in dear Papa's name as well as in mine not to attend the Council of State." The crown prince was likely to be receptive to such rhetoric. What had made him see reason over the past years, he admitted to his wife in April 1864, was "the unspeakably salutary influence of your unforgettable father."[10] The crown prince's loyalty to Albert's teachings remained unshaken by the victorious wars against Denmark and Austria. After a conversation with Frederick William in April 1870, Ambassador Lothar von Schweinitz recorded with palpable chagrin that "the victorious leader on the Bohemian battle fields" still adhered to the ideas of the late prince consort. Frederick William's war diary of 1870–1871 shows how often he pondered Albert's plans, even at the height of the campaign in France and during the negotiations leading to the foundation of the Reich. "What a great mind like that of the enlightened Prince Consort wished and worked for can only gradually come to maturity," he penned on 14 December 1870. "His blessing will not fail to be upon the building of the new Empire." A dozen years later, Albert, now dead for more than two decades, still proved a valued source of inspiration. "I actively remembered your incomparable father today and sought to imagine . . . his position vis-à-vis our current developments," the crown prince wrote to his wife in August 1882. "My conversations with the imagined father were as interesting as we are used to and you could not tell his 71 years from his lively spirit, thank God."[11]

The knowledge of Frederick William's sense of indebtedness to his late father-in-law was by no means restricted to his inner circle and came to be known publicly. The proclamations issued by Emperor Frederick III in March 1888 suggested to the novelist Theodor Fontane that the "Prince Consort Redivivus" had taken over the government. When discussing the same documents, the liberal *Berliner Zeitung* praised them as exactly what one could have hoped for from the "spiritual heir of Prince Albert of Coburg." The classicist Wilhelm Studemund, speaking at the service of commemoration organised by the University of Breslau ten days after the emperor's death, reminded his audience of the "political ideals of his early youth, upon which his thoughtful father-in-law, the Prince Consort Albert of England, had exercised a dominant influence." The extent and duration of this dominance cannot be gauged with mathematical precision, but some of those who knew Frederick William well chose to describe Albert's impact on the Prussian prince in dramatic terms. "I owe it to Prince Albert," the crown prince once declared in a conversation recalled by his erstwhile librarian, "that I have learned to see the world with the eyes of a Western European."[12]

In the very same conversation, Frederick William also insisted that—apart from his father-in-law—it was his wife who had been responsible for his political formation. Alongside his mother and Prince Albert, Princess Victoria was the third decisive force pushing the crown prince's views in a liberal direction. Throughout their life together, Prince Albert's eldest daughter exercised a powerful influence on her husband's politics and it does not detract from the genuinely loving quality of their relationship to observe that this possibility had been clearly present in the minds of those eager to bring Frederick William and Victoria together. A loving and sensitive father, Prince Albert was delighted that the match made in 1855 was a truly happy one, but his fertile and somewhat restless political mind also appreciated the political utility of this marriage. He saw it as a welcome means to further his plan of a liberalized Prussia leading a more closely united German nation. Young Vicky's "special mission" would involve her in "seriousness and difficulty," Baron Christian von Stockmar, Albert's trusted adviser warned from Berlin a few weeks after the engagement. Consequently, no time was lost or effort spared to prepare the fifteen-year-old princess for the tasks ahead. "She comes to me every evening from six to seven, when I put her through a kind of general catechizing," Albert explained to his future son-in-law in November 1855, "and in order to give precision to her ideas, I make her work out certain subjects by herself, and bring me the result to be revised."[13]

The prince consort's efforts did not cease after Princess Victoria left England for her new life in Berlin. "You can say anything to Vicky and will be understood and as far as possible reinforced by her," he wrote to Augusta, explaining how Frederick William was to be counselled from now on. "It will be through her that he is provided with all the advice that is necessary for him, in a form that will not close his heart against it. As regards the kind of advice, I beg you to stick to those very liberal principles which Churches and dogmatizers, as well as politicians, find so hard to digest." Reiterating the role Vicky would play in the shaping of her husband's mind, Albert explained—perhaps a trifle too eagerly—that Augusta was "no longer required to continue irritating him by [her] motherly watchfulness and advice."[14] Throughout the four years between Vicky's departure and Albert's death, father and daughter exchanged hundreds of letters. The prince consort made sure that no political issue was left without comment or exhortation. It was excellent that Frederick William attended ministerial councils; Prussia would never rise by dragging down Germany to its level; Vicky and Fritz were not to lose courage or confidence in the power of the majority; Prussian hegemony in Germany could only be achieved through a freethinking, generous policy. This ceaseless instruction was a huge labour of love, but in Albert's opinion, it was crowned with success. "I am very satisfied with Fritz," he wrote to his brother in July 1861. "It is not possible to develop more steadily and well from a political point of view than he has done lately, or rather, since his marriage. Vicky is clever as she has always been."[15]

Even though the death of her father in December 1861 fell on the young princess like a hammer blow, it did not diminish her cleverness or her determination to change Prussia and Germany through her husband. "Be sure to remain firm and liberal," she implored him in March 1862 amid the escalating conflict between the Prussian government and the liberals in parliament, and this remained the basic tenor of the advice with which she peppered her communications with him over the next quarter of a century. When King William I considered abdicating in favour of his son in September 1862, she encouraged her husband to take over the reins of power. The following year, Vicky urged Frederick William to speak out publicly against the reactionary course steered by Bismarck and thus contributed to the crown prince's fateful declaration at Danzig. She also did her best to manage his circle of advisers. "Would you not like to arrange a little tête-à-tête with a nice and interesting man?" the crown princess wondered in December 1879, and spooled off a list of suitable individuals— almost all of them leading left-liberals: Eduard Lasker, Max von Forckenbeck, Georg von Bunsen, Franz Schenk von Stauffenberg, and Karl Schrader. "Only the healthy liberal principles we find represented amongst the men of the German Freisinn Party can guarantee Germany's inner strength and health for the development of her prosperity and her culture," Victoria reminded him after the left-liberals had suffered a setback in the elections of October 1884.[16]

The ultimate futility of her political efforts made the anguish of losing a beloved husband even harder to bear. "We had a mission, we felt it and we knew it," the bereaved empress wrote to her mother three days after Frederick III's death, "we were Papa's and your children! We were faithful to what we believed and knew to be right. We loved Germany—we wished to see her strong and great, not only with the sword, but in all that was righteous, in culture, in progress and in liberty."[17]

Frederick William's father-in-law and wife were certainly not alone in their belief that the crown prince was committed to progressive and liberal policies. Many contemporary observers considered it a matter of public record that under the tutelage of the formidable Augusta, the adulated Prince Albert, and the dominant Vicky, the heir to the throne had become a dyed-in-the-wool liberal. Frederick William's readiness to surround himself with a coterie of more or less liberal figures—among them Princess Victoria's private secretary, Ernst von Stockmar (the son of Prince Albert's adviser, Christian von Stockmar); Robert Morier, a British diplomat; Franz von Roggenbach, a Whiggish ex-minister from liberal Baden; Max von Forckenbeck, the mayor of Berlin; and the left-liberal deputy Karl Schrader—was seen as further proof of the progressive streak that allegedly ran through the prince's entire life. Frederick William's engagement to Vicky in 1855 had met with hostile mutterings amongst the governing conservative clique, and public celebrations of the marriage three years later were interpreted as demonstrating a desire for liberal change.[18]

A defining climax was reached in 1863, when the crown prince openly opposed Bismarck's attempts to suppress the liberal press. The officers of Potsdam were full of hatred against the "democratic crown prince," Frederick William recorded in his diary on 16 January 1863, and he learned two days later that the left-liberal German Progress Party was counting on him. In July 1863, the then liberal journal *Die Grenzboten,* based in Saxony and therefore beyond the reach of the Prussian censors, praised the "manly defence of the law and of justice" contained in Frederick William's attack on Bismarck. By the autumn of 1863, pamphlets celebrating the crown prince's opposition to the government were circulating in Prussia itself, as were rumours that Frederick William had even joined the Progress Party.[19]

To some observers, the liberal sheen Frederick William acquired during his dramatic falling-out with the Prussian minister-president in 1863 never dimmed. "The crown prince's political thinking is not mine," Bismarck observed four years later. "It is known that the exalted gentleman always wants to govern with the majority." According to an article in the *National-Zeitung* in January 1883, there never had been any serious tension between the "views of the crown princely couple and those of the people." Having identified "English attitudes and ideals" as those of the educated middle class, the liberal paper confidently stated its belief that Frederick William and Victoria's convictions were in line with "our people's hopes for the future." A journalistic introduction to Berlin society could simply observe in 1886 that "amongst the population at large the crown prince is considered a confessor of liberal ideas, often seen as opposed to the current 'reactionary system.' " By the time the liberal daily *Berliner Tageblatt* commemorated the centenary of the late emperor's birth in 1931, Frederick William had fully morphed into a popular freedom fighter. Looking back on his actions in 1863, the paper claimed that the "crown prince of Prussia and Prussian general rose full of outrage against king and government to speak out for the freedom of the liberal press. . . . Thus, in the conflict between ministry and parliament, the crown prince joined the people's side."[20]

Quotable though they are, such unambiguous statements about Frederick William's convictions and intentions exaggerate individual aspects and obscure the hybrid and sometimes contradictory overall character of his liberal beliefs. The "traditional and local influences" that even Augusta had failed to eradicate remained effective and should be taken seriously. They did not, however, prevent Frederick William from subscribing to a large and meaningful portion of the paradigm of nineteenth-century German liberalism. Some aspects of his political convictions—his views on Catholicism, socialism, and full parliamentarization, for instance—do not fit comfortably into the counterfactual reveries of a long-lived Emperor Frederick steering Germany off a pernicious Sonderweg and into the safe haven of modern Western social democracy. That his outlook differed from a post-1945 concept of liberalism does not, however, refute the notion of the crown prince's liberal convictions. Rather, this points to the ways that nineteenth-century German liberalism differed from British or French versions and from the twentieth-century paradigm. It also emphasises the extent to which the crown prince was a typical product of—and participant in—the political culture of his age.

Most fundamentally, Frederick William shared the central aim of early nineteenth-century German liberalism: to implement and safeguard the "legal and constitutional state," a body politic in which the rights of the individual and certain limitations on the exercise of sovereign power were enshrined in a written framework of legal norms and guarded by an elected representation of the people. Reflecting on the great political tasks ahead of him in 1871, Frederick William described himself as "the first monarch to face his people honestly and wholly well-disposed towards the constitutional institutions."[21]

This positive attitude ran like a red thread through Frederick William's entire political life. His respect for the constitution manifested itself in 1849, when the young prince told Gerlach that there had to be an elected parliament, and again in 1855 in his criticism of the vote rigging undertaken by Prussia's conservative government. Having been slapped down by his father for publicly criticizing the Bismarck government in June 1863, Frederick William nevertheless sent a furious letter to the minister-president in which he attacked those whose policy led "from one risky interpretation to another" and ultimately "to the naked and undisguised breach of the constitution." In his correspondence with Eduard Simson, the speaker of the North German parliament during the Franco-Prussian War, the prince conceded that "a new constitution that accounts appropriately and adequately for the liberal demands of our time" ought to be a quid pro quo for monarchical leadership. In April 1880, the crown prince complained bitterly to his wife that in the civil marriage issue, the government was considering certain concessions to the churches. "The worst thing about it," he wrote, "is the undeniable weakening of an existing law through the back door. . . . This is, for my future, an extraordinarily embarrassing, evil trick and mistake." When Frederick William, now a dying emperor, was finally given the opportunity to declare his convictions to the German people, his emphasis was predictable. The first item of his programme insisted that the "constitutional and legal systems of the Reich and of Prussia must grow firm above all in the reverence and customs of the nation."[22]

On the basis of this underlying commitment to constitutional government, Frederick William favoured steady institutional reforms in a liberal direction. A loose page inserted in his diary in 1867 lists a whole raft of proposals ranging from ministerial responsibility and the possible dismissal of civil servants to extending the remit of the Prussian audit office and rural policing.[23] While some of these ideas never received any traceable attention, other items on this agenda exercised the crown prince considerably. The first proposal, for instance, concerned transferring the confirmation of death sentences to the high courts in order to relieve the monarch of this "heavy burden." Frederick William was a self-confessed opponent of capital punishment and intended to make the Prussian tradition of commuting death sentences his regular practice as emperor. When deputising for the injured emperor in 1878, however, he found himself confronted with having to confirm the sentence against his father's would-be assassin. He agonised for days over this decision and talked it over with everyone close to him before reluctantly allowing the execution to proceed.[24]

Another substantial item on Frederick William's list was the reform of Prussia's rural communities (Kreisordnung), which had dragged on since the 1850s. The government's reform bill was eventually carried by an overwhelming majority of liberal and moderately conservative deputies in the lower house of the Prussian parliament in March 1872. When the ultraconservative majority in the upper house subsequently threw it out, the bill acquired a quasi-totemic status in the fight for liberal change. The detailed description of the internal power struggle between Bismarck, the other ministers, and the upper house contained in Frederick William's diary reflects his keen interest in the matter. Eventually, he took the unusual step of attending the crown council of 8 November 1872, where the government's response to the vote in the upper house was discussed. He wanted to throw his weight behind the reform plan. The council's minutes recorded that the "crown prince would not shrink from any legal means to make the upper house accept the Kreisordnung." The measure finally went through after the king had created twenty-six new peers and Frederick William wrote to his father to say that he was delighted with the outcome.[25]

The crown prince was also entirely in tune with the predominant liberal sentiment of the day when a new, vigorous, and organised form of anti-Semitism reared its head in Germany in the late 1870s. Triggered by the economic crisis that followed the so-called founders' crash of 1873 and in the context of growing hostility to the liberals' political influence, anti-Semitism gained momentum. Individuals like the journalists Otto Glagau and Wilhelm Marr, the court preacher and party leader Adolf Stoecker, and the historian Heinrich von Treitschke led a movement aimed at tackling what was portrayed as the "Jewish Question." Anti-Semites weighed in to the public debate with a flurry of articles, pamphlets, and books; by founding pressure groups; and through the "Anti-Semites' Petition" of 1880, which attracted 250,000 signatures. The official and public reaction to this agitation was mixed. The government intervened when anti-Semitic incitement or violence breached existing laws, but did not attack the phenomenon politically. Almost all of the established parties—with the notable exception of the Conservatives—rejected and opposed the demands of the anti-Semites, most prominently the liberals and, above all, their left wing.

Frederick William's reaction to the anti-Semitic movement was public, courageous, and unequivocal. The only member of the royal family to do so and earlier than almost every other prominent non-Jew, he openly demonstrated his disgust for what he regarded as an utterly deplorable phenomenon. As early as December 1879, he attended a concert in a synagogue at the request of the leader of Berlin's Jewish community. He did not find it easy to muster the courage, he confided to his wife, but decided to go because of his dislike of Stoecker and the anti-Semitic league. A year later, his resolve had stiffened. "We are ashamed of the Jew-baiting which goes beyond all decency in Berlin," he wrote from Wiesbaden in November 1880. "Luckily we could attend a concert in a synagogue here to show as far as possible what we think." A few weeks later, Frederick William pasted a newspaper report in his diary about a workers' meeting against anti-Semitism. He added that it was "a remarkable and pleasing fact" that a movement opposing Stoecker's agitation was forming "even amongst workers." Ignoring warnings that his public stance on the issue of anti-Semitism risked his being drawn into a dirty fight, Frederick William stated publicly in January 1881 that he disapproved of and rejected anti-Jewish efforts most emphatically and that he was particularly offended by the introduction of these tendencies into schools and universities. "He hoped," Frederick William was quoted in a newspaper report, "that this evil seed corn, thrown into the nursery of the noble and good, would not come to maturity."[26]

When he was confronted with the anti-Semitic agitation of the late 1870s and early 1880s, the crown prince, in line with his liberal persuasions, opposed the persecution of a religious minority. In the context of the political and governmental campaign against Roman Catholicism, however, Frederick William's beliefs caused him—and the majority of Germany's liberals—to pursue a very different course. The conflict between the Catholic Church and laity on the one hand and the state and the liberals on the other was particularly fierce in Germany. As in many other parts of Europe, it was informed by a bitter ideological struggle between the secularizing forces of liberalism and a resurgent papacy determined to defy its detractors. For many liberals, the fight against Pope Pius IX and his ultramontane church, whose rejection of modern science and dogmatic insistence on papal infallibility enraged them, was a crusade against dark obscurantism and for a free, rational state. The left-liberal politician and eminent scientist Rudolf Virchow gave the conflict its name: Kulturkampf—the struggle for culture.

Bismarck and the German state were brought into the fray by the position of the Catholic minority within the newly founded Reich. Traditionally anti-Prussian and pro-Austrian, bound by ties of religious obedience to the foreign power of the papacy and effectively represented through the Centre Party, which was led by opponents of the chancellor, the Catholics were an inconvenient thorn in the flesh of the new nation-state. The Kulturkampf therefore suited both Bismarck and the National Liberal Party. It conveniently united their uneasy alliance throughout the 1870s, and together they unleashed a campaign against a large religious minority now collectively vilified as a retrograde, unpatriotic, and dangerous enemy of the Reich. From 1871 onward, the governments of the German states initiated a series of legislative measures—among them the introduction of exclusive state supervision of schools, a ban against the Jesuit order, compulsory civil marriage, criminalizing political sermons, forcing seminarians to pass state examinations, and the withdrawal of public funds from recalcitrant clergy. The aim of this policy was to reduce the influence of the Catholic Church over its German flock and to bring priests more fully under the control of the state. Fiercely and imaginatively resisted by the Curia, the German episcopate, the Centre Party, and Germany's Catholics, the acrimonious years of the Kulturkampf ended in a comprehensive failure for the government and the liberal camp.

Frederick William's anti-Catholicism had impeccable credentials. As early as January 1860, in one of his many letters to his daughter, Prince Albert had categorically and emphatically ruled out that a state should agree on a concordat with the pope because the Catholic Church still insisted that it was above the state. Vicky's views on the Roman faith were no less critical: "I consider it both demoralising in the highest degree and blasphemous," she wrote to her mother from a visit to Italy in 1862. "The sad effect it has upon a whole nation is visible here to an extent one can hardly imagine."[27] Frederick William echoed these views wholeheartedly. In November 1864, he wrote to Bismarck to express his hostility to "Jesuits and Ultramontanes," whose increasing influence worried him. Four years later, he deplored that mothers in Schleswig allowed "their children to be confirmed in the enemy Catholic faith," which would have "dangerous consequences for us." During the French campaign, he dreamed of how the future German Reich would free the nation from "despotism and the rule of the black brigade, Jesuitism and orthodoxy would be hit on the head, and the minds would be freed from the tutelage of the Church." Once the Kulturkampf had begun, the crown prince doggedly supported the governmental line. "We cannot and must not back down after we have come this far," he insisted in a letter to Schweinitz, his former adjutant, in February 1875, "and compromising has become completely impossible now that Pius IX has declared war on us in his encyclical."[28]

Even though he did not publicise his anti-Catholic views, Frederick William became a recognised symbol of anticlerical opinion. During his visit to Venice in May 1875, for instance, the local liberals organised a serenade in his honour as a tit for tat for the clerical party's recent public reception of Cardinal Luigi Trevisanato. The painter Anton von Werner, who accompanied the princely couple, recalled that thousands of Venetians shouted "Evviva Fritz," and that the band kept playing the Prussian anthem over and over. Even though the crown prince was embarrassed by this unwanted attention, he stuck to his anticlerical views. Years after the death of Pius IX in 1878 and the breakup of Bismarck's cooperation with the liberals had enabled the chancellor to get the albatross of the failed Kulturkampf off his neck, Frederick William still remained implacable: "I am ashamed that Bismarck is already giving in," he wrote in his diary after a debate on ecclesiastical policy in the Prussian parliament in June 1883, "for why begin a fight against the Jesuits, if you already abandon it ten years later?" The following year, Frederick William observed that the Centre Party deputies in parliament had to be viewed not as Germans, but as strangers. Their presence was the greatest calamity and most insufferable aspect of all.[29]

The crown prince's condemnation of the Social Democrats was similarly dramatic. Established in 1875, when the two formerly competing wings of the workers' movement united, Germany's "Socialist Workers' Party" immediately went on to win twelve seats in the Reichstag elections of 1877. Notwithstanding the party's commitment to a course of legality, the political establishment reacted with shrill alarm to the arrival of an effectively organised working-class party. "Let us hope that the anti-socialist law means the beginning of a radical cure with which we can overcome this evil," the crown prince wrote to Charles of Romania on 19 October 1878. "It will take a lot of effort before we can get rid of this incredibly quickly growing monstrosity, since the teachings of this pernicious clique are selling like hotcakes." Deputising for his injured father, Frederick William wrote to the chancellor on 16 June 1878 to inform him that a senior general had been appointed to command the units that would be deployed "to suppress a possible insurgency in Berlin." If the insurrection were to spread, further troops could be summoned without delay. Such alarmist expressions and exaggerated preparations were clearly influenced by the events of 1878. The year had seen two assassination attempts against Emperor William—both of which were blamed on the Socialist movement—followed by a dissolution of the Reichstag and an election campaign characterized by a frenzied whipping up of fears about the Red Threat.[30]

Frederick William's reactions to the drama of 1878 were not, however, an aberration from an otherwise measured response to the Social Democrats' aims. Rather, the crown prince's attitude toward the Socialist movement had been negative long before Max Hödel and Karl Nobiling fired shots at the emperor. Notwithstanding his widely publicised charitable interest in the social question, Frederick William's views on the political dimension of workers' organisations were no more tolerant than those of most moderate German liberals. When Rudolf von Bennigsen, the leader of the National Liberals, addressed the Reichstag in October 1878, his predictions about the consequences of a Socialist takeover were every bit as lurid as Frederick William's: "I am not talking about the lives which would have been lost in their thousands in such a catastrophe," he exclaimed, "then would also be destroyed forever—along with law, morality and our traditional culture—the larger part of the national wealth accumulated for centuries."[31]

The crown prince had always reacted defensively to what he saw as the Socialist challenge. In 1865 he recorded his determined opposition to giving workers the right to strike. In his opinion, this was above all a means of chastising the bourgeoisie. One of the hopes he placed in the united German Reich, he wrote in October 1870, was that it would serve as a "bulwark against socialism." In 1878 Frederick William described the protesters who interrupted a celebration of Emperor William's recent escape from Hödel's assassination attempt as "pure-bred socialists." Only days later, Nobiling discharged a shotgun at Emperor William and the crown prince had to take over as deputy for his father. His account of the deputyship indicates that Frederick William fully endorsed the government's anti-Socialist legislation. "All parties in the Reichstag, the Progress Party included," the crown prince observed, "recognized the danger caused by the activities of the Social Democrats and were therefore inclined to assist the government in fighting them." On 19 October 1878, Frederick William wrote to his father and regretted that parliament had agreed to soften the anti-Socialist bill's provision for banning Socialist publications. In a letter to Victoria dated 20 April 1880, he expressed disappointment that the law had not been renewed until 1886, as had been demanded, since "this measure paralyses the socialists, even though they still continue their clandestine obstruction." The crown prince's concerns did not ease over the years. The first sentence of Frederick William's diary entry in which he reviewed the 1884 Reichstag elections read: "an enormous danger lies in the growth of the Social Democrats."[32]

Even though the utter rejection of socialism as a political force expressed in these phrases remained unchanged, there are indications that in the course of the 1880s, Frederick William began to doubt the effectiveness of the government's repressive approach. "As we have been predicting for a year, the Berlin elections have turned out considerably more successfully for the Social Democrats than usual," he wrote to his wife in October 1884, and added sarcastically: "I guess under the special protection of the state of siege!!"[33] In spite of such comments, there is no evidence to suggest that the crown prince ever explicitly opposed the periodic renewals of the anti-Socialist law, which the National Liberals helped to bring about in 1880, 1884, and 1886.

Frederick William and the National Liberals, the party that stood for moderate liberalism and cooperation with Bismarck, did not see eye to eye on every issue, though. A marked disagreement can be identified with regard to commercial policy and the introduction of a statute-based social insurance scheme. On both issues, the crown prince's views appear to have been more closely aligned with the left-liberal Secession group, which split away from the National Liberals in 1880 and merged with the radical German Progressive Party four years later.

Unlike the majority of the National Liberals, Frederick William initially opposed Bismarck's turn away from free trade. He criticised the tariffs introduced in 1879 in order to protect Germany's heavy industry and agriculture against foreign competition. Eager to catch up with his wife, whose superior knowledge of these issues he conceded, the crown prince immersed himself in the writings of renowned free traders like Rudolf von Delbrück, Henry Fawcett, and Ludwig Bamberger. The latter's "recent parliamentary speeches," he wrote in May 1879, "have had a very instructive, but repeatedly also a shocking effect on me, because of the thought of how much injury and wrong will now be introduced in Germany." As was so often the case, Frederick William and Vicky fully agreed on this issue. "For many years," she wrote, "free trade has struck me as the only aim of sound national economics," and he thanked her for "listing all those axioms." It should be noted, though, that after these comments, which date from the year when tariffs were first introduced, the topic seems to disappear from the crown prince's political radar. Moreover, as early as September 1880, he distanced himself from the Secession Party's dogmatic opposition to tariffs. "They claim that one has to be a free-trader to be a liberal, which sounds odd," Frederick William wrote in his diary, "especially since America proves the opposite."[34]

The crown prince also opposed Bismarck's legislative programmes for introducing state-regulated insurance schemes to protect workers against the worst effects of accidents, sickness, and old age. The few available sources suggest that he agreed with the left-liberals' concerns about the detrimental consequences of the chancellor's "state-socialism." The "social kingship desired by the state-socialist tendency," Frederick William wrote in November 1884, four months after the controversial accident insurance bill had passed the Reichstag, "is exposed to the onslaught of every kind of interest and will be untenable in the long term." The crown prince's scepticism about the state's role in the delivery of social provision also shines through in his inaugural proclamation. Drawn up in the summer of 1885, it specifically warned against the "expectation that it is possible to end all evils in society through state intervention." True to traditional liberal teachings, he regarded encouraging and supporting the workers' self-reliance as a much more promising avenue. Frederick William also favoured consulting workers directly, as well as reviewing the laws regulating the employment of women and children, work on Sundays, and a maximum working day.[35]

His views on tariff policy and social provision through the state suggest that Frederick William was politically aligned with the left-liberals. He does not appear, however, to have shared their opposition to Germany's colonial expansion. While the available source material does not indicate that overseas imperialism was one of Frederick William's central concerns, it nevertheless points toward a long-term and consistent interest. The generally positive attitude he manifested even before the emergence of a governmental policy in support of imperialist ventures locates him close to the procolonial wing of the National Liberals. In December 1870, for instance, he recorded in his war diary that it might well prove advantageous for Germany to acquire a port in Vietnam by forcing France to cede a naval station there. A few years later, the crown prince, who had been lobbied by interested parties about the importance of German trade concessions in China, unsuccessfully approached Bismarck with a request for further investigation of such schemes. In 1873, the British ambassador Odo Russell, who knew Victoria and Frederick William well, reported that the crown prince favoured Germany's colonial expansion. When drafting an inscription in honour of the Great Elector (1620–1688) three years later, Frederick William made sure to highlight that his famous ancestor had strengthened the Brandenburg navy, secured trade posts in Africa, and even acquired overseas possessions.[36]

Frederick William's views did not change in the course of the 1880s, when Bismarck's backing of overseas ventures resulted in the acquisition of several sizeable colonies. In the spring of 1880, Frederick William criticised the "short-sightedness of many deputies" who frustrated an attempt to "install an active commercial and colonial policy" when the Reichstag rejected a bill to support German trading interests in Samoa. The crown prince was aware of plans to launch the "German Colonial Society" in 1882, and even though he could not be persuaded to become its patron, he did express an interest in its activities. At the height of Germany's colonial expansion, Russell reported to London that Frederick William shared this "national craving." In fact, in May 1884, the crown prince even sent a memorandum to Britain in which he conveyed the German government's expectation that London would be accommodating in connection with Germany's engagement in Fiji, the Congo, and South-West Africa. The draft proclamation for his accession—which the crown prince approved in 1885 after the bulk of the German colonial empire had been acquired—specifically referred to the imperial navy and its "serious responsibilities" which had arisen "through the acquisition of overseas possessions." Though this was not exactly a ringing endorsement of Bismarck's colonial policy, the passage was quickly interpreted by some as indicating that Frederick III intended to "approach the colonial question with the same seriousness as the previous emperor," during whose reign a large overseas empire had been acquired.[37]

═══════

Taken together, the crown prince's views on the constitution, on piecemeal legal and institutional reform, on anti-Semitism, the Kulturkampf, socialism, protectionism, so-called state socialism, and imperial expansion appear to locate him unequivocally within the wide political space occupied by nineteenth-century German liberals. This verdict, although frequently endorsed by Frederick William's liberal supporters and conservative detractors, does not, however, capture the whole picture. The British weekly *The Economist* provided a more subtle account when it considered Frederick William's future in June 1883. As emperor, he would exercise immense authority, "yet no one in Germany appears to know with any certainty how he will use his power. The Prussian system has kept him almost entirely out of public life," the journal observed, "and though he is believed by most Germans to be a Liberal, many others shake their heads, and affirm that he is only a Liberal as a Crown Prince is; that once Emperor . . . he will show himself a true Hohenzollern."[38]

What this article captures is the combination and juxtaposition of forces that defined and limited Frederick William's political outlook. Long before the concept of psychohistory was established, some of Frederick William's contemporaries pointed to the Janus-faced quality of his political personality. Martin Philippson, who published the first substantial biography of the late emperor in 1892, pointed to two very different dimensions of Frederick William's beliefs, which resulted from his two very different parents: "on the one hand aristocratic-soldierly inclinations, on the other modern, educative, free perspectives." In an unpublished biographical essay, Georg Hinzpeter, for many years a tutor in the princely household, similarly explained a few years later that Frederick William's sympathies "always remained attached to the inherited Prussian tradition with all of its narrowness and strictness, while his convictions followed the modern liberal doctrine."[39]

To some observers, the most obvious fly in the ointment of Frederick William's liberalism was his traditionally Prussian attitude toward the military. Even the warm appraisal of the eighteen-year-old prince published in 1849 by the liberal *Deutsche Zeitung* mentioned that he fully shared his father's predilection for the army. Six years later, his mother warned Prince Albert with more than a hint of regret that her son's "preference for military matters had gained a greater preponderance than one should expect." Frederick William's attitude proved resistant even to Vicky's powerful influence. She complained that he could not or would not understand that men's claims such as that a soldier's life was "the only one that becomes a man" or that "death on the field of battle is the thing they wish for" caused her distress. Given these sentiments, it is unlikely that the crown princess would have been as overjoyed as her husband when he was appointed colonel of the First Prussian Infantry Regiment in June 1860. He was in such "a haze of bliss" when he found out that he was actually "quite giddy," he wrote to her. His regiment was the oldest in the army, he added with boyish excitement and saved a particular highlight until last: "By the way, I get to keep the uniform of the First Guards Regiment!!!" The diary entry Frederick William wrote in January 1865 was similarly telling: "Cathedral (alone). [Preacher] Kögel very beautiful, touching, attractive, elating: about marriage and relationship between husband and wife. Not been so edified for years, apart from on the battlefield."[40]

Even though Frederick William's attitude to war itself was dramatically affected by his firsthand experience of what he termed a "horrible activity" during the campaigns against Austria in 1866 and France in 1870–1871, his commitment to the military remained strong. In January 1873, for instance, he commented on the passage of an army organisation bill through the Reichstag: "Hopefully it will lead to the closest cementing together of the individual contingents with our army system as well as to a considerably less restricted power of the supreme commander over them than is the case at present." In his inaugural proclamation published in March 1888, the new emperor described the maintenance of the country's military force as the "necessary and most secure guarantee" of the successful pursuit of the central tasks of government. Literally in his dying days, he still found time and energy to deal with a surprising amount of military detail: officers' brass shoulder pieces were abolished, the drill regime for infantry units was reformed, and more time was allocated to shooting and combat practice.[41]

An heir to the throne so committed to the military traditions of his dynasty could not countenance relinquishing control over the army. When the liberal majority in the Prussian parliament opposed the government's army reforms in May 1861, the crown prince called it "miserable that vital questions of the monarchy should be threatened by factious opponents that know nothing about military things." In 1874 Frederick William's adjutant, Normann, deplored Bismarck's concession of a renegotiation of the military budget in seven years' time and described the compromise as an unnecessary burden on his master's future. He added that "those were badly mistaken" who thought that in this question the crown prince would ever meet the expectations of left-liberal politicians campaigning for more parliamentary control of the military. Hans Delbrück, the military historian and former tutor of Prince Waldemar, recalled Frederick William's frequent declarations that the army must never become a parliamentary force. It was the king's army and had to stay that way.[42] Here was a clear dividing line between Frederick William and the left-liberals. Ever since the conflict of the early 1860s, the Progress Party had campaigned on a platform of subjecting military funding to annual scrutiny and approval by parliament. Even though the 1884 programme of the newly founded German Freisinn Party, which united the Progress and the Secession parties, reduced this requirement to once in every three years, the principle of royal control of the armed forces remained a litmus test of Frederick William's view of parliamentary government. There is no evidence to suggest that he would have been prepared to compromise the fullness of his royal prerogative in this crucial respect.

It also appears unlikely that Frederick William ever wanted to see Germany become, as Emil Ludwig suggested, "like England, a virtual republic"—leaving aside the issue of whether he could have achieved this if he had so wished. In fact, even at the height of the conflict with his father and Bismarck, when he depended more than ever on the encouragement and advice provided by his English wife, he described himself as "the last person who would want to transfer, in a stencil-like fashion, other states' conditions to our own." In spite of the scant and occasionally ambiguous evidence, a convincing case emerges that rather than aiming for a British-style parliamentary system, Frederick William subscribed to the tenets of German *Konstitutionalismus* (constitutionalism). The classic claim that this type of monarchical-constitutional state was particularly suited to Germany's needs was not formulated until Otto Hintze's famous article of 1911. By then, however, its core ideas of a German arrangement combining a strong monarchical executive with parliamentary scrutiny of legislation and governmental action as well as an emphasis on the rule of law had been a long-established creed amongst many moderate liberals and conservatives.[43]

Frederick William's belief in a constitutional—rather than parliamentary—monarchy proved crucially important when, in September 1862, he was confronted with his father's determination to abdicate rather than give in to the Prussian parliament's demand to shorten the term of military service. Frederick William warned the king about "the immeasurable damage such a wicked step as the king abdicating because of a parliamentary resolution would do to crown, country and dynasty." He felt that this would set a very dangerous precedent for the future. When he sent an account of the conversation to his wife, whose advice to seize the opportunity and succeed to the throne he chose to ignore, Frederick William again shuddered at the idea of "the maleficent, wicked step of abdicating which threatened dynasty, house and crown."[44] Other considerations may have played an important role in making up the crown prince's mind—respect toward his father or a realistic sense of the intractability of the political crisis—but it is clear what he chose to emphasise: avoiding the damaging transformation of the Prussian monarchy into a system where parliament had succeeded in forcing out the king.

Moreover, Frederick William's—at best—ambivalent views of the quality of German parliamentary life make it unlikely that he would have been content to see parliament play a dominant constitutional role. Scattered across much of his political correspondence are comments that indicate the disappointment, pessimism, or annoyance the crown prince felt vis-à-vis Germany's parliaments and parties. He was distinctly uneasy about Bismarck's introduction of universal manhood suffrage. It was necessary to guard against it by means of a bicameral system, he wrote to his sister in October 1870. In their periodic dissections of what they saw as Germany's diseased body politic, Victoria and Frederick William would occasionally come back to this issue and describe the German franchise as "damaging" and "a blunder."[45]

The German parties did not offer Frederick William a more edifying prospect either. In Britain, two great and powerful parties truly represented the country. The "immaturity of our compatriots for independent political conviction," the crown prince observed in May 1879, made it appear doubtful, however, whether one should indulge in similar hopes for Germany.[46] "Today I see insecurity and lack of principles both in the political parties and in the population," the crown prince confided to his diary in January 1880. "The leaders appear not to know what they want, or at least have no real desire." Looking back on the completed parliamentary session in June 1883, Frederick William noted that "vanishingly little had been achieved in the course of the fiercest battles." A year later, he bumped into a conservative member of parliament who had annoyed him, and the crown prince asked if he was that "parliamentary blabber-mouth."[47]

Konstitutionalismus offered a way out of the dilemma in which Frederick William found himself. He was caught between his fundamentally liberal outlook and his commitment to maintaining the strong monarchical leadership he considered both central to Prussia's identity and essential because of Germany's deficient parliamentary life. The "optimistic take on our current situation," for instance, which the liberal politician and former Prussian minister Rudolf von Delbrück shared with Frederick William in December 1879, immediately appealed to the crown prince. "Our monarchy, which—unlike in England—will never have to be in hock to the parties, could develop its power," Frederick William summarised Delbrück's thoughts to his sceptical wife. "We should also make sure never to appoint party leaders to ministerial office, which ought to be in the hands of specialists." Agreeing to the domestic condition on which Bismarck reportedly insisted if Frederick William wished him to continue as chancellor was therefore not a big step for the crown prince. During their meeting in March 1886, Bismarck reportedly asked that Frederick William never introduce a parliamentary system. The crown prince readily agreed.[48]

This is not to suggest that the pragmatic rapprochement between the crown prince and the old chancellor was the result of a perfect harmony of political outlook. It was brought about by a heterogeneous combination of personal, party political, and power political factors. The character and extent of Frederick William's liberalism, however, did not make cooperation between him and the Iron Chancellor categorically impossible. In that respect, the crown prince once again proved a fairly typical representative of moderate German liberalism, which also managed to establish a modus vivendi with Bismarck after the Austro-Prussian War and again—with its liberal wings severely clipped—when the National Liberal Party joined the electoral *Kartell* alliance with the conservatives in 1887.

While Frederick William's conventional and relatively malleable liberalism could be accommodated within Bismarck's governmental system, the same was unlikely to be the case for a more unorthodox set of political beliefs to which the crown prince adhered doggedly and surprisingly rigidly. Ironically, what might have destroyed the relationship between Emperor Frederick and Bismarck was the very common denominator that served as the basis for the temporary cooperation between Bismarck and the German liberals: the desire to create and develop a united German Reich.

Heir to an Empire

Wednesday, 18 October 1911, was a memorable day for the good people of Aachen. Emperor William II was visiting the old capital of Charlemagne's medieval empire to unveil an equestrian statue of his father, the late emperor Frederick III. The streets were decorated, the crowds were jubilant, and everything went according to plan. Having finished a nine-course luncheon, the emperor addressed the assembled guests:

> If ever a monarch deserved a monument in Aachen, it is my father, resting in God. Since I was a child I could observe with how much interest he dedicated himself to studying the German emperors and their traditions. . . . When, as a boy, I was in his room and had earned a treat through my good behaviour, he allowed me to leaf through a splendid tome which showed the emperors' jewels, insignia, vestments, weapons and the crown itself in colourful detail. How his eyes sparkled when he told me about the coronation celebrations in Aachen with their ceremonies and banquets, about Charlemagne, Emperor Barbarossa and their splendour. He would always conclude by saying: "All that must come back, the power of the empire must rise again and the lustre of the imperial crown must radiate once more!"[49]

William II may well have had the Aacheners' pride in their city's history in mind when he prepared this speech, but his account captures more than an inconsequential detail. Throughout much of his political life, Frederick William showed an emotionally charged and politically as well as constitutionally relevant commitment to the idea of a German Reich and emperor—its concrete meaning and its outward manifestations. He made no secret of these views, and they did not fail to attract reactions. That he clung to these notions in spite of the largely negative responses he received gives an indication of the depth of his attachment to them.

———

It has been argued that, unlike most German liberals, Frederick William was interested in a united Germany mainly as a "stepping-stone for Prussia and the Hohenzollerns to greater power and prestige." The available evidence supports this interpretation of Frederick William's German nationalism right up until—but not beyond—the foundation of the Reich in 1870–1871. Amid the war scare of 1859, for instance, Frederick William pondered the correct timing of a campaign against France. This should be done carefully, he warned, so that Prussia would not end up fighting for Austria's preservation but for Germany's honour and, implicitly, for Prussian leadership. Two years later, the crown prince asked his father not to ban the black-red-gold German tricolour from a festival to be held in Berlin. He had no sympathy for a flag once proudly waved by the revolutionaries of 1848, he assured the king, but begged him not to offend the many people outside Prussia who were now supporting it. Frederick William made it clear that the Prussian colours must not be pushed into the background and assured King William that he had "his eyes on one aim only: to see your Prussia and your army placed and kept as high as possible above all party opinions." Prussia's position within Germany was also the central concern of a lengthy memorandum on German politics which Frederick William composed in February 1862 to advocate an invasion of the electorate of Hessen-Kassel and the removal of the Austrian-backed reactionary elector Frederick William I. While this might lead to civil war and a division of Germany into two antagonistic camps, the Prussian government "would have not only its own parliament, but the whole of Prussia and considerable sympathies in Germany behind it."[50]

Frederick William developed his ideas about Prussia's political aggrandizement even more clearly during the so-called wars of German unification. To him the German-Danish War of 1864 offered a real opportunity. "If Prussia acts in accordance with that respectable national feeling," he explained to his father in January 1864, "she will gain the emphatic leadership in Germany and will neutralise all the efforts of the governments hostile to her." Before the war against

Austria in the summer of 1866, which Frederick William had tried to prevent, the crown prince had argued strongly against Prussia's annexation of the duchies of Schleswig and Holstein. The Prussian victory over Austria and her German allies, however, made a strong impression on him. During a crown council in August 1866, William I hesitated to accept Bismarck's recommendation to incorporate Hanover, Hessen-Kassel, Hessen-Nassau, and the city of Frankfurt. The king was reluctant to act like the usurper Napoleon Bonaparte. The crown prince, however, "most emphatically recommended the unconditional and complete annexation of those states without any compensation," the council's minutes recorded, "and he declared this to be a duty towards the nation and the army." His father eventually concurred.[51]

After the dramatic events of 1866, the road ahead seemed clear to the crown prince and it led to something greater still than Prussia. "He appears to anticipate Germany's unification under Prussian leadership as something self-evident," the Bavarian minister-president recorded in his diary after talking to Frederick William in April 1868. Talking to Lothar von Schweinitz five months later, the crown prince was even less shy: "I want to wear the German imperial crown," he declared, "and I will wear it."[52]

Prussia's assumption of a German imperial title, which had disappeared when the last Holy Roman Emperor laid down his crown in 1806 and was revived unsuccessfully by the revolutionaries of 1848–1849, was first mooted in 1866–1867. At the time, the idea did not have a fair wind behind it. Bismarck pushed for a federal solution to counter the parliamentary-democratic tendencies aiming for a unitary monarchy. He therefore resisted radical and liberal demands to combine the title emperor for the Prussian king with a German parliament and a responsible national ministry. Plans involving the imperial title, a German cabinet, and a federal upper house were also pursued by a group of German princes close to the Prussian crown prince and centred on Ernest II of Saxe-Coburg-Gotha. While the more strongly federal complexion of their initiative matched Bismarck's intentions, he baulked at the English flavour of its constitutional agenda and its overly romanticized notion of the imperial dignity. For Frederick William, who would have had this kind of empire in mind when he spoke to Schweinitz in 1868, the history of the Holy Roman Emperors was patently a relevant consideration. He somewhat pedantically explained to Bismarck that the title "German

Emperor" never existed. According to a circular issued by Maximilian I in 1508, the correct title was "Elected Roman Emperor, in Germania etc. King."[53]

In 1866–1867 the chancellor stifled the "emperor plan," but he returned to it a few years later as a potentially useful means to overcome a number of domestic problems. During a train journey in January 1870, Bismarck broached the subject with the crown prince. He hoped to use Frederick William to find out the British attitude to this idea. The crown prince immediately sprang into action, and when the British foreign secretary spoke to the Prussian ambassador only four days later, he was fully briefed about the plan to elevate King William to the rank of emperor. Although initially sympathetic, Lord Clarendon eventually expressed misgivings after he had heard about France's opposition to the scheme. This was enough for Bismarck to drop the idea for the time being. Frederick William, whose hopes were dashed yet again, reacted angrily. On 24 April, Schweinitz detected the "bitter feeling that he could not solve [the German question] according to his programme." The next day, Frederick William entered in his diary that his confidant, Morier, had not been aware of "Bismarck's fraud regarding the emperor-idea."[54]

The experiences of the Franco-Prussian War of 1870–1871 strengthened the romantic aspects of Frederick William's attitude to the issue of empire. It is hardly surprising that Bismarck and the crown prince clashed when the topic arose again after the German armies had invaded France. Frederick William felt that he could not trust the chancellor with his own future and his plans for restoring Germany's imperial crown, while Bismarck regarded some of the crown prince's ideas as delusional. The novelist Gustav Freytag, a member of the crown prince's inner circle, recalled a conversation that took place during the campaign in August 1870. Frederick William appeared wedded to "the idea that the king of Prussia would, as emperor of Germany, inherit the thousand-year-old dignities and honours." In September, the crown prince visited the Hall of Mirrors at the Palace of Versailles and recorded his "firm hope that the restoration [!] of emperor and empire would be celebrated here of all places." Nine days later, he tried to overcome his father's opposition to newfangled titles by reminding him that "Germany's imperial or royal crown, more than a millennium old and only dormant since Emperor Francis abdicated in 1806 had nothing in common with the ultra-modern imperial crowns of Austria or France."[55]

Very much aware of the importance of visual symbols and historical arguments, Frederick William criticised the drafts of the new imperial coats of arms that he had ordered from the master of ceremonies of the Prussian court. "I demand especially that ancient coronation crown, because it is the particular attribute of the German imperial dignity and has always been shown on paintings and statues," he insisted on 6 December. A few weeks later, the crown prince and the Grand Duke of Baden coauthored a proclamation for the newly elevated Emperor William. According to this unused document, Frederick William's father would have introduced himself as "a successor of those serene emperors who once bore the crown of Charlemagne." Eventually, when William I was proclaimed emperor, a coat of arms was attached to the drapery behind him. Hastily made from velvet, it was based on a design the crown prince had requested from the painter Ferdinand Count Harrach: a black eagle topped with the medieval imperial crown.[56]

The crown prince's concern to demonstrate the ancient lineage of the Hohenzollerns' brand new dignity did not abate after the official proclamation of William I as German emperor. Frederick William planned a formal coronation, arranged for the production of a montage showing his father in the robes of the old emperors, and made enquiries in Vienna concerning the return of the imperial insignia and crown jewels. Since there was no support for a coronation and the German ambassador in Vienna reported that the Austrians would rather go to war again than hand over the crown jewels, Frederick William was reduced to somewhat desperate measures.[57]

Recalling the opening session of the first German Reichstag on 21 March 1871, the veteran deputy Eugen Richter remembered that William I's throne had been a quaint relic—"the bottom made from stone, the top from metal, a strange thing to behold." Richter believed that one of the ancient emperors may once have sat on it. The use of this antique had been suggested by the crown prince, who persuaded his slightly amused father to honour the "throne of Emperor Henry III" in this way. Frederick William was embarrassed when he later learned that the chair was definitely not the throne of an eleventh-century emperor, but his medieval reveries continued. To commemorate the seventh anniversary of the imperial proclamation at Versailles, he glued a few stanzas by the patriotic poet Max von Schenkendorf into his diary:[58]

Many noble tribes dwell there
In this majestic home,
Amid fine tunes and pious prayer
Stands a ruler's throne:
Most glorious of this whole age
Knightly hero, priest and sage
They call him: German emperor!

The medieval pedigree of his future office was particularly high on the crown prince's agenda in the summer of 1885, when a sudden deterioration of his father's health made Frederick William's succession appear imminent. In July 1885, he was the guest of honour at the twenty-fifth anniversary of the Fifth Westphalian Infantry Regiment. In his short speech, the crown prince expressed his delight that the regiment was now garrisoned in the city of Aachen, "where the bones of Charlemagne rest, whose crown now belongs to my House." In August, Frederick William's dogged insistence on his medieval lineage almost wore out the patience of his adviser Franz von Roggenbach, who, together with Albrecht von Stosch, Heinrich Friedberg, and Heinrich Geffcken, had drafted a number of proclamations for Frederick William's expected accession. After discussing these documents with the crown prince, Roggenbach informed Stosch of Frederick William's determination to accede as "heir of the crown of Charlemagne and the old German emperors, to communicate this claim in a message to the nation and assume the title Frederick IV in succession to Emperor Frederick III." The idea that the crown prince would wish to choose his numeral to link him to a fifteenth-century Habsburg emperor rather than to his illustrious predecessor King Frederick II—the Great—of Prussia struck Roggenbach as utterly absurd. It took two days of persuasion to induce Frederick William to abandon the idea. The issue was still not finally settled, though. When Roggenbach travelled to San Remo in December 1887 to visit the ailing crown prince, Frederick William again suggested calling himself Emperor Frederick IV. Like so many of Frederick William's dreams, this one was also shattered by Bismarck. The question of the unresolved title was raised during a ministerial meeting in February 1888. Bismarck stated categorically that Frederick III was the only possibility, since there was "not the slightest connection" between the old and the new German emperors.[59]

Legally speaking, Bismarck was entirely correct, and it also would have been politically unwise to confront the other German mon-

archs with a symbolism that implied that their erstwhile subordination to the Holy Roman Emperors was to be revived in the new Reich.
Within the wider context of Germany's political culture, though,
Bismarck's rejection of any link appears somewhat disingenuous
and Frederick William's reveries seem less outlandish. In one of his
most famous speeches, the chancellor had himself drawn a direct
line between the medieval emperors and current politics: when Germany's conflict with the papacy escalated in 1872, he had assured
the Reichstag that the country would not go to Canossa—the Italian fortress where, in 1077, Emperor Henry IV had performed an act
of penance before Pope Gregory VII. Bismarck could use this very
successful metaphor because interest in the medieval empire was a
strong, pervasive, and politically relevant cultural force at the time.
The chancellor had probably picked up the reference during a dinner
conversation with Baroness Spitzemberg, who was then in the middle of reading a book by the eminent medievalist Wilhelm von
Giesebrecht.[60]

There was more than just rhetoric to this language of tradition. In
the same year, Bismarck even authorised an expedition to be sent to
Tyre in Asia Minor to bring back the bones of Frederick I. Known
as Frederick Barbarossa, the twelfth-century emperor was believed to
have been buried there after drowning on his way to the Holy Land.
Bismarck was reportedly swayed by the consideration that a government also had to affect the nation's imagination.[61]

Money spent on a search for Barbarossa's bones must have seemed
like a sound investment. The twelfth-century emperor was at the
very heart of the political mythology that imported the Middle Ages
into the nineteenth century. A popular legend held that Barbarossa
was not dead but slumbering inside the Kyffhäuser Mountain in
North Germany; his red beard growing to enormous length and his
head forever circled by ravens, he was waiting for the glory of the
Reich to be restored. As a symbol of German unity and national aspi-
ration, the Barbarossa myth attracted poets, historians, and artists.
Having increased in popularity since the Napoleonic Wars, the Barbarossa theme reached its climax after the Franco-Prussian War. By
1871 the historian Georg Voigt could observe that the emperor's legend had become so widely known that mere hints sufficed to make the
point. This, in turn, allowed Barbarossa to be easily fused with current events. The red-bearded emperor, it was suggested, had risen in
the dignified shape of the aged "Hero-Emperor" William I. The rule

of the white-bearded "Barbablanca" now fulfilled the yearning of more than six hundred years. Through the verses of the painfully prolific Felix Dahn, the phrase gained common currency:[62]

> Who in combat has renewed
> The lustre of the Germans' crown
> Long since widow of the ancients' glory
> Hail to thee, ancient emperor
> Barbablanca, full of triumph
> Saviour of the fatherland.

The medieval halo created for the brand new Reich shone most dramatically from a number of official monuments. The mosaic Anton von Werner designed for Berlin's Victory Column was a prominent early example. Commissioned in 1871, it depicted at its centre a female Germania in medieval garb receiving the imperial crown amid a throng of heroes from the recent war. Barbarossa stands by and gazes upward—presumably at the inevitable ravens. A similar iconography was used for the murals of the imperial palace at Goslar. Restored to what was believed to be its medieval glory, the building was adorned with symbolic historical paintings. The artist Hermann Wislicenus chose to show Emperor William accepting the crown on horseback under a sky filled with medieval emperors. This monumental central painting is flanked by several others depicting medieval scenes including Barbarossa's awakening, Charlemagne's destruction of the Saxons' pagan icon, and Emperor Henry III leading the imprisoned Pope Gregory VI across the Alps. The public use of medieval images for the glorification of the Hohenzollern emperors continued after Frederick William's death in 1888. A mosaic in the atrium of Berlin's Emperor William Memorial Church, consecrated in 1895, for instance, showed William I as the successor of a long line of medieval emperors, among them Charlemagne, Otto I, Henry I, and Rudolf of Habsburg.[63]

———

The crown prince certainly favoured this kind of symbolic and artistic statement. In fact, he advised Werner during the creation of the mosaic for the Victory Column and was also involved in the Goslar project. His imperial notions encompassed more, however, than coats of arms, ancient chairs, Roman numerals, and monumental murals.

To Frederick William, the resurrection of the imperial crown entailed significant constitutional and political consequences. The importance he attached to the dignity and title of the German emperor made him a fervent supporter of increasing the power of the Reich at the expense of its federal units. He was a fierce opponent not only of particularism but even of milder forms of federal diversity, as well as a determined advocate of greater centralisation.[64]

Since Frederick William's rejection of particularism included a hearty dislike even of its Prussian version, the foundation of the Reich can be said to have brought about a dramatic change in his nationalism. He stopped viewing Germany as a means of Prussian aggrandizement and became truly German. The diary entry in which Frederick William recorded his reaction to his new title "Crown Prince of the German Reich" marks a moment of metamorphosis: "I feel exclusively German," he confessed, and added a sentence that seems to anticipate the notorious speech his son would give on 1 August 1914. "I therefore make no difference any more between Bavarians and Badeners or Hessians," the crown prince declared, "and from now on consider every German placed as close to me as I have hitherto considered only my Prussian compatriots."[65] Frederick William's commitment to a more centralised Reich did not merely spring from his exalted view of the emperor's role. It also dovetailed nicely with his occasional sympathies for the unitary left-liberals, his dislike of the strongly federal forces of Political Catholicism, and the somewhat arrogant antipathy he felt toward many of the other German dynasties.

As early as March 1860, Frederick William had mocked the minor German sovereigns and had argued that their small states had better merge into Prussia. During the War of 1866, he was happy to see the "ridiculous German royal titles converted into ducal or grand ducal titles," and expected the Duke of Saxe-Meiningen to come "crawling on his belly, which would be truly German-princely." When, in 1870, some of the southern states dragged their feet during the negotiations that would lead to the foundation of the German Reich, Frederick William came close to threatening military action. He suggested to Bismarck that Prussia should exert the kind of "pressure that the renitent kings could not resist."[66] Even after they had joined the empire in 1871, the crown prince's opinion of the "German-Napoleonic kings," as he sneeringly called them, did not improve: in 1873 Frederick William compared the German princes to wasps whose wings had been ripped off—"as long as they can crawl, they will sting." The crown prince was similarly frank with Bismarck, whose anticentralist views were well known. "You know what I think about the three German kingdoms [of Bavaria, Württemberg, and Saxony] which we received from Napoleon during a most shameful time to assure Germany's fragmentation forever," he wrote in August 1881, and deplored the "daily annoyance these cabinets, replete with their empty titles, cause to the weal of the Reich." Earlier in the same year, he had scoffed at the notion that particularist forces in Hanover were banking on him for the future and ominously added that "the small German princes will have a rude awakening."[67]

As could be expected, Frederick William's relationship with some of the German princes was rather frosty. In the case of King Ludwig II of Bavaria, this bordered on an open hostility sustained by provocative demonstrations. The mayor of the Bavarian town of Füssen was reprimanded by King Ludwig for his excessive protestations of devotion during the crown prince's visit in August 1872. Three years later, when a Munich company producing picture frames was ordered not to call itself "Imperial Royal Court Supplier" and to stop using the Prussian coat of arms, Frederick William demonstratively placed a large order with them. During a conversation with the German ambassador in Paris in August 1874, King Ludwig openly bad-mouthed the crown prince and accused him of planning to deprive the individual German states of their independence.[68]

The sincerity of the crown prince's dislike of the role played by the other German monarchs notwithstanding, these petty antipathies did not constitute the whole picture; they formed merely a contributory part of his wider commitment to furthering the interests of the Reich through greater integration and centralisation. This was a price all separate monarchs would have to pay—including the king of Prussia. In fact, as early as 1871, Frederick William confessed to Chlodwig von Hohenlohe-Schillingsfürst that his father's continued attachment to Prussiandom and the Prussian royal title was giving him cause for concern. When the liberals of Venice serenaded him in 1875 by playing the Prussian anthem "I Am a Prussian, Do You Know My Colours?" he wished they would stop, for this song always brought back to him the days of the most miserable particularism.[69]

For all his delight at the foundation of the Reich, Frederick William was disappointed by the concessions that Bismarck had offered the separate states. The king of Bavaria was to retain command of his troops in peacetime, for instance, and some governments continued with their own diplomatic services. A combination of smaller states would be able to veto Reich government proposals, and the Reich was to be dependent on financial contribution from the separate members. The crown prince had wanted so much more. In a memorandum he sent to Bismarck on 14 August 1870, Frederick William sketched out how Germany was to be united: the leadership and administration of the entire German military was to be transferred to Prussia. There was to be "only one army with one rule book, one type of weaponry and equipment and one principle of promotion and reserves"; the South German states were to join the North German Confederation; and the German princes together with the heads of selected high aristocratic families were to form a German House of Lords. Frederick William repeated his proposal for an all-German upper house on 15 October in a letter to his sister and during a long discussion with Bismarck in November. To demonstrate the extent of his own commitment to a unified Reich, Frederick William even told the Grand Duke of Weimar that he would demand the black-red-gold tricolour as the federal and imperial flag and that the imperial eagle be fixed to the helmets of the entire army. Even though the vagueness of his language makes it difficult to determine his aims precisely, it is probable that he had this kind of centralising, streamlining agenda in mind when he demanded a reform of the "head and the limbs of the resurrected Reich."[70]

With the realisation that his calls were falling on deaf ears, Frederick William's anger grew. These mistakes would render the future construction of the Reich's missing elements incredibly hard, he wrote on 12 December 1870. On the last day of the year, Frederick William felt "actually sick out of revulsion at this lack of determination." Why should we care for Bavaria with her unpredictable king?, he asked, and concluded sarcastically: "They are preparing a lovely inheritance for me here." He was determined, however, not to squander the great opportunity offered by the imperial crown and immediately looked for ways to compensate for the deficiencies he had identified. Since the Reich had been set up so poorly, Frederick William noted on 19 December 1870, the basis of the national edifice must not be neglected and care had to be lavished on outward signs—proclamations, titles, coats of arms, and flags. Beyond this, the crown prince's strategy was straightforward. In order to avoid fanning the flames of particularism even further, one would have to tread softly and avoid meddling with the states' internal affairs, he explained to Charles of Romania in April 1872. This made it even more important, though, "that in the fields of the military, the law and foreign policy a complete unity is manifested and cemented more and more firmly." Six months later, he assured Charles that "the enemies of unity, against whom we are fighting will not measure up to this political power."[71]

Throughout the rest of his life, Frederick William remained determined "to make up for the vile treaties of Versailles" and to bring about a closer integration of the Reich, as he put it in a letter to Stosch in January 1873. "No opportunity must be left unused to act according to this spirit and to gain every advantage over those naysayers."[72] The crown prince therefore warmly welcomed the army organisation bill, which was aired in January 1873. It did not "agree with [his] creed to see a Royal Prussian Army next to an Imperial German Navy and . . . officers and soldiers everywhere wearing double-cockades out of consideration for twenty-seven fatherlands," Frederick William observed to Schweinitz, and hoped that the bill would rectify all this. The crown prince blamed these oddities on Prussian particularism, which clung to a thousand trivialities and "prevented the welding together of the members of the Reich." In the same letter, he expressed his satisfaction that Bismarck now appeared to focus his energies entirely on imperial issues since this was likely to result in the imperial chancellery being eventually complemented by other imperial ministries. Three days later, he told Stosch of his hope that the power of the chancellor would overcome "one-sided Prussian particularism," which had "to end because it plainly [did] not want to know about the Reich."[73]

In August 1873, Frederick William criticised the Victory Column, a monument celebrating the military triumphs of 1864, 1866, and 1870–1871. He deplored the "purely Prussian" character of what he lampooned as the "Victory Asparagus," and feared it would cause bad blood. Two months later, the crown prince looked forward to the creation of an Imperial Supreme Court and a single civil code for the entire nation. In February 1875, he rejoiced in the progress made in this respect. Having witnessed how splendidly the Bavarian city of Augsburg had celebrated the anniversary of the Battle of Sedan, the crown prince wrote to this father to recommend that Lord Mayor Ludwig Fischer be decorated with the "Order of the Crown" in recognition of his keen advocacy of the idea of the German Reich. Another promising means toward greater centralisation was offered by the railways. When he heard about plans to have all of them transferred to the Reich in December 1875, Frederick William told Bismarck that he "wished to inform [himself] more precisely about this important question, which essentially furthers the expansion of the Reich's power."[74]

Frederick William's dogged efforts to strengthen the Reich ranged from the sublime to the faintly ridiculous. In 1876 he noticed that the proverbially thrifty Prussian court still used printed hunting invitations headed "His Majesty the King." The words "and Emperor" were simply scribbled in by hand. The crown prince angrily marked the offending passage in red and blue crayon and wrote "After five years still this" in the margin. When his father referred to his wife as "the queen," Frederick William corrected him and called his mother "the empress." In March 1883, he lost his temper when the Bavarians obstructed the introduction of uniform German postage stamps. The crown prince regarded the death of the childless Duke William of Brunswick in October 1884 as an opportunity to expand the remit of the Reich. Rather than see a different branch of the Guelph family reign there as a sovereign dynasty, Frederick William suggested in November 1884 that the duchy be transformed into an imperial territory—like Alsace-Lorraine—and administered by a regent "on behalf of the Reich."[75]

His views were widely known. The German princes were aware of the crown prince's inclination to make them "kneel before him," as Stosch described it in August 1885, and they warily anticipated Frederick William's reign. When Stosch, Roggenbach, and Friedberg spent much of the summer of 1885 drafting proclamations for Frederick William's accession, they did so partly to avoid a future conflict amongst Germany's crowned heads. The crown prince was eventually prevailed upon to accept the draft proclamation with its promise to respect the constitutional rights of all the separate German states, but this may not have altered his fundamental attitude. "Concerning the position of the future emperor I have often had discussions with my father," Prince William, the future emperor William II, wrote to Bismarck in November 1887. The crown prince had always believed "it was for him alone to command, and the princes had to obey."[76]

On 18 January 1881, the crown prince looked back to the day when King William I had been proclaimed German emperor at Versailles. A decade had passed during which the new state had bedded down, but Frederick William could not disguise his disappointment. "Ten years since the great day of the re-erection of emperor and Reich," he wrote in his diary. "I would truly not have believed then that after such a long time the imperial prestige had gained so little, had understood so little to be feared and respected."[77] Frederick William's choice of the words "fear" and "respect" was not insignificant and points to a further important aspect of his political beliefs—his strongly developed sense of the majesty and power of the monarch.

To the historian, it is striking how many contemporaries commented on this facet of Frederick William's political personality. Bismarck referred to it on numerous occasions. "I know pretty much all the princes in Europe," the chancellor observed in March 1883, "but I do not know a single one whose view of his princely vocation is as exalted as that of our crown prince Frederick William." Bismarck predicted that once on the throne, Frederick William would realise that the rights of the people could only be augmented at the expense of the powers of the monarch and then all of his liberal theories would disappear. When describing a confrontation with Frederick William in his memoirs, Bismarck claimed that decades after the event, he could still recall the crown prince's "hostile expression of Olympian majesty."[78] According to Gustav Freytag, Frederick William was "alive with a princely pride that covets the highest for itself and the highest earthly position was for him that beneath the imperial crown." Karl von Wilmowski, a court official who served both William I and his son, described Frederick William as a man who was full of "all the pride of a Hohenzollern" and held "the rights of the crown in high esteem." The crown prince was convinced that the monarchical principle was a necessary factor of their existence, his librarian Robert Dohme remembered, "and therefore he wanted it robust and authoritarian." The Prussian diplomat Philipp von Eulenburg, who met Frederick William during his regular visits to Bavaria, was struck by the "whole weight of the imperialist sentiment" stored up inside the crown prince. He would rule in a centralised way and remove the undignified titles of the kings of Bavaria, Saxony, and Württemberg, Frederick William had told him. "Where there is an emperor, no kings must rule."[79]

Frederick William's sense of the majesty of his royal status was strongly developed even before its imperial elevation. In 1861 he called his father's coronation a "festive, even sacred act," important for the whole of Germany, "whose future we will one day hold in our hands." Once the experiences of the Austro-Prussian and Franco-Prussian Wars and the heady brew of Frederick William's understanding of the ancient dignity and calling of the imperial office were added to this preexisting outlook, the crown prince developed a somewhat hypertrophic sense of the emperor's proper role and of his own rank. To some extent, this expressed itself in trivial ways. For instance, when discussing the official protocol for saluting, Frederick William insisted in a letter to Stosch in February 1873 that "at most the three German-Napoleonic kings should have precedence over the German crown prince, but no other German ruler or prince." He was reported to be incensed at the preferential treatment enjoyed by Bismarck. "My future subject has a Pullman car and I don't," Holstein quoted him in 1883, and two years later, he recorded the crown prince's outrage at not having been offered a special train.[80]

Such attitudes were reinforced by a side of Frederick William's personality that made him focus strongly on social rank and its outward demonstration. His letters and diaries are full of slightly petty references to medals and decorations. In December 1862, for instance, he rejoiced at receiving the Order of the Golden Fleece from the queen of Spain and explained that he "had really wanted this old order next to the Garter for a long time." Eight years later, the crown prince informed Schweinitz that he was "hopping mad that the Pour-le-Mérite had been wasted on Emperor Alexander, who sends me the fourth class of the Order of St George."[81]

Alongside Frederick William's interest in these fripperies ran his concern for a proper sense of hierarchy. Even accounts of Frederick William as a student mention how highly he rated his own dignity and that he reacted tersely when not shown due respect. In 1864 he recorded in his diary how annoyed he was at his father's decision to ennoble a number of common officers for personal bravery. This, he felt, needlessly increased the size of the poor nobility. The crown prince's friends and family were well aware of his views. Friedberg told Holstein in June 1885 that because of Frederick William's "enormous dynastic snobbery," he would one day appoint a high aristocrat—probably a prince—to lead the government and not "a Müller, Schulze or Friedberg." Prussia's "prejudices about rank and mediatized princes and other princes" ought to be abolished, Queen Victoria suggested to her daughter in June 1885, but she feared that "beloved Fritz [was] rather fond of all these restrictions which give pleasure to no one and are great trouble."[82]

All of this coloured the way in which the heir to the crown envisioned his own reign. A glimpse of his ideas can be gained from a comment the crown prince scribbled in the margin of an article he read in 1878. In this piece for the influential *Preussische Jahrbücher,* the historian and National Liberal Party deputy Alfred Boretius discussed the legal traditions of the Holy Roman Empire. He described how a newly enthroned emperor would traditionally pass judgement on a legal dispute, and observed that right up until the end of the Old Reich, the emperor used to serve as the general judge. Frederick William's comment on this passage reads: "This is how it must be again." Stosch's understanding of Frederick William's political dreams was similar. "What he alluded to in his speech in Aachen," he wrote to Gustav Freytag on 22 August 1885, was "that he is Charlemagne's heir; that is what he wants to call out into the world and make clear to the princes as soon as he inherits the crown. He wants to call himself Frederick IV and in a proclamation to the German people declare himself immediate emperor; the princes and their power are to be broken."[83]

The most revealing account of Frederick William's notion of his imperial office, however, can be found scribbled onto the flyleaves of the 1885 volume of the crown prince's private diary. Written in an abbreviated, staccato-like style, this undated text offers a rare but detailed and candid expression of his political ambitions. The crown prince was clearly exercised by the issue of reestablishing monarchical power vis-à-vis certain deformities of Germany's political life and, above all, alongside the overmighty chancellor. Frederick William started emphatically: "I myself want to be the speaker in my own way, who issues directives, expressions of will to my *servant,*" who should be made to feel that his "omnipotence has been set an objective." If there were to be a conflict with the chancellor, the nation as well as the army and the civil servants would have to be rallied behind the crown. No institution was to rule over the emperor, Frederick William declared, "i.e. Reichstag not decisive with majorities, like its current excesses." What was crucial was the power of the ruler *(Herrschergewalt)* and "not an omnipotent chancellorship, as it has emerged; all strength has to be derived from the former and must remain dependent on it. The empire is to be consolidated; conduct of imperial business by me personally." The army—above all, the officer corps—was to retain its traditional relationship to the emperor, but other aspects of the constitution required change. Amongst the flaws the crown prince identified in Germany's current political situation were universal suffrage and the "location of the centre of gravity in the Reichstag." The parliament had to be "led back to its normal form in order to express once again the dynastic and national convictions of the majority."[84]

Frederick William gave the imperial office a strikingly wide remit. The tasks he set for himself included "steering and calming of the parties," economic and social questions, redrawing the boundaries between royal and ministerial power, and the defence of the most important monarchical prerogatives. The German princes' remaining separate rights were mere "decorative externalities" which Frederick William considered "overcome and ridiculous." The crown prince did not intend to tackle them, though, unless "real questions of power" compelled him to do so. Hoping to avoid a conflict against a united front of Bismarck and the German princes, Frederick William also conceded that his dream of becoming "Frederick IV" was inappropriate. His own view of the "historical connection between today's Prussian-German Empire and the late Roman-German Empire," he observed, struck many as dangerous and impolitic.

It is hard to see which of the various parties at the receiving end of what Jürgen Kloosterhuis has called this "post-absolutist-constitutional Prusso-German empire"[85] would have welcomed a second Frederician era along these lines. Bismarck, parliament, and the German princes all would have been brought to heel within a system dominated by a strong emperor backed by the army, the civil service, and a loyal nation. Frederick William's programme certainly provided a robust solution to an issue that Roggenbach described in October 1885 in a letter to Stockmar: the risk that the position of the crown might degenerate into a "roi fainéant or mock emperor."[86]

The forcefulness of Frederick William's text contrasts starkly with the numerous comments made about the resignation and malleability of its author. Moreover, the focus on communicating and managing the accession in the continued presence of a potentially hostile Bismarck places the document firmly in the specific context of 1885. The Reichstag elections of October 1884, with their successes for the Conservative parties, the Social Democrats, and Stoecker's anti-Semites, and the setback for the German Freisinn

Party had deeply frustrated the crown prince. His faith in parliament was further undermined by what he considered the miserable record achieved when the new Reichstag's first session closed in May 1885. The animus against Bismarck may well have been an aftershock of the crown prince's anger at the lavish honours the chancellor had received on the occasion of his seventieth birthday in the spring of 1885.[87]

A text so clearly of its day—and probably triggered by the tense conversations concerning the draft proclamations in August 1885—does not necessarily represent the definitive formulation of the crown prince's intentions. In spite of these caveats, the imperial dimension of Frederick William's political beliefs was undoubtedly substantial, detailed, and consistent. It should not be relegated to a largely ornamental supporting role alongside his liberal convictions. The fairly illiberal outline of the Frederician empire sketched by the crown prince in the 1885 document arguably contained much more that was irreconcilable with Bismarck's continued tenure of the chancellorship than did the relatively small, irreducible core of Frederick William's liberalism.

CHAPTER THREE

A National Treasure

The crown prince was a national treasure. Widely referred to and perceived as Our Fritz, Frederick William enjoyed enormous popularity and a highly public profile. Ahead of the introduction of a common German currency in 1873, one newspaper printed a reader's suggestion that the new golden twenty-mark coin should be named after him. "Fritz is so popular in the whole of Germany as well as so famous abroad," the writer argued, "that the German Gold-Fritzes would certainly enjoy the same popularity everywhere." The crown prince must have been very gratified when he glued this article into his diary. Accolades were not restricted to the readers' column. "In Crown Prince Frederick William," the daily *Norddeutsche Allgemeine Zeitung* declared in October 1881, "Germany loves and reveres the beacon of an exemplary family life, the ideal of a devoted son, the splendid paragon of indefatigable, self-denying duty, the character steeled through life's struggles and the thunder of cannon, and—as the heir to two crowns—the guarantee of a blessed future."[1] Taken together, these two vignettes—one a quirky suggestion by an eager patriot and one a paean of praise marking the crown prince's fiftieth birthday—contain an almost comprehensive list of the ingredients that went into the creation of a cherished public persona: family values, military glory, dynastic commitment, an all-German appeal, and a folksy popularity were combined by both word and image to create the figure Our Fritz.

The celebrity and public affection enjoyed by the crown prince reflected the many different ways in which he was a participant in the popular and political cultures of his day. This enabled him to play a prominent part in the communication and popularization of the monarchical system and the Hohenzollern dynasty at a time when the importance of different and widening public groups was growing. The monarchs of nineteenth-century Europe were obliged to reckon with them, which meant that a large share of the princely business had to be addressed to an audience and conducted visibly. Kings and queens now operated in a context that "required new strategies of representation and was embedded in changed conditions of perception."[2] Recent work on Queen Victoria's public role, for instance, has pointed to the emergence of a new style of monarchy, in which "royal events were increasingly indivisible from the way in which they were experienced through their media coverage." The development of a "performing monarchy" during the last third of the nineteenth century has been interpreted as part of a political campaign designed to generate continuity and consensus. In order to enable the wider population to identify with the royal families, the latter ended up having to "lead a private life publicly." After all, as the National-Zeitung put it when congratulating Frederick William and Victoria on their silver wedding anniversary in 1883, "a prince's palace will always be more or less a glass house."[3]

By the time this article appeared, a process that intensified and multiplied the public's gaze at the royals' lives was already well under way. The media world was being transformed by the establishment of a much larger, commercialized, and politically more independent mass press aimed at a growing, literate, and enfranchised population. The so-called media revolution of the three decades before the First World War markedly accelerated the expansion of the public sphere that had already been a hallmark of much of the nineteenth century. Whereas in 1870 the German post office delivered about 150 million copies of newspapers to subscribers, thirty years later the figure had increased to a staggering 1.2 billion. Such was the reach of the media, that Germany's reading public became more or less identical with the nation as a whole. This phenomenon linked the development of the media and of the public spheres they sustained with a wider political transformation. Against the background of the introduction of universal—if unequal—manhood suffrage in Prussia in 1848–1850 and of universal equal manhood suffrage in the North German Confederation and the German Reich in 1867–1871, the politics of notables were giving way to an increasingly professional mass politics. If royalty wanted to compete successfully with the other suppliers offering their goods and services to the "political mass market," they had to engage in their own forms of market research, product development, and public relations.[4]

Like most of the royal families of Europe, the Hohenzollerns accepted the obligation to join a reciprocal game of performance and adulation with their subjects. On Sunday, 19 February 1888, a large crowd gathered outside the royal palace in Berlin. Having read the detailed newspaper reports about the dramatic deterioration in Frederick William's health, these Berliners wanted to show their sympathy to the family so gravely affected by the crown prince's illness. Their display of loyal empathy was rewarded when Emperor William appeared at the palace window together with three of his great-grandsons. After a while, the nonagenarian patted the head of one of his great-grandsons and the group was joined first by Empress Augusta in her wheelchair and then by the boys' mother, holding her youngest son. The crowd cheered and then burst into a solemn rendition of the imperial anthem. Naturally, this touching scene was lovingly reported in the press.[5]

The crown prince could not witness the moment himself because he was in San Remo recovering from the tracheotomy he had undergone ten days before. He would have been pleased, however, by this display of popular affection, by the royal family's response, and by the newspaper coverage. Our Fritz was not only genuinely popular, he was also aware of it; his popularity meant much to him and he understood the means by which it was generated.

Communicating the Crown Prince's Image

Frederick William's diaries and correspondence offer ample evidence that his public profile and the response he elicited mattered greatly to him. When, on the way home from church in December 1865, he and his wife were being saluted "noticeably little . . . in spite of our four horses and outrider," he reflected on it in his diary and confessed that it "hurt us both considerably." The following year, however, Frederick William noted that the soldiers he met during the campaign in Bohemia recognised him and expressed their delight at seeing him. This, he admitted, was doing him good. "Often the calls were directed at my person," the crown prince observed with evident pleasure when his party was met enthusiastically everywhere they passed through on the way to France in July 1870. Ten years later, he wrote to Vicky from "dear Nuremberg, where, as before, I was welcomed by an immense mass of people with the liveliest proofs of warm affection." Frederick William's concern for how he was received did not always have happy results, though. Alfred Count Waldersee, the deputy chief of the general staff, complained in 1884 that during manoeuvres the crown prince kept chasing from one point to another in order to be seen and admired by the soldiers and the public. The following year, Holstein recorded in detail Frederick William's anger when even lowly coachmen or hapless sentries failed to recognise him immediately.[6]

Given this awareness of his public profile, it is not surprising that the crown prince had a sound grasp of the crucial role played by journalism in the creation of his image. His diaries and letters are full of references to the press, and he filled large scrapbooks with countless newspaper articles about himself. Scores of cuttings—frequently adorned with marginal comments—were also glued into his diaries.[7] He had a clear idea of the mechanics of news management, analysed its impact, and considered active intervention. "It appears to me that the press barely understands how to do justice to the decisive part played by units of my army in the victory at Sedan," Frederick William noted in his campaign diary in September 1870. "Moreover, I understand well how the old, well-known game has started again at home, whereby my name is mentioned as rarely as possible." In fact, at the beginning of the war, members of the crown prince's circle had given thought to the establishment of a "press bureau" to scan the daily papers, insert suitable texts penned by "hired quills," and do everything to increase Frederick William's popularity, especially in the south of Germany. "This little institution has to remain wholly unknown to the world," Gustav Freytag wrote to Karl von Normann in July 1870. "Everything must appear unforced, as if it were happening by itself."[8]

The crown prince's close attention to his own coverage in the press did not cease when the war ended. After he had given a speech in Wittenberg in September 1883, he wrote two letters to his wife discussing the different reports in a range of newspapers. The *Nationalzeitung* and the *Börsenkurier* had praised the speech, as had other left-liberal publications. The conservative *Kreuzzeitung*, however, had interpreted his words very much in their own way and used them to launch an attack on the *Nationalzeitung*. In November 1886, Frederick William sent two newspaper cuttings to the Prussian minister of justice. The *Hallische Zeitung* and the *Deutsches Tageblatt* had printed an overly melodramatic account of the crown prince's recent visit to Merseburg Cathedral that made him appear to be a religious fanatic. In a covering letter, Frederick William complained about this "hocus-pocus" and asked the minister whether one could take steps to correct this.[9]

Frederick William's appreciation of the importance of the press also influenced the way he dealt with journalists. During the Franco-Prussian War, he allowed two British war correspondents—William Russell of the London *Times* and John Skinner of London's *Daily News*—to join his headquarters, and the crown prince occasionally entertained them at his table. This proved to be a shrewd investment. A few days after the battle of Wörth, for instance, Skinner informed his readers that the "Crown Prince [had] gained a great victory over the ablest general in France." The *Times* also reported the "brilliant victory for the Crown Prince," and Russell declared that "the consideration and gracious courtesy of the Crown Prince [were] quite beyond acknowledgement" and surpassed those of "any Humanitarian in England." Frederick William could not but approve of such delightful guests: they were "agreeable, charming and industriously researching every detail."[10]

This attentive attitude toward journalists continued after Frederick William's return to Berlin. His decision to invite editors and reporters of the leading papers to his palace in Potsdam for an informal meeting caused astonishment at the time. During official functions, he would often wander over to a group of journalists and engage them in conversation. A writer for the *Neue Zürcher Zeitung* recalled how he once asked the correspondents present at a state ceremony if they were happy with the places they had been allocated. When the journalists replied that they were not, the crown prince gave the officials a dressing-down, which ended in: "The gentlemen are more important than you. If they do not write about it, then the whole world will know nothing about what is going on here." While on an official trip to Spain and Italy in 1883, Frederick William made every effort to charm the three newspaper correspondents travelling with him. He joined them for friendly, informal chats and even invited them to dine with him on board the German warship that took him from Genoa to Seville.[11]

The crown prince's desire to shape his public image did not stop at the printed word: he equally appreciated the power of the visual media. Even during his relatively uneventful assignment in the Danish

War, he considered possible means of communicating his achievements through images. In March 1864, Frederick William waited impatiently for drawings he had ordered from Robert Landells, an illustrator working for the *Illustrated London News*. "Sadly the painter did not attend any of the battles I experienced," he sighed, "so that such pictures will have to wait for a later time. It would have been worthwhile to have a skilful military painter come here to record a few moments under our guidance." A fortnight later, he asked the director of the Düsseldorf Academy to despatch their best painter of battle scenes so that the planned assault on the Danish fortress of Düppel could be immortalized. The crown prince invited Landells again during the French campaign. The well-known battle scene painter Georg Bleibtreu also joined his entourage. Landells was awarded the Iron Cross for the bravery he demonstrated when helping wounded Prussian soldiers, and Bleibtreu depicted the crown prince in a number of military contexts. The most important artistic development of the war, however, was the beginning of Frederick William's patronage of the painter Anton von Werner, whom he met at Versailles on 4 November 1870.[12]

Having spent a few weeks at the German headquarters in Versailles at the end of 1870, the twenty-seven-year-old Werner returned to Germany to work on his sketches. On 15 January 1871, he received a telegram from a member of Frederick William's headquarters at Versailles: "H.R.H. the crown prince asks me to tell you that you will experience something worthy of your brush if you can arrive here by 18 January." Werner rushed back and arrived just in time to witness William I's proclamation as German emperor in the Hall of Mirrors. Frederick William was delighted with the "utterly successful sketches" the "painter-genius von Werner" submitted a few days later. It was agreed that a grand historical painting would be commissioned as a present for the new emperor. Throughout the six years it took Werner to complete the painting, the crown prince showed an active interest in its progress, visiting Werner's workshop and asking for alterations and additions to be made. The first version of the painting—the so-called Palace Version—was presented to William I on his eightieth birthday in March 1877. Reproduced many thousands of times, the monumental scene "probably became the most familiar work of contemporary art for two generations of Germans" and powerfully communicated an event crucial to the crown prince's understanding of history and one that he had helped to stage. Werner's later paintings of the same scene—the mural for the Berlin Arsenal and the 1885 version presented to Bismarck—portrayed the scene less realistically. The principal characters Bismarck, William I, and the crown prince now appeared elevated amid a scene of patriotic jubilation.[13]

Frederick William's presence in another historic location was also prominently and evocatively captured on canvas, and the image can be found depicted in almost every hagiographical account of his life, even in books for children: a handsome bearded prince on a white charger, serenely entering Jerusalem while receiving the adulation of a motley oriental crowd.[14] As was the case with Werner's painting of the imperial proclamation, the crown prince had a very active hand in every element of the construction of this image. In 1869 he stood in for his father to represent Prussia at the ceremonial opening of the Suez Canal. Frederick William's grand tour took him via Italy, Greece, and Turkey to Palestine and finally to Egypt. The highlight of the trip was his entry into Jerusalem through the Damascus Gate. Frederick William noted that it was there that "Geoffrey of Bouillon undertook the victorious attack" on the city during the First Crusade and that "no Christian prince ha[d] been allowed to enter since." After meetings with representatives of all the creeds and to the hurrahs of a detachment of Prussian marines, the crown prince—resplendent in his uniform of the Silesian dragoons, adorned with the order of the Black Eagle, the Garter, and a veil around his helmet—entered the city and proceeded to the Church of the Holy Sepulchre.[15]

More than two years after this memorable day, Frederick William and his wife visited Wilhelm Gentz, a well-known painter of oriental themes. After several further inspections of the artist's workshop, a decision was made. "I am to go to Jerusalem," Gentz wrote to his brother in 1873, "because the crown prince desires that I glorify his entry on a white Arabian horse." Equipped with Frederick William's letters of introduction, Gentz departed for Palestine to make detailed sketches of the location, which even involved a troop of Turkish soldiers marching three times through the Damascus Gate. The great success of his painting, which evoked ancient images of Christ's entry into the Holy City, and the wide dissemination of the depicted scene justified these immense efforts. Unveiled in Berlin's National Gallery in December 1876, Gentz's "Entry of the Crown Prince into Jerusalem" won a gold medal. The state purchased it for 16,000 marks and the critics were unstinting with their praise. The contrast between the cultures of the Orient and the Occident, "represented by the German prince," one observer noted, elevated the painting to the rank of a "profound symbol."[16] The theme was echoed more widely by poems contemplating the meaning of Frederick William's presence in the Holy Land. A poem entitled "On the Mount of Olives" opened:[17]

> On the Mount of Olives' height
> Stood the hero, young and grand
> Above the trees and through the night
> His gaze went far into the land.
> Shielded from the city's bustle
> Which the saviour's woe did see
> He listened to your branches' rustle,
> Place of pain: Gethsemane.

The story behind the Sedan panorama demonstrates, however, that the crown prince could not control every canvas. On 1 September 1883, this gigantic portrayal of the decisive battle of the Franco-Prussian War opened in Berlin. A huge circular screen rotated slowly around the paying patriots who watched the spectacle from a central viewing platform. Anton von Werner led a team of painters to create this visitor attraction. Surprisingly, Frederick William never visited the workshop to see the enormous picture take shape and even stayed away from the panorama's official opening. When the disconcerted artist asked the crown princess why this was so, she told him that her husband disliked paintings of battle scenes because of his revulsion at the horrors of war. This account—drawn from Werner's memoirs—was probably coloured by his close relationship with the crown prince. The painter Eugen Bracht, who also worked on the project, gave a rather different explanation. He recalled that once the crown prince had found out that he would not be depicted, he made every effort to have the panorama changed. It had been decided that the painting would focus on the cavalry attack at Floing, but Frederick William urged that the capture of Bazeilles be shown instead, which "would have made him and his staff the centre of the image." Even though Bazeilles—where troops belonging to Frederick William's Third Army had taken a village with considerable brutality—was deemed an unsuitable topic, "the gentleman's vanity proved a difficult hurdle to clear." The committee decided to stand its ground, though, and it was left to Werner "to extricate himself from this embarrassment as best he could."[18]

Until the very end of his life, Frederick William's depiction in portraits and official paintings remained formal, dignified, and full of military splendour. Only two portraits of the crown prince show him in civilian dress: a chalk drawing and a small oil painting both produced by Werner in the private setting of an Italian villa during a visit in October 1887. Public paintings always struck a different note. The most radiant image was perhaps Heinrich von Angeli's portrait of the crown prince. Painted in 1874 when the artist visited Frederick William and Victoria a year after their first meeting in Vienna, the picture shows the crown prince in the dazzling white dress uniform of a Pomeranian cavalry officer. Frederick William is depicted wearing the same uniform and clasping a field marshal's baton in Franz von Lenbach's "Crown Prince Frederick William" (1874). In Werner's paintings—"Baptism in My House" (1880), "Emperor Frederick as Crown Prince at the Court Ball 1878" (1887/1895), and "Prince Henry's Engagement on Emperor William's Ninetieth Birthday" (1887/1889)—Frederick William is again portrayed in uniform and in a formal, slightly stiff pose. Gottlieb Biermann's 1888 portrait shows the emperor in full-dress uniform and holding his field marshal's baton.[19] The image projected through these official paintings became such a well-known point of reference that in 1888 Theodor Fontane could readily refer to one of them in a poem that contrasted the frailty of the emperor's last days with his former magnificence:[20]

> A picture luminous and grand:
> His likeness by master Angeli's hand,
> Orange sash, medals, the helmet shines clear
> A Pasewalker Cuirassier!

The formality and majesty of official portraiture was complemented by the use that Frederick William—along with many other nineteenth-century royals—made of the new medium of photography. In 1854 the Parisian photographer Adolphe Disdéri had patented the *carte-de-visite*, which allowed eight identical photographs to be pasted onto a sheet of cardboard. Now that the photographic image had been made much more affordable than the old daguerreotypes, it quickly turned into a commercial and collectible commodity. Only five years after the invention of the carte-de-visite, photographs of Emperor Napoleon III were sold to the public. The following year, the photographer John Mayall offered a royal album containing fourteen cartes-de-visite of the British royal family for sale: within a few days, wholesalers had already placed orders for 60,000 copies. It is estimated that in the course of the 1860s, about 400 million cartes-de-visite depicting famous personages were sold in England alone. The new craze also gripped Prussia and Germany. Royal images quickly turned into prized and ubiquitous possessions.[21]

While many of the photographic images repeated established formal scenes, poses, and choices of attire, royal photography also adopted more informal, middle-class styles that emphasised the human, homely quality of the exalted individuals depicted. Photographs of this kind enabled ruling families to meet the public's growing interest in their lives by providing images which made concessions to existing conventions but also actively shaped them. Along with his father, who was happy being photographed in civilian clothing or wearing a hunter's hat, Frederick William embraced the opportunities offered by the new medium. There are photographs showing him at the end of a hunt peacefully smoking a pipe next to a dead boar, sitting at home and writing, in traditional Bavarian costume with lederhosen and bare knees in front of a painted Alpine backdrop, reading a book while wearing a comfortable jacket and plus fours, and skating with friends and family on a frozen lake. Many photographs of the crown princely couple tell a similar story. They show Frederick William and Victoria behind a writing desk looking into each other's eyes, the crown princess standing over her newspaper-reading husband with her hand affectionately resting on his shoulder, and Frederick William perched on the armrest of a sofa with Victoria's head leaning against his chest.[22]

The image of family bliss was completed by the many photographs showing the crown prince and princess surrounded by their children. These group scenes often looked lively and warm, with the caring father holding one of the smaller children. Even though in composition these royal family portraits were not unlike those of bourgeois families, they did more than simply record and communicate happiness and affection. They also documented the strength and durability of the dynasty, a purpose most strikingly pursued in the famous "Four Emperors Picture" of 1882. It showed Emperor William holding his newborn great-grandson and putative heir, flanked by the baby's father, the later emperor William II, and his grandfather, the later emperor Frederick III. The photograph was not perfect because it had been taken in a rush in the Potsdam gardens between two thunderstorms, Frederick William explained in June 1882, "but the fact is the main thing and has to compensate for the other deficiencies."[23] Perfect or not, the picture was soon in every shop window.

Public ceremonies were another means by which Frederick William could communicate with the public. In this respect, though, the crown prince had to make do with a somewhat limited stage. Apart from rare and well-publicized events like the imperial proclamation in Versailles or his entry into Jerusalem, he seldom played a central role at great state occasions and was never able to decide how they should be staged. As heir to the throne, he always stood in his father's shadow. His own ceremonial plans—such as introducing a dazzling ritual for official meetings between monarch and parliament or making the "Hohenfriedberg March" the emperor's official hymn to be used like the U.S. president's "Hail to the Chief"—never came to fruition.[24]

Occasionally, the crown prince would use an appearance at a public function to raise his profile a little, but this was usually done so cautiously that it did not cause any ructions. When addressing Berlin's Freemasons in January 1883, for instance, he called for "light and enlightenment" and demanded that there be "no standing still, but progress!" This did not go unnoticed. The left-liberal weekly *Der Reichsfreund* praised the crown prince's "golden words" and hoped he would one day turn them into reality. The conservative *Reichsbote* thought the speech was "quite worrying."[25] The crown prince's remarks at the celebration of Luther's 400th birthday in September 1883 also caused a little stir. His emphasis on the Protestant tradition of freedom of conscience was still cited five years later as indicative of his progressive outlook. Frederick William's address to the senate of the University of Königsberg in November 1885, where he warned the country to stay away from "un-German" national arrogance, triggered a similar response. Liberal voices such as *Die Nation* and the *Weser-Zeitung* commended him for his timely exhortation, but the conservative *Kreuzzeitung* complained that the "Semitic-liberal press" was using the comments for its own purposes. In each of these cases, Frederick William carefully monitored the press reaction.[26]

What really appeared to shape the wider published view of the crown prince's popular personality, however, were not these set pieces but the steady trickle of dozens of trivial stories, anecdotes, and experiences in which Our Fritz played the main role. Amplified by the press and popular publications, these added up to a consistent and attractive message. On a fine May morning in 1859, one author recalled nearly thirty years later, a detachment of grenadier guards was marching from Potsdam to the village of Eiche when they saw Frederick William and Victoria going for a walk, carrying their four-month-old boy in a basket. When he noticed the soldiers, the crown prince ordered them to stop, picked up his son, and introduced him to the guardsmen, inviting each one of them to shake the baby's hand. After that, Frederick William wished the delighted soldiers a good morning and sent them on their way. This was one of many stories that referred to the crown prince's love of children or the ease with which he interacted with common people. One winter's day in the late 1870s, passersby in Berlin stopped outside the entrance to a humble basement dwelling. Word in the street was that the crown prince was there. When a boy had been struck by Frederick William's carriage, the daily *Deutsches Tageblatt* reported, the crown prince had personally brought the injured child to his parents' shabby home and had waited with them until a doctor declared the boy to be unharmed. Frederick William then apologised again and left, only to send a servant the next day to enquire about the boy's recovery and hand over a sum of money.[27]

Ordinary folk who knew how to swim could easily get close to the physically fit crown prince. At midday during the week and at seven o'clock on Sundays, it was reported in July 1883, the crown prince would go to the public baths at Potsdam where he would splash about with soldiers or youths. A favourite manoeuvre of the crown prince's was to press the soles of his feet against those of another swimmer, legs pulled up and hands held. On Frederick William's command, both swimmers would let go, push back, and were propelled backward into the water. Even more widely known than the crown prince's prowess as a swimmer was an Our Fritz anecdote set in Bornstedt, the village outside Potsdam where Frederick William and Victoria owned a country house. In 1882 a telegram was delivered to the village teacher just as the crown prince was inspecting the school. Having learned the shocking news that his aged mother lay dying, the good man was caught on the horns of a somewhat Prussian dilemma: torn between filial affection and the duty of a schoolmaster never to cancel a lesson. He was saved by Frederick William, who told him to rush to his mother's bedside and then taught the class himself. The crown prince's teaching was, needless to say, reported to be nothing short of inspirational. In 1886 a fierce fire tore through the nearby village of Eiche. Taking his responsibilities as the local squire very seriously, Frederick William immediately rushed to help. He ran from house to house to assist with the evacuation. Covered in soot, he took command of the troops that he had ordered in to put out the blaze, pulled down fences and burning roofs himself, and took part in the search for a missing six-year-old boy. The next day, every affected household received twenty-five marks from the crown prince's purse to help with the loss of property.[28]

Many more stories like these could be added to the list. Each of them illustrates one of a catalogue of virtues that cumulatively helped to create and sustain the treasured persona Our Fritz. It appears idle to wonder how many of these anecdotes describe real events and, if so, how big their kernels of truth were. Sometimes, the storytelling obviously developed its own dynamic. A newspaper article reporting the crown prince's arrival in Kempten in August 1872 stated that he had heartily joined in with the choir serenading him. Frederick William stuck the article into his diary and added: "Is not true."[29] Since singing along with a choir was the kind of friendly and folksy gesture for which Our Fritz was known and liked, however, the story nevertheless entered the canon of anecdotes.

The invented story of Frederick William's spontaneous singing thus merely confirms that the image of the crown prince was communicated and popularized by a reciprocal process. It was sustained by certain forms of Frederick William's behaviour, as well as by their perception, embellishment, and dissemination through the public media. This image was significant because of its engagement with cultural and political forces of the present, its partial recourse to an accepted version of the past, and its impact on what was assumed to be a foreseeable future under a new monarch. It connected and reflected aspects of the Prussian imperial monarchy, the Hohenzollern dynasty, and contemporary German society.

A Paragon of Bourgeois Virtue

A crucial dimension of the crown prince's public persona was that he was a man distinguished by almost every bourgeois virtue. In fact, he was frequently described as *bürgerlich* (bourgeois) or even as a *Bürger* (a middle-class citizen). This perception places him in the mainstream of the development of European monarchy after the French Revolution. As the monarchies of the postrevolutionary era underwent numerous and profound changes, the notion of "bürgerlich kingship" emerged as a guiding concept. This transformation was driven by self-preservation. Robbed of the support previously offered by a feudal aristocracy and church, Europe's crowned heads found themselves confronted with the challenges of nationalism, liberalism, and citizens' demands for emancipation. They had to devise strategies to win over the leaders of bourgeois society and attempted to appropriate a bourgeois lifestyle and ostensibly bourgeois virtues. This process was facilitated by the existence of certain shared concerns and beliefs—such as property, inheritance, and family—and accelerated by the "publicity of their existence." Escaping into embourgeoisement and using this development propagandistically was a tempting option for dynastic persons living in "permanent visibility." The end point of this development was a monarch who was explicitly defined as bourgeois. Once kings and queens, as human beings, were indistinguishable from their subjects, they "formed the key stone of a concept for integrating the political public."[30]

Living bourgeois lives in the public eye did not mean, however, that royal families had to abandon their positions of preeminence. On the contrary, their new visibility and their comparability with their subjects almost compelled them to assume a paragon-like status. In the field of bourgeois virtues, they had to lead by example and earn the respect of their audience. Where this was seen not to be the case—as in 1820, when King George IV of England wanted to divorce Queen Caroline—the monarch's suitability for his high office appeared doubtful. "The people wanted George to fulfil his domestic obligations," Leonore Davidoff and Catherine Hall have observed. "Only then could he be a proper father to the country as well. The domestic had been imprinted on the monarchical." George IV was compared unfavourably with his late father, who had impressed the middling sorts by embracing virtues such as honesty and the love of domestic life. In Britain this theme was taken up again by Victoria and Albert. Often credited with establishing the model of family life that endowed the British monarchy with unassailable respectability, Albert was commended for being an excellent husband and father. Queen Victoria understood well that bourgeois virtues paid a political dividend. The newspapers say that "no Sovereign was more loved than I am," she wrote to the king of the Belgians in 1844, "and that, from our happy domestic home—which gives such a good example."[31]

It is tempting to emphasise the connection between Albert's policies, the influence he exercised on his daughter and son-in-law, and the bourgeois quality of Frederick William's image. There was, however, also a strong Prussian precedent that was known to the crown prince and informed his public perception. When Frederick's grandfather, King Frederick William III, succeeded in 1797, the poet Karl von Herklots welcomed him as "Bürger on the Throne," whose pride it was "to be a man." Together with his charismatic wife, Louise, and the ever-increasing number of their children, the king stood for an ideal of decency and unpretentious happiness. This perception was reinforced by reports of the simple life the family enjoyed on their rural estate at Paretz. The narrative of the Bürger king at the head of a perfect family appealed to a wide social and cultural spectrum. In 1798 the romantic poet Friedrich von Hardenberg stated that "the more the royal house, having understood the value of true domesticity, elevated it to the rare height of the throne, the more the great family of the people would recognise itself in this image" and would unite to protect it.[32] Those who preferred more mundane stories could take delight in the news that the royal family drank water rather than wine with their meals and that king and queen addressed each other with the intimate "Du." Years later, when Frederick William III had become an aged widower, people exchanged affectionate anecdotes about the king, who enjoyed walking down Berlin's main thoroughfare, modestly and unguarded, greeting and chatting with passersby.[33]

While the mercurial figure of Frederick William's uncle, King Frederick William IV of Prussia, cannot easily be fitted into the "guiding concept of bürgerlich kingship," Emperor William I was increasingly described in these terms. This was helped by the considerable "talent for affability" he developed in his old age. "He lit the way for the citizenry in bürgerlich virtue: in moral purity, in strength of duty, in unpretentious simplicity, in being true to himself," the liberal daily *Vossische Zeitung* praised the late emperor in an obituary. Other papers recalled his modesty, piety, and work ethic. Even the tender affection between the imperial couple received a mention, which was a trifle rich given the decades of bitterness between William and his wife, Augusta.[34]

A note of caution needs to be added, however, when discussing the phenomenon of nineteenth-century monarchs being portrayed as bürgerlich. Newspapers doggedly labelled modest, dutiful, and family-orientated royals as bourgeois, but the observation that they behaved in this fashion does not mean that these individuals ever perceived themselves as truly bourgeois.[35] This is an important caveat. Crown Prince Frederick William's keen sense of rank and dynastic pride certainly would have stopped him from ever defining himself as a Bürger. It is nevertheless significant that a voice as important within Germany's political culture as the chorus of published opinion consistently praised monarchical figures for the very qualities generally portrayed as epitomising what was best about the Bürgertum (bourgeoisie). The exalted recipients of this kind of flattery were prepared to dance to this particular tune. Whether the smiles on the faces of the noble dancers were real or merely masking their gritted teeth is a different matter. Furthermore, in the case of Crown Prince Frederick William, the bourgeois quality of his persona should not simply be dismissed as a mere façade. The crown prince's publicly projected bourgeois image was more detailed, comprehensive, and consistent than that of his father. Many of the interests and concerns that mattered to him, defined his personality, and informed his behaviour—his attitude toward marital love and fidelity, his view of parenthood and family life, his interest in the arts and a canon of learning—closely fit the paradigm of Bürgerlichkeit—the culture associated with being a Bürger. This culture should be understood as a body of values, of behavioural norms derived from these values, and of a commensurate style of behaviour that characterises even humdrum aspects of life.[36]

For many newspapers, the case was cut and dried. Celebrating the crown prince and his wife in November 1877 on the slightly contrived occasion of the twentieth anniversary of their official engagement, the *Magdeburger Zeitung* praised the "country where bourgeois virtue finds its safest place on the throne." On Frederick William's fiftieth birthday, the liberal *Berliner Tageblatt* declared that "Prussia and Germany welcome in him the free-thinking Bürger," while the *Vossische Zeitung* observed that the crown prince's unostentatious birthday celebrations were "true to his bürgerlich-modest outlook." According to the *Neueste Münchner Nachrichten,* which welcomed the crown prince to the Bavarian capital in April 1883, Frederick William combined "truly chivalrous and truly bürgerlich qualities." Two years later, the *Braunschweiger Tageblatt* observed that "in him bürgerlich thought has reached its most mature and most beautiful development." He had been close to the people, a commemorative volume concluded in 1888, "as the first Bürger and the first head of the family of his nation."[37] In the eyes of bourgeois journalists and presumably their bourgeois readers, the crown prince qualified as bürgerlich because he met, nay, exceeded the conditions derived from a catalogue of behavioural norms that charted Bürgerlichkeit. The praise Frederick William received for being a veritable super-Bürger therefore contains a powerful message about how a particular section of Germany's public wanted to see itself and its monarchy.

The most prominent theme within the bourgeois dimension of Frederick William's image is his excellence as a husband and father, as well as the exemplary quality of his domestic life. Considering how important a "specific family ideal" was to the middle classes, this is not surprising. It formed the very "heart of bürgerlich culture."[38] The well-known story of the family idyll enjoyed by King Frederick William III and Queen Louise reinforced this aspect even further. The author Wilhelm Petsch recalled in 1873 that when the newly wed Frederick William and Victoria moved into their palace in Berlin in 1858, many had wished them the bliss with which his grandparents had been blessed. Now that fifteen years had passed, Petsch was delighted to find that "the crown prince had been generously provided with the old Prussian love." Three years later, the *Madgeburger Zeitung* admired the "shining example of a happy marriage." Looking back after Frederick William's death, writers praised a couple who had gone "through life in loving unanimity" and a marriage not forged by a "policy of courtly calculation" but "truly firm and honestly true until the painful fading of a married life kept pure."[39] The foil for this bürgerlich union, which formed the foundation of the crown prince's admirable domestic life, was the kind of aristocratic marriage implicitly criticised in the comments on "courtly calculation," fidelity, and purity.

The most beautiful accolade for the crown prince and princess, the *Breslauer Zeitung* declared in 1883, was "father and mother." Their family life always had been an example to the German people, the paper explained, and "that, above all, has won them our hearts."[40] As was demanded by the ideal type of a bürgerlich family, the care for their children was perceived to be the essence of Frederick William and Victoria's domestic life. The *Vossische Zeitung* claimed to know that "both spouses most conscientiously supervise the education of their children, their intellectual and physical training as well as the development of their personalities and mutually support each other through their lively conversations." The manner in which the couple dedicated themselves to the education of their children, the conservative *Neue Preussische Zeitung* observed, "has been an example and guide for the whole country."[41]

The amount of detail reported about Frederick William and Victoria's private life together was astonishing. An 1886 publication underlined Victoria's commitment to motherhood by stating—correctly—that against royal convention she had breast-fed some of her children. With his family, the crown prince was a "joyful, joking father," Wilhelm Petsch explained, "but also—when necessary—the serious educator." A popular biography of the crown prince published in 1883 summarized Frederick William's aims for his children's education: "He strove to form them into the foremost Bürger of the state." A visitor calling on the crown prince one day came upon the following scene, described in Oskar Höcker's book of 1888: Frederick William lay on the floor and was happily playing with a cheerful gang of children tumbling all over him. A few pages on, the author reminded his readers of Frederick William's determination to provide "proper schooling" for his children and to send his sons to a grammar school "just like the children of simple Bürger-people."[42]

The reference to the simplicity of his bourgeois life points to another aspect of Frederick William's public image. Many of the stories, reports, and anecdotes in circulation suggest that the crown prince actively contributed to the characterization of his life and tastes as being modest and thrifty. The stationmaster at Dortmund, given less than an hour to organise a meal for Frederick William and Victoria, was embarrassed by the frugality of the food, but the crown prince reassured the poor man: "No, simple and good, that's how I like it." When the crown prince's family spent a holiday on the North Sea island of Föhr in July 1865, the other tourists hardly realised whose company they were in because Frederick William, Victoria, and the children behaved "so simply and frugally."[43]

During the war against Austria, Frederick William made sure to mention to his soldiers that he had run out of tobacco so they would know that he also had to suffer many privations. According to one story, a Berlin ragman, oblivious of who he was talking to, approached Frederick William to ask for some old clothes: the crown prince replied that all the castoffs were needed by his own large family. When visiting Dresden in 1876, Frederick William explored the city on foot, "true to his well-known simple ways." Asked on one occasion why he had only bought twenty raffle tickets, Frederick William admitted that he could not afford more because he had seven children to feed. We are told that the people witnessing the exchange admired his "budgetary prudence." All of this worthy and well-publicised simplicity meant that the crown prince once again emerged as a paragon. Rather than raising more money, "he carefully avoided squandering anything and had to forgo much," a pamphlet stated in 1888. He "provided the whole German nation with an example of how, as a family richly blessed with children, one should live within one's means."[44]

The virtuous themes of family life and unpretentious simplicity were combined and intensified through the well-known symbol of Bornstedt, a country estate outside Potsdam acquired by Frederick William and Victoria in 1867. At this model farm and much-loved retreat, the crown prince played the simple country squire, caring for the locals, sitting alongside them in the pews of the village church, and visiting the school. The young princesses baked cake, their mother fetched the cream from the dairy, and the princes played with the village children. What gave Bornstedt its special resonance with the public, though, was the immediately recognised parallel with the happy family life that Frederick William's paternal grandparents had led at Paretz. Through their "simple, almost bürgerlich" life among the people of Bornstedt, the *Vossische Zeitung* observed in 1883, Frederick William and Victoria were renewing the memory of the "'mayor of Paretz' and his unforgettable wife."[45] A regular highlight each year was the children's party organised by the crown prince and his wife, either in Bornstedt itself or at their nearby palace in Potsdam. Boys and girls from the village, Berlin, and local orphanages were invited for games, cake, and refreshments. Frederick William and Victoria played a hands-on part on these occasions, looking after the children, pouring drinks, offering biscuits, and ensuring that everyone went home with a gift.[46]

These well-known and publicised events not only documented the couple's love of children but also, in the words of one observer, "gave eloquent testimony of the philanthropy felt among the crown princely family towards those who otherwise know nothing but deprivation, need and want." His generosity to poor children and orphans was only one example of yet another of Our Fritz's numerous virtues: charity and social engagement. In addition to the many individual acts of kindness and philanthropy recalled in anecdotes, contemporary accounts frequently point to the "Crown Prince's Donation" *(Kronprinzenspende),* a gift of some 800,000 marks raised by public subscription and presented to Frederick William and Victoria on their silver anniversary. It was pledged to a variety of good causes such as a training facility for nurses, holiday camps and sanatoria for children, temperance organisations, charities seeking to resocialise released convicts, and relief for those affected by recent floods. This illustrated, as one author put it, that Frederick William was "a good, caring father of the country." Announcing the donation, the crown prince expressed his delight that collections undertaken for "noble and charitable ends" had enabled him and his wife to contribute to the common good and thereby to give their anniversary "the most beautiful consecration."[47] A few months later, an earthquake caused great suffering on the Italian island of Ischia. Frederick wrote to the German government in August 1883 to announce publicly that he and Victoria would head the collections organised across Germany to help those affected by the catastrophe. This initiative met "with a most lively response amongst the whole German people."[48]

One of the key bürgerlich virtues listed by Pierer's *Universal-Lexikon* of 1857 was "participation in the furtherance of the public weal." The crown prince fulfilled this duty, not only through acts of charity but also through what was seen as a systematic, earnest, and consistent engagement with various welfare issues. In 1888 the Association for the Welfare of the Working Classes published a booklet specifically in order to "shine a light on his achievements for the good of the people." Several authors contributed warm reports of Frederick William's social programme, as well as his interest in health care, the cooperative movement, housing, vagrancy, and unemployment. Hermann Müller-Bohn's massive tome "Emperor Frederick the Gracious" offers an even fuller account of Frederick William as a champion of popular welfare. It lovingly inventories the crown prince's many commitments, including his support for modern sewerage systems, summer camps for the convalescing poor, and fisheries as a means of providing cheap, wholesome nutrition; his backing of Pastor Friedrich von Bodelschwingh's institutions for those suffering from epilepsy; and even his plans to provide public rain shelters for Berlin's coachmen and troughs for their horses. Frederick William's efforts were certainly recognised. "Always ahead, when it is about offering a home to the true, the good and the beautiful for the welfare of the community," the daily *Berliner Tageblatt* wrote in 1881, "the crown prince has become for all of us a symbol of that modest and yet industrious activity which always puts one's own interests last."[49]

In nineteenth-century Germany, no inventory of Bürgerlichkeit would have been complete without the "canon of bourgeois *Bildung,*" the concern for education, learning, and the arts. It remained, in the words of Wolfgang Kaschuba, "the central axis around which bourgeois life turned." As a result of careful tuition and diligent application, the educated Bürger was expected to develop a discerning knowledge of and respect for history, literature, scholarship, and fine art. Frederick William passed this bürgerlich litmus test much more convincingly than his somewhat unimaginative grandfather or his father, whose ability to sleep through entire theatre performances was legendary. Not only had Frederick William himself received an education orientated on the humanist tradition and culminating in university studies, but he was also known to lavish great care on his own children's tuition at home, at a public grammar school, and at university. Moreover, his interest in cultural and artistic matters remained active and visible. In 1879 Victoria gave Frederick William an old edition of Livy's history of Rome as a birthday present. "As a good German," a contemporary booklet explained, the crown prince "delights in such learned rarities."[50]

Frederick William's reputation as a champion of Bildung and culture rested, above all, on two main pillars: his long-term interest in various aspects of teaching, training, and schooling and his work as patron of the royal museums. The crown prince's support for educational issues went well beyond his paternalistic care for the village school in Bornstedt. Along with his wife, he actively supported Berlin's Pestalozzi-Fröbel-House, opened in 1873. This institution offered kindergarten classes, vocational instruction for boys, home economics for girls, a refectory, and a college for training kindergarten teachers. In 1878 the Crown Prince Frederick William Foundation for Scholarships at the German Crafts Museum was formally incorporated by royal decree. Under Frederick William's patronage, this charitable trust provided bursaries to enable poor talented students to complete their training. From 1881 onward, Frederick William also made an annual visit to Berlin's College of Further Education to conduct examinations, inspect written work, and talk to the staff, even accepting a formal appointment as examiner in 1885. All these activities demonstrated to the public that, as the head teacher of the new Emperor Frederick School in the city of Emden put it in 1889, Frederick William regarded supporting the education of the young "as one of his dearest and most important duties as a ruler."[51]

Returning from a walk along the Rhine one summer's day in 1871, Frederick William found that he had received an entirely unexpected royal decree. His father had appointed him patron (Protektor) of Prussia's royal museums. His previous experience was rather limited and consisted mainly of his support for a German Crafts Museum to be established in Berlin. Modelled on London's South Kensington Museum, it had formally opened in 1868.[52] According to Count Usedom, who served as director-general of the royal museums until 1879, the crown prince initially resented the apolitical nature of his appointment. This did not, however, prevent him from fulfilling his new duties with diligence and seriousness. During Frederick William's tenure as patron the budget of the museums increased more than fivefold and their organisational structure was modernised in 1878. Richard Schöne, who was the crown prince's choice to replace the incompetent Usedom in 1880, gratefully acknowledged Frederick William's backing. Wilhelm von Bode, Schöne's successor, remembered the crown prince as a "warm and energetic supporter of our plans." Nor was the public left unaware of Frederick William's salutary efforts. "Naturally endowed with good taste and artistic sense," the *Vossische Zeitung* noted in January 1883, "the crown prince has . . . been instrumental in bringing about the manifold enrichment recently experienced by our art collections." In his obituary for the late emperor, Richard Schöne bade farewell to a man whose work had been inspired "by the passionate wish to carry advancement, joy, delectation and education into the wider circles of his people through the effectiveness of these institutions."[53]

Numerous further facets can be added to complete the image of a thoroughly cultured man who was friends with painters and poets. In his memorial speech, the historian Hermann Baumgarten mentioned the late emperor's support for the study of history through his sponsorship of source editions, his interest in classical archaeology, and his commitment to the freedom of scientific enquiry. The crown prince's perceived place within a world of Bildung, learning, and art is captured most strikingly in Anton von Werner's painting "Emperor Frederick as Crown Prince at the Court Ball 1878" (1887/1895). Most probably based on a meeting in February 1887, the painting shows Frederick William surrounded by the eminent pathologist

Rudolf Virchow, the physicist Hermann Helmholtz, and the painters Adolf von Menzel and Ludwig Knaus. Frederick William's cultural, artistic, and intellectual interests were thus portrayed as integrating him into society. "Like a modest Bürger he has lived among us for many a year," the *Freisinnige Zeitung* welcomed the new emperor in March 1888, "furthering, together with his wife, arts and sciences and every peaceful human endeavour."[54]

Measured against the yardstick of the culture of Bürgerlichkeit, Our Fritz emerges as a figure of almost frightening perfection. Crown Prince Frederick William had made "all the treasures of the sciences and the arts, all the noble bürgerlich virtues his own," the *Kölnische Zeitung* observed on the day of the emperor's death. Patriotic exaggeration and unrealistic hyperbole notwithstanding, even a royal super-Bürger like Our Fritz offered a means of integrating monarchy and public. "In the crown princely couple," the *Breslauer Zeitung* observed in 1883, "the German people revere the bearer of everything that has always been dear to itself." As Our Fritz, the bürgerlich crown prince played—at least partly—according to "our" rules. He had earned the colossal affection he enjoyed in a meritocratic process through his excellence in a cultural pursuit not of his own devising. This "culture," Thomas Nipperdey explained, is how "Bürgertum constitutes itself." It exists as a "togetherness of virtues and behavioural norms, which reaches far beyond the 'higher' culture, beyond the so-called Bildung and its contents into the elementary areas of life." In their celebration of Our Fritz, powerful voices expressing Germany's political culture could put a bürgerlich seal of approval on the future of their monarchy.[55]

Chip off the Heroic Old Block

The bürgerlich dimension of Our Fritz was only one side of this splendid coin. The obverse bore a regal head and rounded off the crown prince's exemplary Bürgerlichkeit by adding a different set of features. This complementary and sometimes alternative dimension of his public persona was noticeably more heroic and drew strongly on an established canon of kingly virtues. It also integrated Frederick William's image into other aspects of the Hohenzollerns' dynastic legend: not the bürgerlich family idyll of his grandparents' country life, but the glory and suffering of the Seven Years' War and the struggle against Napoleon. On the one hand, this heroic, monarchical version of Our Fritz provided a link between the crown prince and those on the margins of or outside the culture of Bürgerlichkeit. On the other hand, the respect and affection his regal persona commanded even *within* the bürgerlich milieu demonstrates that monarchy could be successfully popularized in simultaneous yet different ways that employed alternative symbolic idioms. The public image of monarchy—generated through projection, reflection, and perception—functioned like a flattering mirror. Standing in front of this looking glass in his frock coat, the German Bürger was delighted to see his crown prince so admirably bürgerlich. Wearing his cherished uniform, the same observer stood to attention, awestruck by Our Fritz's heroism.

The German Bürgertum admired the representatives of the Prussian military state not only because it gave them credit for having won unity and greatness for the nation during the wars of 1866 and 1870–1871. The widespread respect enjoyed by these war heroes also rested on notions of meritocratic entitlement: as in the wars against Napoleonic France, Germany's military leaders were perceived as having measured up to rigorous criteria of success and valiant commitment to the common cause. Moreover, alongside this adulation, a process unfolded which led to a bürgerlich appropriation of the military glory won against Austria and France. After the victorious French campaign the army and the nation were eventually being regarded as identical. The Bürgertum thus ended up admiring what it considered its own deeds when it celebrated the victory of 1870–1871.[56] In the case of Crown Prince Frederick William, two other, older forces are also important to explain the success of his heroic persona: the myths of Frederick the Great and Queen Louise.

Our Fritz's military record was the most glittering aspect of his public image. In the eyes of the German public, the crown prince was a victorious, charismatic, gallant leader of armies, whose contribution to the defeat of the Austrians and the French had been both heroic and crucial. This not only gave Frederick William enormous prestige and popularity but was also seen as proof that he possessed the exceptional level of ability that predestined him for his royal office. Military prowess was clearly one of the kingly virtues whose alleged existence justified for many the belief in the superiority of the hereditary system. Like the Reich itself, Our Fritz was therefore very much a product of war. "We would never have seen the indifferent figure of the Crown Prince Frederick William transformed into the omnipresent, imposing and likeable persona 'Our Fritz,' the icon of the first German army," Georg Hinzpeter wrote as early as 1883, "if external conditions had not forced an opportunity upon him, where his great intellectual talents, his firm will and his generous heart had to show themselves."[57]

There was next to no dissent from this patriotic consensus. It took a conspicuously ungenerous essay published by the novelist Gustav Freytag in 1889 for doubt to be cast on the late emperor's military credentials. Frederick William's performance as an officer had lacked proper professionalism, Freytag claimed, and the crown prince owed the successes of his generalship in 1866 and 1870 to his outstanding chief of staff, General Leonhard von Blumenthal. Freytag's faultfinding not only caused much dismay and failed to resonate amid the public's overwhelming belief in Our Fritz's military excellence, but was also unfair. On the one hand, Frederick William always generously acknowledged the stellar contribution made by senior commanders. When the heir to the throne was made a field marshal in October 1870, he readily conceded that ahead of anyone else this honour should have gone to Helmuth von Moltke, the chief of the Prussian general staff. On 18 March 1888, only days into his own short reign, Emperor Frederick repaid his old debt to Blumenthal by promoting him to the rank of field marshal, too. On the other hand, the crown prince's military record indicated that he was a perfectly competent officer, fully capable of effectively discharging even very demanding duties.[58]

As was to be expected from a future king of Prussia, Frederick William had progressed swiftly and fairly effortlessly through the ranks. After joining the First Guards Landwehr Regiment at the tender age of seven, he was commissioned as a second lieutenant two years later and promoted to captain in 1851. Having commanded a company of the First Guards Regiment, a squadron of dragoons, and a battalion of the Second Guards Landwehr Regiment, Frederick William attended the Berlin War College before being promoted to colonel in 1855 and to brigadier-general three years later.[59] The crown prince's military talents were first tested during Prussia and Austria's joint campaign against Denmark in 1864, when the thirty-three-year old major-general was ordered to serve on the staff of Field Marshal Friedrich von Wrangel. Tetchy, impetuous, and borderline senile, Prussia's octogenarian commander-in-chief required careful handling. Frederick William acquitted himself well. General August von Goeben, who was in charge of a brigade during the conflict, praised the crown prince's intelligence and welcomed his excellent effect on the aged Wrangel. A former Prussian minister-president considered it one of the most precious results of the victory over Denmark that the ability Frederick William demonstrated throughout the campaign had consolidated his position amongst the military establishment.[60]

The crown prince performed equally effectively as commander-in-chief of the Second Prussian Army during the war against Austria in 1866 and at the head of the Third German Army during the French campaign of 1870–1871. While he showed little in the way of strategic flair and had to be talked out of making rash decisions on one or two occasions, he was open to shrewd advice and proved a solid field officer. Physically fit, courageous, and folksy, Frederick William quickly became an inspiration to his troops. At the battle of Nachod, the first serious encounter of the Austro-Prussian War, for instance, he spent a full fourteen hours in the saddle, often exposing himself to considerable danger. Generally maintaining an attitude of quiet imperturbability, he was capable of emphatic firmness when required. "Ride to your countrymen at Froeschwiller and tell them the crown prince of Prussia orders them in the name of their king finally to attack the enemy properly and to throw him back," he bellowed at the Bavarian military plenipotentiary at the height of the battle of Wörth in August 1870. Everywhere the troops were advancing victoriously and only the Bavarians were stalling before the French, he added grimly. This reprimand had been harsh, Frederick William noted in his diary afterward, but a clear word was needed and the outburst had the desired effect. As was shown by his warning against any unnecessary violation of the Belgian border or his scepticism about the effectiveness of bombarding Paris, the crown prince's military judgement was sound on other matters, too.[61]

For the public, the moment when Frederick William was immortalized as a military hero was 3 July 1866, when he led the Second Prussian Army onto the battlefield of Königgrätz-Sadowa to attack the Austrian flank and relieve Prussia's hard-pressed First and Third Armies. The progress of the crown prince's troops had been delayed by communication problems, difficult terrain, and adverse weather conditions, but although it came dangerously late, his intervention sealed Prussia's complete victory over the forces of Austria and

Saxony. The decisive plan for encircling the enemy's main army had been devised by Helmuth von Moltke, yet the account given in Ludwig Ziemssen's life of Frederick William suggests that the real father of the victory was someone else: "And when the heroic prince, together with 80,000 men, stormed towards the fire-breathing heights of Chlum and Rosberitz, grasped the very key of the enemy's position with an iron fist, then the main work of a great day was done." Almost all popular accounts also describe the moving scene of the subsequent meeting between the crown prince and his father. "Unable to utter a word King William extended his right hand to his heroic son," is how one author put it in his book dedicated to Germany's youth. "With tears flowing Crown Prince Frederick William bowed down to kiss it, but the king, crying, pulled him to his chest. Then he removed the Pour le Mérite medal from his neck and hung it on his son."[62]

The Franco-Prussian War added further to Frederick William's laurels. As commander of the Third Army, which combined Prussian and South German troops, the crown prince was hailed as the victor of the early battles at Weissenburg and Wörth. Promoted to the rank of field marshal—an unprecedented honour for a Prussian prince—and highly decorated, Our Fritz became a martial legend. "Right amongst his troops was again Crown Prince Frederick," one account of the battle of Wörth has its readers believe. "Everywhere, where the battle was raging most fiercely, his tall, handsome figure towered over the lines of the combatants."[63] Within weeks of the beginning of the campaign against France, Our Fritz's heroism had launched a cacophony of painful patriotic doggerel. A particularly popular soldiers' song relied on the somewhat predictable solution to the problem of finding a rhyme for Fritz:[64]

> Our crown prince, he's called Fritz,
> And he strikes, just like a blitz
> Right amongst the men of France.
> And whether we did struggle well
> Weissenburg and Wörth will tell,
> Where we had a bloody dance.

Another poem focused rather crudely on the hapless French marshal Patrice de MacMahon, who was defeated at Wörth:[65]

> About our prince a story's told
> Frederick William, he is called

> At Wörth our Fritz smacked the posterior
> Of the Frenchmen's most superior
> MacMahon, MacMahon
> Fritz turns up and he is gone!

From then on, Frederick William's military glory was treated as axiomatic. "He is dear to our people as a victorious general," the *Magdeburger Zeitung* explained in 1877. On his fiftieth birthday, the papers called him a "hero and victor," praised the "ever-lasting laurels" he had gained, and reminded their readers that he had led his troops "from victory to victory." Two years later, the *Breslauer Zeitung* described him as a "genius of a general and brave soldier." The *Vossische Zeitung* observed that Frederick William was "like all Hohenzollerns, a soldier with all his heart" and that he had made a "pre-eminent contribution to the latest great war, through which Prussia's and Germany's greatness was founded." When welcoming the new emperor in March 1888, the conservative *Neue Preussische Zeitung* hailed an outstanding soldier: "Amongst the generals, who gained everlasting glory in great wars, he is of the first rank. No-one can mention the names Königgrätz, Weissenburg and Wörth, without thinking of him, above all others."[66]

A particularly striking feature of Frederick William's military glory was its all-German appeal. If Our Fritz had led them in 1866, a Bavarian soldier told a senior officer in November 1870, they would have beaten "those bloody Prussians." This oft-repeated story epitomised Frederick William's popularity amongst the non-Prussian soldiers, many of whom had fought as Austria's allies only a few years earlier. When he was travelling through Saxony, Bavaria, Württemberg, and Baden in July 1870 to assume his command of the Third German Army for the war with France, the crown prince noticed the warmth of his welcome. Once in the field, he took care to emphasise the inclusive quality of his composite force, which comprised soldiers who spoke a dozen different German dialects and was portrayed as a microcosm of the German nation united in victory. In an order issued on 30 July 1870, he referred to his pride to be leading "the sons united from all the provinces of the fatherland for the common national cause."[67] It was also known that Frederick William successfully pushed for non-Prussians to be decorated with the Iron Cross, a medal which hitherto had been reserved for Prussian recipients. The affection the crown prince quickly commanded amongst his South German soldiers in the field transferred easily to their home countries. The *Allgemeine Zeitung* described the return of the Bavarian troops to Munich in July 1871: "Suddenly everything went quiet for a moment, all eyes were fixed on one point and one man, who rode along in modest dignity, holding his marshal's baton, his face showing that sober faithfulness that surpasses every beauty: it is the crown prince of the German Reich. Like a thunderstorm rages, the jubilations now broke forth from every heart. It was a downpour of joy that reverberated in the skies."[68]

Based on this wartime experience and renewed through the annual trips Frederick William undertook as inspector-general of the South German army contingents, the crown prince's popularity in South Germany remained considerable throughout the rest of his life. "For us in the German South," the *Neueste Münchener Nachrichten* wrote in April 1883, "it is always a happy event to see the very likeable figure of the future emperor again." A French correspondent covering the funeral of King Ludwig II in Munich in 1886 described how the crown prince electrified the crowd that welcomed him with a suitably hushed "There he is." From then on, the journalist felt, the people regarded themselves as Frederick William's subjects. King Ludwig must have turned in his grave. In its obituary of Emperor Frederick, Vienna's *Neue Freie Presse* emphasised that "as the Bavarians' leader in war, as inspector-general of the peacetime army, through the indescribable affability and charm of his character he strengthened the loose bond between North and South." For Munich's *Allgemeine Zeitung,* the late emperor was the hero who built bridges between Prussians and South Germans, who "courted and gained the hearts and minds of our people for German unity; he conquered the South of Germany for the Reich!"[69] Given his commitment to effect a more centralized government of the Reich in the face of particularist foot-dragging, Frederick William must have been particularly pleased about his impact in the South.

As these accounts reveal, it was not only the success of his military leadership that cemented the crown prince's popularity as a general. It was also the style in which he interacted with his troops and with the public that won him the hearts of the soldiers and of large sections of German society. Time and again, published accounts praised Frederick William's *Leutseligkeit,* his approachability and easy manner with ordinary people. A common theme among

the many anecdotes about Our Fritz, this affability was a particularly marked feature of Frederick William's interaction with the
military. He would regularly go swimming with his men. When holi-
daying in July 1865, he also joined a dance organised by sailors. The
relative informality and extraordinariness of life during the French
campaign reinforced this pattern. The crown prince sometimes gave
his pipe to a simple trooper, lay down to rest on the ground with his
men, and occasionally indulged in a bit of horseplay with soldiers
when swimming in a river. He also regularly visited field hospitals to
comfort the wounded and dying. The crown prince's Leutseligkeit
toward the soldiers did not cease when the war ended. During a
holiday in Bavaria in July 1872, for instance, Frederick William invited all the veterans who lived nearby to meet him at Berchtes-
gaden. Wearing the local alpine costume, he chatted with every
soldier, shook countless hands, and plied the men with food, drinks,
and cigars.[70]

The crown prince's interest in and kindness toward the common
people was not seen to be restricted to the military. Whether it was
manifested through sending a new set of bibles to a village school
whose own copies Frederick William had found too worn, speaking
in the Berlinese dialect, interrupting his hunting trip to help fight a
forest fire, or joining the crowds at Berlin's Christmas fair to buy presents for his children: the crown prince's common touch was widely
reported and generally recognised as an essential part of his public
persona. "In his heroic appearance and in the heart-warming
Leutseligkeit of his behaviour were merged the North and the South
of our fatherland in one outstanding personality," the National-
Zeitung explained in June 1888. "The reverence induced by his high
position was mingled in the soul of the people with a feeling of simple
and true love." The liberal weekly Der Reichsfreund reminded its
readers of the many stories about Frederick William's dealings "among
the people and with the people." Always friendly, good, and helpful,
this "gorgeous, radiant hero convinced everyone that the inner core
of his being was the pure, honest love of humanity."[71]

This constant emphasis on the crown prince's ability to condescend
sympathetically and sincerely to people occupying a lower station
than him did more than implicitly endorse a fundamentally hierarchi-
cal model of the relationship between ruler and ruled. It also served
as a permanent reminder of how closely Frederick William's heroic
persona was derived from the preexisting image of Prussia's most

awesome royal icon: King Frederick the Great. In the preface of the 1856 edition of his hugely successful biography of this eighteenth-century monarch, Franz Kugler declared that Frederick the Great remained "close to us as a human being like few others who proudly stand high above the course of history." Frederick II knew, Kugler insisted, how "to penetrate with loving participation the thoughts and needs of even the lowest. He became a man of the people, in the most comprehensive, most noble sense of the word, because he manifested what is dignified clothed in true, simple humanity." Naturally, the great king was also a victorious general, wielding "the sword that enemies forced into his hand." He gave "honour to the German name" so that "German deed and German word would once again, as in days of yore, radiate across the lands."[72]

Kugler's book was first published in 1840 to mark the centenary of Frederick II's accession. Together with a number of publications in a similar vein, it greatly amplified an existing image of Frederick II as a paragon of kingly virtue and a truly popular ruler. This was achieved by casting him in the dual role of heroic warrior and caring, empathetic father of his people: brilliant and courageous, sharing danger and hardship with his soldiers; kind to common folk and always ready to help; modest and thrifty, yet a friend of learning and the arts. The legendary image of the Prussian king had already proved a successful propaganda tool in the eighteenth century, especially among a broader, nonaristocratic public. When it was revived during the first half of the nineteenth century, the myth of the Old Fritz quickly emerged as a dominant and widely perceived symbol of glorious Prussiandom and popular monarchy.[73]

It was only a short step from venerating the Old Fritz to adoring Our Fritz. The rhymester Edmund Höfer expressed the feeling with little grace but undeniable clarity:

> We young ones we can do it,
> God's thunder and God's blitz;
> And though we lack the old one,
> We do have our young Fritz!

Wilhelm Petsch's poem "Hail Our Fritz, the Young One!" in which the "young Fritz" is described as a "true scion of the old," and Georg Lang's verses "The Old and the Young Fritz" struck the same patriotic note. In 1875 Theodor Drobisch even published a richly illustrated children's book on the topic. *The Old Fritz and Our Fritz* brought together two groups of biographical poems highlighting the links between these two royal figures. The readiness with which connections were made between the existing Frederician myth and the figure of the crown prince demonstrates the persuasiveness of the established narrative of dynastic virtue and superiority. Like a well-hewn building block in an arch, the heroic persona Our Fritz was made to fit its dynastic context perfectly. Once in place, it served to strengthen the overall structure. In turn, the myth of the Old Fritz greatly facilitated the success of Frederick William's own public image.[74]

The crown prince's integration into this dynastic narrative was bought at a price, though, carrying with it the risk of limiting the range of his political appeal. As yet another Hohenzollern monarch, Our Fritz generally failed to find favour with the Social Democrats. We have never expected much "from the heir of a royal dignity 'by the Grace of God,' " the weekly *Der Sozialdemokrat* observed drily a fortnight after Frederick William had succeeded his father. The Socialist writer Max Maurenbrecher, a contemporary, produced a two-volume study to demonstrate that the "Hohenzollern Legend" had been created entirely to conserve the monarchical system and prevent change. By the same token, however, the dynastic story helped to make the crown prince more acceptable to right-wing sceptics. The myth of Old Fritz shone in such a patriotic, martial, and monarchical light that those baulking at Frederick William's liberal reputation could always focus on Our Fritz's heroically Frederician dimension. They were thus able to display monarchical loyalty while avoiding unpalatable politics. "On the eve of the sombre day, when the dark shadows of death receive the deceased into their realm, his majestic image once again stands before us," the *Norddeutsche Allgemeine Zeitung*, a leading organ of the conservative *Kartell* of governmental parties, wrote on the day before Emperor Frederick's funeral. "It recalls the memory of the battle-hardened general, who was passionate about the fatherland's greatness and reputation, the heir of the name and spirit of his great ancestors."[75]

The myth of Frederick the Great proved, however, to be a wonderfully flexible travelling companion for the German Bürgertum as it progressed along the road of its own political development. During the first half of the nineteenth century, before Old Fritz was yoked to a conservative cart, many liberals had interpreted him as a symbol of progressive, enlightened thinking that could even be deployed to challenge the rigid conservatism of their day. When Frederick William acceded as Emperor Frederick III in March 1888, an attempt was made from within the left-liberal camp to score a political point by reaching back to this older version. "The name defines his programme," the liberal *Vossische Zeitung* declared when welcoming Frederick. "The new emperor has chosen the name of his great ancestor, the enlightened spirit who called himself the first servant of his state, who was a protector of liberty, a keeper of the people's weal, a supporter of arts and sciences, in spite of all the glory on the field of honour." In a similar vein, Arnold Perls, a well-known left-liberal journalist, offered readers of the *Berliner Zeitung* an unflinchingly partisan interpretation of the emperor's proclamations, which he saw as containing the "neo-Frederician wisdom of governance."[76]

The surprising malleability of existing dynastic narratives is also demonstrated by the connections that contemporaries drew between Our Fritz and his grandmother, the sainted Queen Louise. The main vehicle for integrating the image of Our Fritz with the Louise myth was, of course, the story of Bornstedt, which was widely seen as a reincarnation of Louise's idyll at Paretz. In the setting of Bornstedt, the themes of simplicity, princely thrift, Leutseligkeit, and concern for the common people could be drawn as a mimetic version of the queen's family home. This offered softer, warmer colours than the sometimes acerbic model of the old bachelor Fredrick the Great. Through their warmth, family values, sympathetic condescension to simple people, unpretentiousness, and love of children, a strong connection was already established between Frederick William and his grandmother. Both of them, for instance, were known to have enthralled crowds by publicly kissing children: Louise during her entrance into Berlin in 1793 and Frederick William during a visit to Italy in 1878.[77]

The myth of Queen Louise comprised more facets, though, than just maternal kindness and domestic bliss. In the emergence of a "Cult of Louise," the heroic national struggle against the French and the queen's suffering, sacrifice, and early death also played a crucial role. Having died—as the legend would have it—essentially of worry and grief for her family and country during a time when Prussia was suffering war, defeat, and ignominy at the hands of Napoleon, the queen occupied a preeminent position within a national and monarchical cult of the dead.[78] Inspired by the terrible fate the crown prince and emperor had to endure in the final year of his life, observers were struck by the parallel between the "Noble Sufferer" and the late lamented queen. "As our thoughts rest on his death bed," the rector of Halle University declared in his memorial oration in June 1888, "another image of suffering arises: the likeness of that beloved queen, who saw nothing but the humiliation of her country and died of it without abandoning hope." For the author Bruno Garlepp, Frederick William resembled Louise because "they both sank into the grave before they could fully develop their deeds." With the benefit of hindsight, Frederick William and Victoria's move into the crown prince's palace in Berlin struck one observer as a terrible premonition, for there resided "the spirit of Louise, the sufferer on Prussia's throne, glorified through pain and death."[79]

A final though unspoken parallel between Louise and Frederick William completes the crown prince's set of kingly virtues: his beauty. Already attractive as a boy, Frederick William's good looks as a man were proverbial. An observer watching him walking around Nancy in the summer of 1870 described him as "the very image of robust, unconscious beauty—so free and kind his gaze, so fresh and unforced every movement." Once Frederick William was a mature man, accounts of his beauty stuck closely to the topos of a Germanic knight. "Like a Nordic hero from days long gone his appearance radiates forth from among the group of paladins surrounding the revered figure of Emperor William, the White-Beard," is how the *Berliner Tageblatt* described the fifty-year-old crown prince. In March 1888, the *Freisinnige Zeitung* recalled his return from France in 1871: he was "the original image of masculine strength and beauty as a radiant hero, tanned by the sun, returning from campaigning in faraway lands." Conservatives like Heinrich von Treitschke and left-liberals like Arnold Perls were united in praising Frederick William as manly and handsome. For Robert Dohme, Frederick William had been "one of the most beautiful men who ever lived—even as a corpse he still radiated an almost unearthly beauty and mildness." While the crown prince was generally talked about as a strapping warrior, Dohme especially remembered—and this was also a well-known detail in the iconography of Frederick the Great—the crown prince's blue eyes: wonderful, soulful, and intelligent.[80]

Adulation of this kind illustrates how the heroic dimension of Frederick William's public image led to a blurring of the line between patriotic loyalty and fantasy. Toward the end of Frederick William's life and increasingly after his death, the metaphors used to describe him often hailed from the realm of legend. Riding in the procession celebrating Queen Victoria's Golden Jubilee in 1887, he reminded spectators of the medieval swan knight and was greeted with shouts of "Lohengrin." Later in the year, the society hostess Anna von Helmholtz also referred to him as "the swan knight, on whom rests the hope of every ideal endeavour." Praising the late emperor in a memorial sermon, a preacher at the Württembergian court invoked the famous dragon slayer and called Frederick III a Siegfried-like figure. The well-known war correspondent Archibald Forbes saw him as "our modern King Arthur."[81]

This tendency further emphasises the different effects caused by the bürgerlich and heroic dimensions of the persona Our Fritz. The former suggested a fundamental sameness between the crown prince and Germany's wider society: Frederick William's eminence appeared as the result of the kind of effort and self-discipline that was principally open to everyone. The latter reinforced a perceived notion of fundamental difference because it highlighted an extraordinariness derived from inherited, supernatural, or God-given qualities.

Frederick William's Dynastic Project

The appeal of his great dynastic past was certainly not lost on Frederick William himself. Given his acute sense of inherited rank and his passion for history, it is not surprising that his ancestry occupied him deeply. To the crown prince, the history of the Hohenzollern family was not a matter of purely private interest. He clearly believed in the value and necessity of educating German society by sharing the Hohenzollerns' dynastic story. Frederick William's thinking about the means by which the greatness of his dynasty should be communicated to the wider public was anything but modest. It encompassed a wide spectrum of processes and media that comprised historical scholarship, museum projects, monuments, and truly majestic building programmes. Viewed as a whole, Frederick William's plans added up to a dynastic project of remarkable proportions.

As a student of his family's history, the crown prince paid particular attention to three of his ancestors: the Great Elector, Frederick William (1620–1688); King Frederick the Great (1712–1786); and Queen Louise (1776–1810). In March 1860, he invited the historian Johann Gustav Droysen to discuss plans for a biography of the Great

Elector. Fifteen months later, Droysen informed a colleague that the crown prince had secured enough funding for work to start on a twenty-volume edition of sources and material. The first volume of *Documents and Files on the History of Elector Frederick William of Brandenburg* was published in 1864. Another twenty-two volumes would follow in the course of the next sixty-six years. The crown prince also persuaded his father to order the building of a monument to the Great Elector and personally laid the foundation stone on 18 June 1875—two hundred years after his ancestor's famous victory in the battle of Fehrbellin. At the same time, the crown prince also initiated a programme of collecting together in one place every edition of every publication of the works of Frederick the Great.[82]

Notwithstanding his respect for the Great Elector and Frederick the Great, it was Queen Louise who occupied a special place in Frederick William's heart. On 19 July 1860, the fiftieth anniversary of her death, he visited her mausoleum in the gardens of Charlottenburg Palace to lay wreaths on her tomb. Together with his father, he went there again to draw strength and inspiration before leaving for France at the beginning of the War of 1870–1871. Frederick William also marked the seventieth anniversary of his grandmother's death in a letter to his father. Most importantly, though, over many years, the crown prince devoted a significant amount of his time to collecting a wealth of historical material about Queen Louise. He often visited the archive of the royal house to read documents and make long, handwritten excerpts. He also contacted other princes such as the Grand Duke of Mecklenburg-Strelitz and the Duke of Saxe-Altenburg to request Louise's letters and documents deposited in their family archives. He collected photographs of Paretz, as well as scholarly articles and studies about Queen Louise. Frederick William even compiled a large collection of newspaper articles written in 1876 on the occasion of the queen's hundredth birthday. The material thus garnered in the course of more than a decade fills two large boxes. Even though this collection was clearly a labour of love, a letter from Frederick William's close confidant Ernst von Stockmar shows that it was not undertaken without ulterior motives. Stockmar praised the crown prince for having assembled these documents so methodically and industriously. "If this material is put to proper use," he concluded, "a quickening of the feelings for dynasty and fatherland must be the result, and Your Imperial Highness will find in this a due reward."[83]

In the Hohenzollern Museum, German patriotism and dynastic loyalty received a physical focus. Housed at Monbijou Palace in the centre of Berlin, the museum grew out of a display of "historically remarkable items" related to the history of Prussia and its dynasty. The exhibition, originally organised to raise funds for a charity, was the brainchild of the chamberlain and librarian Robert Dohme, who had spent many years compiling inventories of the royal palaces. Having visited dynastic museums in Paris, Copenhagen, and Hanover, Dohme regretted that the Hohenzollerns had so far failed to make their countless memorabilia accessible to the public. He was convinced, after all, that no people had more reason to be proud of their monarchs than the Prussians. When the crown prince learned of Dohme's ideas, he reacted with enthusiasm and promised his full support. The 1868 exhibition consisted of fourteen rooms in which items commemorating Prussia's military history as well as its kings and queens were shown. The display proved to be a great success and, after two visits, King William was persuaded to abandon the reservations he had initially raised against the project.[84]

Buoyed by the emperor's change of heart, Dohme concentrated on expanding the collection and turning the temporary exhibition into a proper museum. The eventual success of this plan, Dohme recalled in his memoirs, was "entirely due to Crown Prince Frederick, who, as patron, became the real founder of the museum." Frederick William's "restless zeal for the project, his comprehensive knowledge of the history of his house and his deep piety for the ancestors" had been crucial. The crown prince threw himself into the task of setting up the museum. He raided his personal belongings and acquired new items which he then transferred to Monbijou, very often attaching handwritten explanations to each artefact or relic. His visits to the nascent museum were numerous, and when the press started reporting on his activities, people from all over the country began sending in their own souvenirs. "Spent a long time arranging things in the collection in Monbijou," the crown prince wrote in his diary during the final hectic period just days before the opening in March 1877. "There will be a greater wealth of material than I had expected."[85]

The museum formally opened on Emperor William's eightieth birthday on 22 March 1877 and became a great success—not least because visiting it was made effectively compulsory for soldiers and schoolchildren. According to their relative importance, the

Hohenzollern rulers and their wives were allocated one or more rooms. The museum was packed with paintings, furniture, and artefacts, but also with countless personal items chosen to convey a sense of human interest, familiarity, and closeness within the overall context of showcasing the dynasty's peerless achievements for the fatherland. Visitors could marvel at coronation robes, death masks, the stuffed horse William I rode in 1866, locks of hair, toys, snuffboxes, painted Easter eggs, and every other form of patriotic bric-a-brac. Over the years, the museum changed and expanded. The space allocated to Frederick the Great grew from two rooms to six. Queen Louise went from two rooms to four. Eventually, space was also set aside for the late Emperor Frederick III. The comment his room attracted from a contemporary travel guide marked a posthumous triumph for him: "Touching intimacy between royal house with the old king (Frederick William III), with the old emperor and with the crown prince, the creator of the museum."[86]

Historical studies and a public museum were not the only media Frederick William employed for his dynastic project. He also was acutely aware of the grandest medium of dynastic display: public architecture. Of the three major architectural initiatives he pursued, though, only one was even begun during his lifetime. Work on the restoration of the Castle Church in Wittenberg commenced in 1885, but Frederick William did not live to see its completion in 1892. The crown prince's plans for a separate Hohenzollern crypt or sepulchral monument were never realised, and the great Protestant cathedral of which he dreamed was built by his son.

Consecrated in 1503, Wittenberg's Castle Church occupies a special place in the history of the Reformation. It was to its door, so the story goes, that Martin Luther nailed his ninety-five theses in 1517. When Prussia acquired Wittenberg along with the rest of Electoral Saxony in 1815, the church still bore the scars of the city's recent bombardment. Its hasty rebuilding in time for the tercentenary of the Reformation in 1817 marked only the beginning of Prussia's attention to its new possession. During the following decades, the church was gradually transformed into a Protestant monument. In 1821 Wittenberg's Luther monument was erected. A metal church door bearing the text of the reformer's theses was installed in 1858. The 400th anniversary of Luther's birth in 1883 provided yet another stimulus for this development. By then, the crown prince had already emerged as the driving force behind the effort to restore this iconic building.

In the autumn of 1880, Frederick William explained his intentions to the architect in charge of the project. He wanted to celebrate the greatness of the Reformation by "founding in Wittenberg a pantheon of German spiritual heroes" that would "remind every visitor of that great age."[87]

After Frederick William had visited the Castle Church in April 1880, he noted in his diary that plans for the "beautification and monumentalization of the cradle of the Reformation, which is so soberly bare" were being considered. From then on, he vigorously pursued the issue, compiling a large portfolio of documents, drafts, and letters; developing detailed architectural proposals; monitoring plans; and suggesting specific changes. Once governmental funding had been secured and work had started, the crown prince also travelled to Wittenberg to inspect the site. Frederick William's central idea for the redesign of the interior was to flank the statues of Luther and Melanchthon with those of the "most eminent contemporaries, who fought and created in this place." The walls were to be decorated with the coats of arms and mottos of those German princes who adopted Protestantism in 1540.[88]

The somewhat obscure date of 1540—the year a Protestant church order was introduced in Brandenburg—was selected for a good reason. This reference point enabled the crown prince to give the history of the Reformation in sixteenth-century Germany a hefty pro-Hohenzollern slant. Statues of the Hohenzollern princes Albrecht of Prussia and Elector Joachim II of Brandenburg were given prominent locations on the gallery of princely guardians of Protestantism— alongside such luminaries as Frederick the Wise of Saxony and Philipp of Hessen. Frederick William thus continued a policy started by his uncle, King Frederick William IV of Prussia. The Hohenzollerns were to be portrayed as the political, genealogical, and spiritual successors of the electors of Saxony, thereby buttressing their claim to be Germany's foremost Protestant dynasty. The crown prince's plans for communicating this dynastic message through the medium of the "cradle of the Reformation" did not stop there: the tower of the church was to be topped with an imperial crown, the gallery was to bear a Hohenzollern coat of arms, and the weather vane was to be fashioned in the shape of a Prussian eagle. Even though only the last of these ideas was realised, Frederick William's project was in sympathetic hands. When the restored church was solemnly inaugurated in October 1892, his son, Emperor William II, spared no expense in order to use the occasion as a demonstration of the Hohenzollerns' preeminence among Germany's Protestant dynasties.[89]

Frederick William's plans for a Hohenzollern crypt as a national monument also took their cue from his uncle. King Frederick William IV had wanted to house the remains of the various Hohenzollern electors and kings with more dignity than in the somewhat dilapidated undercroft of Berlin Cathedral. Work to erect a mausoleum next to the cathedral began in the 1840s, but the planned Prussian version of an Italian Camposanto was never finished and lay abandoned for almost three decades. When, in the 1870s, a new attempt was made to address the unsatisfactory situation, Frederick William seized upon this great opportunity. He was less interested in the building itself, but focused almost exclusively on its historical, dynastic, and pedagogical functions. The historian Hans Delbrück, for many years a member of Frederick William's household, gave a detailed account of the crown prince's intentions: "The Hohenzollern crypt was to be a shrine commemorating Prussian history. Every soldier serving in Berlin, every Prussian coming to Berlin and viewing the tombs of his kings, should simultaneously gain an immediate understanding of the wonderful course of the history of the state tied to this dynasty."[90]

Frederick William spent more than a decade perfecting his scheme. His fundamental idea is outlined in a handwritten memorandum dated March 1876. Every Hohenzollern ruler was to be given his own bay above the subterranean resting place of his remains, each of which was to be decorated with the finest examples of German art, but strictly according to the taste of the ruler's age. There also should be space for mottos, favourite sayings, and inscriptions offering concise summaries of the ruler's deeds and achievements. The bays should be arranged in strictly chronological order and room should also be made for rulers whose bones remained interred elsewhere. Once the basic structure of the plan was in place, the crown prince worked tirelessly on the detail. The vast material assembled comprises detailed notes on suitable kinds of stone, mosaics, and ornamental styles, as well as lists of dozens of tombs and monuments from all over Europe and across the ages. He collected drawings and photographs and eventually settled on specific recommendations. The memorial for Elector Frederick I (1371–1440), for instance, was to be fashioned after the tomb of Jacopo di Lusitania in the Church of

San Miniato in Florence. Most care of all, however, was lavished on the inscriptions, which would offer the visitor a summary of the ruler's life. Frederick William carefully researched every single one, drafted and redrafted them, and eventually sent them out to historians and confidants to invite their comments. Sometimes he felt overcome by the weight of his task. "Where Frederick the Great is concerned," he admitted to Stockmar in February 1882, "I have, after years of trying, given up on composing an inscription for him like the ones for the other monarchs; for his greatness cannot be captured in brief, concise sentences, nor am I able to reflect the huge variety of his achievements in a few words."[91]

The crown prince persevered with the crypt plan, even after the building project had once again run into the sand and even when he was in the throes of his fatal illness. Some of his notes on Italian and British tombs and monuments date to the summer of 1887. In his recollections, Robert Dohme described a poignant last meeting only days before Emperor Frederick's death. Having prepared a small print run of the final version of the inscriptions, Dohme met the emperor to point out a few mistakes he had spotted in a particular excerpt. Frederick III collected the relevant paperwork from his desk, handed it to Dohme, patted him on the shoulder, and then shook his hand.[92]

The crypt church was never built, but once again his son realised—in his own inimitable style—what his father had planned. December 1901 witnessed the completion of Emperor William II's artistic pet project—the dynastic gallery of thirty-two statues of the rulers of Brandenburg-Prussia, hewn out of finest Carrara marble and placed inside semicircular bays along a thoroughfare in Berlin's Tiergarten Park. With all the historical details carefully researched and every ruler shown as a handsome young man, this sculptural display was designed to connect the people enjoying a leisurely stroll with the history of Brandenburg-Prussia as manifested through its dynasty.[93]

Alongside and closely connected with his plans for a dynastic crypt, Frederick William also envisaged a complete rebuilding of Berlin's cathedral. The architect Julius Raschdorff recalled a long visit the crown prince and his wife paid to his office in December 1881, which led to a number of smaller commissions. At Frederick William's request, Raschdorff later produced detailed plans for the capital's new cathedral. The drawings he published in 1888 under the title "A Concept by His Majesty the Emperor and King for the

Construction of the Cathedral and the Completion of the Royal Palace in Berlin" document how the new building was to communicate a political message: the unity of the Reich was embodied in the person of the emperor and linked to the Prussian monarchy. A bridge across one of Berlin's main streets was to connect the huge new cathedral directly to the royal palace. Under its three domes the cathedral was to accommodate three separate spaces: a sepulchral or crypt church *(Grabkirche)*, a central ceremonial church *(Festkirche)*, and the preaching church *(Predigtkirche)* for the use of the cathedral parish. Both the cathedral and the royal palace were to be dwarfed by a gigantic new campanile, and a large equestrian statue of Emperor William was to be placed in front of the central arch. Within three weeks of his father's death, Frederick William, now Emperor Frederick III, ordered that the question of a rebuilding of Berlin cathedral "be addressed immediately."[94]

An undated memorandum in Frederick William's own hand provides a detailed insight into his plans for the new building. It was to have the capacity for at least 3,000 worshippers or participants in "great occasions of state or of the court." The cathedral was to house "monuments for all the previous generations of the royal family" and also for distinguished generals, statesmen, poets, and artists. Moreover, it would contain "tablets and headstones in honour of our electors and kings as well as their spouses and offspring." Integrating his plans for the dynastic crypt into a grand building project allowed Frederick William to dream of an overall complex that would fuse aspects of the Pantheon and Westminster Abbey. So grand were his ambitions that Frederick William felt the need to consider slightly misleading ways of announcing the "rebuilding of the present cathedral" in order "to allay the fears of those who think that a protestant St. Peter's cathedral following the example of the Roman one is to be built in Berlin." He remained engaged with this project until his dying days. On 18 April 1888, the emperor asked Dohme to read the ministerial report on the cathedral project and then incorporated the chamberlain's comments into his reply to the ministry. Yet again, Emperor William II picked up the threads after his father's death. During the ministerial council of 30 June 1888, the new emperor declared that respect for the late emperor commanded him to ensure that Frederick III's plans for Berlin's cathedral be executed exactly as detailed by Raschdorff. This proved to be easier said than done, though, and it was not until 1905 that the new cathedral was finally consecrated.[95]

An exploration of the roles played by Crown Prince Frederick William in the communication and popularisation of monarchy and dynasty thus suggests that, in this respect, his widely assumed status as a political nonentity needs to be reconsidered. In terms of projecting his own image, he emerges as an imaginative operator within a society and political system where different and increasingly important public spheres were reached and shaped by a variety of media. The crown prince's flair for communication tasks is further vindicated by the broadly successful record of his dynastic project, whose major components were all completed and eventually contributed to the ever firmer establishment of the "Hohenzollern Legend" as a narrative intended to consolidate the Reich's monarchical system.

Through the press, popular publications, pictures, speeches, scholarship, museums, architecture, and Frederick William's behaviour on the public stage, the persona Our Fritz was integrated into a reciprocal relationship with Germany's wider society. While the crown prince could not exercise complete control over his public portrayal, he utilised his ability to influence it. He clearly had a hand in generating successful images of himself and of the dynasty, but these were also conditioned by what the different audiences wanted and expected. The content, quality, and texture of the crown prince's public image generated by this process demonstrate that Frederick William participated in older dynastic continuities as well as in contemporary developments. The former allowed him to be perceived as a heroic other, endowed with kingly virtues and the manly beauty of a Nordic legend. The latter highlighted that, as someone who lived a life of bürgerlich perfection, the crown prince was essentially of the people—only much better. It remains interesting to note, though, that for all the importance of the meritocratic virtues of the bürgerlich world, the tale of a hero descended from a dynasty of heroes had not lost its magic.

By combining these two dimensions seamlessly, the public story of Our Fritz demonstrates a characteristic feature of political myths—the ability to integrate apparent contradictions through a narrative process.[96] That these two fundamentally contradictory perceptions successfully complemented each other to the benefit of the popularity of Our Fritz points to the readiness of Germany's society and political culture to combine bürgerlich confidence and aspirations with a sense of monarchical awe. Equally, Frederick William's capacity to integrate these perceptions, both of which generated monarchical strength and popularity, suggests that his rule would have enjoyed very firm public support.

Photograph of Crown Prince Frederick William (1874). The public loved Frederick William for his approachability, kindness, and good looks. Many commented on his gentle and beautiful eyes. AHH (Inv.-Nr. B 1185).

Portrait of Emperor William I by G. Richter (1876). William I was a parsimonious man of stern, military bearing, but he came to be revered as "Barbablanca," the ancient Emperor Whitebeard, dutifully guarding his people. BPK, Nr. 10000907.

Photograph of Crown
Princess Victoria by E.
Bieber (1875). Intelligent,
headstrong, and forever
pointing out Britain's
superiority, Crown Princess
Victoria was heartily
disliked among Prussia's
political and courtly elites.
BPK, Nr. 70002648.

Photograph of Otto
von Bismarck by Linde
Photographers (1864). "This is
not a minister, but a dictator,"
Crown Prince Frederick
William said in describing the
powerful chancellor in 1885.
BPK, Nr. 00001420.

The Proclamation of the German Empire by Anton von Werner (1877). The crown prince not only helped to stage the ceremony in Versailles but also ensured that generations of Germans could picture the scene when he invited von Werner to paint it. Image after Hermann Müller-Bohn, *Kaiser Friedrich der Gütige. Vaterländisches Ehrenbuch* (Berlin, 1900), 398a–b (author's collection).

Crown Prince Frederick William's Entry into Jerusalem, November 1869 by Wilhelm Gentz (1876). Frederick William personally commissioned this monumental painting to capture and publicise the moment of his ceremonial entry into the city of Jerusalem on a white charger. BPK, Nr. 00025412.

Portrait of Crown Prince Frederick William by Heinrich von Angeli (after 1874). This portrait, which showed the crown prince wearing the shimmering breastplate of the Pasewalk Cuirassier Regiment, was so well known that it was even mentioned in popular poetry. Stiftung Preussische Schlösser und Gärten Berlin-Brandenburg.

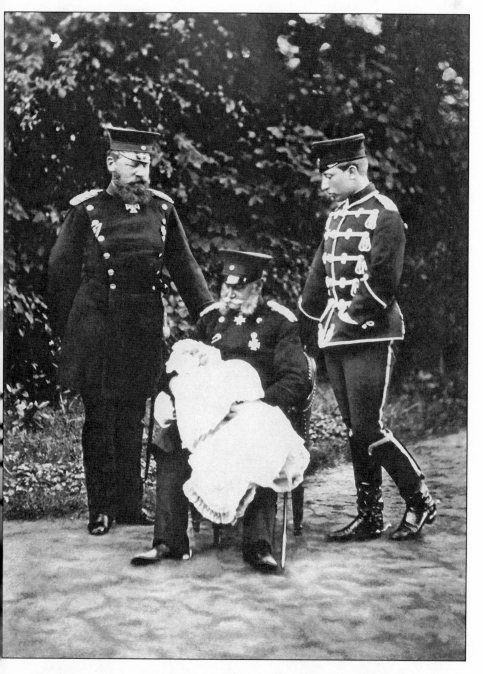

The "Four Emperors Photograph" by Hermann Selle (1882) depicts great-grandfather, grandfather, father, and son. This demonstration of the assured future of the Hohenzollern dynasty became a near-ubiquitous patriotic souvenir. BPK, Nr. 10000909.

Photograph of Crown Prince Frederick William and his family (about 1866). Barely distinguishable from a depiction of bourgeois family bliss, the crown princely couple were happy to show how affectionate and close they were to their children. BPK, Nr. 50110020.

With Frederick William perched on an armrest and Victoria's head leaning against his shoulder, this photograph conveys a sense of intimacy and informality (about 1870). BPK, Nr. 10013668.

Emperor Frederick as Crown Prince at the Court Ball in 1878 by Anton von Werner (1887/1895). In an attempt to depict the crown prince's commitment to German culture, this painting shows Frederick William surrounded by some of the most eminent German scientists and artists of the age. BPK, Nr. 00017226.

The Crown Prince in the School in Bornstedt by Ernst Henseler (1898) portrays
the best known of the many popular anecdotes about Our Fritz: after a village
schoolmaster had to rush to his mother's deathbed, the crown prince swiftly
stepped into the breach and taught an unforgettable history class. Image after
Hermann Müller-Bohn, *Kaiser Friedrich der Gütige. Vaterländisches Ehrenbuch*
(Berlin, 1900), 422a–b (author's collection).

Showing Frederick William in traditional Alpine costume—complete with lederhosen and a "chamois-tuft" hat—this carefully staged photograph of the Prussian crown prince would have appealed to Bavarians. AHH (Inv.-Nr. B 1186).

The garden parties Frederick William and Victoria organised for the children of Bornstedt Village and orphans from Berlin were well known and widely publicised. After a watercolour by W. Hoffmann, from Oskar Höcker, *Kaiser Friedrich als Prinz, Feldherr und Herrscher* (Berlin, 1888), 192a (author's collection).

Front cover of Theodor Drobisch, *Der Alte Fritz und Unser Fritz. Ein Buch für die Jugend* (Dresden, 1875). This children's book of poems on Old Fritz and Our Fritz illustrates how the crown prince's popularity was fuelled by the patriotic myth that had grown up around his famous ancestor King Frederick the Great. Image provided by Staatsbibliothek Preussischer Kulturbesitz, Berlin.

Design for Berlin's new cathedral, western aspect. The bombastic plans for rebuilding Berlin's cathedral associated with Emperor Frederick III caused some people to fear that he aimed at nothing less than a Protestant counterpart to Rome's St. Peter's Basilica. From Julius Carl Raschdorff, *Ein Entwurf seiner Majestät des Kaisers und Königs Friedrich III. zum Neubau des Domes und zur Vollendung des Königlichen Schlosses in Berlin* (Berlin, 1888); image provided by AHH (Inv.-Nr. K Deu Berlin 1888 1).

Photograph of Sir Morell Mackenzie by H. Mendelsohn. Frederick William and Victoria praised the gentleness and tact of the British physician, but many contemporaries reviled him as a dissimulating charlatan. Image after H. R. Haweis, *Sir Morell Mackenzie: Physician and Operator; A Memoir* (London, 1893), St. Andrews University Library.

The Emperor Frederick monument in Cologne. After Emperor William II vetoed a prizewinning design for a monument showing his father surrounded by workers, citizens, and soldiers, the city of Cologne had to make do with the patriotic norm—an equestrian statue by Peter Breuer (author's collection).

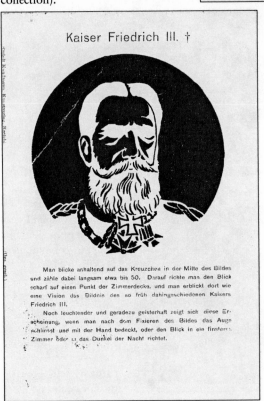

The Emperor Frederick monument in Wiesbaden. According to a local paper, the people of Wiesbaden barely recognised their "simple and liberal Emperor Frederick" in the imperious figure created by the sculptor Joseph Uphues (author's collection).

"Vision Card" of Emperor Frederick III. An interactive keepsake for the mournful patriot: focus on the centre of the image for a minute and a ghostly likeness of the departed emperor will be imprinted on your retina (author's collection).

CHAPTER FOUR

The Politics of Succession

Frederick William's public image portrayed an ideal ruler, a man full of virtues and endowed with almost superhuman gifts. Insiders saw him in a much less flattering light. It is rather poignant to observe that—with the exception of his wife—this publicly adored figure had almost no wholehearted supporters or real friends amongst those who knew him personally. He was painfully aware of his isolation. When saying farewell to Albrecht von Stosch after a meeting in June 1886, Frederick William became tearful and told the general that he had "now grown entirely lonely." Stosch was not unaffected by the crown prince's plight: "I guess you will have witnessed a Good Friday dirge in a Roman Catholic cathedral," he wrote to Karl von Normann. "I have always found them very moving. And here I had exactly the same emotion; the endless lamentation of a soul." Neither such moments of empathy nor the closeness of the relationship that had linked the two men since 1865, however, stopped Stosch from expressing his low opinion of Frederick William's political talents with astonishing frankness. Writing to Gustav Freytag in 1873, he argued that the succession of "the young master" would mean a weakening of the current political situation. In November 1881, he deplored the crown prince's "barrenness of spirit," and after perusing Frederick William's letters six years later, he criticised their superficiality and facile arbitrariness.[1]

These and Stosch's many other critical comments formed part of a wider picture. Using more or less lurid colours, both the crown prince's friends and his foes depicted him as comprehensively lacking in political talent. Frederick William's brother-in-law, the Grand Duke of Baden, described him as too soft, helpless, uninformed, sluggish, and spineless. Baron Franz von Roggenbach thought the crown prince was incapable of manly resolve and expected that, as emperor, he would waste time and goodwill on mere ceremonial trifles. Gustav Freytag commented on the "weakness of this peculiar personality," and expected little more of his reign than "quaintness, court frippery and decorations."[2] All of these damning verdicts came from Frederick William's circle of "friends." Others were even more outspoken. Bismarck variously called the crown prince delusional, lazy, stupid, haughty, and keen on flattery. The diplomat Philipp von Eulenburg was repulsed by what he saw as the crown prince's "autocratic desires clothed in sentimental liberality" and his "personal vanity which values hurrahs, bouquets and gestures of prostration." According to Bismarck's son Herbert, Frederick William was characterised by "measureless personal pride and the most complete lack of judgement." His accession to the imperial throne would be like giving a fragile work of art to a "foolish, bloody-minded child." Friedrich von Holstein described the crown prince as a mixture of "weakness and pusillanimity."[3]

These damning verdicts came on top of several other factors that diminished Frederick William's political clout: his widely known periods of depression and inaction; his tendency to absent himself from the hateful "cage" that was Berlin through ceaseless travelling; the general hostility toward his allegedly dominant wife; the suspicion that he was unduly "prompted from over the water," as Morier put it in 1863; and the determination of both his father and the chancellor to deny him any significant influence. All of this meant that Frederick William's power to shape political developments was severely curtailed.[4]

The crown prince was aware of this, but he resisted advice from both his wife and Stosch that he should improve his standing by rattling the cage a little. Instead, he was disarmingly and fatalistically open about his predicament. Wilhelm Bode, one of the directors of the royal museums, recalled that Frederick William told him more than once that his own endorsement was actually counterproductive. "I am your undoing, Bode. Believe me, if it had not been me who warmly recommended this request to my father, it would have been approved." Frederick William was not even his own man when deputising for the injured emperor. In November 1878, he complained to Hohenlohe-Schillingsfürst that his father kept interfering with the conduct of business and wished that the emperor would formally take over again. "You also have to consider that I am not inclined to have matters decided for me by a majordomo," he told Stosch in October 1880. "I am thus resigned, without good courage or confidence."[5]

In spite of these substantial limitations on Frederick William's ability to play an active role, he was a figure of crucial political importance. Few actors on Germany's political stage could afford to ignore the crown prince when making strategic and tactical plans for the future. His approval was a precious asset for any political party, grouping, or individual, and even the public perception of his support—correct or not—was seen as valuable. This meant that Frederick William was frequently confronted with more or less welcome attempts to sign him up to a particular agenda. Methods employed ranged from gentle persuasion to fairly rough wooing. In February 1884, Roggenbach likened the parties' attempts at "catching the future ruler in their nets" to a "great wrestling match."[6]

Roggenbach's description of Frederick William as the "future ruler" points to the dynastic element at the heart of the crown prince's political relevance. Within the monarchical systems of Prussia and the German Reich, the person on the throne could make a real difference—even if that person were weak and led by others. No one knew this better than Bismarck, who had defended, re-created, and operated these systems for years. "The position of the king of Prussia is, thank God, so strong that the monarch's individuality will not only make itself felt, but has to make itself felt," the chancellor explained in 1883. "Every one of our rulers has always been mindful to show at the very moment of accession, that he has taken over the reins of government, that a new regime has begun."[7] Bismarck expected more often than not that the next new regime would naturally retain the old chancellor and that the structures in place would limit the extent of any desired change. The potential for a significant reorientation was nevertheless patently inherent in the dynastic principle. This fundamental openness of the political future attracted both enemies and defenders of the status quo to the next person on the throne. In addition to his dynastic position, Frederick William's high profile and enormous popularity also proved to be valuable political resources. By the 1880s, the various party political antagonists regularly peppered their public confrontations with claims and counterclaims about the crown prince's alleged endorsement.

Roggenbach's great wrestling match was fought out in two distinct bouts. The first, begun in 1879–1880, saw the left-liberal forces of opposition attempting to change the balance of political power. Using the galvanizing effect of Frederick William's seemingly imminent succession, they hoped to form a liberal *Kronprinzenpartei* (Crown Prince Party), strong enough to turn his accession into a moment of political sea change. The second bout saw fighters such as Bismarck, the crown prince's more conservative advisers, and the National Liberals frustrate their opponents' endeavours. They did so by weakening the left-liberals and creating an alternative, party-political constellation that was believed to be compatible not only with the new reign but also with much of the old system. Both halves of Roggenbach's mixed metaphors convey significant aspects of the overall process. The wrestling match points to the robustness of a political fight in which few holds were barred. The piscatorial image of catching prey in nets also repays closer scrutiny; the fish is clearly what it is all about, but it does not do much and has little say in what is going on.

"Policy of the Future": The Left-Liberals and the Crown Prince

In August 1883, *Der Sozialdemokrat,* the weekly paper of the German Socialist Workers' Party, offered a trenchant analysis of what it called the "liberal policy of the future." This plan was based on two assumptions, the paper explained: on the hypothesis that the eighty-four-year-old emperor would soon die and on the "myth of the liberal crown prince." This universal myth, which had kept the patient peoples of the world calm as well as disappointed for centuries, was not merely hallowed by its great age. In the case of the German crown prince, it was also fuelled by his known animosity toward Bismarck. This dislike sprang not only from the envy experienced by the rather soft crown prince when contemplating the Iron Chancellor, the paper explained, but also from the thin liberal veneer that the imperious Vicky had applied to him. Going back all the way to the Danzig speech of 1863, the liberals were now prospecting Frederick William's life for anecdotes proving his opposition to Bismarck. The *Sozialdemokrat* wryly offered to provide dozens more of these stories—and authentic ones to boot—but it doubted the robustness of the liberals' plans. The views of the "liberal crown prince" were harmless, the paper concluded, and the "policy of the future" rested on "very, very shaky foundations."[8]

By the time this article appeared, the political scene had been buzzing for some time with rumours about the formation of a Kronprinzenpartei and self-styled "ministers of the future." Since King William was already sixty-four years old when he was crowned in 1861, the intentions of his successor had long been a topic of speculation. In 1863 Bismarck explicitly invited Frederick William to prepare the transition toward a future government based on his own principles. Four years later, the minister-president referred to Rudolf von Bennigsen and Max von Forckenbeck as the crown prince's future ministers. From 1866 onward, the crown prince met the latter so frequently and shared so much sensitive information with him that this confidence "almost filled [him] with grave worries about the future," Forckenbeck admitted to his wife.[9]

During the 1870s, however, the notion of a liberal opposition pinning its hopes for changing the status quo on the crown prince seemed far-fetched. The bulk of German liberalism—with the notable exception of the radical Progress Party—willingly supported Bismarck's course. Rather than beating the chancellor's government, some of the liberal leaders were looking to effect gradual change by joining it. This constellation changed in 1878–1879, when Bismarck shifted the direction of his domestic policy and altered the pattern of party-political alliances, on whose support he relied. By ending his close cooperation with the National Liberals, implementing policies likely to fragment their party, and passing legislation with the support of the Centre Party, the chancellor unwittingly turned the crown prince's friendship into a prized and tactically important political commodity.[10]

On 30 August 1880, twenty-eight deputies from the left wing of the National Liberals seceded from the party and subsequently formed their own parliamentary caucus under the name "Liberal Union" *(Liberale Vereinigung)*. More widely known as the "Secessionists," this group comprised some of the most prominent liberals of the day, including Max von Forckenbeck, Heinrich Rickert, Franz Schenk von Stauffenberg, Ludwig Bamberger, Georg von Bunsen, Ludwig Virchow, Eduard Lasker, and Karl Schrader. The members of this new breakaway faction had been increasingly alienated by Bismarck's championing of protectionist tariffs and state monopolies,

as well as by his persecution of the Social Democrats and the dé-
tente with the Catholic Church. Dissatisfied with what struck them
as their own party leadership's conciliatory reaction to this caesura
in the domestic politics of the Reich, the Secessionists declared that
they were committed to "firm resistance against the retrograde movement." This involved standing up for free trade, the protection of
constitutional rights, and the defence of the state's "inalienable rights"
against clerical interference.[11]

The central strategic aim of this group had already been aired more
than a year before. In May 1879, Forckenbeck addressed a meeting of
the Städtetag (cities' league), where representatives of seventy-two
German cities publicly protested against Bismarck's commercial protectionism. Speaking as mayor of Berlin, Forckenbeck urged the German middle class to form a single great and comprehensive party
united by its commitment to liberal principles. A few days later, Forckenbeck and Stauffenberg resigned from their offices as speaker and
deputy-speaker of the Reichstag to show their opposition both to the
government's policies and the sense of drift within their own party.
Plans for a secession of the left wing gathered pace after the National
Liberals' poor performance in the Prussian parliamentary elections of
October 1879. On 19 August 1880, Heinrich Rickert addressed a
meeting in Danzig and repeated the call for a united liberal party to be
based on free trade and the fight against clerical interference, as well as
commanding "a majority against Bismarck's current plans." The manifesto the Secessionists issued a few days later to explain their decision
to break away struck the same note. It described the defence of "the
political liberties that were not easily won" as the "common task of
the entire liberal party." Efforts to bring about a liberal unification intensified further after the strong showing of both the new Liberal
Union and the even more radical Progress Party at the Reichstag elections of 1881. Some of the left-liberal leaders, most prominently Eduard Lasker, now saw an opportunity to combine the 162 deputies
from all the different liberal caucuses into a phalanx capable of wrest-
ing real power from the chancellor.[12]

Bismarck was well aware of these plans. As early as July 1879, he
had drawn the emperor's attention to "that small number of ministers
of the future, who assume that, once God calls upon him to rule, His
Imperial Highness the crown prince will appoint a liberal ministry."
These "future calculations," the chancellor added a few days later,

were actively spread by men like Forckenbeck, Rickert, or the progressive deputy Albert Hänel. He believed that rumours of this kind were thriving because there were various links with the crown prince's household. In order for this threat to Bismarck's position to materialize, two conditions had to be met. First, the crown prince had to be linked and seen to be linked to this project, for the hopes of uniting the fragmented body of German liberalism hinged on the promise of a new dawn. Soon, very soon perhaps, the new ruler and his party could make a fresh start in German politics. Second, the forces of liberalism had to overcome their differences and form the "greater liberal party or at least a union of all parliamentary groupings," which Lasker called for in November 1881. The stakes were high. "The election results show," he continued, "that unifying and goal-orientated action can make an absolute liberal majority in the Reichstag possible, even under unfavourable circumstances."[13]

If hearsay was anything to go by, the chances of enlisting the support of the crown prince for this venture were rather high. As early as November 1878, the Württembergian minister-president confirmed to a colleague that Stauffenberg and the left-wing National Liberals were indeed being supported by the crown prince. Three years later, the Austrian ambassador in Berlin reported to Vienna that the German liberals were "banking on the great age of Emperor William and the free-thinking direction of his heir and successor." There was certainly much in Frederick William's life story that provided grist for the political rumour mill. His liberal reputation dated back more than thirty years, had been reinforced by his marriage to Victoria, and became a matter of public record when he distanced himself from Bismarck in 1863. At that time, the Prussian government had carefully archived letters and pamphlets in which it was claimed that the crown prince provided "moral support of great importance" for the opposition and had even become a "secret member" of the radical Progressive Party. Though he never again challenged his father's government in public after 1863, Frederick William's liberal tendencies and the frequently strained nature of his relationship with Bismarck were hardly secrets. Moreover, Frederick William's own behaviour was partly responsible for keeping alive a general belief in his liberal outlook.[14]

Networking and personal contacts provided one means by which Frederick William's liberal reputation was sustained. Ever since the early 1860s, the crown prince had remained in touch with a number of liberal politicians, whom he met in private both in Berlin and during his many trips. He would invite them discreetly to seek their opinions and to keep abreast of current political developments. Frederick William's interlocutors would often leave charmed by his direct and affable style. In August 1866, Forckenbeck gave his wife a detailed account of his first meeting with the crown prince. He had been led into a plain room in the palace at 9:45 p.m. and was initially quite nervous about talking to Frederick William. The crown prince's charm, simplicity, and liberal outlook quickly reassured him, though, and Forckenbeck spoke openly for three-quarters of an hour. Ludwig Bamberger's description of a meeting in March 1884 is remarkably similar: a one-hour conversation that was quite informal and ranged over a great many issues left the deputy with the impression of having met a modest, straightforward, liberal man.[15] Forckenbeck—along with Franz von Roggenbach and Karl Schrader— became a close confidant who met Frederick William on numerous occasions stretching over the next twenty years. There were also several other leading liberals whose encounters with the crown prince were important and frequent enough to be recorded in diaries and letters: Rudolf von Bennigsen, Georg von Bunsen, Hermann Schulze-Delitzsch, Franz Schenk von Stauffenberg, Rudolf von Delbrück, Rudolf Gneist, Wilhelm Grabow, Gustav von Mevissen, August von Saucken-Julienfelde, Kurt von Saucken-Tarputschen, Karl Twesten, and Rudolf Virchow.

Moreover, Frederick William occasionally made public gestures and utterances that functioned like a dog whistle. He never engaged directly with contentious aspects of governmental policy, but those whose ears were finely tuned to the language of Germany's political culture could make out a clear tendency. In November 1868, the crown prince and his wife wrote to Berlin's mayor, Carl Theodor Seydel, a member of the Progressive Party, to offer their public endorsement of the city's commemoration of the 100th birthday of the Protestant theologian Friedrich Schleiermacher. Orthodox-conservative circles had previously made every effort to stop the honouring of this liberal and reform-orientated thinker. Between 1879 and 1881, Frederick William took a public stance against the rising tide of political anti-Semitism. Roggenbach rated this as a highly political act: "Never has the indistinctness of the crown princely microcosm been so firmly punched through," he wrote to Stosch in 1881, "as in this attack against the anti-Semites' movement." In January 1882, the crown prince went out of his way to praise "the leadership of Berlin's civic administration for the shrewd and methodical care" it took of the capital's inhabitants. This stood in marked contrast to Bismarck's verdict. Ten months earlier, the chancellor had used a widely noted Reichstag speech to attack Berlin's city government for being run by a progressive cabal. In January 1882, Frederick William used his address at the opening of the new building of Berlin's Masonic lodge to call for social, cultural, and scientific enlightenment and progress. Ludwig Bamberger, who had recently given a celebrated funeral eulogy for the liberal deputy Eduard Lasker, received an invitation to the crown prince's ball in February 1884, and in October of the same year, Frederick William sent another letter to Berlin's civic authorities to thank them for their "sound management of the administration."[16]

The crown prince and left-liberal party politics were linked by more than personal acquaintance and a sympathetic general attitude that manifested itself in some of Frederick William's public gestures. There was also concrete agreement on four specific political issues: First, the crown prince shared the left-liberals' opposition to protective tariffs and studied Bamberger's speeches and writings on this issue. Second, they were united in hostility to Bismarck's programme of state-regulated social insurance. In 1884, Bamberger, who had coauthored the tract "Against State Socialism," sent Frederick William a copy of the pamphlet. The very next day, he was invited to discuss the question further. Third, they both resisted a swift dismantling of the anti-Catholic legislation introduced in the 1870s. These concerns found their way into the Secessionist manifesto of 30 August 1880, which stated that ecclesiastical freedom had to be regulated by state legislation. This dovetailed with Frederick William's fairly implacable attitude toward the Roman Church. As late as 1883, the crown prince found it shameful that Bismarck was giving in to the Jesuits after a mere ten years of fighting. A fourth and final area of agreement was the left-liberals' belief in a more-centralised German Reich. In February 1884, Bamberger included the "fight against particularist tendencies" in an early draft of the programme for the united left-liberal party. Two months later, the party weekly *Die Nation* proclaimed that "Germany's true interest would not suffer if the imperial power were to be strengthened in a more unitary direction."[17]

The Secessionists' campaign to win Frederick William's active support for the Kronprinzenpartei proved a more difficult task, though, than is suggested by this auspicious context. Still reeling from the death of his son Waldemar in March 1879, the crown prince was in a deeply pessimistic mood when he first became aware of the thrust of this political development. His diary entries in May 1879 nevertheless document that he was interested in Forckenbeck's efforts to form a "great liberal party" and resented the attempts to smear Berlin's mayor as an extremist. Victoria immediately started dreaming about a mighty party on whose support Frederick William could count: "Would not 'our' liberal party grow and grow, gather more and more people round it, would not Bismarck have to reckon with it?" she asked. The crown prince, however, was more sceptical. He told his wife that he could not say whether Forckenbeck's step would heal any rifts. Given the Germans' political immaturity, he doubted that a "great liberal party" could ever be viable. Even though "a truly liberal party in Germany" used to be his dream, Frederick William explained on 24 May, all work on this edifice had been smashed to pieces by Bismarck. After a long conversation with the East Prussian liberal Kurt von Saucken-Tarputschen in September 1879, the crown prince was still downbeat. The conservatives were likely to do well in the upcoming Prussian elections and it was as yet unproven that the leading liberals were more than mere theoreticians.[18]

In light of all this gloom, Forckenbeck had a mountain to climb when he met Frederick William on 27 December 1879 for a conversation that lasted more than two hours. The crown prince wanted to know if one could count on this planned party and if a liberal regime in Germany could be built on it. Forckenbeck explained that Bismarck's tariff policy had finished the National Liberals, but he assured Frederick William that "work was quietly going on towards the foundation of a great, free-thinking party" that would certainly prove viable. A fortnight later, the crown prince met the railway director Karl Schrader, another prominent Secessionist, and after the meeting, he wrote to Victoria that he felt less worried.[19]

In a further move to win over the crown prince, the leading left-liberals agreed in March 1880 not to make their opposition to the seven-year army budget the official reason for their decision to quit the National Liberals, although they were deeply uneasy about the

Reichstag giving up its control over military expenditure for such a long period. Resisting the army bill would have been seen as unpatriotic and could have alienated the crown prince. The bill passed on 6 May 1880, with the votes of almost all the National Liberal deputies. Using a Kulturkampf-related issue as a trigger for breaking away from the National Liberal Party proved a much better tactical move. In August 1880, only days before the Secessionists left the National Liberals, Stauffenberg joined the crown prince on a railway journey and briefed him for more than two hours about the next steps and the plans for the new party.[20]

Even though the liberal Bavarian baron did his best to explain that the Kronprinzenpartei required a process of slow and steady construction, Frederick William remained cautious. This is a "party in swaddling clothes," he wrote to Victoria afterward and described its future development as highly questionable. The official announcement of the group's decision to secede did not lift the crown prince's pessimistic mood either. He wondered on 9 September 1880 whether this division of the National Liberal Party merely added to the general confusion. In the following days, he also criticised the Secessionists for failing to explain their concerns with sufficient clarity and noted a rumour that the prominent deputy Heinrich Rickert did not regard this as the way to form a united liberal party.[21]

Only after the Secessionists and the Progressive Party had made significant gains in the Reichstag elections of October 1881 did the crown prince begin to sound more hopeful about the future of the great liberal party. On 8 December 1881, Schrader told him that the different liberal caucuses in the Reichstag were moving closer by the day and were beginning to unite. He also explained that Bennigsen, the leader of the rump National Liberals, was convinced that all liberals belonged together and should act accordingly. "The united liberals, 150 men strong, believe that they can exercise great influence both inside and outside of the Reichstag as early as this winter," Frederick William wrote in his diary on 11 December 1881. Six months later, the crown prince noted that Bennigsen agreed with the Secession's Heinrich Rickert and Eugen Richter of the Progressive Party on a matter of fiscal policy. He took this to be an indication that "the great liberal party thinks in a rather uniform way."[22]

The language the Secession liberals were using at the time to woo the crown prince can be gleaned from an article published in November 1882 in the widely read British journal *Fortnightly Review*.

Georg von Bunsen's essay "The Liberal Party in Germany" offered the next monarch the loving yet self-confident embrace of Germany's liberals. Bunsen described them as a group to whom "loyalty to their sovereign [was] not instinctive only, but reasoning." To save the monarchy, to save society, and "to draw the balance, as it were, between the advanced democracy of the West, and the informal despotism of the East," the author claimed, "Liberalism can only be enlisted." Bunsen explicitly conceded that a strong executive was necessary. Having mentioned more than once how "aged"—indeed, how "venerable"— Emperor William, that "true specimen of the *ancien régime*" was, the essay finished by outlining "a future, not, perhaps, so far distant." Then the party "of faith in the improvement of men, of law and organisation, and consequent stability; the party of national unity without uniformity; the party that continues the saving traditions of the dynasty of Hohenzollern" would hold "the destinies of Prussia and of Germany in their hands." Unsurprisingly, claims like these enraged the political opponents of the left-liberals. In January 1883, the Centre Party's *Germania* grumbled about the "pestering behaviour of a party seeking to drag the name of the future leader . . . into the arena of political strife." A year later, Friedrich von Holstein accused the left-liberals of behaving like "royalists of the future," and Emil Pindter, editor of the pro-Bismarck *Norddeutsche Allgemeine Zeitung*, decried their use of the crown prince as a "means of progressive agitation."[23]

The leaders of the Secession would hardly have found these attacks particularly stinging. Ever since the autumn of 1881, with the fair wind of a successful Reichstag election behind them, the left-liberals had intensified their efforts to forge a united liberal Kronprinzenpartei. They were quite open about their intentions. "We admit it fully and unabashedly," their party newspaper, *Die Tribüne*, declared in October 1882. "Liberalism cannot achieve anything in matters of law or of the state, if it fails to win the ear and heart of the king." The liberal party had made suggestions for a long time, the article continued, and now it was hopeful that before too long it would win "the ear and heart of the king, so that its suggestions will turn into achievements."[24]

Invoking the name of the crown prince was a conspicuous feature of the left-liberal campaign. In October 1882, the progressive weekly *Der Reichsfreund* highlighted Frederick William's outspoken attacks on the anti-Semites and his praise for Berlin's city government. The

paper insisted that these demonstrations illustrated the vast difference between the views of the future ruler and those held by the chancellor and the Conservative Party. The *Berliner Zeitung* reminded its
readers in January 1883 that the crown prince had never left anyone
in doubt "that he did not want his views identified with Bismarck's."
Even though the chancellor's wrath has been directed at "Forckenbeck, or Georg von Bunsen, Virchow or Mommsen," the left-liberal
daily argued, "these men have retained the favour of the crown
princely couple, then as now." Two months later, the *Reichsfreund*
described Frederick William's speech at the recent opening of Berlin's
Masonic lodge as "a suitable motto for any association of men of the
Progress party," and looked forward to the day when the next ruler
would turn these words into reality. In a piece entitled "Crown Prince
and Chancellor," published in January 1884, the *Reichsfreund* went
so far as to claim that Frederick William was actively pursuing a political strategy directed against Bismarck. The article, which was also
disseminated as a separate pamphlet and reprinted by other papers,
observed that the conservative press was falsely trying to portray
Frederick William as a supporter of the chancellor. But the more it did
this, the *Reichsfreund* gloated, the more the crown prince demonstrated his refusal "to represent the chancellor's current policies."[25]

In the very same month that the *Reichsfreund* made this bold claim,
the formal process of creating the united liberal Kronprinzenpartei
began. Hopes of including the National Liberals had to be abandoned when the decidedly pro-Bismarck Johannes Miquel emerged
as that party's leading man in 1883 and steered it firmly toward
renewed cooperation with the chancellor. The Secessionists did, however, remain interested in a merger with the more radical Progressives,
and this wish was warmly reciprocated. On 10 January 1884,
Bamberger, Bunsen, Forckenbeck, Rickert, and Schrader agreed to
convene at the end of the month to discuss their relationship with the
other liberal parties. Even before their meeting could take place,
though, Eugen Richter, the leader of the Progressive Party, asked his
party colleague Albert Hänel to initiate negotiations about a possible
fusion with the Secessionists.[26]

Hänel was a shrewd choice. As the leading representative of the
"moderate Progressives," he had long since struck Bamberger as a

person who could facilitate the union. The crown prince also thought highly of Hänel and described him as a "person of significance" with the perspective of a statesman. If the liberal party were to show some unity and cohesion, Frederick William noted in August 1882, this would be very much Hänel's achievement. After preliminary talks with Rickert, Bamberger, and Schrader, Hänel met Forckenbeck on 30 January 1884. He persuaded him to agree to a fusion including Richter, whose relationship with Forckenbeck was anything but cordial. The "necessity of uniting before the accession of the crown prince . . . who had to find a strengthened liberal party already in place in order to reckon with it" and the pressure of the upcoming Reichstag elections played a crucial part in hurrying the process along.[27]

The subsequent negotiations about the joint party programme and the new name were kept to a small number of key individuals who completed their work very swiftly. By 5 March 1884, the parliamentary caucuses of the Liberal Union and the Progressive Party separately voted in favour of a merger on the basis of a concise party manifesto. The men drafting this document had done their best to make Frederick William an offer he could not refuse. The most noticeable concession was offered by the Progressives in connection with military policy. They abandoned both their earlier demand for a reduction of military expenditure and their insistence on an annual vote on the military budget. Instead, the fifth item of the programme of the new *Deutsche Freisinnige Partei* (German Free-Thinking Party) called for "maintaining the full military power of the people" and for the army budget to be authorized by the Reichstag once every three years. Further points concerned the introduction of a responsible Reich ministry, defence of the rights of parliament, protection of civil liberties, strengthening of the Reich's control of the railways, opposition to "state socialism," and rejection of economic policies favouring special interests. "All of this," the document concluded, "for the consolidation of Germany's national unification, in loyalty towards the emperor and on the constitutional basis of the federal state."[28]

When the new parliamentary session opened on 6 March 1884, the caucus of the newly formed Freisinn Party comprised more than 100 deputies and was the largest in the Reichstag. "It is intended that firm ground be regained for liberalism," Frederick William noted in his diary when commenting on the new foundation on the same day. "May this fusion have a healing effect; right now it is opposed by many hostile elements, which means that a healthy fruit can only ripen slowly." The new party's journalistic organs were in no mood for slow ripening, though. They noisily entered the fray. "The German Bürgertum can now decide if it is ready to step out of its political apathy," *Die Nation* declared on 8 March 1884, and called on the Bürgertum to defend the very basis of its political and social existence. A few days later, the weekly began its account of a fairly contrived anecdote about the crown prince with the words "an exalted gentleman, to whose name our people's most beautiful memories and no less beautiful hopes are linked." On 16 March 1884, the *Berliner Zeitung* argued that the formation of the Freisinn Party was tantamount to the beginning of a British parliamentary system in which majority parties were ready to take on political responsibility. With a less-than-subtle nod to the crown prince, the paper added that "one should not forget that an aversion to British ways may not be shared everywhere and forever." A few weeks later, Theodor Barth responded pugnaciously to those who attacked the Freisinn Party for advocating a more centralised Reich. "The time is perhaps not very distant, when liberalism, as it did before, must act in favour of Germany's unity," he wrote in *Die Nation*. "The bearer of the German imperial crown . . . will recognize then who his most unselfish and most determined supporters are."[29]

The Freisinn Party's confident strutting on the political stage in the spring of 1884, however, proved a mere flash in the pan. Increasingly faint echoes of the original Kronprinzenpartei project still reverberated in 1885 and beyond, but its advocates were doing little more than whistling in the dark. Even before the party suffered a severe electoral setback in the Reichstag elections of October 1884, its leadership knew full well that they could not wholly count on Frederick William. "You were asking me about the current political views of the crown prince," Schrader replied to Stauffenberg in August 1884. "Sadly, I can tell you less than I could have done some time ago, since I have not seen him and the crown princess for some time." Schrader then explained that Frederick William and Victoria had become careful concerning their relations with "liberal people." The crown prince also may have had concerns about the Freisinn Party's radical nature and its views on military affairs. Above all, Schrader admitted, "we are not offering the future ruler what must be crucial to him: a firm party, able to take over the government and supported by the people." He predicted that the future emperor would not be able to part with Bismarck any time soon.[30]

Frederick William had not lost all his sympathy for the left-liberals. He regretted the outcome of the elections in October 1884, in which the Freisinn Party dropped to sixty-seven seats while National Liberals, Conservatives, and Socialists all increased their parliamentary representation. "The total defeat of the Freisinn deeply depresses me," he wrote to Victoria in November 1884, and stated that the two of them were amongst the few "still clinging to an old free-thinking view." These feelings did not translate into action, though, but reinforced the crown prince's resignation. Bismarck has been indoctrinating the country for such a long time, Frederick William wrote to Victoria a few days later, that it was now almost impossible to repair things. On the same day, Holstein noted in his diary that the crown prince was in "a condition of dissatisfied resignation," declaring himself to be "a used-up man" and that "it would be best to renounce the throne and let [his] son rule, who [was] in tune with the new ways." When, on top of the left-liberals' electoral defeat and Frederick William's lack of fighting spirit, Emperor William's failing health made the succession appear imminent, the Secessionists privately gave up hope. "Pass on my regards to Rickert and tell him that I have also had no hope whatsoever of a change of system when the succession comes," Schrader wrote to his wife in July 1885. "For our policy we have to rely on ourselves, then as now."[31]

The original plan to create a Kronprinzenpartei—a union of all the parliamentary forces of German liberalism allied with the crown prince and ready to govern with him as a responsible majority party—failed quickly and on a number of counts. In spite of this, the idea was to have a remarkable and somewhat ghoulish career after its own political death in 1884 and even after the demise of its eponymous protagonist in 1888. The original scheme had a number of fatal political flaws. The gap between the left-liberal camp and the National Liberal rump turned out to be unbridgeable and widening. The Secessionists were a top-heavy, elitist group without a wider popular and organisational base. They lacked noncommissioned officers, Bamberger complained in December 1880. These logistical, financial, and staffing problems became particularly acute during election campaigns, which helps to explain why the Secessionists and the Progressives were so eager to join forces ahead of the 1884 election. The left-liberals' inability to match, let alone improve, their earlier success at the 1884 Reichstag elections also played an important role.[32]

The central weakness of the plan, however, was its reliance on what *Der Sozialdemokrat* mocked as the "myth of the liberal crown prince." On the one hand, as the Socialist weekly pointed out in August 1883, Frederick William had no power over the government and no influence. "In order to make people talk about him every now and then," the paper acidly remarked, "he has to engage in the silliest nonsense, clearly the result of the deadliest boredom: playing schoolmaster, splashing about with soldiers in the swimming pool and more such things." On the other hand, since the crown prince's antipathy to Bismarck had reportedly failed to produce even a single significant deed in more than two decades, his liberalism struck the Socialist weekly as far too "harmless" to provide a solid foundation for an ambitious "policy of the future." This verdict implied not only that Frederick William was too weak to effect real change but also that reports of his liberalism were greatly exaggerated. Underneath what *Der Sozialdemokrat* called the crown prince's "liberal-conservative-parliamentary coat of paint" there was certainly much that could not be easily reconciled with central tenets of left-liberal politics.[33]

The Secessionists' careful tiptoeing around military issues, Bunsen's assurance that everyone believed in a strong executive, and the numerous references to the future monarch's central role suggest that the men behind the Kronprinzenpartei plan were not unaware of these tensions. Whether they had done enough to reconcile Frederick William to periodic parliamentary control of military budgets, to government by majority parties, and to responsible ministries is a moot point. It appears clear, however, that they knew their political relationship with the crown prince was not as harmonious and that his relationship with Bismarck was not as dysfunctional as their own publicity campaign suggested.

The crown prince's own politics were somewhat bigamous throughout the period. On the one hand, he had numerous meetings with leading left-liberals whose aims he understood perfectly well. On the other hand, he remained in contact with Bismarck and allowed himself to be drawn into the chancellor's nets. Frederick William's relationship with the protagonists of the Kronprinzenpartei was probably sustained by more than unalloyed political agreement. Victoria's emphatically left-liberal convictions played an important role, as did a little vanity. Albrecht von Stosch observed as early as 1870 that "all this intercourse with the liberals only appeals to the gentleman because they court him and make him feel powerful."[34] That the relationship between the crown prince and Bismarck never collapsed was due to the fact that the left-liberals' scheme was not the only one afoot.

Containing the Succession: Bismarck's Fight against the Kronprinzenpartei

The left-liberal attack against Bismarck's monopoly on power was certainly well-timed. It was launched during a period when the chancellor's position in domestic politics was unprecedentedly weak. The cluster of measures Bismarck pushed through in 1878–1879 ended the increasingly fraught "Liberal Era," during which he had relied on the support of the National Liberals. Some of the government's initiatives now required the votes of the Catholic Centre Party. Initially, the changed constellation produced a number of successes for the chancellor. The newly elected Reichstag passed the anti-Socialist law in October 1878. Protectionist tariff legislation was approved in July 1879, and in the autumn of that year, the free-trading liberals suffered a sharp setback in the elections for the Prussian parliament. In the spring of 1880, the renewals of both the seven-year army budget and the anti-Socialist law cleared the Reichstag. Thereafter, however, the government hit the buffers. Instead of delivering a reliable vehicle for his policies, the realignments of 1878–1879 left Bismarck mired in frustrating and unsuccessful parliamentary squabbles. In the course of 1880 and 1881, the Reichstag rejected governmental bills to introduce biennial budgets and to provide financial guarantees for German commercial ventures overseas. It also blocked a package of fiscal reforms and scuppered Bismarck's proposed National Economic Council by refusing to fund it.[35]

After the elections in October 1881, which had been billed as a plebiscite for or against the chancellor, Bismarck's relationship with the Reichstag reached a low point. Lothar Gall even argues that, as far as the chancellor was concerned, the elections "destroyed any possible parliamentary base" and made even his most devoted supporters wonder if Bismarck would ever again "find a firm political footing." The results were truly awful for the government. Three years after the anti-Socialist law had been passed, the Social Democrats returned as many deputies as they had in 1877. The Secessionists won forty-six seats; the Progressive Party increased from twenty-six to sixty seats. Parties considered close to the chancellor lost about half of their support. Overall, a potentially pro-Bismarck combination of 125 Conservatives, Free Conservatives, and National Liberals now faced 272 hostile Centrists, Secessionists, Progressives, Poles, and Social Democrats. Though deeply embittered by this crushing defeat, the chancellor insisted on ploughing on with essentially the same raft of policies that had met with such dogged opposition before the elections. The results of this strategy were not surprising. "We are now reaping the fruits of our parliamentary tactics and are suffering defeat after defeat," Agriculture Minister Robert Lucius observed in May 1883.[36]

For Bismarck, the crisis went even deeper than the failure to get a series of bills onto the statute book. The narrowness of his support reminded him acutely of the precariousness of his own position and of the fragility of the Reich's governmental system. In January 1881, well before the calamitous elections of October 1881, he declared that "his party consisted only of the king and himself." Given that William I was only weeks away from his eighty-fourth birthday, and in view of the Secessionists' attempts to sign up the next ruler, this was hardly reassuring. To the chancellor, the succession and the parliamentary crisis appeared interlocked. At a ministerial meeting in January 1881, he observed that the very deputies who were currently opposing his proposal of a state monopoly on tobacco also "had an eye on ministerial posts under the crown prince." In June 1881, Bismarck complained that no one in parliament offered any support because plans were being hedged to form a future ministry headed by liberals such as Bennigsen, Stauffenberg, and Forckenbeck. "We have no time to lose," the chancellor wrote to a ministerial colleague in May 1882, "and have to remember that with every session the opposition counts on the succession and on the removal of the current government." On some occasions, these apprehensions assumed almost apocalyptic dimensions. "I am saying this without bitterness and entirely calmly," Bismarck declared in December 1883, "from my perspective Germany's future is black. Once Forckenbeck and Virchow get their hands on the tiller and receive backing from above, the whole thing will fall apart again."[37]

Three elements combined to give the Kronprinzenpartei plan its lethal potential: the formation of a powerful party uniting all liberal forces, the risk that the crown prince's moderate liberalism might be radicalised by Freisinn seduction and matrimonial bullying, and the absence of a strong parliamentary combination committed to supporting the chancellor. To be successful, a strategy designed to avert this danger and put in place a viable alternative for the future would therefore have to achieve three interlocking outcomes: preventing or at least weakening the "great liberal party," detaching Frederick William from the left-liberals, and creating a powerful and biddable parliamentary combination acceptable to both the old chancellor and the new emperor.[38]

Bismarck realized as early as 1879 that the Liberals, who were then very much at the heart of his parliamentary problems, could also be part of the solution. The crux of the government's difficulty, he believed, was its lack of a dependable majority amongst the parties in the Reichstag. The passage of the government's tariff legislation in July 1879 had been secured by the votes of the Conservatives and the Catholic Centre Party, but regardless of how many concessions were made to them, the Centrists would never become reliable supporters. An alternative majority could only be imagined if the Conservatives could be linked to "the honest part of the National Liberals." In their present shape, however, the National Liberals could not be counted on because the chancellor regarded "the Progressives wearing a National Liberal mask, the men of the cities' league and the 'great' liberal party—that is to say: the republicans—as equally unreliable and perhaps even more dangerous supporters than the Centre." The decision by these "masked Progressives" to secede from the "honest" National Liberals in August 1880 therefore offered Bismarck a political opportunity. In the course of the following years, he would try his best to damage the former and eventually reel in the latter.[39]

Otto von Bismarck was a renowned hater of his enemies and pursued some of them with unbridled venom. Although there were several others who deserve a mention in this context, the chancellor lavished exceptional loathing on the liberal British statesman William Gladstone and the Freisinn deputy Eduard Lasker. His anger reached its furious peak during the years after 1880, when Gladstone began his second premiership and the left-liberal Secession embarked on its policy of courting the crown prince. Bismarck was convinced that the "crazy professor" and "dilettante," who was now leading the

British government, would exercise a calamitous influence on European politics and ruin his own country. In spite of this—or, rather, because of this—the chancellor did not find Gladstone entirely useless. The prime minister played an important role in Bismarck's campaign to frustrate the policies pursued by Lasker and the other left-liberals.

Lasker had been the target of Bismarck's ire for many years. He believed that the influential liberal deputy, with whom the chancellor had clashed fiercely over the tariff question, held antimonarchical views and called him a political disease, a parasite, and a "stupid Jewish boy." Lasker's leading role within the Secessionists and his efforts to forge a "great liberal party" only confirmed Bismarck's suspicion that he was championing the introduction of a British parliamentary system in Germany. It therefore did not take the chancellor very long to coin what he considered an apt and suitably pejorative designation for the Secessionists. In December 1880, the *Norddeutsche Allgemeine Zeitung,* a paper entirely in Bismarck's pocket, set the tone of the public debate by calling the group around Lasker, Bamberger, Rickert, Forckenbeck, and Stauffenberg the "Gladstone Ministry."[40]

This label did more than simply tinge the left-liberals in an unpatriotically foreign hue and allude to the influence of the unpopular crown princess, whose admiration for Gladstone was widely known. It also linked the Kronprinzenpartei to a regime that Bismarck was actively portraying as utterly disastrous. The chancellor calculated that once it was understood that the Secessionists' alleged British lodestar had deprived his own country of firm leadership, brought on moral corruption, and increased the risk of revolution, left-liberal principles would be discredited and wider support would rally to his own cause. Over the coming years, diplomatic reports, the Bismarck press, and the chancellor's own briefings for the emperor and crown prince all featured endless stories about Britain's political downfall: worries about the Irish question, agricultural evictions, the Phoenix Park murders of 1882, defeats in foreign affairs, colonial setbacks, and the damage caused by electoral reform. In February 1884, Bismarck wrote a particularly lurid analysis in which he predicted that Gladstone's principles would "decompose and republicanize" Britain. At the emperor's behest, this document was sent to the crown prince. An article in the progovernment weekly *Die Grenzboten,* which appeared in May 1884 just after the formation of the

Freisinn Party, drew the battle lines very clearly. It contrasted the timeless achievements reflected in Bismarck's speeches with the glib parliamentary rhetoric of orators like Lasker and Gladstone. Even though the *Grenzboten* article then listed a raft of problems likely to be caused by Gladstone's administration, it ended with a reassuring quotation from the equally pro-Bismarck *Kölnische Zeitung:* "Gladstonianism is as much in decline in Britain as the related dogmatism of Richter, Bamberger and their associates in Germany."[41]

The unfriendly reference to Lasker in this article was unsurprising but in poor taste. Only a few months earlier, on 5 January 1884, the politician had suddenly died of a heart attack while on a trip to the United States. On the one hand, this event was to highlight the potential fragility of Bismarck's position. The liberal deputy's death caused widespread public mourning and triggered expressions of respect across party boundaries. The chancellor was also shocked to learn that several of his ministerial colleagues were minded to attend Lasker's funeral. Holstein took this as a sign that the political class was beginning to ingratiate itself with the coming regime. "Everything is smiling towards the future," he noted in his diary on 27 January 1884. The ministers had read the crown prince's view correctly. Frederick William regretted the passing of this "selfless man of true conviction," from whom he had expected much for his future. On the other hand, Lasker's death offered Bismarck an opportunity to show his power and demonstrate the futility of any opposition. Backed by the emperor, who had requested that no civil servant attend the funeral, the chancellor effectively ordered his colleagues to stay away from the ceremony. Holstein conveyed Bismarck's message to Heinrich Friedberg, the Prussian justice minister who was on friendly terms with the crown prince, and to Gustav von Sommerfeld, a member of the crown princely household. He urged them to prevent Frederick William from taking any steps that would bring on the chancellor's wrath. Bismarck prevailed and the liberals had to lay one of their most distinguished parliamentarians to rest without a single official gesture of respect. "E. Lasker was buried in the Jewish cemetery today with great participation of the public," the crown prince noted in his diary on 27 January 1884, and added lamely that he "joined them in spirit." He had always thought highly of Lasker, Frederick William sheepishly told Bamberger during a private meeting a few days later, "but it had been strictly forbidden from above to show any form of sympathy."[42]

Bismarck also used Lasker's death to drag his campaign against the Kronprinzenpartei onto the parliamentary stage. A few days after Lasker died in New York, the United States House of Representatives sent the Reichstag a message of condolence in which the deceased was praised for "his firm and constant exposition of and devotion to free and liberal ideas." Bismarck ordered that the resolution be returned to Washington. When the Reichstag reconvened on 7 March 1884, Rickert, Hänel, and Richter fiercely attacked the chancellor's action. A week later, Bismarck responded to the issue in person. Ignoring the liberals' fury and fortified by one and a half bottles of Mosel wine, he chided Lasker's political allies for abusing the privileged position of standing by a friend's grave for purposes of agitation. He then criticized Lasker's consistent opposition to the emperor and himself, accused him of leading the left wing of his old party astray, and declared that he had no reason to feel any gratitude toward the deceased. For all its crassness, Bismarck's attack was not without a tactical purpose. He had singled out Lasker's role in splitting the National Liberals as particularly deplorable. This had destroyed any chance of cohesion amongst the parliamentary caucuses and was responsible for the current fragmentation. The chancellor explained afterward that his main object had been to encourage the moderate National Liberals around Bennigsen. Now that the Secessionists had fused with the Progressives and become open enemies, he told Holstein, he would attempt once more to form "a large, moderate middle party."[43]

Immediately after the Lasker affair, the chancellor focused on the next bone of contention. When the programme of the left-liberal German Freisinn Party was published in March 1884, Bismarck latched onto its call for a "responsible Reich ministry." This was done in order to mobilise the forces of federal diversity against the centralism of the new party and of its alleged patron, the crown prince. The Secessionists had attacked the alleged disjointedness of the Reich's internal structures for many years. In his widely read pamphlet *Die Sezession*, Bamberger had subjected what he considered the halfheartedness of Bismarck's unification of Germany to a withering attack. In order to avoid uncomfortable obstacles, the chancellor had retained "twee and cumbersome deadwood" and had spared "dynastic self-love." This had led to a frustrating mess: "Bavarian reserved rights with baroque party prerogatives, Württembergian special privileges, tincy-wincy territorial sovereignties, the Imperial Territory of Alsace-Lorraine clad in a nebulous stately garb—all excellent, the motlier the better, only dogmatic fools demand unity and uniformity."[44]

This kind of sarcastic rhetoric made it easy for Bismarck to mobilise the individual German governments against the threat the Freisinn allegedly posed to their future status. On 14 March 1884, the chancellor met the Saxon envoy to affirm his commitment to the various German dynasties and express concerns for the time "when the emperor passes away and the crown prince does not only surround himself with liberalizing advisers and ministers, but paves the way for unitary tendencies." Bismarck asked the envoy to convey the suggestion to the Saxon government that joint action be taken against this danger. After some time-consuming procedural toing and froing in the Reich's federal council—which confirmed the validity of Bamberger's comments—Bismarck eventually succeeded in pushing all twenty-five representatives of the various German governments into endorsing a public repudiation of the Freisinn Party's constitutional aims. "It will not be erroneous," their joint statement declared, "to see in the establishment of such a [responsible] ministry as the new progressive party desires the means of subjugating the Reich's government under the majority resolutions of the Reichstag." Change on this scale, it was argued, risked the disintegration of the young state. The following day, Bismarck explained to the Württembergian envoy the reasoning behind the unusual step of directing a federal declaration against a party programme: "In view of the crown prince's close relationship with Forckenbeck and other members of this party [and] in view of the unitary views and endeavours," it was his duty to "throw up a dam against the dangers threatening the Reich at the succession."[45]

The left-liberals took up Bismarck's challenge. The policy of the next ruler could not be shackled by declarations in the federal council, Theodor Barth insisted in *Die Nation* on 12 April 1884, and he promised the Freisinn Party's support in defence of German unity. In a lively Reichstag debate on 9 May 1884, Richter referred to the federal council's attack on the Freisinn Party's programme and accused the chancellor of trying to block the future of liberalism in Germany. The cap fit and Bismarck wore it with pride. "I regard it as my life's task," he replied to Richter, "as my duty to emperor and country to fight against this liberalism until my last breath." To struggle against the phantasms of parliamentary rule, he shouted, was his "damned duty and obligation as the emperor's servant."[46]

The main item of parliamentary business on that day, however, was the renewal of the anti-Socialist law. By then, Bismarck approached even the alleged Socialist threat in terms of its usefulness as a stick with which to beat the left-liberals. So fierce was his rejection of the Freisinn that he had briefly toyed with the idea of countering it by easing the oppression of the Social Democrats. During the elections for Berlin's city council in October 1883, there had already been complaints from the Progressive Party that the government was damaging them by giving the Socialists an unusually free rein. It appears that at the beginning of 1884, Bismarck even considered dropping the anti-Socialist law altogether. The middle classes would then be purged of their progressive leanings by their naked fear of socialism. In a rapid volte-face, the chancellor then decided that the law was crucial. On 16 March 1884, Bismarck visited the crown prince and suggested that the Reichstag might have to be dissolved if it voted against renewing the anti-Socialist law. The chancellor kept these rumours going during the run-up to the crucial vote in May and further increased the pressure by recalling Emperor William from his vacation at Wiesbaden to ensure that he would be available in case his signature on the decree of dissolution were suddenly needed.[47]

Bismarck's tactics in connection with the anti-Socialist law were designed to damage the left-liberals in two ways. He put tremendous pressure on the fault line that separated those in the party who were implacably opposed to the law from those who were prepared—for a variety of reasons—to support the government bill. In the end, the Freisinn caucus could only resolve the issue by arranging for a number of deputies to absent themselves from the crucial vote. Most left-liberal deputies still voted against the bill, but they did so, Bamberger noted, in the hope that they would be defeated and avoid the dreaded dissolution.[48]

Even more strikingly, though, Bismarck used the debate about the renewal of the anti-Socialist law to identify the left-liberals with the kind of fundamental danger to the state previously associated exclusively with socialism. In fact, the two speeches he gave on 9 May 1884 painted the Freisinn in even more threatening colours than the Social Democrats. The chancellor described Russian nihilism as "a climatic aberration more of progressive liberalism than of socialism." The former was "much more dangerous for the future calm and development of our state than social democracy, because it operated in a more sophisticated way." The Socialist Party was not really so dangerous, he explained, and claimed that he did not fear that "it would poison our blood and marrow. Yet I believe that the party of progressive liberalism is capable of this; its poison is more powerful than that of the socialists." Ultimately, however, both evils were linked. "All I can do," Bismarck concluded, "if, as seems possible, elections may not be far off, is to end with this urgent request to the voters: if you wish to be rid of the socialist danger, do not vote for a progressive deputy!"[49]

As the renewal of the anti-Socialist law passed the Reichstag by 189 to 157 votes, the chancellor had no need to call an early election. This gave him time to pursue yet another scheme that would damage the left-liberals' prospects. On 24 April 1884, he confirmed by telegram that the holdings of the Bremen merchant Adolf Lüderitz at Angra Pequena in today's Namibia were placed under the protection of the Reich. Between May and August 1884, the German flag was hoisted in Togoland, the Cameroons, and Angra Pequena. German colonies in East Africa and New Guinea acquired between February and May 1885 rounded off a hectic and dramatic period of sudden imperial expansion. Even though an organized and vocal German colonial movement can be traced back to the 1840s and became increasingly active in the course of the 1870s, the chancellor had long been staunchly opposed to any German involvement in imperialist ventures. As a consequence, the Reich possessed not a single overseas territory at a time when the "Scramble for Africa" and for other colonial prizes was already well under way. The question why Bismarck was suddenly converted to approving a policy of colonial acquisition has triggered a lively historiographical debate. A whole bundle of domestic and foreign policy factors has been identified that enabled and motivated the chancellor's new departure. One of the many uses of the colonial policy was undoubtedly its potential impact on the Reichstag elections in October 1884. "The whole colonial story is a fraud," Bismarck admitted to a colleague in September 1884, "but we need it for the elections."[50]

A particularly attractive feature of the electoral effect of the colonial issue was that it worked particularly to the detriment of the left-liberals. The existing agitation in favour of an active German imperialism was whipped up considerably once the actual acquisition of colonies had begun. The imperialist frenzy—expressed and sustained by large sections of Germany's published opinion—not only benefitted a government that was reported to have acted robustly to protect the country's future, but also threw the rigidly anticolonial stance of the Freisinn Party into sharp relief. Government-inspired papers quickly seized on this. They warned the electorate against returning a strong opposition to the Reichstag and accused the left-liberals of doing everything to prevent the great "national deed" overseas. Their arguments, based on the "narrow-minded thinking of accountants," endangered the nation's future. The prominent geographer Friedrich Ratzel wrote a pamphlet lambasting those "envious critics" and "Reich-sourpusses" who failed to understand the importance of the colonial question and indulged in "petty wars of words" and "superficial and loquacious parliamentarism."[51]

Bismarck himself used every parliamentary opportunity to attack the left-liberals' uncompromising anti-imperialist pronouncements. When addressing the Reichstag's budget committee on 23 June 1884, he described Bamberger as an opponent of "every kind of overseas development of the German nation." The chancellor observed that Bamberger's comments would make sense "coming from the mouth of a foreign statesman, but sounded surprising coming from the mouth of a representative of the German nation." Eugen Richter, Bismarck commented, appeared to desire a situation "where Germans abroad had to approach foreign authorities cap in hand to ask for protection." Three days later, the chancellor delivered a long speech in the Reichstag. He began by accusing Bamberger of having "inflicted the curse of ridicule" on Germany's colonial endeavours. The rest of the speech was almost entirely dedicated to portraying Bamberger, Richter, and Rickert as naïve and pettifogging opponents of the colonial programme. The final session of the fifth Reichstag closed on 28 June 1884. When the newly elected sixth Reichstag convened on 20 November, the left-liberal caucus was reduced by forty-one deputies.[52]

———

Damaging the prospects of the Freisinn Party was only one aspect of Bismarck's struggle against the Kronprinzenpartei scenario. Another weapon in the chancellor's armoury was weakening the links between the crown prince and anyone suspected of left-liberal leanings. The colonial policy with its emphasis on Germany's need for overseas territories did just that, since Frederick William certainly did not share the Freisinn Party's dogmatic hostility to Germany's colonial expansion. On the contrary, he had been critical of the Reichstag's refusal to support German trade activities overseas in 1880 and was, according to the British ambassador in Berlin, fully caught up in the colonial excitement that gripped Germany in 1884. Moreover, the colonial agenda, which had already led to tensions between Berlin and London, proved a welcome embarrassment for the crown princess. "No question is as suitable as this," Holstein gleefully observed in June 1884, "to put the future empress with her British tendencies in the wrong in front of the German people."[53]

In their attempts to isolate the crown prince as much as possible from liberal influences, Bismarck and his supporters went even further and even targeted individuals known to be close to Frederick William. The most prominent amongst the chancellor's victims was the general and admiral Albrecht von Stosch, who had been a confidant of the crown prince since the mid-1860s. In 1866 Stosch acquitted himself very well as quartermaster-general of the Prussian Second Army, commanded by the crown prince. During the Franco-Prussian War, he served with distinction as commissary-general of the German armies and subsequently as chief of staff of the German army section at the Loire. His abilities as a soldier greatly impressed Emperor William, who remained a lifelong supporter. With the backing of both the emperor and the crown prince, Stosch was appointed chief of the German admiralty and minister of state in 1872.[54]

Bismarck did not oppose this choice, but it is fair to assume that pleasing William I and Frederick William was not the chancellor's only consideration. He was also keen to place Stosch in a position where a close eye could be kept on this very energetic, ambitious, and well-connected man. Predictably, the relationship between the chancellor and the navy minister quickly turned sour. Bismarck was suspicious of Stosch's standing at court and his constructive working relationship with almost all the parties in the Reichstag. Increasingly obsessed with the idea that Stosch was planning to unseat him, Bismarck eventually attacked his minister during a budget debate in March 1877. Referring to a financial concession that Stosch had made to the budget committee, he accused him of paying more heed to "the authority and persuasiveness" of the progressive leader Eugen Richter than to the chancellor's.[55]

In Bismarck's book, providing a link—however tenuous—between the crown prince and left-liberalism was an unforgivable sin that deserved nothing short of a political death sentence. He therefore refused Stosch's request to retract the insinuation and forced the minister to tender his resignation. Emperor William's refusal to let Stosch go triggered a resignation from the chancellor, which was also denied. Locked into a frustrating relationship by the emperor's insistence that they both continue in their respective offices, the two men struggled on. Bismarck did his best to damage Stosch's influence by excluding him from ministerial meetings and denying him access to certain official papers. Worn out by internal hostility and tired of the public and parliamentary attacks on his stewardship of the navy, Stosch eventually insisted on resigning in March 1883. On the day of his resignation, Stosch informed Robert Lucius that he was aware of the efforts "to give the crown prince as conservative a surrounding as possible," and complained bitterly about the attempts "to damage his reputation by calling him a liberal." Even though Stosch spent the bulk of his time thereafter on his estate in the Rhineland, the connection with the crown prince was never severed. On 31 March 1883, as a little gesture of defiance against the mighty chancellor, Frederick William and Victoria invited Stosch for a private farewell dinner.[56]

Since Stosch was not fully out of the picture, Bismarck's guns remained trained on his perceived rival. The extent of the chancellor's concerns can be gleaned from Holstein's diary. In January and February 1884, the foreign office councillor mentioned plans for Stosch's chancellorship and even a "future ministry Stosch-Forckenbeck." In June 1884, Bismarck set aside a paragraph of the Reichstag speech in which he attacked the left-liberals' anticolonialism in order to smear Stosch. Observing how popular the former navy minister had been with the opposition, he declared that the Freisinn deputy Heinrich Rickert and others had been plotting to install Stosch in the chancellery. The admiral may or may not have been aware of these schemes, he claimed, but the conspirators counted on his participation, power, and connections.[57]

Even though both Richter and Rickert denied any knowledge of such a plan, the Bismarck press ran with the story. "Mr. von Stosch was not only in touch with the so-called court liberals, Messrs. Rickert, von Bunsen, von Forckenbeck and others," the *Norddeutsche Allgemeine Zeitung* explained on 5 July 1884, "he also supported them politically and was prepared to place his connections at court at their disposal." In order to oppose the German government, a heterogeneous coalition—resembling Gladstone's majority—had allegedly been forged: "National Liberals, Progressives, Secessionists and Ultramontanes closed ranks . . . and the role of Mr. Gladstone was reserved for the then chief of the admiralty." Stosch was incandescent that ahead of the crown prince's accession attempts were made to "kill him morally," and he angrily denied any association with radical opponents of the government. He wrote furious letters to the paper's editor, to the war minister, to the chief of the military cabinet, and to Frederick William. Even though none of these letters elicited a fully satisfactory reply, the attacks on Stosch eventually ceased.[58]

As the admiral noted himself, the attempts to lower his political standing formed part of a wider process of transformation. In order to bring about a rapprochement between Frederick William and Bismarck, significant changes were made to the group of court officials and confidants who surrounded the crown prince. "Stosch, Eulenburg, Mischke, Normann gone—a very considerable improvement of the political situation," is how Holstein smugly summarised the results of these efforts in May 1884. The foreign office councillor, who had long been worried about the tensions between the crown prince and the chancellor, believed that they were caused by ambitious troublemakers in Frederick William's household. The crown prince's chamberlain, Count August zu Eulenburg, who was allegedly feeding "distrust on both sides," was the first to go. He succumbed to a cooperation between Holstein and his friend, Count Götz von Seckendorff, the crown princess's chamberlain. The joy caused by Eulenburg's departure in 1882 ended, though, when he was replaced by Karl von Normann. An old friend of Stosch's, Normann had been a member of the household since 1864 and was believed to hold anti-Bismarck views. He was not only rumoured to have his eye on the chancellorship; he also was allegedly close to Forckenbeck, Bamberger, and Virchow. The vacancy left behind by Normann's promotion was filled by the conservative Gustav von Sommerfeld. In February 1884, Frederick William's adjutant Albert von Mischke, who was a friend of both Normann and Stosch, fell victim to a whispering campaign.[59]

The isolated Normann only held out until May 1884 before he was finally dislodged. His standing with Frederick William was unusually strong because, as Stosch put it in July 1883, "the crown prince's entire greatness in the political and intellectual realms consist[ed] of

Normann." According to Holstein's diagnosis, it was the chamberlain's hubris that caused his downfall: "When Normann believed that the great democratic party was behind him, he swelled with pride," he commented, "and did no longer want to share his domination of the crown prince with the crown princess." This made it easy for Seckendorff to turn the crown princess against Normann. The diplomat Count Hugo von Radolinski, who the emperor appointed to succeed him, was not only a very close friend of Holstein's; he also had been carefully vetted by Bismarck, who was immensely grateful for Radolinski's willingness to enter this "pig of a business." The chancellor promised him an excellent diplomatic appointment afterward, "even if [he] had to kill someone for it." Normann's removal completed the changing of the crown prince's guards. It did not go unnoticed. The newly appointed men are conservative, Karl Schrader observed in August 1884, "and they appear to consider it their duty to free their employers from liberal influence."[60]

Bismarck went further than damaging the left-liberals' prospects and purging the crown prince's environment of putative liberals. He also strove to involve Frederick William actively in governmental initiatives and institutions. The visit of King Alfonso XII of Spain to Germany in September 1883 provided the chancellor with a welcome opportunity to draw the crown prince into his orbit. After attending German army manoeuvres and exploring the possibilities of a Spanish-German alliance, Alfonso returned home via Paris, where he was mobbed by an anti-German crowd. Infuriated by the king's decision to accept the honorary colonelcy of a Prussian regiment garrisoned in Strasbourg, Parisians hurled abuse at Alfonso and attacked his carriage. Bismarck believed that this provocation required a response. On 16 October 1883, he sent Frederick William a long letter suggesting that the crown prince should soon make an official, high-profile visit to Spain. The chancellor clearly was doing his utmost to charm Frederick William. The letter was timed to arrive on the crown prince's birthday and included Bismarck's "most humble congratulations." Unusually, the chancellor also decided to approach Frederick William before informing the emperor. He would not dare to involve His Majesty, Bismarck wrote, unless he was assured that Frederick William approved of this plan. To add even more drama, the chancellor insisted that journeying overland through France was out of the question and that a German warship would be summoned to convey the crown prince. Frederick William was more than happy to accept this task and his joy certainly was not dimmed by Bismarck's suggestion that the visit should be marked by lavish ceremonies and splendour.[61]

It was hardly a secret that the chancellor regarded the Spanish trip as a means of beguiling the crown prince. Holstein's diary entries show that Bismarck had told him about his intention to flatter Frederick William's princely sensitivities and that the chancellor expected some sort of gratitude for treating the crown prince to an "unusually interesting journey, to a triumphal procession through Spain and Italy." On 29 November 1883, a fortnight after Frederick William had embarked on his trouble-free, four-week trip, Bismarck mocked the crown prince's "love of approbation" in a private conversation. Frederick William enjoyed making a good impression and would "cut an imposing figure next to the little Aztecs." The chancellor therefore did his best to smooth over the various tiffs that caused considerable bad blood ahead of the crown prince's departure. He also worked hard to spare Frederick William any embarrassment when a visit to the Vatican was suddenly added to the itinerary.[62]

Even though the emperor's refusal to allow his son to take Prince William to Spain had greatly upset the crown prince and he subsequently grumbled about his unexpected mission to Rome, Bismarck's Spanish-charm offensive was at least partially successful. On 17 November 1883, he exchanged warm farewell telegrams with Frederick William. Upon his return, the crown prince submitted a long report, which Bismarck honoured with a fourteen-page reply. Eight months later, Frederick William presented the chancellor with a copy of his travel diary and a photograph. This provided Bismarck with yet another opportunity to praise the crown prince's signal contribution to Spanish-German relations.[63]

By the time the chancellor received his copy of the Spanish diary, he had long since embarked on yet another scheme to attach the crown prince to him. On 12 April 1884, Bismarck called on the crown prince and invited him to accept the presidency of the Prussian Council of State. Frederick William agreed immediately. The Council of State was a committee of notables and senior officials with the remit to scrutinize legislative proposals and advise the government. Set up by royal decree in 1817, it lost most of its raison d'être when the Prussian parliament was established in 1848. The council had never been formally abolished, but by the mid-1880s, it had not met for more than twenty-five years. Bismarck's decision to revive it caused general bafflement and a great deal of scepticism. Ministers foresaw unnecessary complications, deputies worried that it would diminish the status of the parliament, and even the emperor raised serious doubts. None of this stopped the chancellor; it did not even slow him down very much. On 16 March 1884, Bismarck surprised his colleagues by announcing his plan. A mere six weeks later, Emperor William's formal authorisation completed the process of reactivating the council.[64]

While there may have been other motives as well—the need for an independent body of expert advisers and the idea of developing the Prussian council into a Reich body that would clip the wings of the Reichstag have been mentioned—this initiative should predominantly be seen in the context of Bismarck's concerns about the succession. The Bavarian diplomat Klemens von Podewils-Dürnitz was not the only contemporary who considered this body of appointed dignitaries a "specifically conservative element with the essential task of acting as a counterweight to a possible Freisinn ministry." Bismarck made similar comments when speaking to the Saxon envoy, but a slightly different motivation appears more convincing. Rather than containing the excessive liberalism of a future Freisinn regime, the Council of State plan was meant to help prevent it. Johannes Miquel, the mayor of Frankfurt and leader of the National Liberals approved of the scheme for this very reason. He told Stosch on 25 April that he saw it "as a shackling of the crown prince against his leftward drifting ideas for the future."[65]

The plan appeared to work. In June 1884, Minister Lucius noted in his diary that the left-liberals had been "a little chagrined since the crown prince ha[d] taken over the presidency of the Council of State, while Bismarck's relationship with the crown prince ha[d] become more intimate." During a formal dinner in October 1884, the industrialist Louis Baare, who was a member of the council, told Frederick William how delighted he was that he had accepted the chairmanship and asked if he could be open as to why this was so. When Frederick William said he could, Baare told him: "It makes me happy because Your Imperial Highness has now made a clean break with Forckenbeck and his lot." The crown prince's response was tight-lipped: "Sure enough, you do speak openly."[66]

The chancellor had planned to flatter the crown prince by repeating the little touch that had worked so well when he suggested the Spanish trip to Frederick William in 1883. The first session of the council should take place on 18 October 1884, Bismarck wrote to a court official, because of its "historical importance" as the birthday of His Imperial Highness, the crown prince. For some reason, this could not be arranged, but having to chair the meeting on 25 October 1884 did not appear to diminish Frederick William's enjoyment of the occasion. He presided over an illustrious body of ministers, mayors, civil servants, parliamentarians, high-ranking officers, scholars, and industrialists. The membership of the council was overwhelmingly conservative, but a handful of prominent National Liberals had thoughtfully been appointed.[67]

The crown prince's excitement about his new position proved short-lived. Having to sit in the committee room and missing the lovely sunshine outside was irksome, he wrote to his wife on 1 November 1884. Neither the emperor, who welcomed the crown prince's initial dedication, nor Bismarck had expected Frederick William to stay the course. When discussing his son's chairmanship of the council in April 1884, the emperor had wondered how long it would be until Frederick William was fed up with the task. Bismarck replied that the crown prince had attended ministerial meetings in the 1860s, but yawned so much that he almost dislocated his jaw and then stayed away. Somewhat more charitably, Martin Philippson, a liberal contemporary, suggested that Frederick William's growing dislike of his appointment reflected his concerns about the council's antiparliamentary effect. Neither the reasons for the crown prince's disenchantment nor the fact that the council's sessions had effectively petered out by 1886, however, appear to have interested Bismarck very much. By the end of 1884, so many central planks of the Kronprinzenpartei project had been broken that the chancellor could concentrate on building an alternative.[68]

Weakening the left-liberals and depriving them of their dynastic Jacob's ladder were important aspects of Bismarck's strategy. These measures needed to be complemented, however, by bringing the "honest part" of the National Liberals back into the chancellor's fold. Only with their deputies could he build a reliable parliamentary majority that would both underpin the succession and keep its potential for systemic change within acceptable limits. Bismarck was helped in this endeavour by developments taking place within the National Liberal Party after 1880. Bennigsen, the party leader, initially tried to steer a compromise course designed to prevent further defections on either wing of the party. The new programme, which was formulated in May 1881, held out a hand of cooperation to anyone striving for similar aims. It was meant to pacify the growing body of National Liberals who were hoping to see their party return to a closer relationship with the government, but it was vague enough to keep alive the Secessionists' dream of an eventual reunification. Since this evasive document ended up being understood differently by almost every reader, it created little clarity.[69]

Bismarck sensed that there was much to play for and he certainly did not want to leave the field to those striving to unite a "great liberal party" on a left-liberal platform. Within weeks of the Secessionists' breakaway, the chancellor invited Bennigsen to renew their old cooperation. If they shunned the left-liberals, the chancellor proposed, the National Liberals could form a powerful alliance with the moderate conservatives. Bismarck was happy to offer the exclusion of the ultraconservatives from this combination and even dangled the carrot of a pseudoparliamentary system. In a message conveyed to Bennigsen in September 1880, he suggested that if such an alliance were established, the government would only table measures on which the united middle parties had previously agreed. In his Reichstag speech of 5 May 1881, the chancellor went out of his way to praise Bennigsen, calling him "the fellow-fighter to whom [he] was indebted for his real support and to whom the German Reich owe[d] so much in respect of its creation and consolidation." Bismarck declared that—because of his "personal feelings" for Bennigsen and because of the damage it would do to Germany's parliamentary development—he would find it painful if the National Liberals were to grow apart from the government. Such an estrangement, he warned, would destroy the plans he was attaching to the hope that the National Liberals would merge with the Right rather than with the Left. The chancellor ended by addressing Bennigsen directly: "Do not let the Left beguile you!"[70]

Even though this appeal did not yield any direct results, Bismarck continued to invest in his relationship with the liberal leader. Their meeting in February 1883 left Bennigsen very satisfied. The harsh criticism of Lasker voiced by the chancellor during his provocative Reichstag speech of 13 March 1884 stood in marked contrast to his description of Bennigsen as "my political and personal friend" in the same speech. Two months later, Bismarck once again made his political feelings toward the National Liberals perfectly clear. He conceded that there had been a split, but added: "My fondness towards these gentlemen, my respect for them and the regret with which I think back to the good relations with this party are not dead. I maintain to all of those who have remained National Liberal and have not gone over to the Progressive Party exactly the same political friendship, as soon as they are ready to re-connect, and I am not ashamed of it."[71]

Bismarck had made very considerable progress between these two speeches on 13 March and 9 May 1884. On 23 March 1884, a delegation of forty-two leading National Liberals from the south of Germany issued the Heidelberg Programme, which had been drafted by the party's new leading man, Mayor Johannes Miquel of Frankfurt. The programme emphatically backed the German military, praised Bismarck's foreign and social policies, formally endorsed the tariff legislation in place, and insisted on the necessity of renewing the anti-Socialist law. In a direct snub to the Freisinn Party, which had been formed only weeks earlier, the declaration explicitly ruled out any fusion with other parties. In his speech to the regional party conference in Neustadt on 14 April 1884, Miquel struck an even more decisive note. He declared that the National Liberals considered Bismarck "a shining example to all the great and powerful men" and hoped that there would soon be "a secure and determined parliamentary majority of middle parties to work with the imperial chancellor if at all possible." Even though the party leadership in Berlin dragged its feet for a while, by the beginning of May 1884, the National Liberal caucuses in the Reichstag and the Prussian parliament had agreed a joint statement welcoming the document. The men behind the Heidelberg Programme had done their best to make Bismarck an offer he could not refuse.[72]

He did not refuse it. He had invited it. Bismarck told Holstein that the reference to "his friend" Bennigsen in his Reichstag speech in March 1884 had been made specifically to encourage the National Liberals. Shortly after the Heidelberg meeting, the chancellor sent Miquel a message asking him to attend a private meeting. The National Liberals were also mentioned during the chancellor's conversation with the crown prince on 12 April 1884. Bismarck and Frederick William not only discussed the Council of State but also considered the time after Emperor William's death. The crown prince declared that he would be delighted to retain Bismarck as chancellor and planned to appoint Bennigsen and Miquel to be in charge of Prussian affairs. Bismarck replied that he had no objections to governing with the National Liberals, but warned against going further to the Left. Forckenbeck and his party would soon bring on the republic. After this exchange, the crown prince and the chancellor reportedly parted on excellent terms, the former even walking the latter to the door.[73]

At this frantic time, Bismarck was simultaneously pursuing two more initiatives. They also helped to underpin his policy of reattaching a purged National Liberal Party to his government. In April 1884, the chancellor was busy putting the finishing touches to his sudden reactivation of the Prussian Council of State. This provided him with another opportunity to reward the National Liberals for their recent return to the Bismarckian camp. Very few liberals were selected to sit among the dozens of dignitaries that constituted this body, but Bennigsen, Miquel, and the Rhenish financier Gustav von Mevissen made it onto the list. This distinction not only highlighted the special regard in which the chancellor held them but also brought the National Liberals into contact with the crown prince.

On 24 April 1884, one month after the Heidelberg declaration, twelve days after he and Frederick William agreed on the future appointment of Bennigsen and Miquel, and four days after Emperor William formally approved the Council of State plan, Bismarck sent the telegram that marked the beginning of Germany's colonial venture. The government's decision to enter the imperial game gave a dramatic boost to the German colonial movement and to the parties most closely involved with it—the National Liberals and the Free Conservatives. Being able to present themselves as the true advocates of the nation's vital interests overseas not only made the National Liberals appear attractive in the eyes of the electorate—and the crown prince—but also provided yet another link between the National Liberals and Bismarck's government. In his Reichstag speech of 1 December 1884, Bismarck made it very clear that the government's gift of a colonial shot in the arm did not come free of charge for the parties that benefitted from it. It had to be reciprocated with firm and disciplined parliamentary support. "To be able to pursue a successful overseas policy, every government . . . has to be backed by a parliamentary majority which is not torn apart and diminished by parties, which does not depend on the momentary disgruntlement of individual parties. Without having such a reserve in the background we can pursue no colonial or overseas policy."[74]

The National Liberals were prepared to accept this political deal and joined an increasingly firmly integrated governmental front. Committed to defending the status quo, the National Liberals largely abandoned their political struggle against the forces of the Right and directed their fire against the left-liberals, the Socialists, and the Centre Party. The patterns of electoral contests illustrate this trend very clearly. In 1881, the National Liberals had competed with Conservatives in seventy-two seats and with left-liberals in sixty. By 1884, these figures had changed to forty-two and ninety-one, respectively. By the time Bismarck had successfully triggered the 1887 elections, the National Liberals, the Free Conservatives, and the German Conservatives, who had been briefed about the chancellor's intentions, quickly agreed to a formal arrangement—the so-called *Kartell*. According to the terms of this alliance, the parties involved refrained from standing against each other in individual constituencies and agreed on single candidates for seats held by their opponents. The National Liberals' reorientation paid a handsome electoral dividend. From forty-seven seats in 1881, they went up to fifty-one in 1884 and to ninety-nine in 1887.[75]

Having analysed how the National Liberals and the left-liberals responded to the risks and opportunities of the early 1880s, the historian Felix Rachfahl pointed to a fundamental difference: "The National Liberals henceforth counted on the governing statesman, i.e. on the present; the Freisinn, however, counted on the future." This interpretation, though insightful, underestimated the depth of the chancellor's stratagem. Bismarck was as aware as any left-liberal politician of the political implications of the impending succession. He was not merely consolidating his regime for the time being but was also preparing a viable political future for himself and—by extension—for the National Liberals. A united parliamentary majority of the Conservative and National Liberal caucuses committed to supporting Bismarck was probably enough to secure his position even after the succession. For the crown prince to be reliably won over to this combination, however, would be the icing on the cake.[76]

There were some indications that Frederick William was already leaning that way. In April 1884, well after the Heidelberg meeting, the crown prince suggested to Bismarck that he was planning to appoint Bennigsen and Miquel to ministerial offices. In June 1884, he

wrote a brief reflection on the National Liberals' recent program-
matic changes. His summary was broadly positive and referred to
their intention "to suppress parliamentary hostility to the Reich government" as well as to a "moderate party of the middle helpful to the
government without party consideration." The crown prince also appears to have been favourably impressed with the performance of the
National Liberal members of the Council of State. Their contributions made committee meetings interesting, he wrote to Victoria in
October 1884: "It is amusing how [the ultraconservative] Minister
von Puttkamer gets uneasy, as soon as Miquel or Bennigsen or Mevissen speak." In November 1884, Holstein reported that the crown
prince spent the council meetings listening "in raptures to the liberal
speeches by Bennigsen, Miquel and their associates." A residual
amount of equivocation nevertheless remained. Frederick William
described the National Liberals' election campaign as sad, shameless, and base, and after meeting the leading left-liberal Karl Schrader,
he wrote to Victoria that "Heidelbergery" had greatly damaged the
well-intentioned Freisinn Party. These last twinges of left-liberal
sympathy were to fade, though, and gave way to a steady firming up
of the relationship between the crown prince and the chancellor's
camp.[77]

In retrospect, this development appears almost overdetermined.
The election results clearly played a crucial role. At the 1884 elections,
the Freisinn Party suffered a serious setback. In February 1887, it was
virtually destroyed when a pro-Bismarck juggernaut was returned in
the shape of the Kartell, which controlled 220 of the Reichstag's 397
seats. "The crown prince will now be spared any kind of embarrassment," the leading left-liberal Ludwig Bamberger observed when
commenting on the outcome: "He will do what Bismarck wants."
Drawing on information obtained from "a well-informed German,"
the *New York Herald* provided the most candid summary of what
the chancellor had achieved. In order to curb the crown princess's
left-liberal proclivities, the paper argued in March 1887, "Bismarck
brought about the late elections and forced the issues in such a way as
to obtain a strong government majority of National Liberalists." The
demolition of the Freisinn Party and this new majority secured the
chancellor's future. "When the crown princess begins to rule Germany, she will find a majority too strong to be lightly dismissed, and
of liberal but not dangerously radical tendencies." Bismarck had supplied Victoria with "a new set of friends sufficiently to her taste to

make it hard for her to quarrel with them. There is no mistake so great as to suppose that Prince Bismarck is not providing for the future."[78]

The 1887 poll had come about because of the Reichstag's refusal to pass the renewal of the army bill. Bismarck had introduced this new *Septennat* proposal, which fixed the military budget for a further seven years and increased the size of the armed forces in the autumn of 1886. He had done so more than a year ahead of schedule because he wanted to fight an election on this issue amid rising foreign political tensions and rumours of a possible war. Determined to reshape the parliamentary landscape, the chancellor brushed aside every offer of a compromise and seized the earliest opportunity to dissolve the Reichstag. Bismarck's tactics were successful, but neither subtle nor unexpected. As early as December 1885, Bennigsen confidently anticipated that the chancellor was preparing the ground "to dissolve [parliament] at the right moment and appeal to the country's healthy national forces." The frenzied patriotic appeal raised in the run-up to the so-called Septennat elections enabled the "healthy national forces" of the Kartell to justify their formation of a united block that would deliver the reliable majority of which Bismarck had dreamed in 1879.[79]

Moreover, Bismarck had chosen his ground well. The crown prince had a strong track record of supporting earlier army bills. When he learned of the dissolution of the Reichstag in January 1887, Frederick William could not bring himself to condemn the measure. In his diary entry, he merely recorded his apprehension about a possible new "conflict period" and wondered what Bismarck might do if the elections failed to produce "a more pliable Reichstag." After a long meeting with the crown prince on 26 January 1887, the chancellor smugly told his press agent Moritz Busch that his relationship with Frederick William and Victoria could not be better. Bismarck was sure that he would stay on. This time it was the Kartell press that used the crown prince in their electioneering. An article from the *Kölnische Zeitung* which Frederick William pasted into his diary in February 1887 accused "progressive newspapers" of "offending the crown prince, our most senior field marshal, by claiming he was opposed to the Septennat." This was surely a falsehood, the paper argued, and declared that "the crown prince wholly and entirely back[ed] the Septennat and the entire army bill."[80]

The pressure on Frederick William to move toward the National Liberals and the chancellor also came from another direction. Ironically, this was also urged by the very adviser Bismarck had always regarded with fierce suspicion. Ever since the spring of 1884, Albrecht von Stosch had been busy facilitating such a rapprochement. In April 1884, he reassured a worried Miquel that the crown prince's political instincts were opposed to the Left. Two years later, Stosch sought to convince Frederick William that the government's social insurance schemes were successfully regaining the trust of the workers who were no longer listening to Socialist agitation. When the two men met again a few weeks later, Stosch insisted that Bismarck had to be retained and recommended Bennigsen and the Free Conservative Adolf von Arnim-Boitzenburg as future ministers. After the electoral success of the Kartell in February 1887, Stosch redoubled his efforts. In March 1887, he travelled to Frankfurt to negotiate with Miquel. His aim was to "link the National Liberals to the crown prince." Stosch told Freytag that he had "pulled a lot of strings" and hoped that the "puppets would now do their duty." Even a man as determined and resourceful as Stosch could not overcome every obstacle, though. "The mistress does not know what she wants and so the husband acts helplessly and cluelessly alongside her," he wrote to Normann in April 1887. "It shines through that he would have liked to confer with Miquel and Bennigsen, but he was not allowed to do so."[81]

By the spring of 1887, Victoria's disapproval was probably no longer the main reason why Frederick William did not meet with the National Liberal leadership. Ever since January 1887, the crown prince had been troubled by a persistent hoarseness. When the usual remedies failed to help the patient, a specialist was consulted who discovered a growth inside the larynx and decided to remove it. In March and April 1887, Frederick William was subjected almost daily to a very painful procedure during which a red-hot platinum wire was inserted into his throat in a vain attempt to destroy the tumour. Within a few weeks, a committee of physicians was convened. It was their view that the crown prince's condition was malignant and that only risky surgery could save him.

Bismarck's reaction to this course of events surprised even his own family. In May 1887, his son William wondered why his father displayed such mood swings in relation to Frederick William's situation. A few weeks later, Philipp von Eulenburg noted with some consternation that the chancellor had wept when he learned the gravity of the crown prince's illness. Although he did not wish to diminish this beautiful expression of emotional attachment, the diplomat continued, he suspected that Bismarck's frustration about the political consequences of Frederick William's fatal illness may well have played a role, too. "The chancellor had prepared brilliantly for Frederick William's reign," J. Alden Nichols has observed, "and now it was not to be." After Bismarck had toiled for years to set up the liberal-conservative constellation that allowed him to govern effectively under the new emperor and his wife, fate had ripped the raison d'être out of his policy. The news that the crown prince was doomed reached the chancellor only weeks after he had finally closed the net around the future ruler. Did Bismarck shed tears of sorrow or tears of frustration?[82]

CHAPTER FIVE

Illness and Reign

The eighteen months that preceded Frederick William's death in June 1888 were a period of unremitting ghastliness. In the throes of increasingly unbearable physical and mental anguish, the dying man was subjected to a variety of cruel, dishonest, and calculating forms of behaviour. Among his tormentors were numerous organs of published opinion, actors on and behind the political stage, members of his family and household, and even the medical men by his bedside. Engaged in bitter fights over political power and driven by personal vanity, they invaded the crown prince's privacy, dashed his hopes, disrespected his dignity, and exploited his weakness. His father's death on 9 March 1888 finally brought Frederick William to the throne. Since the dying new emperor was unable to impose his will, however, the ninety-nine days of his reign witnessed more callous intrigue and relentless jockeying for future positions. Throughout this maelstrom of misery, Frederick William behaved with such fortitude, self-discipline, and generosity of spirit that Noble Sufferer became a widely used epithet for him. His desperation rarely broke through and did so only when he was confiding to his wife or trusted friends. "That I have to suffer such a terrible, revolting disease and be so revolting to all of you and a burden," Frederick William sobbed in Victoria's arms in November 1887. "Why is heaven so cruel to me? What have I done to be thus afflicted and damned?" When his old chief of staff visited him in May 1888, the dying emperor saw no use in pretending: "My dear Blumenthal," he scribbled on a piece of paper, "it is almost unbearable."[1]

The last year of Frederick William's life was not only characterized by great woe but also by a striking paradox. Many of the circumstances of his existence during those months were dramatically
and profoundly new. From the spring of 1887 onward, his life was
dominated by his illness and doctors' orders. As the crown prince
was absent from German soil between June 1887 and March 1888,
his failing father and even Bismarck exercised less control over him
than ever before. When Frederick William returned to Germany, he
did so as emperor and king, finally endowed with the powers and
independence that he and his wife had craved for so long. Yet, in spite
of the novelty of these circumstances, the issues and constellations
which haunted Frederick William in his final year were old and hackneyed. The ghosts of years past, which now returned in an even more
frantic form, included the public hostility to Frederick William's alleged Anglophile tendencies and the influence of foreigners, aggressive attempts to claim him for a party-political agenda, the dominant
roles played by his wife and by Bismarck, the political fallout of an
anticipated succession, and the dysfunctional relationships with his
father and his eldest son. Even the Battenberg marriage affair reared
its odious head again.

By preserving beyond the watershed of his accession the very feature that had defined his decades as crown prince—his powerlessness—
Frederick William's illness turned his short reign into a dispiriting
experience of déjà vu. The implacable progress of the emperor's condition forced those who viewed his reign as a fleeting opportunity to
achieve their aims to act with hasty exaggeration. Those who regarded the accession of the voiceless emperor as an unfortunate irritation merely played for time and prepared for the future.

Fleeing the Disease: Frederick William's Journey to San Remo

In October 1881, Frederick William turned fifty. Even the man who
was Our Fritz did not prove immune to the effects of middle age. The
crown prince's physical constitution was no longer as sturdy as the
descriptions of him as a Nordic hero and glorious warrior suggested.
He frequently suffered from colds and throat complaints. Often he
had to rest several times a day and he was also beginning to put on
weight. After he had contracted measles in April 1886, Frederick
William took a long time to recover. General Stosch and Ambassador Lothar von Schweinitz met the crown prince in May 1886 and

noticed how much Frederick William had aged. Both men commented on the greying of his famous beard. The periods of depression and the dark moods that affected Frederick William with increasing frequency after the death of Prince Waldemar in 1879 are also likely to have drained him of energy. By 1887, the royal physicians were thus used to the crown prince's regular ailments, and it took a long time for the hoarseness that affected Frederick William in the winter of 1886–1887 to strike anyone as alarming.[2]

A heavy smoker throughout his adult life, the crown prince was used to recurring bouts of hoarseness. Anton von Werner noticed as early as May 1875 that Frederick William was almost voiceless when he arrived in Venice. In February 1886, the crown prince decided not to join a skating party in order to protect his sore throat. The cold persisted until April 1886 and in the autumn of that year his throat was again affected. This time the condition could not be shaken off with the aid of the usual remedies. The crown prince was barely able to say a word at a ball given by War Minister Bronsart on 31 January 1887, and his voice had not returned in time for the carnival ball at the palace on 11 February. When, at the beginning of March 1887, hoarseness still forced Frederick William to cancel appointments, Dr. August Wegner, the physician-in-ordinary to the crown prince, decided to call in a specialist for diseases of the throat. On 6 March 1887, Professor Carl Gerhardt of Berlin's Charité Hospital examined Frederick William. Using a laryngoscope, Gerhardt discovered a "pale, slightly uneven protuberance in the shape of a tongue or lobe." The growth measured about two by four millimetres and was attached to the left vocal cord. After unsuccessful attempts to excise it by means of a wire noose and a circular scalpel, the professor resorted to galvanocautery. A platinum wire rendered red-hot by electrical current was inserted into the crown prince's larynx to burn and destroy the lesion. This painful procedure was repeated more than a dozen times between 14 March and 7 April 1887. When the course of treatment finally appeared to have removed the growth, Gerhardt gave the crown prince permission to leave for a long-planned trip to the spa resort of Bad Ems.[3]

In his subsequent account of the crown prince's illness, Gerhardt explained that the weeks Frederick William spent relaxing at Bad Ems without any further treatment had a diagnostic purpose. If the growth were to return, this would considerably heighten the professor's fears that the crown prince's condition might be malignant. On

29 April 1887, the crown princess sent her mother an upbeat letter from the resort; Frederick William's throat appeared to be improving steadily and he was feeling well. But Victoria's optimism was soon to be dashed. The hoarseness reappeared, and when Gerhardt examined the crown prince upon his return on 15 May 1887, he found the lesion bigger than before. At Gerhardt's suggestion, the distinguished surgeon Ernst von Bergmann was summoned. He examined Frederick William the following day, diagnosed cancer, and urged an immediate operation. On 18 May 1887, a group of six doctors, including the laryngologist Adelbert von Tobold, convened and unanimously endorsed Bergmann's view. A surgical procedure to open the larynx and remove the affected tissue was scheduled for 21 May 1887. While it offered the only hope of curing laryngeal cancer, the operation nevertheless carried a significant risk of the patient dying under the knife or shortly afterward.[4]

On the eve of the planned operation, however, the eminent British laryngologist Morell Mackenzie arrived in Berlin. His involvement had been recommended by Wegner on 16 May during a meeting with Gerhardt and Bergmann, both of whom had accepted the proposal. The crown princess gladly complied with the doctors' suggestion and sent a telegram to her mother requesting that she arrange for Mackenzie to be despatched immediately. Even though contemporaries as well as historians have closely—and sometimes furiously—scrutinised Mackenzie's role, motivation, strengths, and shortcomings, a number of key questions still remain controversial or unresolved. Did Mackenzie owe his invitation to the crown princess? Did he arrive in Berlin with a clear brief to prevent the planned operation? Why did he resist the cancer diagnosis for so long—way beyond the point of reasonable doubt—and why did he remain so unbelievably sanguine about his ability to cure Frederick William?

Wegner's decision to propose Mackenzie may have been influenced by his well-founded expectation that Victoria would welcome the presence of a British specialist, but there is no clear evidence to prove that the crown princess instigated the recommendation. It is perfectly plausible that the physician only became aware of Mackenzie when he consulted the Englishman's recently translated compendium on the diseases of the throat. That the crown princess may have privately mentioned Mackenzie's name to Wegner cannot be ruled out, though. Such a suggestion would certainly have been made very discreetly since Victoria patently appreciated that summoning a British specialist was politically sensitive. In a letter of 17 May 1887, she told her mother that many in Germany would criticise her for recommending a foreigner and asked the queen to make it look as if she had sent Mackenzie. Regardless of who first thought of involving the Englishman, it is clear that the German doctors attending Frederick William were not only fully aware of his invitation, but formally requested and approved it.[5]

Everything had been prepared for the operation on Frederick William's throat when Mackenzie alighted from his train in Berlin on the afternoon of 20 May 1887. Two rooms in the crown prince's palace had been set aside and the floors scoured with carbolic acid. Instruments, bandages, and other equipment had been delivered. The German doctors were confident that their diagnosis was correct and all they expected from Mackenzie was a formal endorsement. Gerhardt recalled afterward that he and Bergmann had agreed to invite the Englishman "because we regarded the laryngoscopical findings and the development of the illness as so clear and evidential, that everyone who could use a laryngoscope had to come to the same conclusion." Within hours of Mackenzie's arrival, though, this certainty had been pricked and the operation was postponed, never to be performed. This marked the beginning of the bitter struggle between Mackenzie and his German colleagues, yet not everyone in Berlin was appalled by this turn of events. Bismarck, for his part, was firmly opposed to a risky surgical procedure. He preferred, as he later put it in a letter to the crown princess, "to face the dangers of the disease rather than the dangers of the operation." Understandably, Victoria also was utterly frightened by the prospect of surgery and relieved by its postponement. "You can image that this is not an easy operation or a small one," she had written to her mother on 17 May. "The idea of a knife touching his dear throat is terrible to me."[6]

It has been argued that Mackenzie prevented the operation after having been made aware of these concerns and that he arrived in Berlin knowing "very precisely what was expected of him." For political and personal reasons, it is suggested, both the chancellor and the crown princess had decided against the operation with its risk of a quick death and preferred a gamble: that old age would carry off Emperor William before the crown prince succumbed to his cancer. If successful, the gamble would put a dying Frederick William on the throne. His reign would probably be quite brief, but it would make Victoria an empress and delay the accession of the immature Prince William.[7] It strains credulity, though, to argue that Mackenzie participated in this alleged scheme from the very start, knowingly undermined a correct diagnosis, and sought to prevent the proposed cure for purely nonmedical reasons. Such a strategy would also have sat uneasily with the suggestion Mackenzie made on 20 May 1887: Having contradicted the German doctors by stating that the growth did not appear to him to be malignant, he recommended that a tissue sample be analysed microscopically. The tiny portion of the growth which Mackenzie successfully removed on 21 May was then examined by Professor Rudolf Virchow, the leading authority in the field of cellular pathology. Virchow could not identify any signs of malignancy, but had he done so, Mackenzie would have found it very hard to resist the pressure for immediate surgery.

A less Machiavellian explanation appears more credible here—at least when accounting for the developments before Frederick William's cancer diagnosis was confirmed in the autumn of 1887. Bismarck, who had not been involved in Mackenzie's invitation, was hardly a warm supporter of the Englishman and appears to have been motivated by his instincts. To avoid any responsibility, he would emphatically resist endorsing the English doctor's planned treatment, the chancellor told Lucius on 7 June 1887, but if he found himself in Frederick William's position, he would first try everything else and would undergo surgery only "under the most extreme circumstances." The crown princess was also afraid of the dangerous operation and clung to the hope that Frederick William's condition was not malignant after all. "I hope and trust and believe that there is no such danger at present," she wrote on 17 May, and reiterated two days later that she did not apprehend that the swelling was "of a cancerous kind." Delighted to be offered a ray of hope, Victoria immediately embraced Mackenzie's optimistic prognosis and informed her mother on 24 May that "we need not be anxious any more, and only most careful and conscientious to effect the best possible cure."[8]

As for Mackenzie, it cannot be determined whether or not he sincerely believed before November 1887 that he was capable of curing what he described as a nonmalignant swelling. He may have made an honest mistake and found himself confirmed in his error by Virchow's reassuring findings. Alternatively, his medical experience may well have led Mackenzie to decide that the crown prince's cancer simply could not be cured—neither through the high-risk external surgery urged by the German doctors nor through his own, largely placebo-like treatment. In this case, Mackenzie's ministrations in the course of the subsequent year were primarily a psychological exercise in palliative care. As such, they were not without merit. Those to whom it mattered most—Frederick William and Victoria—drew much solace from Mackenzie's care and considered themselves in very good hands. Mackenzie's pleasant manner and his optimism, ill-founded though it was, sustained them for several months. The Englishman's many public detractors and personal enemies, however, reached a different and much harsher conclusion. For them, he was a dishonest, self-promoting charlatan on the take, who spun along his pitiful patient until it was too late, while extracting exorbitant fees, securing a knighthood for himself, and persistently leaking intimate details to the press to raise his own profile. Some of the invective hurled against Mackenzie was obviously spiteful and fabricated, but not all the criticism was devoid of justification.

By proposing that a tissue sample be examined microscopically, Mackenzie had wrong-footed Gerhardt and Bergmann. Holstein could hardly believe that "the other asses" had not thought of this before, and called this omission a "sad reflection on the Berlin doctors." Although they accused Mackenzie of having removed nothing but a minute sample of surface tissue and criticised his excessive reliance on Virchow's cautiously phrased findings, the German doctors were grudgingly beginning to leave the field to the confident Englishman. When meeting his colleagues on 25 May 1887, Mackenzie insisted categorically that the growth in Frederick William's throat was benign and proposed treating it through the mouth rather than by external surgery. "If the prince were to come to my clinic in London like any other mortal," he told the Prussian justice minister Friedberg two days later, "he would be entirely cured within four to six weeks."[9]

Frederick William was more than willing to do this. In Britain he could combine his medical treatment with his long-planned attendance at the celebrations of Queen Victoria's Golden Jubilee on 21 June 1887. The trip encountered some resistance, though. Wegner was worried that the swelling in the crown prince's throat might suddenly threaten suffocation. Prince William was eager to attend the jubilee in his father's stead, and there was a general reluctance to see the crown prince out of the country in view of the emperor's frailty. William I, however, was not minded to deny his son's wish and resisted various attempts to persuade him to withhold his permission. Mackenzie's ascendancy was assured after he removed two further tissue samples on 8 June 1887. Virchow again reported that there were no signs of malignancy and even sounded a decidedly optimistic note about the nature of the disease. Mackenzie and Frederick William agreed that Virchow's findings should be published to reassure the worried public. On 13 June 1887, the crown prince left for Britain. He would not see his father again.[10]

The events surrounding Frederick William's intention to travel to London in June 1887 threw some of the key features of his life into sharp relief. A fifty-six-year-old grandfather suffering from a serious illness, the crown prince still required his father's permission to attend the clinic of his chosen doctor. Even though the emperor granted his son's request, his reaction to Frederick William's plight was and remained strangely detached. Bismarck called on the emperor immediately after he realised that a life-threatening operation on the crown prince was planned and urged him to receive the doctors the following morning before deciding whether to allow the operation to go ahead. William reportedly replied that this would be inconvenient as he was planning to inspect troops in Potsdam. Only when Bismarck insisted did the emperor reluctantly agree to be briefed, but the doctors would have to come early so that the inspection would not be compromised. When approving Frederick William's request to travel, the emperor remarked that this was perhaps his son's final wish. Witnesses were struck that he made this observation without showing any deeper emotion. In September 1887, the emperor received Frederick William's chamberlain, who had just returned from Britain, but William showed little interest in the medical reports and complained instead about the high costs of his son's stay. "This gives you an idea," Holstein commented wryly in his diary, "how crowned fathers and their heirs may have dealt with each other during the middle ages."[11]

The emperor's lack of feeling also contributed to an exacerbation of the disagreeable role played by Frederick William's eldest son, whose relationship with his parents had long been troubled and mutually hurtful. Once the news of the crown prince's serious illness had spread, unscrupulous careerists everywhere suddenly turned to the young prince who might soon be on the throne. Prince William responded to such opportunistic adulation by greedily assuming the role of the coming man. He had few qualms about elbowing his father aside. Without consulting his parents, he asked the old monarch to appoint him—rather than the ailing crown prince—as the emperor's official representative at the Jubilee celebrations. The emperor obliged without seeking his son's opinion and Prince William immediately communicated his appointment to the British court. Frederick William was terribly upset about this attempt to cut him out of a grand dynastic event that was close to his heart. He wrote to Queen Victoria on 30 May 1887, confirming his intention to attend the celebrations and requesting that she continue to consider him the official representative. The queen was only too happy to rap the knuckles of her insolent grandson, who ended up apoplectic with anger at being relegated to a minor role during the festivities.[12]

The Jubilee celebrations witnessed Frederick William's last great public performance in the heroic role of Our Fritz. As the grand procession marking Queen Victoria's fiftieth anniversary on the throne wound its way through the streets of London on 21 June 1887, the crown prince outshone almost every other visiting dignitary. "That the English people scarcely regard him as a foreigner was proved by the loud acclamations of welcome that greeted him from the crowd along Constitution-Hill," London's *Daily News* observed. "His tall figure looked almost gigantic in the white uniform of a Cuirassier of the Guard with the Imperial crest on his helmet, and he sat with the firm ease of a born cavalry soldier." A German tourist described his excitement as the group of princes approached the window from which he was watching the procession: "It did not require a long search to identify the man whom we were more eager to see than the queen with all her splendour. On a white horse, in a white cuirassier uniform . . . , rode the German crown prince. . . . 'Lohengrin,' shouted Mrs. Semon. 'Lohengrin,' the other women joined in, enthralled by admiration and enthusiasm." Felix Semon, an eminent British laryngologist of German-Jewish origin, who had followed the story of the crown prince's illness with close interest, could not share in the joy of the people standing next to him. Frederick William's sallow complexion and the strained rigidity of his bearing caused him grave concerns. "This is not Lohengrin," he muttered, "this is the Commendatore from Don Giovanni."[13]

Semon's reference to the stony figure of death from Mozart's opera stood in sharp contrast to Mackenzie's well-publicised optimism. He examined the crown prince as soon as he arrived in London on

14 June 1887, and pronounced a reassuring verdict. The following day, the *Pall Mall Gazette* echoed Mackenzie's view in a suspiciously well-informed article. Then Frederick William's medical treatment began: astringent powders and ferric chloride were applied to Frederick William's larynx. Further tissue samples were removed and galvanocautery was used once again. Although none of these measures was innovative or sophisticated, Mackenzie's comments on his patient's progress remained consistently sanguine. The crown prince's condition was definitely not malignant, Mackenzie wrote to the editor of a German journal on 8 July. The following day, he shook Frederick William's hand and warmly congratulated him on the return of his voice. A week later, the doctor arranged for Frederick William to pay his only visit to Mackenzie's London Throat Hospital. The crown prince proved a good sport and wove his affable magic as of old. He had kind words for a sick little girl, chatted sympathetically with the outpatients, and "expressed himself greatly pleased with all he saw." On 8 August 1887, Mackenzie assured the crown princess that he had never been more hopeful about Frederick William's prospects than now. The throat specialist's confidence was obviously infectious and his grateful patient, who was feeling better at the time, asked Queen Victoria to reward Mackenzie with a knighthood. Convinced that the doctor had saved her son-in-law's life, the queen decided to ignore her prime minister's warning that it was still early days. On 8 September 1887, Mackenzie was knighted.[14]

When set against the background of the queen's thankfulness that "beloved Fritz" should have "recovered his dear health so much," Dr. Wilhelm Landgraf's reports make for very sombre reading. Mackenzie had been reluctant to accept the presence of Professor Gerhardt's assistant in Britain and did his best to keep him away from the patient and undermine him in a variety of underhand ways. In spite of this, Landgraf doggedly stuck to his orders. He examined Frederick William seven times between 17 June and 23 August 1887, openly shared his concerns with Mackenzie, and sent detailed reports to Berlin. Unlike Mackenzie, Landgraf recorded a steady worsening of Frederick William's condition. The removed tissue quickly regrew and the disease was spreading. Landgraf's careful observations fuelled the growing hostility to Mackenzie amongst the German medical establishment and eventually the wider public. Since he could not match Mackenzie's supple persuasiveness and allegedly annoyed Frederick William with his clumsiness, however, the German doctor had no impact on the crown prince's treatment and eventually returned to Berlin on 3 September 1887.[15]

By then the crown prince had already embarked on his increasingly desperate flight from the disease. Frederick William's tendency toward frequent and escapist travel had attracted comment for some time. Stosch deplored as early as February 1880 that the crown prince "was touring round the world" instead of participating in events, and this pattern became even more pronounced in the course of the 1880s. Now a combination of fearful restlessness and Mackenzie's pseudomedical recommendations concerning the healing qualities of this or that climate turned Frederick William into a wretched knight errant in search of a cure. Having travelled from Berlin to London on 13 June 1887, he moved to the mild sea air of the Isle of Wight on 28 June. In line with Mackenzie's belief in the efficacy of a bracing mountain climate, Frederick William then spent the time between 9 and 29 August in Braemar in the Scottish Highlands. When the weather there turned autumnal, Mackenzie recommended relocating to the Tyrolean Alps. On 3 September, the crown prince left London and reached the resort of Toblach four days later. Unable to stand the cold at 1,200 metres above sea level for more than a few weeks, Frederick William moved on to Venice, where he arrived on 6 October 1887. A week later, he travelled to Baveno on the Lago Maggiore. Buoyed by the mild weather, the beautiful gardens, and Mackenzie's reassuring comment that "the Crown Prince's throat [was] in a very satisfactory state," Frederick William and Victoria decided to remain there for several weeks. When the crown prince finally took up residence in the Villa Zirio in San Remo on 3 November 1887, he had reached the farthest point of his pilgrimage.[16]

The arrival at San Remo on the Italian Riviera marked the end of more than one road. Within days it became clear that Mackenzie's policy of unwavering optimism was no longer sustainable. Even as late as 30 October 1887 he had claimed that there was "little to indicate, either to the illustrious sufferer himself or to others, that a change for the worse had occurred." On 5 November, however, Mackenzie responded to an urgent call from his assistant Mark Hovell and rushed to San Remo to examine the crown prince. He diagnosed the presence of a large growth with a "distinctly malignant look" and broke the dreaded news to his patient. Suddenly, Mackenzie was keen to share responsibility and requested the involvement of other doctors. The Viennese laryngologist Leopold von Schrötter and his colleague Dr. Hermann Krause from Berlin were summoned and confirmed the cancer diagnosis. Because of the advanced stage of the disease, now only the extremely risky removal of the entire larynx offered a faint hope of a cure. Frederick William received his doctors on 11 November. He stoically listened to their unanimous report and then ruled out the surgical option. If a further growth of the tumour were to threaten suffocation, however, he would agree to undergo a tracheotomy. The crown prince understood that he had received a death sentence. His diary entry for 11 November calmly summarizes the day's events and ends: "I will thus have to put my house in order."[17]

The following weeks brought occasional improvements in the crown prince's well-being, which encouraged Mackenzie to backtrack tantalizingly from his cancer diagnosis. An article in the *British Medical Journal* of 7 January 1888 stated that he considered the crown prince's symptoms compatible "with the more severe form of chronic laryngitis" and, ten days later, Mackenzie told Queen Victoria that he "fully believed that there was nothing malignant" about Frederick William's disease. In spite of these astounding statements and the puzzling fact that the microscopic examination of expectorated tissue had still not yielded an unequivocal diagnosis, the crown prince's condition deteriorated relentlessly. This led to acrimonious bickering between Mackenzie and Victoria on the one hand and the surgeon Friedrich Bramann on the other. The latter, an assistant of Ernst von Bergmann's, had been despatched to San Remo by the emperor to be on hand in case the tracheotomy needed to be performed before Bergmann himself could be at the scene. In spite of Bramann's urgent warnings, Victoria and Mackenzie refused to summon Bergmann until the situation was so acute that Bramann had to act himself. The young surgeon operated on 9 February 1888 under the most trying circumstances. Considering it undignified for her husband to be placed on a table, Victoria insisted that the operation be performed on a bed and Mackenzie only abandoned his opposition to the use of chloroform at the very last moment. So immense was the strain on Bramann that he was reportedly carrying a revolver to kill himself if the operation had failed. In spite of all this, the procedure went smoothly: an incision was made into Frederick William's windpipe and a tube was inserted. The crown prince could now breathe much more easily, but what was left of his voice fell silent forever.[18]

The tracheotomy did not bring Frederick William even the temporary improvement normally expected from this procedure. He continued to feel weak, had no appetite, and could not sleep. He coughed up fresh blood and blood-streaked sputum, suffered from severe neuralgic pain, and had fever. Moreover, the atmosphere in the Villa Zirio was poisoned by the unseemly rows between the two medical factions. Bergmann, who arrived on 11 February, and Mackenzie could barely stand to be in the same room, let alone agree on a line of treatment. They fought over the shape of the tube and ignored each other's requests. Mackenzie tried to get rid of Bergmann as soon as the crown prince's surgical wound had healed and refused to accept that the professor's microscopic examinations had finally proved that this was a case of cancer. Only when the distinguished anatomist and oncologist Heinrich Wilhelm Waldeyer arrived in San Remo on 3 March 1888 and unequivocally confirmed the presence of cancer cells did Mackenzie concede the true nature of the crown prince's condition. On 6 March 1888, the doctors called a truce. After signing a written undertaking to recommend Frederick William's return to Germany in the spring or if his health deteriorated further, Mackenzie was again entrusted with the crown prince's treatment. In order to spare the patient's feelings, the doctors also agreed to treat Waldeyer's report as strictly confidential.[19]

In his account of Frederick William's illness, Bergmann emphasised with noticeable satisfaction that the attempt to keep Waldeyer's findings out of the press was actually successful. This was no small achievement since media interest in the ailing crown prince had become frantic. Unfettered by considerations of veracity, sensitivity, or compassion, the newspapers feasted on the unfolding tragedy of an ancient emperor and his doomed son apparently locked into a macabre race. Frederick William was "dreadfully annoyed by all the foolish articles about himself in the German newspapers," Victoria wrote to her mother from Baveno. "They are as tactless as they are impertinent and unfair."[20]

At San Remo things went from bad to worse. As soon as Frederick William and Victoria had moved into the Villa Zirio, the hotel opposite was crawling with reporters who even perched on the roof to observe the house. Some American papers allegedly sent female journalists whose charm might elicit exclusive information. No story seemed too banal or too outlandish. According to one paper, the arrival of a second shipment of German beer in January 1888 indicated that the crown prince's health was improving. Other papers carried the bizarre story that all of Frederick William's front teeth had been extracted to allow a better view of his larynx. The reports became noticeably more mawkish after the publication of the cancer diagnosis on 11 November 1887. Up until this point, the bulk of published opinion had taken its cue from Mackenzie's optimistic statements and had confidently expected the crown prince's speedy recovery. Now the mood changed markedly, and the callousness of the press as well as the obvious indiscretion of many of the people surrounding them became a constant source of upset to the crown princely couple: "The newspapers are filled with absolute lies and yet one does not know whether it be wise or advisable to contradict them," Victoria complained. "They are for the most part very spiteful innuendos."[21]

The bluntness with which the *Reichsanzeiger,* the official organ of the German government, announced on 12 November 1887 that the crown prince suffered from a "carcinomatous" affliction stunned even the doctors on whose confidential report the announcement was based. The German press reacted with anger against Mackenzie, who was now subjected to fierce and sometimes scurrilous attacks. The longer the rumour mill was grinding out stories, though, the more the general oscillation of hope and despair filling the newspaper columns acquired a familiar party-political pattern. The left-liberal weekly *Der Reichsfreund* illustrates this trend. On 7 January 1888, it attacked the conservative *Sonntagsfreund* for mentioning the crown prince only to call him fatally ill, while openly courting Prince William as the next emperor. *Der Reichsfreund* followed this up with a string of encouraging reports about the health of the "beloved man." It culminated in the claim that Professor Waldeyer had found no trace of cancer in Frederick William's expectorations. In return, conservative voices accused the liberal camp of downplaying the severity of Frederick William's condition because of their political investment in his reign. "The crown princess and her democratic following are spreading shameless lies about the crown prince's condition," Holstein observed in November 1887. "Their aim is to prevent that the crown prince be made to renounce the crown because of his incapacity." Prince William shared this analysis of what was happening to his father and tastelessly quipped that "they would even place his corpse on a horse, like El Cid at Valencia."[22]

The cruelty of William's comment epitomises the most disagreeable aspect of his behaviour throughout his father's illness. As soon as he became aware of the seriousness of the crown prince's condition, William showed a hard-nosed eagerness to position himself as the new monarch-in-waiting. His instinctive reaction to the cancer diagnosis of May 1887 had been to communicate it to the officer corps in order to convey to them a sense of his own increased importance. William's actions ahead of the Jubilee celebrations and during his short visit to San Remo in November 1887 also reflected this. Having obtained the emperor's permission, William travelled to the Villa Zirio on 9 November to ensure his father's correct treatment and gather reliable information. His peremptory attitude and his attempt to assert himself by citing the emperor's orders greatly upset both his parents. His son could barely wait for his death, Frederick William told his chamberlain on 10 November. Less than a fortnight later, the crown prince was accidentally handed a letter in which William mentioned that he had been appointed his grandfather's deputy. In view of William's previous behaviour and amid rumours that the ailing crown prince might be forced to renounce the throne, it is hardly surprising that Frederick William was beside himself when he learned about this fait accompli. He raged against being treated like a dead man. Even though Frederick William briefly considered travelling to Berlin to protest, he was quickly dissuaded from taking any such steps and accepted that sending a note of complaint to Bismarck was all that could be done.[23]

Frederick William's anger about his son's letter had been exacerbated because the news had struck him like a bolt from the blue. In an attempt to spare her husband any excessive excitement the crown princess had decided not to show him Bismarck's official notification of the appointment. That Victoria was screening Frederick William's correspondence confirmed Prince William's negative opinion of the situation in San Remo. He considered his father a noble but helpless victim, suffering at the hands of his reviled mother who abused her dominance to serve her own interests as well as those of her British homeland. After William had vented his anger about the Jubilee affair in a conversation with Radolinski in July 1887, the chamberlain noted how "terribly he hated" his mother. Subsequent developments had only served to aggravate these feelings. After the deputyship incident, the prince took the extraordinary step of formally warning the German foreign office against sending any confidential information to the crown prince. Since his mother was opening all the letters, everything would automatically be betrayed to Britain. By February 1888, Holstein observed, there was nothing but "wild hatred" between Prince William and the crown princess.[24]

The painful relationship between mother and son was certainly made worse by deep-seated personal factors, but William's loathing of his mother was part of a wider phenomenon. The events since Mackenzie's arrival had caused a shrill intensification of the dislike of Victoria that had long since existed amongst court circles and many members of the political class. Positioned at the centre of his web of informants, Holstein recorded every rumour, story, and outburst with grim satisfaction: the crown princess had reportedly tried hard to get her husband to make a will in line with her specific wishes; Bismarck observed that Victoria yearned to be free of Frederick William; the crown princess despised her husband and was cheerfully anticipating never having to return to Germany. In September, Holstein included a long letter from Toblach in his diary. The sender—most probably the chamberlain Moritz von Lyncker— provided a memorably bilious account of Victoria in which he accused her of indifference, cruelty, selfishness, frivolity, and adultery: "I cannot describe how this woman is getting on my nerves," he wrote. "I cannot bear the permanent smile on her face any longer; this woman has smiled every bit of sanity out of her house." In November 1887, Emil von Albedyll, the chief of the emperor's military cabinet, accused the crown princess of lying about her husband's health. She was merely keeping her "foot in the stirrup" so that she could actually govern herself. Bismarck read Victoria's intentions differently, but was equally damning. She did not have the ambition to be a ruler, he told Lucius in March 1888, "she was mainly selfish and pleasure-seeking. The position of a widowed empress would be most convenient to her."[25]

Though much of this invective against the crown princess was born of spite, opportunism, and Anglophobia, Victoria had given her enemies much to work with. Her unquestioning belief in Mackenzie's superiority and her adoption of a public pose of rigidly cheerful optimism alienated many and was increasingly unbelievable. Her decisions to travel to Toblach, Venice, and Baveno—where she spent considerable time walking in the mountains, shopping for antiques, and sightseeing, while frequently leaving her exhausted husband behind—were certainly ill-judged. These and other oddities should, however, be viewed in the context of her very real desperation at seeing her husband threatened with a lingering death and all her life's hopes dashed. Denial, bewilderment, and the urge to experience a kind of normality for the last time may all have played a role. Most importantly, however, she appears to have been a devoted carer for her sick husband when it really mattered. Ernst von Bergmann, who had little reason to flatter Victoria, wrote to his wife to praise the crown princess's tenderness, ceaseless activity, and self-denial: "This is the expression of the innermost heart," he concluded. As he had done for three decades, Frederick William felt nothing but deep and loving gratitude to his wife: "My beloved Vicky has cared for me with incomparable courage and the greatest perseverance," he wrote to Queen Victoria on 29 December 1887. "I have no words to express how much I admire her stance, the greatness of her soul and how infinitely grateful I am that she never wavered for a moment but always courageously kept her head."[26]

The Left-Liberals and Empress Victoria during the Ninety-nine Days

On 3 June 1887, Emperor William boarded the sloop *Pommerania* to inspect the naval squadron anchoring in Kiel Harbour. Determined to remain visible to his sailors, the ninety-year-old trooper braved the cold wind and refused to take shelter in the cabin. He never fully recovered from the severe cold he caught that day and by the autumn, his end seemed near. The emperor "might be found dead in his bed any morning," Emil von Albedyll observed in mid-November and suggested that measures ought to be put in place to prepare for the inevitable. Unwilling to countenance the idea of a dying emperor "sitting in Italy with his neck slit open," Albedyll urged that power should pass from the emperor straight into the hands of Prince William. The chief of the military cabinet was not alone in advocating that Frederick William be excluded from the succession, but Bismarck would not hear of it. Should the old emperor be incapacitated, Prince William would deputise for him, but this delegated authority would cease at the very moment of the old emperor's death. There could be no vacuum, Bismarck insisted in February 1888: "The crown slips through the keyhole of the sick room. In the meantime the ministry continues with governmental business until it receives further orders from the sovereign." This is precisely what would happen.[27]

On 7 March, Prince William returned from his second visit to San Remo to find his grandfather on his deathbed. At 8:30 a.m. on 9 March 1888, three weeks before his ninety-first birthday, William I peacefully passed away. Two hours later, a telegram from Berlin arrived at the Villa Zirio. The recipient did not need to open the envelope to learn its content: it was addressed to "His Majesty the German Emperor and King Frederick William." "Today my beloved father closed his eyes forever," the new emperor later wrote in his diary. "Thus I ascend the throne of my fathers and that of the German emperors. May God help me to fulfil my duties conscientiously and for the good of the narrower and wider fatherland." At midday Bismarck addressed a special session of the Reichstag. In hushed silence, the deputies listened to the official notification of Emperor William's death. "As a result of this event," the chancellor declared, "the Prussian crown and, according to Article Eleven of the Reich constitution, the imperial title have passed to His Majesty Frederick III, king of Prussia." Having first invested his wife with the Order of the Black Eagle and then appointed Mackenzie his physician-in-ordinary, the new emperor left San Remo on the morning of 10 March. At 6:30 p.m. on 11 March, Bismarck and the other ministers boarded the emperor's special train at Leipzig Station to meet their new sovereign. Five hours later, Frederick III arrived at Charlottenburg Palace, a few miles outside Berlin. A crowd of several thousand well-wishers had braved a blizzard and waited late into the night to welcome him.[28]

The warmth of the public reaction on Frederick's return to Germany remained undiminished throughout the emperor's short reign. Every day, people gathered outside the palace gates, bringing flowers and eagerly awaiting news from within. On the few occasions when the emperor was well enough to travel to the capital, the public response was overwhelming. "I have seen every great public ceremony in Berlin during the last thirty years," the correspondent of the London *Standard* reported after Frederick had visited his mother on Good Friday, "but I have never seen such a crowd of human beings as had assembled today to witness the emperor drive back to Charlottenburg. . . . The hurrahs and 'hochs' of the multitude were endless, and the general enthusiasm surpassed description." Within minutes, all the florists were sold out and the path of the imperial carriage was strewn with flowers. When Frederick relocated from Charlottenburg to Potsdam aboard the steam yacht *Alexandra* two months later, the water's edge was lined with people waving flags, throwing flowers, and cheering him. Initially, the German press also spoke with one voice of patriotic piety. The left-liberal *Freisinnige Zeitung* welcomed the "darling of the people" and the ultraconservative *Neue Preussische Zeitung* observed that "every child in Germany joyfully babble[d]" Frederick's name.[29]

It did not take long, however, until the reporting on the new monarch acquired the bitter taste of party strife. In April 1888, the *Grenzboten*, an influential rightwing weekly, launched a furious attack against the left-liberals and their press. It was "unheard of for a party to claim a regent as its own" and the Freisinn Party ought to be ashamed of the "cynical and tasteless manner" in which "they were seeking to identify the new emperor and empress with their own beliefs." The day would come, the *Grenzboten* warned on 12 April 1888, when the "loyal mask will be torn off the faces of the progressive agitators by people who carry their love for the monarchy in their hearts and not on their tongues." The conservative *Neue Preussische Zeitung* shared this view and explained that "this new leftist loyalty to the crown [was] a ploy in the hope of winning support to develop a parliamentary system."[30]

Everything, so it appeared, was now grist to the left-liberals' mill. On 11 March, the *Freisinnige Zeitung* lauded Frederick for his decision not to impose a national protocol for the mourning of his father since this represented a break with the tradition of the state's arrogant nannying of its citizens. The *Vossische Zeitung* explained on 12 March that the emperor had called himself after Frederick the Great to demonstrate his intention to be "a patron of liberty" and a "protector of the people's weal." At the end of the month, the *Reichsfreund* trawled the past decade for progressive statements by the new emperor. Beginning with the crown prince's stance against anti-Semitism in 1878 and ending with his rejection of national arrogance in 1885, it proudly listed a total of nine separate instances where he had delighted the left-liberals and annoyed the conservatives. Ten weeks later, the *Reichsfreund* reminded its readers of the "consoling and liberating" speech the crown prince had given at Danzig twenty-five years before and hailed the emperor as "the most loyal protector and preserver of the people's constitutional rights."[31]

Nothing highlighted the parties' different responses to the succession more clearly, though, than their different interpretations of the new emperor's proclamations. The documents "To My People" and "To the Imperial Chancellor" were published on 12 March 1888, but had not changed since being crafted in the summer of 1885. Based on drafts by Roggenbach, Stosch, and Friedberg, these texts offered a high-sounding but bland commitment to peace, tolerance, piety, and constitutional government. Bismarck found the proclamations entirely unobjectionable, but their political meaning turned out to be very much in the eye of the beholder. The liberal press celebrated the pronouncements as evidence of the emperor's commitment to radical change. "This is the language of a prince who has shed the traditions of the old police state," the *Vossische Zeitung* rejoiced. The *Berliner Zeitung* welcomed this "strictly liberal statement" and pointed to its allegedly pro-parliament and anti-Bismarckian edge. According to the *Frankfurter Zeitung,* the proclamation encouraged "the great mass of the free-thinking bourgeoisie who have nailed their colours to the mast of legitimate progress." In his assessment of Frederick's "world historical proclamations," Arnold Perls, the left-liberal editor of the *Berliner Zeitung,* claimed that "no prince could have been expected to speak out more emphatically for liberty and for the rights of the people alongside the rights of the crown."[32]

It is hard to believe that the papers supporting the Kartell of National Liberals and Conservatives were responding to the same proclamations. The *National-Zeitung* saw no indication "of a break with the domestic policy pursued to date," and the *Neue Preussische Zeitung* welcomed the "unshakable commitment to the foundations on which the Prussian state has rested securely hitherto." According to the *Konservative Korrespondenz,* the new regime would remain firmly grounded on "the fear of God, faithful duty and strong authoritarian government."[33]

The state of the emperor's health soon emerged as another political battleground. Many observers had been pleasantly surprised by Frederick's appearance when he returned to Berlin. Initially, he was certainly invigorated by his new task. There were also periods of remission. The emperor's admirable self-discipline, Victoria's stubborn optimism, and Mackenzie's silver-tongued equivocation could not hide the fact, though, that Frederick was a dying man. Too fragile to venture out into the cold, he had to watch his father's funeral procession on 16 March 1888 through a palace window. His nights were broken by coughing. Swallowing became increasingly difficult. He was often feverish and his strength was ebbing away. Crown

Prince William eventually took on many routine items requiring monarchical approval, but even this left the emperor with more business than he could handle. Frederick made a heroic effort to receive ministers and other visitors, deal with paperwork, and show himself to the public, but the situation was hopeless. "The newspaper reports about the despatch of several hours of business are pure nonsense," Stosch wrote to a friend after a visit to Charlottenburg. "The emperor falls asleep when a report lasts for more than a few minutes, is often too weak to write and must then try to communicate through facial expressions and signs. It breaks your heart."[34]

As Stosch suggested, a number of liberal papers conveyed a very different impression. On 16 March, the *Berliner Zeitung* rejected the worrying account of the emperor's health recently given in a national liberal paper. "There is currently no talk of any serious symptom of disquiet," the left-liberal daily insisted and observed that dark rumours could "only hail from other quarters than the medical authorities." The *Reichsfreund* assured its readers that it was full of "firm, confident hope that he [would] recover completely" and be restored to the German nation, "whose pride and hope he is, for many blessed years of health and strength." Ten days before Frederick's death, the *Vossische Zeitung* still maintained that all the stories about a deterioration of his health were without foundation and that the emperor's throat showed no more signs of malignancy. An article in Berlin's democratic *Volk-Zeitung* clearly demonstrates the party-political dimension of the issue. Even savage tribes "would look askance at the unspeakable emotional callousness of subjecting a seriously but not hopelessly ill man to a daily certification of the inevitable proximity of his death," the paper argued. The Kartell newspapers, however, were doing this without so much as blinking.[35]

Comments like this triggered a livid reaction from the Kartell press. The *Grenzboten* was beside itself about these "insolent and deceitful 'Court Jacobins,'" and condemned the travesty of "democrats donning the garb of loyalty." Some of this anger resulted from the widespread belief that a left-liberal conspiracy was pulling the wires inside Charlottenburg Palace. Fuelled by Frederick's decision to recommend Virchow, Schrader, and Forckenbeck for decorations, the rumour mill kept on turning. On 22 March 1888, Bismarck told his ministerial colleagues that Mrs. Schrader, Baroness Stockmar, and Mrs. von Helmholtz were scurrying out of the room when he called on the empress the previous day. Since all of these ladies had more or less impeccable left-liberal credentials, it seemed clear that a clandestine web had been spun. General Alfred von Waldersee noted with shocked consternation that these forces had made "themselves felt so quickly and so thoroughly." On 8 April 1888, Bismarck's wife, Johanna, expressed her fears about a future "ministry Forckenbeck-Schrader-Virchow" and Crown Prince William claimed that nothing but mischief was coming out of Charlottenburg. At the end of May 1888, he informed the Grand Duke of Baden that he had identified the rotten apple. "The spring driving everything is the Freisinn deputy Schrader, whom Mama receives every now and then and who also remains constantly in touch with her through his wife—an acquaintance of Mama's."[36]

In 1935 the historian Gisbert Beyerhaus published an essay on the role of the left-liberals during Frederick's short reign. Using language no less dramatic than that employed by the liberals' enemies in 1888, he warned against underestimating the Freisinn Party's fighting spirit and called the ninety-nine days "German liberalism's last decisive battle for political power." The liberals aimed at nothing less than overthrowing or at least fatally undermining Bismarck, Beyerhaus claimed, and they were not content to restrict themselves to passive resistance or a few pinpricks. This interpretation was largely based on the recent publication of Ludwig Bamberger's diaries, which revealed that throughout the latter part of Frederick's reign, the prominent Freisinn deputy had secretly acted as Empress Victoria's adviser. This cooperation certainly did not justify Beyerhaus's troubling belief in a fully fledged Jewish-Masonic conspiracy which "subterraneously" connected 1888 with Bismarck's fall in 1890. It is true, however, that in response to the political situation after Emperor William's death, the left-liberals did engage in a certain amount of scheming and networking.[37]

At the end of March 1888, Henriette Schrader, Bogumilla von Stockmar, and Anna von Helmholtz set up a committee to organise an address directed at the empress. Signed by several thousand "liberal women," this declaration was meant to be a formal expression of their devotion to Victoria and a counterweight to the increasingly hostile Kartell press. "It is terrible here in Berlin," Henriette Schrader wrote to her sister on 20 March. "There is a party which even agitates against the emperor. . . . Emperor William is regarded as a saint and commemorations upon commemorations are organized with great ostentation. The current emperor Frederick III is entirely ignored by many." Even though the address initiative was strictly in female hands and was ostensibly nonpolitical, leading left-liberals kept an eye on its progress. The text of the address was far too formal, Karl Schrader wrote to Bamberger on 26 March 1888, but the main thing was that it was done and that it attracted a sufficient number of signatures. Schrader welcomed the initiative because of his concerns that the momentum of the accession might fade away again: "It will be the task of our party to communicate the spirit of the imperial proclamations to the wider population without giving up on any of our views." This was hardly the language of dagger-wielding conspirators. The emperor's condition had clearly dashed the left-liberals' political hopes for the short term. In the past, her husband had always told her how the Freisinn Party would one day play a crucial role in persuading the new emperor gradually to emancipate himself from Bismarck, Henriette Schrader wrote to her sister on 30 March 1888, "but now they are thinking of the sick man; this paralyzes everything."[38]

An assessment of Bamberger's role as Victoria's adviser yields a similarly mixed result. There was some networking, undisguised loathing of the "reptiles" of the Kartell press, and hostility to ultra-conservatives such as the Prussian minister Robert von Puttkamer, but the reach of these activities remained limited and the tone of Bamberger's guidance was surprisingly moderate. The link between Bamberger and Charlottenburg Palace was established on 31 March 1888 when he attended a dinner party for Mackenzie organised by Anna von Helmholtz at Victoria's behest. A few days later, Bamberger invited the Englishman to dine at his house. When Empress Victoria learned that the deputy was concerned about the imperial couple's relationship with the press, she set up a line of communication. On 26 April, her confidante Bogumilla von Stockmar called on Bamberger, who happened to live close to the Stockmar residence. This visit marked the beginning of a busy exchange of letters and secret messages between Bogumilla, "the neighbour," and the "friend" in the palace.[39]

On the one hand, Victoria used the connection to unburden herself by writing long, passionate letters, which she knew would reach a discreet, sympathetic, and intelligent reader. She drew comfort from Bamberger's sensitive responses, which she regarded as rare acts of chivalry. On the other hand, the deputy provided sensible advice. On 30 April, he regretted the vile attacks against the imperial couple, but insisted that "big issues" could not be tackled at the moment. There was only one duty now: "to protect the calm of every breath on the sickbed." Since there was only one "all-powerful enemy: the disease," he repeated a fortnight later, the emperor had to be spared fierce conflicts. Any attempt to effect significant change—such as a change of the ministry—was unrealistic.[40]

Bamberger did, however, have a hand in forcing the resignation of the liberals' bête noire, Robert von Puttkamer. The Prussian parliament had recently censured the conservative minister for governmental gerrymandering and had retrospectively cancelled the election of his younger brother. In line with Bamberger's recommendations, the emperor sent the minister a pointed reminder of the importance of free elections. When he attempted to justify himself and received an ungracious reply from the emperor, Puttkamer had no option but to resign. Bamberger's delight was just as great as the outrage of conservatives such as Crown Prince William and General Waldersee. On 8 June, the "neighbour" smugly noted in his diary that the emperor had acted precisely as he had suggested.[41]

It was, of course, perfectly clear to Bamberger that the action against Puttkamer had been taken by Victoria and not by the dying emperor. The empress enjoyed damaging her enemies, Bismarck announced to his colleagues on 7 June 1888, and suspected that Karl Schrader had drafted the letters that had brought down the minister. "Thus Her Majesty has tidied everything up," was Lucius's reaction when he saw the official announcement of Puttkamer's resignation. This appraisal of Victoria's role was just one example of the public and personal antipathy against the empress. For decades, Victoria had been accused of dangerous political views, dominating her husband and foreign loyalties. As stories from Toblach, Baveno, and San Remo spread, the image of Victoria as a selfish harpy was painted in increasingly lurid colours. Amid the feverish atmosphere of Frederick's unreal reign, some of Victoria's critics lost all their inhibitions. The couple were mocked as "Frederick the Brit" and his wife, Mrs. "Ma-kennt-se"—the latter being both Berlinese for "one knows her" and a pun on the English doctor's name. Pictures of Victoria and Mackenzie were circulating which labelled them as "regicides." She was accused of adultery and of spending vast sums on English workmen decorating the palace. "The emperor is internally and externally a broken man," Stosch wrote to Normann on 17 March 1888, "and his wife is a fury." Holstein noted on 15 May 1888 that the empress was now "reaping what she had sowed with her de-monstrative scorn for everything German."[42]

For some observers, the combination of Victoria's strongly held views and her husband's weakness defined Frederick's reign. Walder-see believed that "it would be a terrible misfortune if we now had a healthy Emperor Frederick. Led by his wife, he has all it takes to derail the German Reich." Even the shrewd diarist Baroness Spitzem-berg deplored the damage done to Frederick's reputation by his wife's actions. Victoria had torn down Frederick's "glorious and saintly halo" by dragging the dying man into the dirt, she wrote in June 1888. "How could she, if she loved him, have put him into situ-ations like during the Battenberg question and now in the Puttkamer affair?"[43]

It is not surprising that Spitzemberg classed the Battenberg issue as a cardinal sin. Nothing Victoria did as empress caused more harm to her reputation than her decision to reengage actively with her old project of marrying her daughter Viktoria to Prince Alexander von Battenberg. The sound of warning bells had already been deafening in 1886, when Duke Ernest of Coburg, Prince Albert's older brother, anonymously published the pamphlet "Co-Regents and Foreign Hands in Germany." Peppered with a fair sprinkling of private infor-mation, the duke's booklet offered an Anglophobe attack against a baneful web of intrigue that was damaging Germany and allegedly spun by female members of the British royal family. The author claimed that some German parties were still banking on English in-fluences that would one day lever them into power, and he called upon the nation to rise up against these machinations.[44]

Even though Bamberger sent Victoria a copy of the tract in April 1888, the empress was not swayed by such alarming symptoms of the political mood. Her almost obsessive commitment to this increasingly bizarre marriage quest exceeded all bounds of reasonableness. She therefore had to bear a fair share of the responsibility for the aggres-sive reaction she encountered in 1888. In order to understand why the Battenberg issue triggered such an enormous amount of heat and fury—involving a veritable press war, party-political invective, diplo-matic complications with two great powers, and the threat of resigna-tion from the chancellor—it is necessary briefly to consider the earlier stages of this affair.[45]

Alexander von Battenberg was a man blessed with panache, charm, and dashing good looks. In spite of his parents' morganatic marriage, which somewhat tarnished his aristocratic status, he had excellent links to both Tsar Alexander II and Queen Victoria, whose daughter Alice had married his uncle. In 1879 the tsar installed the twenty-one-year-old officer as prince of the new state of Bulgaria. Instead of acting like a Russian puppet, though, Alexander went native and rebelled against the country's satellite status. Confronted with Russia's open hostility, he developed an understandable interest in consolidating his position by means of a dynastic link. Luckily for him, three Victorias warmly reciprocated his matchmaking intentions: Queen Victoria, Crown Princess Victoria, and her second daughter, the nubile Princess Viktoria—known as Moretta.[46]

During his visit to Balmoral in 1879, "Sandro" had charmed the queen, who also appreciated that a union between him and Moretta would serve British interests by containing Russia's ambitions in the Balkans. Moretta's motives were less complex: she was seventeen years old and madly in love. Her mother occupied a remarkable middle position. On the one hand, she was infatuated with Sandro. In a letter to Bamberger, she described him as "a hero, also a martyr, a brave, able, excellent man, the very example of a son and brother—noble, chivalrous, gifted and sensitive. At the same time beautiful and attractive." More than one observer believed that Moretta was not the only one who had fallen in love with Sandro. On the other hand, the crown princess also welcomed the foreign political dimension of the marriage. In 1883 she advocated "tearing Bulgaria out of the Russians' claws" and hoped to "increase German influence there in conjunction with Britain, Austria and Italy."[47]

Few things could be more abhorrent to Bismarck than Sandro and Moretta's romance with its implied risk of a formal dynastic link with Alexander's Bulgaria. Sandro was not only vociferously championed by the three Victorias; as an enemy of Russia, he had also become the darling of the German left-liberals. Moreover, the chancellor's foreign policy pivoted on the notion of Germany's complete lack of interest in the Balkans. Since he had worked hard to unite Russia, Austria, and Germany in the Three Emperors' Alliance of 1881, he was determined to avoid any unnecessary aggravation of the tsar. Alexander pursued his courtship in defiance of Bismarck's wishes and from the spring of 1883 onward, he and Moretta considered themselves informally engaged. As efforts at firming up this arrangement were being made behind the scenes, opposition to the Battenberg marriage was forming. A powerful faction within the

Prussian royal family opposed the marriage on grounds of dynastic propriety. The emperor, his wife, their daughter Louise, and their grandsons William and Henry regarded the morganatic Battenbergs as of insufficient rank and considered Alexander a dubious, debt-ridden womaniser. Crown Prince Frederick William was caught between a rock and a hard place. For several years, he vacillated between supporting his wife in her passionate quest to make this marriage happen and obedience to his father, whose views on the Battenbergs' inferiority he shared.

Sandro and Moretta met again in the spring of 1884 and may even have exchanged rings. In the teeth of growing resistance, the crown princess worked feverishly to close the deal. When Alexander von Battenberg visited Berlin in May 1884, the battle lines were drawn. Emperor William and Bismarck resorted to more or less direct threats against the prince. Frederick William, however, ignored his father's opposition as well as his own misgivings and treated Sandro with conspicuous warmth. "The crown princess has once again changed his mind," Holstein observed on 12 May 1884. Undeterred by the emperor's implacable hostility and Alexander's forced abdication in 1886, Victoria doggedly persisted in her efforts to broker the match. She assured her husband in September 1886 that Sandro would be a real support and a faithful son to him and an example to William and Henry. Since nothing could be done as long as Emperor William forbade the marriage, though, the crown prince eventually persuaded his wife to put the matter on ice until the succession.[48]

When the time finally arrived, Victoria knew that she had to move fast. Within days of Emperor William's death, Sandro received a letter from the new empress informing him that his marriage to Moretta would soon be arranged. The ex-prince of Bulgaria, who was now eking out a fairly penniless existence in Darmstadt and was happily falling in love with an opera singer, reacted with some trepidation. Fully aware of the fragility of the new regime as well as of how much Bismarck and the new crown prince hated him, he tried his best to withdraw. He even managed to persuade Queen Victoria to urge her daughter not to push this issue any further. The empress would not relent, though, and soon Berlin was abuzz with rumours. "Suddenly the Battenberger is to receive a senior military command. A huge slap in the face of the tsar," Herbert von Bismarck wrote to his brother on 28 March 1888. Three days later, a telegram was indeed sent to Sandro summoning him to see the emperor on 2 April. Frederick informed Bismarck during a meeting on 31 March that Prince Alexander was coming to receive a senior commission and be decorated with the order Pour le Mérite. These measures were preparatory to further steps. When Bismarck insisted that this would seriously damage Russo-German relations and force him to resign, the emperor agreed to cancel Sandro's invitation. If Holstein's account is to be believed, this change of heart triggered a stormy confrontation between Victoria and Frederick. She reportedly accused her husband of callously sacrificing their daughter's happiness, whereupon a distraught and breathless Frederick ordered her out of the room. The telegram postponing Sandro's trip was despatched, but Holstein did not think that this would be the end of the matter: "The empress will try everything to achieve this marriage."[49]

Holstein was right. The events of 31 March marked the beginning rather than the end of the public outcry caused by the Battenberg question. Within days, newspapers all over Germany were up in arms. Some attacked a dangerous British-Freisinn clique allegedly operating at the highest level and bent on damaging Germany's vital interests by forcing out the chancellor and destroying Russo-German relations. Others furiously defended the imperial couple against their vile detractors. Contrary to appearances, however, the drama of the *Kanzlerkrise* (Chancellor Crisis) was stage managed by Bismarck—the putative victim of the supposed conspiracy—and was not the result of dark forces bent on his destruction. Victoria's relative passivity during the crisis did not mean, however, that she had abandoned Sandro to the arms of his soprano. As late as 4 June 1888, Bamberger still felt duty-bound to caution the empress that yet another renewal of her efforts to marry Moretta to Sandro would have calamitous consequences. He predicted that "the authority and position of even the most exalted persons wishing [the marriage] would be forever undermined" and warned Victoria that her defenders would be reduced to a miserable and embarrassed silence.[50]

Against the background of a widespread belief in a Freisinn conspiracy centred on the empress, it appears ironic that it was the left-liberal "co-regent" Bamberger who gave Victoria such stern and effective words of warning against the Battenberg marriage. Bamberger's action suggests that there was nothing amounting to a left-liberal plan to "derail" the Reich during the ninety-nine days. Frederick's illness proved to be an "all-powerful enemy" indeed, and it destroyed any hope of a dramatic change of track. This did not mean, however, that the old *Kronprinzenpartei* had given up all of its political ambitions or that the popular, liberal icon Our Fritz had become irrelevant to their plans. Even as part of a lamented past, he would still be at the heart of a liberal "policy of the future."

Bismarck, the "Kanzlerkrise," and the Politics of a New Succession

The ninety-nine days appeared to agree with the chancellor. Victoria was struck by the septuagenarian's visibly good health. "I never saw him looking stronger," she noted on 19 March: "as hale as a bell—rosy in the face." The journalist Moritz Busch, who met Bismarck on 7 April 1888, also noticed how well the chancellor appeared. The long anticipated succession did not seem to inconvenience him in any way. "Everything is going easily and comfortably with the exalted gentleman," he informed the ministers four days after the old emperor's death, "like a game of roulette." In retrospect, Bismarck even opined that in his entire career, business was never conducted "as smoothly and agreeably as during the 99 days when Emperor Frederick reigned." The imperial couple treated him with respect, and he repaid them with courtesy. "Prince Bismarck has been civil and nice and I think feels quite at his ease," Victoria informed her mother on 16 March. Two months later, the empress's view had not changed. "I cannot reproach the chancellor," she confided to Bamberger, "he is not as petty as the other ministers, he is more generous and the emperor's illness affects him much more." The peculiar Indian summer in Bismarck's relationship with Victoria and Frederick culminated in a memorable scene on 14 June 1888. As Bismarck was about to leave Frederick's bedside for the last time, the emperor placed his wife's hand into the chancellor's. Bismarck understood and declared: "Your Majesty can be assured that I will never forget that Her Majesty is my queen."[51]

It is fair to say that the chancellor's attitude toward Emperor Frederick's tragedy was not as callous as that of his son Herbert or General Waldersee, but his treatment of the imperial couple nevertheless resulted from calculation and cunning rather than from sincere devotion. Immediately after Emperor William's death, he had consulted Bergmann who confirmed that the new emperor would not survive the summer. "In reality," Bismarck told the French ambassador on 10 March 1888, "we are entering a feminine reign—or rather interregnum—of a few months." In the knowledge that Frederick's time on the throne was going to be no more than a brief intermezzo, the chancellor could approach his new monarch with mellifluous dissimulation. With an unerring eye for the political realities, he concentrated his efforts on the empress. The behaviour he was adopting toward her was that of a "love-struck greybeard," Bismarck admitted to Lucius. Heeding Disraeli's advice that flattery for royals should be laid on with a trowel, Bismarck performed some astonishing stunts. The British ambassador observed that during a formal dinner on 25 April the chancellor "ardently did his best to be amiable and agreeable." At the end, "he selected a large bonbon adorned with a photograph of the Empress and, after calling Her Majesty's attention to it in some graceful words, unbuttoned his coat and placed it next to his heart." Though barely believable, Bismarck's charm offensive was not without effect. Even when looking back on her husband's reign, Victoria still commented on the consideration and graciousness shown by the chancellor.[52]

The story was more complex, though, than that of a consummate performer duping a gullible empress. On the one hand, Victoria was not wholly taken in by the chancellor. On 9 May, she criticised his "high-handed rule," under which Germany's politics had become very bitter. After reading Bamberger's incisive letters, she also knew what to think of Bismarck's claims that the other ministers were frustrating his honest efforts to comply with the emperor's request that medals be given to Schrader, Bunsen, and Forckenbeck. Moreover, Victoria commented on the insincerity of Bismarck's behaviour during and immediately after his last meeting with Frederick. Rather than affected by grief, he struck her as vigorous, lively, and relieved. On the other hand, the velvet glove of flattery was not the chancellor's only means of influence. Since Emperor William had left no money to either Victoria or her daughters, the question of their financial security in the future weighed heavily on Frederick's and Victoria's minds. Bismarck had already anticipated in February 1888 that Victoria could be generously provided for during the emperor's "short reign," and now he played this trump card very effectively. Bismarck's flattery was to be laid on with a golden trowel.[53]

It was against this background that the most dramatic and Machiavellian political scheme pursued during the ninety-nine days unfolded. The so-called Kanzlerkrise started during the eventful meeting between Bismarck and the imperial couple on 31 March 1888 which resulted in the sudden cancellation of Alexander von Battenberg's invitation. What followed was a political spectacle made up of a mixture of uncommonly duplicitous and disrespectful means and motives. Even the hard-boiled Holstein found it unpalatable. "Is this not a farce?" he asked, as the crisis was petering out ten days later. "Each seeks to con the other; the most conned is the poor emperor." As with so many other aspects of Emperor Frederick's short reign, this farce was made up of ingredients that had already been the standard fare of the years before 1888: a scheming chancellor, a largely passive and almost powerless Frederick, a willing horde of rent-a-pen hacks, the public vilification of the Englishwoman Victoria, the chancellor's concerns about his own future under the next monarch, and efforts to damage the left-liberals while consolidating the governmental camp. The only innovation was the peculiar understanding between the chancellor, who orchestrated the brouhaha, and Empress Victoria, its main target.[54]

Before Bismarck left the palace on 31 March 1888, the emperor asked him to submit his case against the Battenberg marriage in writing. Over the next few days, the chancellor not only composed a memorandum but also mobilised the sworn enemies of the Battenberg project. Grand Duke Frederick of Baden approached Prince Alexander's uncle, the Grand Duke of Hessen-Darmstadt, with an urgent request to lean on his nephew. On 4 April, Crown Prince William sent the hapless Battenberg a fierce letter which the chancellor had drafted for him. Everyone working for this marriage would be regarded as the enemy of his country and treated accordingly, William threatened. On the same day, the emperor received Bismarck's thirty-page memorandum. Any friendly gesture toward Prince Alexander—let alone a marriage—was likely to cause grave offence to Russia, the chancellor warned. If such a step were taken, he would be forced to step down. On 5 April, Bismarck went public. The government-inspired *Kölnische Zeitung* reported in its morning edition that Bismarck was considering resigning. Even though "health grounds" were officially cited, the paper revealed that the real reason was an "undisclosed conflict." The tension was further ratcheted up by a telegram sent to the German ambassador in London on the same day. Count Hatzfeldt was instructed to inform the British government that a successful outcome of the allegedly anti-Russian marriage project so doggedly pursued by Queen Victoria would force Germany to protect its interests by moving closer to St. Petersburg.[55]

Empress Victoria had not been idle either. Immediately after the meeting with Bismarck, she sent Sandro an extraordinary letter suggesting that he and Moretta secretly elope. He could then pursue a military career abroad. On 4 April, however, she instructed Chamberlain Radolinski to make preparations for the engagement to be celebrated on 12 April 1888—Moretta's twenty-second birthday.

The stage appeared set for an almighty clash between the empress and the chancellor, but then the Battenberg question suddenly took a most unexpected turn. On 5 April, Bismarck was received by Victoria. Rather than tear into each other, the two struck a deal. The chancellor made some conciliatory noises about not wanting to stand in the way of Moretta and Sandro's private happiness forever. Then he suddenly offered to arrange for nine million marks to be released from the late emperor's estate. This would enable Frederick to settle dowries of two million on each of his daughters and gift one million to his wife. The empress now agreed to postpone the marriage until after Frederick's death and invited the chancellor "to rail against her to his heart's content and afterwards blame her for everything." Later on the same day, as public excitement about the report in the *Kölnische Zeitung* was intensifying, Victoria sent her mother a telegram: "Please be in no anxiety. Crisis of Chancellor is an invention; we have never been on better terms." Five days later, she reiterated that "all this row [was] made for a purpose, and [was] really very silly." The empress's belief that her mother needed reassuring about the political situation reflected the ferocity of the press campaign that was unleashed after 5 April. Prime Minister Lord Salisbury nervously warned the queen on 8 April that she might encounter "some disrespectful demonstration" during her planned trip to Germany. The monarch was not so easily frightened, though, and insisted on visiting her "poor sick son-in-law."[56]

Salisbury clearly believed Bismarck to be at the heart of the journalistic storm that was now sweeping the Reich. The chancellor has "a vast corrupt influence over the press and can give enormous circulation to rumours," he informed the queen. This appeared to be borne out by the tone adopted in numerous Kartell organs. The

Battenberg marriage would becloud "our otherwise clear friendship with Russia," the *Kölnische Zeitung* predicted on 9 April. "Not only peace but Germany's political honour is at stake. It would be one more tragedy of fate for the House of Hohenzollern if Bismarck had to end his long service over a personal and emotional matter.... If it takes place, the Princess Viktoria and her mother will have to bear the full responsibility for it." On the following day, the conservative *Dresdener Nachrichten* printed a brazen attack against the empress under the headline "No Petticoat Politics! And No English Politics in Germany!" Having been personally briefed by the chancellor, the journalist Moritz Busch contributed a double salvo in the *Grenzboten*. On 12 April, he called the Battenberg prince a pawn in the Freisinn Party's evil scheme to remove the chancellor, even at the price of a possible war against Russia. A week later, Busch attacked the empress, "who has remained an Englishwoman" and was still doing her duty for Britain by furthering an initiative designed to damage Russo-German relations. "The marriage between Battenberg and our emperor's daughter," he reminded his readers, "was suggested by his mother-in-law and is keenly desired and vigorously pursued by his wife."[57]

As Kartell activists in Berlin, Leipzig, and Breslau were circulating petitions calling on the emperor to reassure the nation by declaring Bismarck irreplaceable, the left-liberal press rode to the rescue of the imperial couple. Displaying the sudden conversion to the cause of monarchical government which their political opponents found so nauseating, the Freisinn Party now declared to be scandalized by Bismarck's attack on the crown's prerogatives. The *Frankfurter Zeitung* regarded the whole affair as an attempt by the chancellor to cement his omnipotence under the new regime and suggested that his resignation might enhance the dynasty's prestige. According to the *Freisinnige Zeitung*, the emperor's freedom of action would be diminished to an unacceptable extent once a minister was declared indispensable. The *Vossische Zeitung* saw no danger to the Reich in the planned marriage. "What is crazy and unheard-of in the kingdom of Prussia," the *Reichsfreund* declared on 14 April, "is that those on the government's secret payroll and their intrepid sidekicks have got this rumpus going to conjure up outrage for the benefit of our premier statesman and against our emperor and empress." Even the doughty old radical Eugen Richter publicly struck the pose of a defender of the dynasty: "A shameful agitation against the crown and the imperial house has recently been started in Breslau and Leipzig," he exclaimed in the Prussian parliament. By opposing it, the Freisinn Party had proved its loyalty to the royal family. It was the *Freisinnige Zeitung*, Richter claimed, that had "unmasked and rejected the disgraceful attacks launched against the empress by liars and embezzlers."[58]

The Kanzlerkrise was thus characterized by a number of remarkably counterintuitive features: Empress Victoria protested that her relations with the chancellor were never better than while she was being pilloried by the Bismarck press; the Kartell parties openly attacked the dynasty and tried to force the emperor's hand by plebiscitary means; and the left-liberals rallied to protect the monarch's prerogative. The crisis also appeared to make no sense at the international level. The brusque warning about the serious consequences of the marriage which Bismarck sent to the British government on 5 April was met with an icy reply from Lord Salisbury, who refused to assist the chancellor in his attempt "to gratify the malignant feelings of the Russian Emperor." If German cooperation could only be had at the price of kowtowing to Russia, Britain would have to do without it. Two days later, however, Queen Victoria informed the German government that she was opposed to the Battenberg marriage. According to the British ambassador, Herbert von Bismarck was delighted to receive this news and promised to act on it. Yet on 8 April, the chancellor still briefed Moritz Busch to attack both Empress Victoria *and* her mother for supporting the marriage. In fact, Busch's anti-British polemic in the *Grenzboten* only appeared eleven days later. By then, Bismarck's behaviour in the Kanzlerkrise had seriously damaged Anglo-German relations.[59]

Even Russia, whose sensitivities Bismarck was ostensibly trying his utmost to protect, presented anything but a straightforward case. Rather than react with indignation at the possibility of Battenberg's visit to Charlottenburg, the Russian foreign minister calmly assured German ambassador Lothar von Schweinitz that such an event, though regrettable, would not make him doubt Germany's friendly attitude toward Russia. Clearly annoyed, Bismarck informed Schweinitz on 8 April 1888 that he would not be able to frustrate Empress Victoria's plans without a little assistance from St. Petersburg: "The ladies and England would then emerge victorious from the fight." After all, Bismarck grumbled, he could not be "more Russian than the Russian government." To make matters worse for the chancellor, the Pan-Slavic press, pouncing at the opportunity to needle their old enemy, loudly proclaimed Russia's complete lack of interest in the entire affair. The weakness of the Russian card that Bismarck played to justify his official case against the Battenberg marriage was obvious. The chancellor was putting on a show, Holstein commented, "the Russian danger is not as bad as all that." Queen Victoria, who now opposed the marriage as ill-advised, also was not convinced that it would lead to international complications: "Surely the prognostications of such great European changes arising out of a marriage are absurd," she observed on 13 April.[60]

The Kanzlerkrise ended as abruptly as it had started. It was simply called off. On 10 April 1888, Bismarck and Empress Victoria had a long meeting. In the course of this two-hour conversation, he gave her some advice on how to invest the money and insisted that the Battenberg marriage would dishonour the Hohenzollerns. He would not rule out, though, that it might yet take place: discreetly and at an unspecified future date, perhaps under a different emperor. Reportedly, they also agreed to keep the outward appearance of a conflict going for a little longer. When Bismarck was received by the emperor on the following day, he was handed a note enquiring if the meeting of the previous day had satisfied him that all the differences in connection with the Battenberg marriage had been resolved. Having confirmed that this was the case, Bismarck received another piece of paper stating that the matter was now resolved and that it would be handled in line with his wishes. The chancellor informed his ministerial colleagues of this outcome and arranged for the petitions in Leipzig and Breslau to be called off, but decided not to publicise his victory lest he be accused of crowing. The right strings were pulled, though, and the press furore soon petered out. Less than a fortnight later, Bismarck publicly pressed Victoria's image to his heart and a further ten months on, Sandro happily wed the celebrated soprano Johanna Loisinger. Moretta did not have to wait too long either: in 1890 she married the entirely uncontroversial Prince Adolf zu Schaumburg-Lippe.[61]

Even though the bizarre manoeuvre that was the Kanzlerkrise only made sense in the context of the impending succession of Crown Prince William, other factors may well have played a part. Bismarck was certainly vain enough to resent the idea that after five years of resisting the Battenberg marriage he would finally have to accept defeat. His decision to whip up a huge frenzy to rule out any possibility of the project ever being renewed may also have been caused by his suspicion that Victoria would not abide by the terms of a confidential deal. One could not rely on a woman's word, Bismarck explained to Roggenbach after conceding that his demands had been met at the very beginning of the crisis. It is important not to forget that underneath his charming façade, Bismarck still held Victoria and her husband in low regard. During a private dinner party on 11 April 1888, he spoke unguardedly about the couple, calling Frederick unbelievably submissive and dependent, "like a dog." Victoria, in contrast, was a "wild woman" whose "unbridled sensuality" and erotic infatuation with Prince Alexander repulsed him. The main effect achieved by the Kanzlerkrise only becomes fully visible, though, when it is read against the background of the policies the chancellor had pursued between 1880 and 1887 in relation to Crown Prince Frederick William's anticipated succession.[62]

Then, as later, Bismarck was looking for a united parliamentary basis that would strengthen his position vis-à-vis the incoming monarch. It was therefore of concern to him that relations amongst the parties united by the 1887 Kartell arrangement had grown noticeably hostile. The National Liberals and the moderate Free Conservatives were fiercely opposed to what they saw as the German Conservatives' reactionary clericalism, their budding cooperation with the Catholic Centre Party, and the growing influence of well-connected ultraconservative cliques. The increasingly intransigent stance taken by the right-wing German Conservatives could seriously inconvenience the government—as was shown in February 1888 when they scuppered the bill to abolish primary school fees. What was worse, their catchy charge that the National Liberals were bent on devaluing the true conservative idea in order to lure conservatives into "the great National Liberal mish-mash swamp" put pressure on a possible fault line within the Kartell.

The Kanzlerkrise went a long way toward firming up the chancellor's party-political support. Not only did all the Kartell parties unite on an unequivocally pro-Bismarck platform but the crisis also disciplined the right-wing conservatives. Confronted with the question of whether or not they would back the chancellor and his defence of Russo-German relations against a plot hatched by the left-liberals, Empress Victoria, and Perfidious Albion, the German Conservatives had little choice. Their hatred of the Freisinn Party, of "the Englishwoman," and of Bismarck's possible replacements—the names of Bennigsen and Roggenbach were touted in the press—became the nose ring by which Bismarck led them back into the fold of the Kartell.[63]

At the heart of Bismarck's efforts to consolidate his support was the concern about his relationship with the next emperor. Ever since the early 1880s, he and his son Herbert had worked hard and sometimes obsequiously to draw Prince William into the Bismarckian orbit. Toward the end of the 1880s, however, the prince became increasingly close to Alfred von Waldersee. This ambitious general was clearly angling for the chancellorship and challenged Bismarck by advocating a more hawkish foreign policy. Waldersee also introduced William to the circle of ultraconservative, anti-Semitic Protestant zealots around the court preacher Adolf Stoecker. The prince's attendance at a high-profile meeting of the Waldersee-Stoecker group in November 1887 was widely taken to signal his break with the Bismarcks in favour of a decidedly more right-wing affiliation.

Determined not to give up without a fight, Bismarck used the Kanzlerkrise as a means of realigning William with himself. Holstein realised immediately that the manoeuvre was not aimed at Battenberg, but at the succession. It was all about Bismarck's desire to curry favour with the crown prince, he observed on 3 April 1888. Bismarck's "seemingly furious resistance" to the marriage, he later explained, was fuelled by the chancellor's fear of William. On 17 April, Holstein commented wryly on the strange sight of "the Bismarcks, father and son, waiting hand and foot on the crown prince." William was kept closely involved in the fight against the alleged marriage intrigue. The chancellor even invited the crown prince to flex his muscles by signing a bombastically aggressive letter. When reminded of his hatred against his mother and Alexander Battenberg, William's response was almost Pavlovian. The Reich "avoided by a hairsbreadth a catastrophe, which would have culminated in the resignation of our Iron Chancellor," he informed the Duke of Coburg on 3 April. "The reason behind this is the name 'Battenberg' and Mama the driving force, naturally with England in the background." Nor was the crown prince likely to remain unimpressed by the spectacle of the nationwide press campaign in support of the irreplaceable Bismarck.[64]

Once the Kanzlerkrise is seen primarily as the chancellor's attempt to regain the position of trust with the crown prince that he enjoyed before the Stoecker affair, Empress Victoria's willingness to play her part appears less puzzling. According to J. Alden Nichols, "such an attempt to educate Crown Prince William and compromise the reactionary Junkers could easily have charmed and intrigued" Victoria and could have persuaded her "to approve scurrilous press attacks on herself." While the correctness of this interpretation can only be surmised, it is entirely plausible to argue that both the emperor and his wife would have been prepared to go to considerable lengths to bring about a change in their son's outlook and behaviour. They had grave doubts about William's readiness to succeed to the throne and their distrust in the crown prince manifested itself strikingly in the first telegram the new emperor sent to him: "I express the firm confidence," Frederick wrote with more than a hint of exhortation, "that in loyalty and obedience you will be an example to all." William felt the sting of this communication, but he failed to get the point.[65]

Within weeks of Frederick's return to Berlin, the papers reported with some disbelief that on 1 April 1888, the crown prince had given a crass toast in honour of Bismarck's seventy-third birthday. Flogging a hackneyed simile, William had compared the Reich to an army whose commander had fallen. Since "the first officer was lying gravely wounded on the ground," he explained, 46 million hearts now had to rally to the standard bearer—"our great chancellor"—upon whom everything depended. Frederick sent his son a tart rebuke for this public diminution of the emperor on account of his ill health. William defended himself with the feeble explanation that he had been misquoted, but this episode failed to chasten him. Holstein sarcastically noted on 11 April that William was "developing the attractive affectations of a ruler." These involved more than just rudeness and self-importance. William instructed the commanding officer at Charlottenburg Palace to have the premises occupied and sealed off as soon as the emperor was dead. Through informers within their household he also spied on his parents, who were fully aware of his attitude. "William fancies himself completely the emperor—and an absolute and autocratic one," Victoria complained to her mother on 12 May and added a week later that he was "in a ring, a coterie, whose main endeavour [was] as it were to paralyse Fritz in every way." The empress was bitter, but knew that there was little she or even Frederick could do. "People in general consider us a mere passing shadow, soon to be replaced by reality in the shape of William," she had written within days of returning to

Berlin. The imperial couple had no alternative but to cooperate with the chancellor in the faint hope that his attempts to prepare William for the throne might bear some fruit.[66]

The modus vivendi offered by Bismarck came with a price tag, though, and on the chancellor's own terms. Where matters of substance were concerned, Bismarck quickly dropped his mask of studied politeness and revealed the power politician underneath. Frederick and Victoria realised this soon after their arrival in Berlin. Two imperial bills that had passed the Federal Council and the Reichstag in February 1888 were waiting to be signed and proclaimed by the emperor. On 22 March, Bismarck informed a ministerial meeting that Frederick had initially refused to sign both the law lengthening Reichstag sessions to five years and the one extending the anti-Socialist law by a further two years. Reportedly, the emperor had based his decision on a catalogue of left-liberal arguments.[67]

This attempt to impose a retrospective veto on legislation has been regarded as a sign of Frederick's tendency toward an anti-parliamentary and essentially autocratic form of "personal regiment." Although this interpretation may be putting too much weight on a single decision, it is clear that Frederick's refusal to sign was neither constitutional nor politically acceptable for Bismarck. As soon as he learned about the emperor's decision, the chancellor went to Charlottenburg. Even in retrospect, Victoria vividly recalled Bismarck's furious stare, his stern reminder that the emperor had no right to obstruct these laws, and the threatened resignation of the entire ministry. When the empress immediately gave in and instantly secured her husband's signature, Bismarck calmed down. He "retracted his claws," Victoria remembered, "like a tiger, which changes its mind and will not pounce on its prey."[68]

Where the disagreements concerned smaller issues, the chancellor's opposition was less ferocious, but as effective. Even though he went along with most of the names on Frederick's long list of promotions, ennoblements, and decorations, Bismarck carefully intervened to make sure the outcome was not too unpalatable. He eventually agreed to award medals to Forckenbeck and Virchow—the former was officially decorated for his services to flood victims and the latter for his scientific achievements—but several others were blocked. For men like Bunsen, Schrader, and Stauffenberg, the ninety-nine days came and went without official recognition. Bismarck tried to cover his tracks by first appearing sanguine about the proposals and subsequently blaming the rejections on the intransigence of his colleagues, but this was a transparent ruse. Even Holstein felt uneasy about this barefaced demonstration of the emperor's impotence and observed that "these few small decorations" would hardly have caused any damage.[69]

Frederick's wish to mark his accession with the traditional gesture of an amnesty was treated in a similarly mean-spirited manner. "Fritz devoted himself to it and wanted to see it extended to political refugees and to other political crimes," Victoria recalled, but the chancellor did not want to hear about it. "It is a peculiar act of grace," Bismarck told ministers on 22 March, "to let a gang of criminals loose all over the country." With the threat of resignation always hanging in the air, the emperor had to watch his amnesty being pared to the bone. As Frederick had feared, the liberal public noted with disappointment that the amnesty of 1 April not only excluded prostitutes and vagabonds but also all convictions for political crimes and especially the Social Democrats.[70]

Harsh though it may seem, it is probably fair to say that a few medals and a carefully circumscribed amnesty were the full extent of Bismarck's concessions to the dying emperor. Frederick's opposition to the law extending the sessions of the Prussian parliament to five years also turned out to be no more than a minor irritation. As king of Prussia, he was legally entitled to reject this measure, which he regarded as an unfortunate infringement of the rights of the electorate. On 26 May 1888, Frederick made use of this prerogative and refused to sign the law which Minister Puttkamer had submitted to him. The monarch's resistance crumbled quickly, though, and the very next day, Justice Minister Friedberg prevailed upon him to change his mind and sign the document. A further delay was caused when Bismarck unexpectedly suggested that Frederick was within his rights to postpone the public proclamation of the law, but on 7 June, even this formality was completed.[71]

The chancellor's seemingly unhelpful suggestion throws some doubt on the purity even of Frederick's and Victoria's only substantial political achievement since Bismarck's mercurial intervention points to a connection between the emperor's final concession and Puttkamer's removal. The latter was edged out of office by means of various communications about electoral issues exchanged between 27 May and 6 June—exactly the span of time during which Bismarck had managed to stave off the enactment of Puttkamer's electoral law.

Rather than mark a defeat for Bismarck, the fall of the reviled minister of the interior thus appears to have formed yet another part of the
chancellor's policy of succession.

It is true that the empress celebrated Puttkamer's political demise
as a "great step," that Bamberger and the Freisinn Party considered
it a highly welcome event, and that it was accompanied by howls
of fury from the crown prince and Waldersee, but the chancellor's
role—as it had been so often—was rather murky. When addressing
the other ministers, Bismarck spoke about his efforts to persuade
Puttkamer to fight for his post and railed against the empress, her
left-liberal coterie, and the cruelty of Puttkamer's treatment. A closer
analysis suggests, however, that the chancellor had every reason to
desire the removal of a minister who was not only a doctrinaire conservative but was also known to have recently encouraged Crown
Prince William to rule without the support of a mighty chancellor.
Thus, Puttkamer fell and his political assassination was conveniently
blamed on the same Anglo-liberal clique which Bismarck had resisted
so valiantly during the Kanzlerkrise.[72]

The chancellor's ministerial colleagues may not have fully understood that removing Puttkamer was part of Bismarck's preparation
for the next reign, but they certainly noticed that his replacement was
handled with the future firmly in view. "He is approaching these issues with an eye on the heir to the throne," Lucius wrote on 10 June
1888, after Bismarck had ruled out Bennigsen as Puttkamer's successor. "Some time ago he had prepared himself for a few national-
liberal ministers in case of a longer reign of His Majesty, but now he
is making provisions for a ministry which is robustly conservative,
but not ultra."[73]

As these machinations were being pursued, Frederick had entered
the final phase of his agony. The emperor and his entourage had left
Charlottenburg and relocated to Potsdam on 1 June 1888. There he
resided at his old home, the New Palace, which had officially been
renamed Friedrichskron in April. Although Frederick enjoyed returning to the familiar building and its gardens, he was now sinking
fast. On 8 June, the doctors diagnosed that the wall of the emperor's
oesophagus had been perforated. Four days later, Frederick was
driven through the Potsdam parks for the last time. On 13 June, he
received his final official visitor, King Oscar of Sweden. The emperor
had hoped to welcome the king wearing the uniform of the Pasewalker Cuirassiers, but he had collapsed several times trying to put

it on. The audience with Oscar lasted barely more than a minute. Victoria's distress was now almost unbearable: "My days and nights pass I know not how! I hardly leave Fritz's room," she wrote to her mother. "He is a perfect skeleton now and his fine thick hair is quite thin. His poor throat is such a painful and shocking sight, that I can often hardly bear to look at it, when it is done up, etc. I have to rush away to hide my tears often." Emperor Frederick died two days later, on the morning of 15 June 1888.[74]

CHAPTER SIX

Contested Memory

On the morning of 15 June 1888, a scattering of journalists and members of the public were waiting outside Friedrichskron Palace, hoping for news of the dying emperor. The correspondent for the London *Times* described an idyllic scene: the air rich with the scent of blossom; the matin bell chiming from a distant village church; the songs of larks, cuckoos, and wood pigeons mingling in the groves. Suddenly, the royal standard was lowered to half-mast. The falling blade of a guillotine could not have given a "more painful shock to the sorrowful onlookers," the journalist remarked. Within an instant, though, the silence of their dumbfounded grief was broken "by the clatter of horses' hoofs and on looking up they beheld a squadron of the Hussars of the Guard in their scarlet jackets rapidly dispersing like the leaves of a fan to take possession of all the points of access to the huge Palace area." Within half an hour, the troopers were reinforced "by a splendid company of infantry," and together they sealed the premises "hermetically as well against ingress as egress for some time after the emperor's death." Acting on orders previously lodged by Crown Prince William, the troops had been anticipating the moment for some time. They were now deployed with indecorous haste because the new emperor feared that an attempt could be made to smuggle papers documenting the extent of purported Freisinn conspiracy out of the palace. No one was allowed to leave—not even ministers, doctors, or members of the imperial household. Rumours that Mackenzie was hiding the late emperor's memoirs nearly led to the English physician's arrest.[1]

William II's attempt to control his father's posthumous impact was characteristically brusque and insensitive. He was not, however, alone in bringing a political edge to his father's memory, nor were his suspicions entirely without foundation. But the horse had bolted long before. Crown Prince Frederick William and Victoria had deposited three boxes containing confidential papers in a strong room in Windsor Palace as long ago as July 1887; two further shipments were sent to England in May and June 1888. Claims that Empress Victoria had purloined incriminating paperwork were nevertheless wide off the mark. In spite of her grave misgivings about the new regime, she quickly agreed to repatriate all the documents, gave her permission for them to be vetted by ministers, and voluntarily deposited the bulk of them in the Prussian Royal Archives. Even this proved insufficient, though, to prevent the late emperor's private writings from being used in a manner that greatly irked his successor. Within a few months, the Freisinn deputy Constantin Bulle celebrated the unauthorised publication of Frederick's war diary of 1870–1871 at a political meeting. In the shape of the diary, a voice had risen from the grave, he declared, to ensure that the late emperor's image would never fade. In an attempt to prevent that voice from resonating too widely, William II and the chancellor once again resorted to the big stick of the state.[2]

The military occupation of Friedrichskron Palace, the reaction to the publication of the crown prince's war diary, the governmental reprisals against those responsible, and the event at which Constantin Bulle spoke were all measures adopted during the bitter quarrel over the late emperor's public memory. The two parties involved in this conflict—the left-liberals and Empress Victoria on the one hand; the new emperor, Bismarck, and the governmental camp on the other—entered the fray with passion and resourcefulness. They all believed the stakes to be high. The ninety-nine days had added sympathy, monarchical awe, and tragedy to the warm popularity and heroic glamour that had already been the hallmarks of Our Fritz. In his persona were assembled all the ingredients of a powerful political myth. Depending on its composition and on who championed it, this myth could have very different effects. It could either help attract a mass following to a reinvigorated left-wing opposition or further strengthen the conservative narrative of the Hohenzollern legend through the addition of yet another glittering chapter.

The political potency and urgency of the Frederick myth was a direct function of the high profile of the official and popular cult of monarchy. The first phase of the contest is therefore squarely located within the political, legal, and cultural context of imperial Germany. The left-liberals' bid to fashion the image of Emperor Frederick according to their own strategic interests and the countermoves pursued by forces defending the status quo only made sense under the circumstances of William II's rule. Once the events of 1918 had swept the imperial order away, Frederick's memory was once again open for reconsideration. The mechanisms which had previously secured the dominance of one of the competing interpretations were no longer in place. As a result of critical perspectives and new freedoms of analysis, a changed complexion of Frederick's prevalent image emerged. The passage of time and intervening events meant, however, that the Frederick myth turned from a hotly contested political concern into one of speculative historical interest.

Commemorating the "People's Emperor"

Ludwig Bamberger and other prominent left-liberals accepted that Frederick's illness was an enemy that could not be defeated. It destroyed any hopes for political change in the short term which the Freisinn Party may still have entertained. The stricken emperor could not implement any radical reforms. This realistic appraisal did not mean, however, that the left-liberals had given up their political ambitions for the medium and long term or that Frederick and his reign were unimportant for their plans. On the contrary, the carefully constructed memory of the change that had supposedly been prepared for so many years and was then tragically denied in 1888 became a precious political resource. In a cruelly ironic twist, the Noble Sufferer's agony and death even increased its political value. The status of the memory was now protected by piety and sympathy, while its content could be defined without fear of contradiction by the man himself. What the *Sozialdemokrat* had mocked as the "myth of the liberal crown prince" in 1883 was exalted by the heartrending events of 1888.[3] In the hands of those determined to change the Reich's political status quo and shape a new regime, the myth of the sainted, late-lamented Noble Sufferer, of Our Fritz, and of the liberal emperor could be a sharp weapon.

Ever since the early 1880s, the party dubbed the *Kronprinzenpartei* had claimed to have the ear of the crown prince, who purportedly shared their views on a number of key issues. In spite of electoral setbacks and the private realisation that Frederick William's enthusiasm for the "great liberal party" was on the wane, these claims were assertively repeated as soon as Emperor Frederick had succeeded to the throne. To the considerable annoyance of the political Right, the Freisinn Party's press organs now posed as the only political force loyal to an imperial couple they portrayed as firmly committed to a left-liberal agenda. This was done for a purpose.

As early as 26 March 1888, Karl Schrader contacted Bamberger to explain his view of the tasks now facing the left-liberals: to maintain the momentum caused by the succession and to disseminate the spirit of Frederick's proclamations amongst the population at large. Schrader's letter pinpointed the strategic consideration at the heart of the Freisinn campaign for the control of the myth of Emperor Frederick: the memory of Our Fritz was able to convey the political beliefs of a liberal elite to the wider public. "He has done enough to gain glory," Henriette Schrader wrote to a friend two days before the emperor's death. "Once he is gone, the people, who are not yet capable of political thinking, will weave a myth around him, which stirs imagination and may perhaps awaken more within them than enlightenment and teaching."[4]

Since the people in their simplicity could not be trusted to do all that weaving and awakening unaided, the interested parties applied themselves to the business of mythmaking. Now German liberalism would have to play a long game, Schrader explained to Stauffenberg shortly after Frederick's death: "We who revered our dear Emperor Frederick more than all the others and were closer to him, we also have the sacred duty, above all others, to adopt the realization of the aims to which he pledged his entire strength during his last months of unspeakable physical and mental suffering." This was also what Empress Victoria rightly expected of those, "who truly loved and understood the emperor." In a letter she sent to Henriette Schrader on 8 August, Victoria provided a clear indication of the activities she had in mind: "All over Germany an association could be formed, which calls itself 'Emperor Frederick Association' and pursues all the objectives hinted at in Emperor Frederick's programme," she suggested. The network should use journalistic organs such as *Die Nation*, the *Vossische Zeitung*, and Berlin's *Volkszeitung*, and its main objective would be "to convey to the masses the idea of changing Germany in a liberal direction."[5]

Karl Schrader immediately pushed ahead with this initiative. Victoria was "firm in her thoroughly liberal views on religion, politics, social and economic affairs," he wrote to Stauffenberg three days later. She could be "an inestimable treasure for the German nation," but she required assistance and "specifically—since there is no help from above—from the people and especially from us . . . who agree with her and Emperor Frederick's lifelong views." The best service to be rendered to Germany, Schrader argued, was to keep alive Frederick's memory as a ruler who was truly popular and who loved the people: "Around this a better development that springs from the people can and must crystallize, and we have to make this possible by maintaining the people's awareness of him."[6]

In the course of the following years, the determination not to let the liberal emperor sink into oblivion led to a variety of activities. These were not only designed to maintain his high profile but also to counter efforts to belittle his political relevance. By stressing Frederick's left-liberal credentials, his close connection with the people, and the lasting value of his legacy, the emperor's obituaries in the left-liberal press marked the first step in this posthumous initiative. The *Vossische Zeitung* claimed that "everyone knew that his ear belonged to the poor, the persecuted and to those in need." It confidently predicted that Frederick's spirit would live on and that "the golden treasure of his thoughts" would become Germany's yardstick. It was a great blessing, the venerable Berlin daily explained, "that he could validate with the imperial title the wealth of great ideas and noble suggestions which he carried within him." The people "waited and hoped for him, when, during the last decade, an all-too-heavy burden chafed their necks," the *Volkszeitung* observed, and *Die Nation* described how the "hearts of the oppressed" had rallied to Frederick. The *Freisinnige Zeitung* predicted that the principle of the equality of all political parties, to which the deceased had dedicated his final efforts, would "for all times be a precious legacy for the German people." By the time the weekly *Der Reichsfreund* appeared, the tone of the liberals' rhetoric had risen to a quasi-religious crescendo: "His name and his example are our banner and watchword in all the struggles ahead of us, with this sign we must and will conquer."[7]

The publication of extracts from the diary which Crown Prince Frederick William had kept during the Franco-Prussian War triggered the next wave of liberal outpourings. "Every line, every word of this text is of inestimable value," the *Berliner Zeitung* enthused on 21 September. "Pallid envy and political injustice seek to darken the noble image which resides in the hearts of every good German and every friend of liberty," the *Vossische Zeitung* observed, but they have been rebutted by "Emperor Frederick's own words . . . which truly contain a political legacy worthy of . . . serving as the touchstone of future policy." The diary showed that "lofty and free-thinking tasks" had filled the crown prince's soul in 1871, the *Freisinnige Zeitung* declared. The *Volkszeitung* called it a "signpost towards the path on which the people can reach only freedom and peace," and insisted that "the shortest reign of any German emperor, of any Prussian king, will last the longest in people's memory." Resorting to characteristically bombastic pathos, the *Reichsfreund* concluded its examination of the diary by proclaiming that "the struggle for the rights and liberty of the people will be won under Emperor Frederick's banner." A similar spirit of hyperbole breathed through the articles occasioned by the anniversary of Frederick's birthday on 18 October. His government had remained a torso, the *Berliner Tageblatt* conceded on 18 October 1888, but it was a torso "of such incomparable magnificence and beauty" that even the most remote posterity would be "enthralled with admiration."[8]

A number of publications that were rushed out in 1888 reinforced the message communicated by the Freisinn press. Arnold Perls's *Emperor Frederick and the 100 Days of His Government: A Booklet of Commemoration Dedicated to Every Free-Thinking German* lovingly inventoried the whole gamut of Frederick's liberal deeds, from the Danzig speech in 1863 to his imperial proclamation twenty-five years later. "He belonged to us, to the entire people," Perls claimed and declared that the throne of this "free-thinking, far-sighted prince" rested "securely on the rock of his people's love." The pamphlet *Emperor Frederick the Noble Sufferer, His Doctors and Mackenzie's Book* struck a similar note. Its author, the physician J. L. Kleyst, called Frederick a "people's emperor in the true sense of the word," insisted that he would have fulfilled the people's hopes, and described his diary as a "great monument." The booklet *Emperor Frederick as Friend of the People* aimed to "throw light on his achievements in the field of popular welfare." Edited by the liberal economist Viktor Böhmert, it featured contributions by the Freisinn politicians Karl Schrader, Georg von Bunsen, and Eduard Eberty. The liberal journalist Ludwig Ziemssen even managed to complete a book-length biography of the emperor before the year was out. His message was more subtle, but still recognisable: "The ideal of a gracious, mild, earnest, enlightened ruler—this is how his image is deeply carved into his people's soul," Ziemssen concluded and declared that Frederick would always remain amongst the German people—"never fading, unforgettable."[9]

The first anniversary of the emperor's death was a natural occasion for the smooth continuation of the Freisinn Party's campaign beyond the "Year of the Three Emperors." Accordingly, June 1889 yielded another flurry of articles. The *Berliner Zeitung* gave up half its front page to a poem in which Ludwig Ziemssen pledged: "What you desired, before you had to leave / To your ideals, we will forever cleave!" The *Freisinnige Zeitung* printed a similarly lyrical attack against the "guileful lies" viciously but vainly spread to damage Frederick's reputation, which "radiated brightly with the clarity of heaven." The *Volkszeitung* recorded its gratitude that over the past year the emperor's "shadow had fought, victoriously and irresistibly, alongside those committed to the freedom and welfare of the people." The offerings printed in the *Berliner Tageblatt* and the *Vossische Zeitung* were no less fulsome. *Die Nation* declared that Frederick's commitment to "humane morality and liberal progress" had made him the very "embodiment of a cultured prince of peace," and this was how he continued to live "in the imagination of the masses."[10]

The left-liberals had more strings to their bow. Under the leadership of Mayor Forckenbeck, Berlin's city administration lost little time in launching other commemorative initiatives. By the beginning of October 1888, a committee had agreed to commit public funds to an "Emperor Frederick Foundation" dedicated to popular good causes chosen by Empress Victoria. Frederick's widow was delighted by this gesture and appreciated its political dimension. "The town of Berlin is going to hand over to me 575 hundred marks for charitable purposes in memory of our beloved Fritz," she informed her mother. "Some of the kind gentlemen from the town said they hoped I would look upon it as a silent protest against all that had been said and done to hurt and pain us." At the same time, the city council also initiated a public subscription for the building of a monument in honour of the late emperor.[11]

Taken together, these two steps amounted to anything but a "silent" protest and were interpreted as moves designed to embarrass the new regime. The Badenese diplomat Adolf Marschall von Bieberstein observed that these "demonstrative" resolutions, which had been passed without so much as consulting the emperor, were bound to make a "painful impression." It was therefore hardly surprising that William II politely but firmly turned down the formal request to permit the erection of an Emperor Frederick monument paid for by Berlin's citizenry that Forckenbeck submitted in May 1889. He was grateful for the offer, the emperor wrote a year later, but he did not want to deny himself the pleasure of erecting such a monument himself. As it turned out, William II managed to delay his gratification until 1904, when Berlin's Emperor Frederick monument was finally unveiled.[12]

An even more eye-catching aspect of the left-liberals political celebration of the life and legacy of Emperor Frederick were the large public events to mark the anniversaries of his birthday. "In many places, in large cities and small communities speakers have again attempted to place the image of the noble one in front of the souls of their listeners," *Die Nation* reported in October 1888. It was Theodor Barth, the editor of the weekly paper, who gave the memorial speech at the event organised by Berlin's *Freisinniger Verein*. Eighteen hundred people had thronged into the great hall of the Bock brewery to hear Frederick described as one of the "martyrs for freedom" treated shamefully by those who oppose "the reform of Germany in a liberal spirit." The representatives of the state shunned the memorial celebration taking place simultaneously at Gotha, but—according to the *Gothaisches Tageblatt*—this did not diminish the occasion in any way. The venue was filled to capacity and the "core of the citizenry" had turned out. Many were reportedly moved to tears by the pledge "to fight and to struggle fearlessly and persistently with [Frederick's] spirit in mind." Only then, the speaker declared, would there be truth in the chosen motto: "Loyalty to the emperor—even beyond death." Reichstag deputy Constantin Bulle, speaking at the memorial event hosted by Bremen's Freisinn association in 1888, warned the spiteful clique bent on diminishing Frederick's image that their efforts would be futile. The emperor would not be remembered "as the sick ruler in Charlottenburg," but would "continue to live amongst us as the passionate fighter for German unity, political freedom, social progress."[13]

In October the following year, the *Freisinnige Verein der Halleschen Thorbezirke*, the *Deutschfreisinnige Arbeiter Verein*, and the *Handwerkerverein* staged similar celebrations in Berlin. On 23 November 1889, the latter association also held an "Emperor Frederick Celebration" where a portrait of the emperor was unveiled and the statutes of the Emperor Frederick Charitable Foundation for Orphans were published. Karl Schrader spoke at this occasion. He reminded his audience that the "duty to keep his memory sacred in the sense in which he wished it" involved striving for "the great aims which he set for us." Schrader, a wealthy railway magnate, also declared that it was not the great of this world, but the poor who were remembering the late emperor most loyally and gratefully. Even in October 1890, the commemorative ceremony organised by the Freisinn association in the town of Görlitz still attracted hundreds of participants. If the evening's speaker is to be believed, the crowd that had filled every last seat of the Reichshalle regarded themselves as the "loyal keepers of Emperor Frederick's legacy for his people" and wished to renew their "mutual covenant."[14]

After 1890 the intensive campaign to establish Frederick III as a political myth with a clearly oppositional edge lost some of its momentum. Left-liberals nevertheless continued to invoke the late emperor in order to gain political advantage and to highlight the shortcomings of his successor. In 1894, for instance, the historian Ludwig Quidde published his sensational tract *Caligula: A Study in Imperial Insanity*. Ostensibly an investigation of the mental state of the infamous Roman emperor who purportedly appointed his horse to a seat in the Senate, this brazen attack on William II went through thirty-four editions and sold hundreds of thousands of copies. Quidde chose the contrast between "Caligula" and his flawless father, "Germanicus," as the starting point for his condemnation of the unstable and dangerous son. Germanicus, who had been "the people's favourite," had succumbed to "a malignant fate" while still in the prime of life. He had won "the confidence of the common soldiers in many campaigns, . . . but the people did not only view him as a military hero, he was popular in the best sense of the word." If Germanicus had ever ruled, Quidde maintained, "it is likely that he would have inaugurated a period of greater happiness and freedom."[15]

Anniversary years also provided welcome opportunities for renewing the left-liberal claim on Frederick's memory. In 1898 the Reichstag elections happened to be scheduled for the day after the tenth anniversary of the emperor's death. Determined not to waste a serendipitous opening, the *Berliner Tageblatt* observed that "just in these hours of anxious expectation before the election day, [Frederick's] magnificent proclamations force their way into our conscience again." The paper rounded off its reflections on Frederick III with a poem: "An emperor of spring/You did but briefly reign/A freedom-minded king/Accepting of your pain." The eyes of the *Volkszeitung* were equally firmly fixed on the elections. The radical daily insisted that there was no better way of proving oneself worthy of Emperor Frederick's memory "than by making proper use of the most important, highest, most sacred political rights of the German people." According to the *Vossische Zeitung*, nobody ever doubted the late emperor's determination to implement a liberal reform of the Reich. The *Berliner Zeitung* was confident that he would have turned out "an effective workman practically serving the liberal idea."[16]

By the twenty-fifth anniversary of Frederick's death, the drama of the ninety-nine days was clearly receding into a distant past. Now, even the efforts of the indefatigable Karl Schrader came to an end. Having worked hard to use this occasion in order to renew Frederick's public memory, he died at the age of seventy-nine, just over a month before the anniversary day. Schrader left behind a half-finished appreciation of Frederick III which he was writing for the *Berliner Tageblatt*. To honour not just the late emperor but also the "worthy man, who was almost the last witness, the last of the circle of the emperor and the empress," the paper decided to publish the fragment found amongst Schrader's papers. Since this text broke off before Frederick William's Danzig speech of 1863, it did not raise what the *Neue Preussische Zeitung* called "a variety of disagreeable recollections." The ultraconservative daily refused to stir these up itself, but feared that "the left-wing press [would] probably look after that sufficiently." It certainly did. The liberal weekly *Die Hilfe* delivered a swipe against William II by emphasising that Frederick III had shown "the calm and deliberate attitude of a truly constitutional ruler" who "did not consider the cultivation of militarism the main, let alone the only task of state and society." The late emperor did not have "low regard for civic liberty," the *Frankfurter Zeitung* observed in a similar vein, while the *Vossische Zeitung* declared that Frederick "deeply felt the need to give succour to the poor and disenfranchised and also to pave the way for liberty." His body has fallen to dust, the paper concluded, "but his spirit will live on and his memory will last down the generations."[17]

Defeating the Liberal Myth of Frederick III

Emperor William II succeeded to the throne determined to strike down the cabal that he believed had exploited his late father's weakness for its own selfish and nefarious purposes. The order to have Friedrichskron Palace sealed off and searched was only the first blow; it was immediately followed by an attack directed against Mackenzie and all of those who had—for whatever reason—clung to an increasingly unbelievable optimism concerning Frederick's physical condition. Within hours of the emperor's death, the English doctor was summoned to meet both William and Bismarck and received an order to submit a report on Frederick's illness. Mackenzie agreed, but was nonplussed when less than twenty-four hours later he was instructed to complete the document immediately. The Englishman hurriedly scribbled a paragraph in which he wisely avoided the trap laid for him by confirming that Frederick had indeed died of cancer. Thereupon, he was invited to attend the late emperor's postmortem examination. In spite of his mother's passionate pleas that her late husband's body should not be touched, William II decided that an autopsy should take place. Three weeks later, a full report on this examination was published as part of a 103-page publication entitled *The Illness of Emperor Frederick III.*[18]

This booklet brought together the accounts of all the German doctors involved in the case and was clearly intended to emphasise the correctness of the German diagnosis while vilifying both Mackenzie and—by extension—those who had backed him. Victoria begged her son to forbid a publication that would be "unbearably painful" for her, but William again chose to ignore his mother's wishes. In July 1888, the pamphlet was published by the official Imperial Printing Office. The German government did, however, prove only too willing to attempt the suppression of a publication when Mackenzie rushed out his equally partisan rebuttal a few months later. In August 1888, the new emperor upset his mother again. The historian Heinrich von Treitschke had recently published an essay in which he argued that years of idleness had caused Crown Prince Frederick William to lose touch with reality and had rendered him unable to understand the ideas of a new age. William's decision to put his appreciation of Treitschke's work formally on record sent a strong message. This was reinforced by the emperor's decision to evict his mother from Friedrichskron Palace in September 1888 and change its name back to New Palace *(Neues Palais)*. Empress Frederick—as Victoria called herself after her husband's death— eventually settled in Kronberg, near Frankfurt, where she oversaw the construction of a splendid new palace. Completed in 1894 and named Friedrichshof in honour of her late husband, it became Victoria's home until her death of breast cancer in 1901.[19]

William II, Bismarck, who remained as chancellor, and the Kartell of National Liberals and Conservatives were all eager to prevent the left-liberals from defining Frederick III as their patron saint. The bitterness of the ensuing conflict suggests that the Freisinn Party's campaign had touched a raw nerve. The more outspoken the left-liberals' claims became, the more angrily national-liberal and conservative voices sought to refute them. In June 1888, the Free Conservative *Deutsches Wochenblatt* charged the Freisinn Party with repeatedly spreading lies "until its supporters are finally convinced that only disease and death prevented Emperor Frederick from appointing a Rickert-Bamberger-Richter ministry." Three weeks later, the *Grenzboten* attacked the story of Frederick's liberalism by accusing the Freisinn Party of "every possible lie and dissimulation." The exaggerated praise for Frederick's diary, the *Neue Preussische Zeitung* explained in September 1888, sprang from "the repulsive endeavour to advertise the Freisinn's wares at any cost." The *Reichsbote* reminded its readers of that party's "disgusting" attempts to exploit Frederick's short reign. The most acerbic attack on the "fairy tale" of the left-liberal emperor came in the shape of the widely read pamphlet *Also a Programme from the 99 Days*, published in October 1888. From behind a thin veil of anonymity, Duke Ernest of Coburg accused the Freisinn Party of having engaged in years of backstairs intrigue that were now followed by "transparent electoral tactics." He ended by outlining a scurrilous dystopia of organised high treason and the destruction of the Reich, which he claimed would have been the result of a Freisinn government.[20]

Duke Ernest was by no means the most highly placed individual incensed by the left-liberals' political use of Emperor Frederick. In October 1888, William II complained to Bismarck about an article from the *Berliner Zeitung* in which Frederick III was warmly commemorated; the tone adopted by the Freisinn paper, the young emperor fumed, was close to lese majesty. When William met Mayor Forckenbeck and a delegation of city councillors a few days later, he gave free rein to his annoyance. The manner in which some Berlin papers had recently intruded into affairs of his family was unacceptable, the emperor protested. He insisted that the "continuous use of quotations from his most exalted late father against his person must finally cease. It offended him most profoundly as a son and was highly unsuitable." William then exited without shaking Forckenbeck's hand.[21]

Although some observers considered this outburst ill-judged—especially since the mayor had come to present William with the city's gift of a fountain to adorn the palace square—others thought the Freisinn Party deserved what it got. Envoy Marschall von Bieberstein observed that the left-liberals only had themselves to blame for getting their knuckles rapped, and even sympathizers such as the radical *Volkszeitung* suggested that some of the recent provocations had been unnecessary. The Freisinn Party's weekly *Die Nation* was not cowed, though, and repaid William with carefully worded insolence: "How does our party's press normally talk about the dynasty?" it mused a week after the emperor's outburst. There had been "nothing but reverence" for William I and "enthusiastic love" for Emperor Frederick and his wife. And the current emperor, the article concluded, "is being treated with the kind of respect the laws and good manners of a monarchical state command."[22]

Forckenbeck only experienced William's wrath to the extent of having to forgo the pleasure of an imperial handshake. Other supposed friends of the late emperor Frederick did not get off so lightly. By the time of William II's tirade against the Berlin papers, Friedrich Heinrich Geffcken, a fifty-seven-year-old retired law professor, had already spent a month in prison. He had been arrested only days after the moderate monthly *Deutsche Rundschau* had published extracts from Crown Prince Frederick William's war diary. Geffcken, who had copied passages from the diary the crown prince had lent him in the 1870s and arranged them for publication, was the main victim of the persecution unleashed by Bismarck and the emperor. Three months of incarceration in Berlin's Moabit Prison left Geffcken a broken man. The professor, who had known Frederick William since their student days at Bonn, was by no means the only target. Other old confidants of Frederick and Victoria such as Roggenbach, Stosch, Morier, and Baroness Stockmar were also drawn into the criminal investigation. With the backing of the emperor, Bismarck applied every legal and political means at his disposal in an attempt to destroy what he saw as a conspiracy of the late emperor's "good friends," whom he described as a gang of "malcontents, toadies and intriguers."[23]

Given the hotly contested politicisation of Emperor Frederick's memory, it is not surprising that the publication of passages from the diary he kept during the foundation of the Reich caused a huge stir. The Freisinn press immediately seized upon Frederick William's criticisms of Bismarck and his characteristically vague comments on the need for liberal change and constitutional government. The left-liberal *Börsen-Courier* went so far as to claim that the Freisinn Party no longer needed an election manifesto. Frederick's diary alone was sufficient. What delighted the left-liberals made others suspicious. Marschall von Bieberstein found it "barely believable" that this veritable shopping list of Freisinn demands should now appear so neatly packaged in a document dating back to 1871. Bismarck's response was explosive; several months later, the topic still agitated him so much that the governor of Alsace-Lorraine thought he might be mentally deranged. The "legend" of the liberal emperor had to be destroyed, the chancellor told him, because it was dangerous for the entire dynasty. Bismarck regarded the publication as part of a coup against his own position. The diary entries highlighting Frederick William's keen support for the Reich and Bismarck's alleged foot-dragging might be used to diminish the chancellor's own standing as the "Founder of the Reich." In order to fight this perceived danger, Bismarck embarked on a fairly brutal twin-track strategy: he went after the individuals he suspected of being involved in this ploy and he publicly damaged the standing of what he saw as the iconic centrepiece of their policy—the figure of Emperor Frederick.[24]

At Bismarck's behest, Emperor William, who was also boiling with rage, ordered a criminal investigation on a charge of treason. A search of the offices of the *Deutsche Rundschau* identified Geffcken as the person responsible for submitting the diary extracts. His residence in Hamburg was searched, and the professor himself was arrested. A week later, Bismarck personally wrote to the Imperial Justice Ministry to recommend further searches in line with leads already identified. Unearthing the plot between Geffcken and his correspondents would not only help with the current investigation, the chancellor explained, but would also be of political importance "for the entire future of the Reich." A judge entered Roggenbach's house on 14 October 1888, and several documents were confiscated. Roggenbach himself was interrogated on 6 November. The investigating judge also interviewed Stosch, Gustav Freytag, and Bogumilla von Stockmar. The authorities found precious little on which to base their case, but Bismarck persisted. The chancellor wants to see Emperor Frederick "utterly extinguished from the minds of men and the pages of history," the Freisinn politician Georg von Bunsen explained to Robert Morier in December 1888. That was why "Roggenbach, Stosch, Mrs. von Stockmar, Geffcken and others [were] treated as suspects." The formula was simple: "Something always sticks, even if the trial against G. has to be dropped."[25]

Bunsen's prediction proved correct. On 16 December 1888, the prosecutor Hermann Tessendorff submitted a lengthy writ to the Imperial Court indicting Geffcken for betrayal of state secrets; three weeks later, the judges dismissed the case. Though embarrassing for the government, this setback was hardly surprising since the legal case against Geffcken had always been weak. In a lecture to a party gathering, the Freisinn lawyer Richard Grelling had already demolished every conceivable indictment on 10 October 1888. The Prussian justice minister could not but agree; Friedberg admitted in December that he was unable to think of how the accused could be found guilty.[26]

For Bismarck, however, there was always the court of public opinion and the politics of smear. On 14 January, the prosecutor's submission was published together with extracts from private letters written by Geffcken and Roggenbach. Eugen Richter condemned the Bismarck press for exploiting this material by extracting from it "a poisonous distillate of 50 lines . . . so that the writers appear either as madmen or as criminals." Using a tellingly familiar phrase, an article published in *Die Grenzboten* a few days later mocked Emperor Frederick's circle of friends as "malcontents, toadies and intriguers." Roggenbach understood that these attacks were by no means an unfortunate by-product but formed a central part of the campaign: "Once a ruthless historical verdict had been passed against a dead, defenceless hero and emperor, the next thing was to sacrifice his entourage on his grave," he wrote to the Grand Duke of Baden in November 1888, "and to resort if not to physical then at least to moral killing."[27]

Roggenbach's comment points to the second and even more scandalous aspect of Bismarck's campaign: the public diminution of Emperor Frederick. The Badenese politician was not the only one to realise that this was the chancellor's intention. "Prince Bismarck, his clique, the government and society here (with few exceptions) are bent on tearing down beloved Fritz's memory, which is idolised by the people," Empress Victoria complained to her mother on 2 November 1888. The chancellor wanted to prove that Frederick "would have been a danger for Germany, that he would not have protected her interests, and that his Liberal ideas, his sympathisers and his friends would have been the ruin of the state." Bismarck began his public campaign to devalue the left-liberals' icon with a thunderbolt. On 27 September 1888, he published—with Emperor William's permission—the report on the publication of the diary which he had written four days previously. Bismarck had opened his account by stating that the crown prince had been extraneous to the key negotiations in 1870. Information had been withheld from Frederick William on King William's orders, Bismarck explained, because it was feared that the crown prince would leak secrets to the Francophile British court. There also had been concerns that the crown prince's involvement would have damaged relations with the other German monarchs because of his belief in violent means suggested to him by incompetent advisers. Later in the document, the chancellor referred more bluntly to Frederick's intention "to breach the treaties with the South German allies and betray and violate them."[28]

The accusation that the crown prince could not be trusted to keep state secrets even in times of war was unheard-of, but cleverly chosen. It chimed with the prejudice that the late emperor had been too Anglophile for his own good and for that of the fatherland. This particular stake was driven in even deeper. On 16 December 1888, the pro-Bismarck *Kölnische Zeitung* published an article stating that in 1870 the British diplomat Robert Morier had passed German military secrets to the French. Morier angrily challenged this unfounded allegation, but Foreign Minister Herbert von Bismarck rudely refused to set the record straight. The purpose behind this smear, directed against someone who was known to have been a lifelong friend of Frederick William, was only too clear. In January 1889, the diplomat Baron Otto von Loë, a Catholic opponent of the chancellor, wrote a letter of support to Morier. He explained that "in order to diminish the late emperor Frederick in the eyes of his admirers" Bismarck had tried to portray one of Frederick's close friends as a "cruel enemy of Germany." For Loë, this was an "attempt to profane the dead."[29]

Having received the nod from above, the Bismarck press joined the fray. *Die Grenzboten* could find nothing especially profound or original in Frederick William's diary and thought it unlikely that its publication would improve the late emperor's reputation "anywhere beyond the circle of certain parties." The *Hamburger Nachrichten* claimed that military operations had been hampered by Frederick's "soft nature." According to *Die Post,* the crown prince actually had been an obstacle on the path toward unity. The *Dresdner Nachrichten* claimed that after 1871 he spent his time "passively vegetating in cloud-cuckoo-land" and the *Kölnische Zeitung* accused him of failing to know the difference between fantasy and reality. For the left-liberal *Die Nation,* which collected all these attacks in October 1888, it was clear that the Bismarck papers were not simply after Geffcken—they wanted to condemn Emperor Frederick.[30]

Bismarck's attack against the Freisinn and the memory of Frederick III coincided with a governmental victory in the Prussian elections on 6 November 1888. The left-liberals lost 11 seats and only returned 29 deputies to the new parliament, while the combined Kartell caucus increased from 267 to 279 members. This was not enough, however, to alleviate the profound unease that the chancellor's crusade against the late emperor had caused, even amongst the political Right. The Free Conservative *Deutsches Wochenblatt* criticised the Bismarck press for "speaking about the dead monarch in a manner that was only too likely to weaken the monarchical spirit." The historian and Free Conservative Reichstag deputy Hans Delbrück was similarly appalled by Bismarck's report of 23 September: "Faced with this wicked document," he wrote, "a German patriot has no choice but to cover his head and fall silent." Even the ultraconservative *Neue Preussische Zeitung* was concerned that the steps taken by the government might damage the monarchical feeling in the country and drag the emperor's name into the mire of party strife. The chancellor may well have shrugged off comments like these, but they were not exclusively directed at him. When the Grand Duke of Baden and Roggenbach considered the issue, they agreed that "the young emperor's permission to have his father and mother dishonoured and the beautiful figure of the crown prince . . . dragged in the dirt of calumny by attacks carried out in his name" was causing "damage to his own reputation and of the monarchical spirit." William II was sensitive to this kind of argument and decided not to lend any further support to Bismarck's actions.[31]

This did not mean that the new emperor simply dropped the issue of his father's memory or adopted an uncritical view. It was known, for instance, that William approved of Gustav Freytag's reminiscences of the crown prince, which were published in October 1889 and attracted attention because of their unflattering tone. Rather, a sceptical attitude toward Emperor Frederick's political role needed to be embedded in a wider context of monarchical respect and filial piety. The politically dangerous myth of the liberal People's Emperor *(Volkskaiser)* could not be fought by denigration alone. This would harm the institution of monarchy itself. A complementary strategy was required: the propagation of a popular but harmless countermyth. The well-established heroic image of Our Fritz, with its strong links to Frederick the Great and Queen Louise, provided an excellent basis for this endeavour. Moreover, the pronounced identification with his dynastic past—which the late emperor had shown throughout his life—and his willingness to project the image of a radiant hero meant that this version of his memory was arguably more truthful than the liberal counterpart it was designed to crowd out. Once the theme of the Noble Sufferer stoically enduring his grim fate was added to those of the glorious warrior and the kindly monarchical father figure, the memory of Frederick III could simply be slotted into the Hohenzollerns' patriotic narrative.[32]

The Kartell papers helped to disseminate this version of the late emperor from the very moment of his death. The crown prince had been a mature man "when he first draped the victor's laurels around his head," *Die Post* observed on 16 June 1888, but "within the German people he continued to live as a youthful hero, an Achilles in body, with blonde hair and fiery eyes, a young man." On the eve of Frederick's funeral, the *Norddeutsche Allgemeine Zeitung* evoked the "memory of the war lord, tested in battle and enthralled with the fatherland's greatness and prestige, of the heir to the name and spirit of his great ancestors, . . . of the imperial sufferer, who parted from us as a hero, a martyr." The *Reichsbote* predicted in October 1888 that Frederick's memory would carry on "in the noble, exalted shape of the heroic victor of Königgrätz and Wörth" and as "the admirable hero patiently bearing his terrible suffering."[33]

Although scant, the attention conservative papers paid to the tenth anniversary of Emperor Frederick's death also matched this image.

The *Neue Preussische Zeitung* called him William I's "all-popular and formerly flourishing son, the victorious general Frederick." According to the *Reichsbote,* Germany suffered a double loss in 1888: "The old emperor William, who completed the great work together with his chancellor Bismarck, and Emperor Frederick, who contributed to it as a general." Twenty-five years after Frederick's death, the *Neue Preussische Zeitung* still remembered "above all the general of the Second Army of 1866, whose intervention secured the most glorious victory in Prussia's history . . . and the general of the Third Army of 1870, who adorned his standards with the laurel of Weissenburg and Wörth." The *Norddeutsche Allgemeine Zeitung* similarly reminded its readers of a man whose head was "richly adorned with the laurels of war" and who remained "right up until his last days a prince and soldier from top to toe."[34]

William II did his best to consolidate this image. After the unveiling of the Emperor Frederick monument at Wörth in October 1895, he pledged "within sight of the noble victor, our immortalized emperor, to keep what he fought to gain and to protect the crown which he forged." Half a year later, the emperor launched the battleship *Emperor Frederick III.* It was named, he declared, after a man who "enjoyed the privilege to have stood at the head of Germany's united armies in order to gain unity for our fatherland and to secure the imperial crown for our house for all eternity." When unveiling his father's monument in Berlin in October 1904, William spoke about the "Siegfried-like form and comely looks" of this "high-minded hero who fought his father's battles to pave the way for the Reich." Once the "storms of war" had abated, though, Emperor Frederick—like his great ancestor and namesake—tended and furthered "the peaceful arts." Addressing the people of Aachen seven years later, after he had unveiled yet another monument in honour of his father, the emperor reiterated that it was "on the bloody field of battle" that Crown Prince Frederick William "had helped to obtain the imperial crown for his venerable father and unity for the German people." William II gave the fullest account of his version of Emperor Frederick's memory in the recollections he published after his abdication in 1918: "My father lives in the mind of his own and of succeeding generations as the victor of Königgrätz and Wörth who helped to forge Germany's Imperial crown; as the amiable and popular Crown Prince; and, as Emperor . . . as the man of sorrows, who bore with noble fortitude sufferings that carried him off before his time."[35]

In shaping his father's public image, William II did not have to rely on words alone. One of the most eye-catching ways in which the political culture of the German Reich expressed itself was a veritable craze for monuments. By the end of the First World War, the country was adorned with hundreds—maybe thousands—of statues, busts, towers, colonnades, arches, and plaques honouring the nation's greats. Emperor William I and Bismarck led the field by a comfortable margin, but the widespread devotion to Emperor Frederick III also left traces in bronze, marble, and granite. Files in the Prussian State Archives indicate that in Prussia alone, permanent memorials to Frederick III were installed in more than 150 different cities, towns, and villages. Veterans of the 1870–1871 war assembled around a bust of the late emperor in the Berlin suburb of Wilmersdorf as early as October 1888. More than twenty-five years later, a huge equestrian statue of the emperor was unveiled in the city of Stettin and dominated the Königsplatz until its destruction in the Second World War.[36]

As emperor and king, William II had the power to control this increasingly omnipresent medium. He could ensure that the authorised version of the myth of Emperor Frederick would be literally carved in stone. Karl Schrader appreciated the importance of this visual form of commemoration. Even before the veterans of Wilmersdorf congregated around their humble memorial of Frederick III, the Freisinn deputy anticipated that monuments would be used in a manner inimical to the left-liberal agenda. "They will build him some equestrian statues," he predicted to Stauffenberg in August 1888, "but this will not perpetuate his memory, at least not in the way in which it should be done."[37]

This, however, was precisely how Emperor William intended to commemorate his father, and he used his prerogative to sanction the building of statues of members of the royal family accordingly. As a first step, William asserted the priority of his grandfather's memory by insisting that monuments in honour of his father could not be erected in places that were still without an Emperor William monument. Second, the emperor kept a close eye on the design and symbolic content of the monuments for his father. They had to depict him as the embodiment of military glory, as a youthful crown prince, and preferably on horseback. On this, William and his chancellor were agreed. In August 1889, Bismarck observed in a formal submission to the Prussian council of ministers that one could not ignore "the regrettable but historical fact" that Frederick had not been able to do anything as emperor that would "justify an emperor-monument." The late monarch was entitled to the nation's gratitude, Bismarck explained, but his claim rested on the "support which he, as a general, lent his father in 1866 and 1870/1 in connection with the foundation of the German Reich." The only kind of monument that was justified, Bismarck concluded, would be one "honouring the crown prince as the general and politician he was then."[38]

Files from the emperor's civil cabinet document how closely William scrutinised the various proposals. The proportions of a bust of Frederick to be displayed in the East Prussian town of Tapiau in 1904 struck him as incorrect, so the emperor personally marked up a photograph of the model and explained the necessary changes. The monument envisaged for Magdeburg in 1906 had its cherubs removed, garlands added, and Frederick's thighs slimmed down. The patriots of Wanne were given the go-ahead in 1913, but only if wreaths on the pedestal of their memorial were removed and the granite cut rather than polished.[39]

The emperor was not merely concerned with aesthetic detail; the monuments also had to tell the correct story. The first great statue dedicated to Frederick III was unveiled at Wörth in October 1895. After making a few minor alterations, the emperor accepted a design showing the crown prince on horseback atop a rocky outcrop fronted by two Germanic warriors shaking hands. This set the tone for future sculptures. The statue erected in Wiesbaden two years later represented Frederick standing and clasping his marshal's baton. William praised the work of sculptor Joseph Uphues, but—according to the *Wiesbadener Tageblatt*—the locals did not recognise their "simple and liberal Emperor Frederick" in this "greatcoat-shrouded, cannon-barrel-booted, pompous" figure. Nor did the people of Cologne get the monument they wanted. The winning entry of their competition had shown Frederick standing amid two groups of figures: soldiers on the one hand, workers and middle-class citizens on the other. In July 1900, William declared that only an equestrian statue would do, and imposed the design by the Berlin sculptor Peter Breuer. The management of the Baltic resort of Misdroy learned in April 1903 that their statue of Frederick in civilian clothes was unacceptable. His Majesty insisted on a military greatcoat.[40]

The pious and respectful devotion to his father that Emperor William displayed on grand occasions was also more than an expression of filial affection, compliance with the rules of decorum, and the public maintenance of a popular monarchical feeling. Presenting himself as the devoted fulfiller of Emperor Frederick's most treasured concerns was another way in which Emperor William could domesticate his father's memory. This proved particularly easy in projects where father and son agreed. A fortnight after Frederick's death, William II attended a meeting of the Prussian council of ministers and committed himself to building Berlin's new cathedral in the grand manner supposedly favoured by the late emperor. Two months later, William reiterated in a formal order that the design produced by the architect Raschdorff "according to the intentions of Their Majesties, My father, the Emperor and King Frederick, resting in God, and My Mother, the Empress and Queen Frederick should form the basis for any further progress irrespective of modifications and alterations which may prove necessary."[41]

It did not take long for a considerable body of opposition to the proposed scheme to build up. A ministerial commission, the Berlin chamber of architects, the academy for civil engineering, and even the press voiced their reservations about the architectural merits and financial implications of the Raschdorff plan. It was known, however, that William II remained committed to the project. "The noble emperor Frederick devoted himself on his sickbed to this issue as much as time and his strength would allow it," the *Schwäbische Merkur* observed in September 1889. "His son considers it his father's legacy to erect the building by following in his footsteps; and that means according to the beautiful plans devised by Frederick III together with the architect Raschdorff." Eventually, William was forced to accept that the Prussian parliament's refusal to commit more than 10 million marks meant that changes were inevitable. Instead of the original Frederick III-Raschdorff design with its triple-nave cathedral, huge campanile, bridge, and price tag of 22 million marks, a single building with just one central dome was erected. Raschdorff remained as chief architect, while William actively superintended the project. In correspondence with his mother, he insisted on the continuity of the new design with his father's wishes. The piece of parchment that was ceremoniously encased in the foundation on 17 June 1894 told a similar story. Its inscription, composed by the emperor himself and published in a governmental paper two days later, traced the idea for a new cathedral to William II's great-uncle, King Frederick William IV, and his grandfather, Emperor William I. "Within days of his accession Our much-loved father, Emperor and King

Frederick III ordered that preparations for the building be resumed, yet a harsh fate denied him its execution," William had written. "Thus the fulfilment of this legacy has fallen to us."[42]

It was hard to surpass the symbolic power of literally building a cathedral on a statement that tied Frederick III to the Hohenzollerns' dynastic tradition. In terms of immediacy and visibility, however, the room dedicated to Frederick III in Berlin's Hohenzollern Museum won hands down. By sticking precisely to the same kitschy culture of display that characterized the presentation of all the other Hohenzollern monarchs, the newly added room conveyed the key elements of the authorised version of Frederick III. The contents emphasised his continuity with his predecessors on the Prussian throne and his military achievements. There were numerous loyal addresses and letters of congratulation to mark birthdays and anniversaries, royal photo albums, toys, and childhood uniforms. As befitted the commemoration of a Noble Sufferer, the room featured a crown of thorns—a souvenir Frederick William had brought back from his trip to the Orient in 1869. Visitors to the museum could also marvel at a wreath of dried leaves adorned with a ribbon commemorating the victories of Düppel and Königgrätz, a chandelier lovingly crafted from a grenade that had missed the crown prince in 1864, and—rather poignantly—the pipe he used to smoke during his campaigns.[43]

Trite though it may appear, it was this version of Frederick's memory that prevailed in imperial Germany. In spite of the best efforts of Empress Frederick and the erstwhile Kronprinzenpartei, Frederick III did not emerge as the anchoring point of an opposition party pushing for liberal change and a socially aware, more democratized form of imperial rule. Perhaps counterintuitively, it was the late emperor's continuing popularity and relatively high public profile that ended up diminishing his political relevance. The edges with which the left-liberals sought to equip their version of the Frederick myth lost their sharpness because the "victor of Wörth" and Noble Sufferer was smothered in patriotic treacle. Almost all of the scores of statues, plaques, and obelisks were initiated and paid for by local veterans' associations and civic committees. These groups were eager to establish memorials reflecting a wider patriotic consensus rather than inviting party strife. This general trend was illustrated by events in Wittenberg. In 1890, the leader of the local Freisinn section and town councillor Gustav Matthesius suggested that a

Frederick monument be erected on the Schlossplatz. This was "initially pursued as a party matter in a less than tactful manner," the Prussian minister of the interior reported in 1893, but it soon became clear "that the necessary funds could not be raised in this way and a wider committee was formed which was headed by Mayor Dr. Schild."[44]

Within weeks of Emperor Frederick's death, the market was supplied with a steady stream of hagiographical accounts of his life. These numerous books, booklets, and brochures celebrated a glorious, noble, and tragic prince and monarch. In doing so, they also helped to disseminate and consolidate the harmonious, heroic, and sanitized version of Frederick's memory. With very few exceptions, these publications downplayed or omitted every controversial aspect. An unusually dedicated reader could have perused the biographies of Emperor Frederick by Adami (1888), Höcker (1888), Hottinger (1888), Brunold (1889), Hiltl (1889), Seidel (1890), von Felseneck (1899), Hoffmeyer (1901), Garlepp (1911), and Epstein (1913) and would still have remained almost entirely ignorant of the bitter rift between the crown prince and his father in 1863. The same spirit of patriotic decorum pervaded the work of the teacher Hermann Müller-Bohn, who was probably the most successful contemporary biographer of Emperor Frederick. Between 1889 and 1914, this prolific panegyrist of the Hohenzollern dynasty published numerous editions of several near-identical biographies of the emperor, all of which would have made excellent presents. Entitled *Our Fritz: German Emperor and King of Prussia, Emperor Frederick the Gracious: A Patriotic Book of Honour,* and *Emperor Frederick—a Memorial,* these massive and richly decorated tomes provided a wealth of detail and boundless loyal edification. Above all, the books incorporated Frederick III firmly into the Hohenzollerns' dynastic story. "We find that in a peculiar way ... Emperor Frederick combined the characteristics and merits of his ancestors," Müller-Bohn observed at the end of *Emperor Frederick the Gracious.* The author proved his contention by ploughing through a list of no fewer than six of Frederick's monarchical predecessors who had purportedly bequeathed eleven separate virtues to him.[45]

In retrospect, it appears almost overdetermined that the attempt to establish the myth of Frederick III as a force of political opposition in imperial Germany would not succeed. As images of the past are not rigidly fixed but malleable and permanently contested, the shape and application of historical memory is determined by the distribution of political, cultural, and social power within a society. It is not surprising that those who wielded this power used it in order to gain mastery over political myths that were generally deployed to justify political aims. Confrontations of this kind were particularly fierce in imperial Germany, it has been argued, because bourgeois forces realised that control over political myths was a substitute for direct participation in the exercise of political power. They could be used to push the aristocratic elites of the Reich in ever new directions. The left-liberal attempt to appropriate and define the memory of Frederick III was certainly undertaken in order to push a political opponent in a different direction, which also explains the vehemence of the reaction. Moreover, this was not—or at least not exclusively—a substitute for political participation, but also a means to widen the Freisinn Party's popular appeal.[46]

In a contest between the forces of Germany's left-liberals on the one hand and the combined strength of the emperor, government, national-liberalism, and conservatism on the other, however, the odds were fairly overwhelmingly stacked against the former. The Freisinn Party's opponents not only commanded incomparably more powerful means of influencing the formation of Frederick's public memory; the left-liberals also entered a period of steady political decline. There were pockets of resilience—at the level of city government, for instance, or in some regions—but the national influence of this increasingly fragmented political force was on the wane.[47]

Moreover, the attempt to establish the memory of a dead monarch as a vehicle for systemic change was further undermined by the gradual emergence of the Social Democrats as the most vibrant opposition to the status quo. Their scepticism about the depth of Crown Prince Frederick William's supposed liberalism and their generally antimonarchical attitude effectively immunized them against the myth of a "people's emperor" whose heart beat for the poor. In March 1888, *Der Sozialdemokrat* described Frederick III's proclamations as full of platitudes and claimed that the Social Democrats had never expected him to "take a decided position in the social struggles of our age." After the emperor's death, the Socialist weekly "very much doubted that Frederick III would have truly fulfilled the hopes bourgeois liberalism had placed in him." When the Reichstag passed an appeal asking the government to erect a Frederick III monument ten years after his death, the Social Democrats refused to endorse it. "Our principles and views on the current system of rule and the leading personalities make it impossible for us," Deputy Paul Singer explained, "to authorize funds dedicated to purposes of monarchical ovation."[48]

The fact that only the Social Democrats refused to put their names to this petition showed how uncontroversial the public celebration of Frederick III had become. With the support of anti-Semites, Conservatives, Free Conservatives, Centrists, National Liberals, the Freisinn, and even the Polish minority, the Reichstag not only voted to provide the funds for this monument but also gave William II full authority over its design and location. The emperor chose the Munich-based sculptor Rudolf Maison to create the statue, which was placed on the banks of the river Spree in the very heart of Berlin and eventually unveiled in October 1904. The monument showed Frederick wearing the uniform of the Pasewalker Cuirassiers, complete with marshal's baton and spiked helmet and, of course, on horseback. Notwithstanding the political intention behind the design of this and all the other monuments in his honour, it would be hard to argue that the man who posed for Heinrich von Angeli's imperious portrait in the very same uniform would have objected to being immortalized in this way.[49]

After the Reich: Remembering Frederick since 1918

After the defeat of the Reich in the First World War and William II's escape to his Dutch exile, Germans had every reason to be sceptical about heroic Hohenzollern emperors with spiked helmets and shimmering breastplates. To many, the dynastic tradition that had produced William II now appeared deeply flawed and responsible for bringing about the calamities of war, defeat, and disorder. In this context, the notion of a different trajectory offered by previous monarchs gained new relevance. The interwar period therefore witnessed a revival of interest in Frederick III and the question of the alternative he might have provided. The monarchical myth was revisited at a time of transition. The imperial regime had changed from a political and legal reality into a recent historical past. Yet only three decades had passed since the ninety-nine days and, for many, the memory of Emperor Frederick remained a vivid and personal experience. Because of this immediacy, the engagement with the Frederick myth that took place during the interwar period was still marked by a flicker of passion and engagement that could not be rekindled after the Second World War.

Within months of William II's abdication, the linguist Eduard Engel republished those extracts from Frederick William's war diaries which had caused such a stir when they were first printed in the *Deutsche Rundschau* in 1888. With a preface dated "the day of Emperor Frederick's death" in 1919, the booklet made no bones about its intention to show how much better Germany would have fared with Frederick, whose commitment to left-liberal principles was "incontestable." There would have been no Anglo-German hostility, no Russo-French alliance, and consequently no world war. As Britain's ally, Germany might have been compelled to make do with a smaller fleet, Engel conceded. But it "would have been and remained bigger than the one we have now," he added acerbically in the very month when the German navy was scuttled at Scapa Flow. In 1922 the monthly *Deutsche Revue* published the lengthy "Memories of Emperor Frederick," penned by Robert Dohme in the autumn of 1888. Dohme had been one of the crown prince's close confidants for many years; his recollections painted an affectionate image of the deceased and dwelled on the callousness displayed by William II at the beginning of his reign.[50]

In 1926 a comprehensive edition of the crown prince's diaries of the War of 1870–1871 superseded Engel's slender volume. Having compared the various manuscripts of the diary and lovingly improved Frederick William's occasionally clunky prose, the archivist Heinrich Otto Meisner presented a 500-page tome to the public. The moment had now come, he declared, when the diary could be "revered by the German people with undivided piety as a precious monument of a noble heart and German conviction." In 1929 Meisner delivered a second volume of the crown prince's diaries covering the years 1848 to 1866. A further two years later, he published *The Prussian Crown Prince in the Constitutional Struggle 1863*. This collection of documents focused specifically on Frederick William's opposition to the repressive policy that was pursued by Bismarck and authorised by his father.[51]

On the one hand, Meisner's work was completed against the background of renewed public interest in Frederick III, which expressed itself with surprising strength at the centenary of the emperor's birth in 1931. On the other hand, the subject was also beginning to attract stronger historiographical interest. For more than thirty years, historical research on Frederick III had been stifled because the polemical controversy following his death had made this topic politically sensitive. Notable early efforts had been tainted by ulterior motives. In 1889 the novelist Gustav Freytag, who had been close to Frederick III over several decades but was now firmly in the Bismarckian camp, published a slim volume of "commemorative leaves." Entitled *The Crown Prince and the German Imperial Crown,* the book made blunt statements about Frederick William's vanity, his mediocrity as a general, and Victoria's dominance. Stosch claimed that Freytag wanted "to hamper the legend-making by which the Freisinn [was seeking] to shroud itself in a monarchical cape." As could be expected, the work was vigorously attacked by Frederick's defenders. The left-liberal *Breslauer Zeitung* found it "hurtful" and rejected Freytag's judgement as compromised. Writing in *Die Nation,* Karl Schrader contradicted Freytag's criticisms one by one. Even the conservative historian Hans Delbrück resented the attempt to expose Frederick's every weakness.[52]

The biography of Frederick III which Martin Philippson published in 1893 was a much more substantial work than Freytag's essay, but it also had a partisan background. The author had cooperated closely with Schrader, who not only commented on the manuscript but also encouraged Empress Victoria to support the scheme. Philippson also tried to approach Roggenbach in order to secure additional material for the book and offered him the right to vet the final text before publication. The result was predictable. "Philippson has deftly painted all the good and beautiful things one can say about the gentleman in the brightest colours and has left everything weak and inadequate in the darkest shadow," Stosch commented after reading the book. "He reports much that is wrong, but with such confidence and such positive evidence that his hero appears even more glorious."[53]

The polemics of the years immediately after 1888 soon gave way to a sterile consensus of dynastic decorum endorsed by the historiographical establishment. In 1901, for instance, the *Historische Zeitschrift,* the premier journal of historical scholarship in Germany, published reviews of a new edition of Philippson's biography and Herman Müller-Bohn's *Emperor Frederick the Gracious.* Professor Georg Kaufmann of Breslau University attacked the former for taking Frederick William's side in every conflict with William I or Bismarck. Philippson's biography was "not the book about Emperor

Frederick that we need," the professor concluded. Müller-Bohn's *Patriotic Book of Honour,* however, was praised as a "beautiful work which one would wish to see widely disseminated amongst our families." The numerous popular biographies of Frederick published during William II's reign thus merely offered florid reiterations of a patriotic story and did little to rescue the memory of the late emperor from the purely formulaic. Even though Margarete von Poschinger's three volumes of 1899–1900 struck a balance between the bürgerlich-liberal and conventionally heroic aspects of Frederick's life by providing bounteous information on both, they did not break this mould either. The readability of Poschinger's work was greatly reduced by the author's decision to rely entirely on compiling scrupulously sanitized source material, which allowed her to fill more than 1,300 pages without offering a single original interpretation. A further problem that limited the incisiveness of this work was Poschinger's closeness to Bismarck, whose endorsement of her project she proudly alluded to in the preface.[54]

The end of the German monarchies in 1918 opened up new perspectives and brought with it unprecedented scholarly freedoms. The dynamic that forced the exiled emperor to abandon his attempts to prevent the publication of the final volume of Bismarck's memoirs, which quickly sold more than 300,000 copies, also invigorated engagement with Frederick III. Prompted by Meisner's 1926 edition of the crown prince's war diaries, the theologian Friedrich Curtius published "Emperor Frederick and the German People" in the catholic monthly *Hochland.* This article by the son of Frederick William's old tutor passionately endorsed the interpretation of the late emperor as a bürgerlich liberal. It elevated him to the status of a moral beacon. The author described the monarch as at one with the German nation, its culture, its bourgeoisie, and its left-liberal politics. Moreover, Frederick III was ethically opposed to Bismarck and alienated from his son. It was fair to demand, Curtius concluded, that the German people defend Frederick's memory and that "it declare itself for him, just like once it paid homage to the victor of Wörth." The left-liberal historian Johannes Ziekursch, whose political history of the Bismarck era appeared in 1927, approached the topic with much less pedagogic emphasis. Soberly weighing up Frederick's generosity of spirit, decency, and moderate liberalism against his resignation, irresolution, and powerlessness, Ziekursch painted a sympathetic but largely demystified portrait of the emperor.[55]

By the 1930s, the renewed interest in Frederick had grown sufficiently to produce two full-scale biographies. Both were written with literary ambition and from a liberal standpoint. Though the authors had trained as historians, neither was part of the academic establishment and they found themselves increasingly marginalised and persecuted as Germany's attempt at liberal democracy was failing. In 1931 the Jewish teacher and biographer Eugen Wolbe published *Emperor Frederick: The Tragedy of One Passed-Over*. Described as the first modern biography of the emperor and promising to remedy the absence of an objective account of his life, this pacily written life portrayed its tragic hero with great warmth and his liberal inclinations with undisguised sympathy. Wolbe made it clear that Frederick's premature death marked the beginning of a calamitous development. He devoted the final lines of his work to Victoria's worries about Germany's growing Anglophobia, "which Emperor Frederick's successor failed to rein in." Werner Richter's *Frederick III: Life and Tragedy of the Second Hohenzollern Emperor* conveyed a similar image of liberal righteousness and tragic failure. The historian and journalist had fled Nazi Germany in 1936 and finished his book in exile two years later. According to Richter, the conviction that "right surpasses might" ran through Frederick's life like a "straight, unbroken line of development," from the eighteen-year-old's insistence that a parliament was essential to the dying emperor's dismissal of the election-rigging minister Puttkamer. Identified with such a "fundamental law," Frederick had clearly become a symbol against lawless violence of the Nazi state.[56]

Not all the historiographical attention devoted to Frederick III during the interwar period was so friendly. Seeking to provide a psychological explanation for William II's character flaws, Emil Ludwig's sensational study of 1926 presented the public with an unflattering account of the last emperor's father. Ludwig described Crown Prince Frederick William as a weak man. Pompous, authoritarian by nature, suffused with ideas of divine grace, and seeking distraction on endless travels, he was pushed into liberal ideas by a powerful spouse. Irresolute though he was, he nevertheless chafed under the yoke of his position and vented his frustration by treating his eldest son badly. When Friedrich Curtius attacked what he considered Ludwig's spiteful account of the crown prince, the latter hit back by questioning Frederick III's liberalism. It amounted to little more than the "romantic-dynastic-democratic imperial dream" of a prince who "wanted to wear scarlet and crown and adorn his wife with it" but was never prepared to be merely first amongst equals. Frederick William was fortunate, Ludwig harshly concluded, that his father's longevity protected him against ever having to deliver on the expectations associated with his rule. Some conservative historians were similarly scathing when commenting on the edition of Frederick William's war diaries. Kurt von Raumer observed in the *Historische Zeitschrift* that the diary could not be read without revealing—"with shocking clarity"—the crown prince's lack of political talent, naïve ignorance, childlikeness, and obsession with trivialities. Writing in the *Preussische Jahrbücher*, Hans Rothfels concluded that the diary proved the charge of Frederick William's susceptibility to "petticoat influences." Rothfels also claimed that it illustrated the crown prince's lack of originality, focus, and political instinct.[57]

The centenary year of Frederick III's birth, 1931, thus came at a time when his memory had acquired a hybrid quality. On the one hand, it was no longer protected by patriotic decorum and monarchical power. The emperor's life lay open to critical investigation. Hundreds of pages of his private papers were now in the public domain. Moreover, neither the liberal nor the heroic-patriotic version of Frederick's myth retained the power to enthral that they may once have possessed. On the other hand, the responses to the centenary would show that the process of disenchanting the memory of Our Fritz was not yet complete. For some of the older individuals involved, the myth still had the immediacy and lustre of a firsthand experience. Even the theatre director and writer Ludwig Sternaux, who at forty-six years of age did not even belong to the oldest generation, vividly recalled the cultish veneration of Emperor Frederick: men proudly sported an "Emperor-Frederick-beard" and women wore brooches made from coins minted during his brief reign. The emperor's omnipresent picture lay amongst the family photos, as if it belonged to them. His own youth was still full of these memories, Sternaux explained in his piece for the Berlin daily *Der Tag* in 1931. The former diplomat and Reichstag deputy Hans Arthur von Kemnitz had waited as a seventeen-year-old in the snow outside Charlottenburg Station in 1888 to witness Emperor Frederick's arrival from San Remo. In his article for the same paper, Kemnitz emphasised Frederick's immediate, overwhelming, and natural popularity that would have expressed itself in celebrations and fêtes everywhere, "if our old Reich still existed today."[58]

The end of Hohenzollern rule in 1918 did not mean that the political purposes once served by the Frederick myth disappeared with it. Rather, by 1931 a reversal of fronts had occurred, which led liberals and monarchists to rediscover the usefulness of Frederick's persona. Now it was the forces of the political Right who ensured that the emperor's 100th birthday did not pass without celebrations. Monarchist organisations like the right-wing *Nationalverband Deutscher Offiziere* (National League of German Officers) and the *Preußenbund* (Prussia League) seized the occasion to stage events in pursuit of their own agendas. Like France's restored Bourbon dynasty after the fall of Napoleon, the monarchists of Weimar Germany had learned nothing and forgotten nothing. By brandishing the old image of the military hero, they were hoping to undermine the republican status quo. On 16 October, a group of officers—among them Emperor William's second son, Prince Eitel Friedrich—convened in the Marble Hall of Berlin's Zoological Garden to commemorate Emperor Frederick and listen to a speech by the Reichstag deputy Friedrich Everling. This well-known monarchist insisted that Frederick had been a soldier above all else and had proved his heroism by enduring his "unheard-of fate." On 18 October, the *Preußenbund* organised a patriotic pilgrimage to Frederick's tomb in Potsdam. Under the watchful eyes of members of the *Stahlhelm* (steel helmet) paramilitary, thousands of veterans marched to Frederick's mausoleum. Former crown prince William and his brothers attended the festivities. William II had sent a telegram from the Netherlands to commemorate his father, "the heroic victor of the decisive battles during the genesis of the German Reich, the pious sufferer on the imperial throne." The sermon was preached by the former court chaplain Johannes Vogel, who praised the military heroism of the "Siegfried-like" figure, the fortitude with which he bore his fate and his gentle humanity. Lest anyone might think Our Fritz a Republican, though, Vogel snapped that he would have locked up "international democrats, if they had turned practical, before they knew it."[59]

The Democrats, thus threatened, begged to differ. "Many things would have turned out differently if Emperor Frederick had lived," the *Berliner Morgenpost* declared on 18 October 1931. Remembering him was now "a means of comparison and a force to guide us," the paper observed, but "the fulfilment of the patriotic hopes once associated with his person, [was] now incumbent upon the people." Writing in the *Berliner Tageblatt,* the prominent left-wing journalist and lawyer Rudolf Olden enlisted Emperor Frederick even more clearly for the democratic cause. Anyone with firsthand experience of the current Hohenzollerns would find it hard to believe, Olden claimed, that there once was a Prussian crown prince who rose "against king and government in order to demonstrate for the freedom of the liberal press." If he had lived, history would have taken a different route: Central Europe would have turned to the West, would have experienced "a happy period of civic development," and "democracy would have matured."[60]

The decades after 1931 were lean ones for the memory of the penultimate Hohenzollern monarch. National Socialist mythmaking had no use for Anglophile liberals or noble sufferers. Frederick III did not fare much better in the Federal Republic of Germany, which has been described as a "largely myth-free zone." Berlin's large Prussia exhibition of 1981 entirely ignored Emperor Frederick. Werner Knopp, the director of the foundation responsible for Prussia's cultural heritage, noted this with more than a hint of bitterness and declared that this neglect—precisely 150 years after Frederick's birth and in a museum that the crown prince had helped to establish—would have upset the sensitive monarch. This "cold and smooth country celebrates anniversaries only reluctantly," Knopp grumbled.[61]

It did not take too long, though, until the slight of 1981 was atoned. In 1988–1989 an exhibition on the emperor's life was organised by the Prussian State Archives to mark the centenary of Frederick's death. After a month in Berlin, it travelled to Westphalia, Bad Homburg, and Bonn, where it closed in October 1989. Almost all of those who commented on the exhibition were attracted by the lure of an unrealised superior alternative embodied by the tragic monarch. "German history would naturally have taken a different turn, if this ruler had reigned for longer," insisted a commentator on WDR radio. The government weekly *Das Parlament* similarly pondered how "the history of the German Reich and of Europe" would have changed if this "liberal minded emperor had been able to act true to his principles." The *Bonner Rundschau* suggested that Frederick might have been the man to complement Bismarck's foreign policy with "an urgently needed more liberal concept of domestic politics." According to the *Rhein-Zeitung*, the emperor was even counted amongst those paving the way for the rule of law in a democratic state.[62]

Such fulsome endorsements of the progressive version of the Frederick myth more than a century after the emperor's death marked only a partial victory for the liberals who had worked so hard to establish it in the 1880s and 1890s. They had wanted to create a political tool to prevent precisely the kind of development that became the main reason for the resurgence of the legend of the missed opportunity. The story of the liberal emperor returned as a symbol of remorseful failure, not as the sign of a victorious campaign. Such is the tragedy of Frederick's life: when he is remembered at all now, it is for what he might have done but could never accomplish.

Conclusion

The death of Emperor Frederick III was a godsend for purveyors of devotional trinkets. Soon the market was flooded with countless commemorative knickknacks. In addition to the many medals, prints, and tankards, mourning patriots were offered a "vision card" dedicated to the late, lamented monarch. This remarkable gimmick featured a portrait of Frederick in the shape of a strongly contoured black-and-white negative. A set of instructions below the drawing invited the spectator to focus closely on a tiny cross at the centre of the image while slowly counting up to fifty. After that, on gazing up to the ceiling, "one will behold, as in a vision, the likeness of the Emperor Frederick III, who departed this world so soon." An even "more luminous and downright ghost-like effect" was promised to those who first stared at the image and then covered their closed eyes with their hands. This interactive keepsake does not simply demonstrate the physiological impressionability of the intent observer but also offers a salutary warning to the biographer: if one peers at historical figures for long enough, one may end up seeing their phantasmic outlines in all sorts of places. While inevitably emphasising the life and relevance of its subject, a scholarly biography must take care to avoid the optical illusion that results from imprinted retinas and find other means to account for the importance of its subject.

In the case of the highly visible Frederick III, there is an obvious risk of exaggerating his importance. After all, it can be argued that his direct impact on the world around him and the subsequent course of German history was very limited. Crown Prince Frederick William may have planned to make changes after his succession; a number of developments might have been facilitated by Frederick III's reign; and after his death interested parties voiced extravagant claims about the difference the ninety-nine days would make in the long term. It nevertheless remains true that almost none of this came to pass. A number of factors and events combined to deny the crown prince and emperor real political power and active influence: the irresolution, resignation, and docility that formed part of his personality; the powerful, dominant individuals determined to keep him on a tight rein; a framework of dynastic and constitutional rules that deprived the position of the crown prince of direct power; the inability of the political forces championing the crown prince to gain parliamentary dominance; and, ultimately, his fatal illness. As a consequence, Frederick III's historiographical footprint has been small. Those looking for a chapter on his ninety-nine-day reign in the standard textbooks will in most cases be disappointed.[1]

The observation that Frederick III was not amongst the key figures who shaped Germany does not, however, relegate the story of his life to the status of a moving illustration of the human condition to be cited merely for the sake of completeness or in order to sustain counterfactual parlour games. A careful reading of Frederick's biography reveals much about the functioning of the Hohenzollern monarchy and dynasty within the politics and political culture of Prussia and Germany. Once the developments triggered by his long-awaited succession, his contribution to defining the public image of monarchy, and the striking similarities between him and his son are taken into consideration, it becomes clear that Frederick's role was important at the time and had significant consequences. This is particularly apparent in areas—such as the popularisation of the dynasty—where he was relatively free to apply the talents he possessed. Paradoxically, even the personal limitations that Crown Prince Frederick William brought to his position can be helpful here. Extraordinary contingent factors resulting from an individual's outstanding aptitude—such as rare tactical cunning, unusual ruthlessness, or singular energy—easily obscure the analysis of structural or systemic aspects of the topic. That Frederick William was equipped with a more ordinary measure of ability facilitates the appraisal of the normal workings of the monarchical system of which he was a pivotal part.

William I's quip that he found it hard being emperor under Bismarck has become almost proverbial. The frequent descriptions of the chancellor as an overmighty grand vizier or majordomo reflected this widespread belief in the completeness of Bismarck's power. Yet the fragility of his position was demonstrated all too clearly by the anticipated succession of Crown Prince Frederick William throughout much of the 1880s and then, from 1887 onward, by the expectation that his son would soon ascend the throne. Within a system of hereditary monarchy, the chancellor's tenure essentially depended on the unpredictable timing of the Grim Reaper. As William I was entering his ninth decade, the belief in the imminent accession of a new monarch whose abilities were not rated highly and whose future decisions were hard to forecast—Bismarck described Frederick William variously as either sound and sensible, radically liberal, intrinsically authoritarian, or unable to resist his wife's wishes—coloured much of the political agenda. From 1879 onward, this impacted directly on the formation and programmes of political parties, shaped electoral tactics, led to institutional change, motivated significant foreign policy ventures, and caused the removal of ministers and court officials. Frederick William's cancer diagnosis triggered a new flurry of tactical manoeuvres. Bismarck, individual ministers, and the various parties realised that they had to trim their sails to a different wind.

The recurrence of succession constellations and their capacity to set the agenda before the accession of the new monarch underline the fundamental openness of the Prusso-German monarchical system to change brought about by the vagaries of dynastic inheritance. It is also worth noting that the parties and the Reichstag played very important roles in the various tactical responses to anticipated successions. Both the left-liberals and Bismarck regarded the formation of party alliances capable of delivering strong electoral results and a dominant position in parliament as crucial weapons in their fight for political hegemony.

The Hohenzollern monarchy's ability to accommodate change was also illustrated by the public image of Crown Prince Frederick William and by the ways in which it was generated and communicated. The persona Our Fritz reconciled a remarkably wide spectrum of virtues and distinctions that corresponded to both contemporary tastes and historical tradition. In this figure, a narrative of meritocratic middle-class culture and informed engagement with the needs of modern society was seamlessly intertwined with the heroic story of the noble warrior and exalted scion of a great dynastic line. Through this combination, Crown Prince Frederick William helped to strengthen Hohenzollern rule by making it appear compatible with a political culture whose public discourse was increasingly characterised by bourgeois values. Crucially, this was achieved without conceding too much in the way of royal prerogative or monarchical awe.

The manner in which the celebrity figure Our Fritz was created and sustained points to the integration of the Prusso-German monarchy into the developing modern media system and the public spheres it created. On the one hand, there was in Crown Prince Frederick William a monarchical actor with a flair for public relations and a desire to maintain a certain image of himself. It is a moot point to enquire to what extent this was driven simply by the crown prince's "love of approbation," as Bismarck supposed,[2] or by a deliberate attempt to communicate the prospect of a different political future. While there is no unequivocal evidence to suggest that Frederick William was systematically constructing a bürgerlich-liberal image of himself for political ends, the forces of party-political liberalism clearly tried to benefit from this portrayal of the crown prince. On the other hand, the persona Our Fritz was not, of course, purely a product of Frederick William's efforts. It was coauthored by the media and by other interested parties using that media. The crown prince's image was a public commodity over which the depicted royal could not exercise complete control. It frequently showed aspects that were simply projected onto Frederick William, whose highly public profile and important future role promised maximum visibility.

As a result of his great popularity, his winning ways, and his unequivocal commitment to the nation-state created in 1870–1871, Frederick William also contributed significantly to the consolidation of the Reich identity, especially in the non-Prussian parts of Germany. The warmth of feeling toward him as the leader of the South German troops during the Franco-Prussian War and as a regular visitor afterward was powerfully expressed after his death. "While our simple country folk possessed in the prince a talisman against un-German influences and siren calls, his noble personality made him the bulwark of every lofty and ideal endeavour to the intellectual nobility," Munich's *Allgemeine Zeitung* observed in June

1888 and mourned the "German crown prince," who had won Bavarian hearts and minds for national unity. Whereas in Prussia Emperor William II had kept his father's funeral almost indecorously low-key and hidden from public view, the Bavarian government came under massive pressure to stage a grand ceremony in memory of the late emperor. A combination of popular demands and urgent advice from within the Bavarian civil service forced the ministry in Munich to scale up the commemorative celebrations. The "spectacular act of national loyalty and solidarity" that followed marked the incorporation of the imperial dimension into the symbolic language of the kingdom of Bavaria.[3]

The posthumous rise of Frederick III's political profile continued as the antagonists joined the fray of a public and noticeably fierce contest over the late emperor's memory. Both the left-liberal grouping around the Freisinn Party and Empress Victoria and the conservative-governmental camp around William II and Bismarck spared no effort in championing their own versions of the Frederick myth and in challenging that of their adversaries. The intensity of this conflict confirmed the political relevance of the Our Fritz persona and demonstrated that the different political actors were heavily committed to the politics of memory. They took a keen interest in which version of the past was being communicated to the public, as well as in the management of that message. The left-liberals not only used their party press, but staged large-scale commemorative events with a quasi-religious character to tie a political narrative to forms of organised remembrance. William II, who had "an acute and romantic sense of dynastic responsibility,"[4] patently felt the sting of his father—a king and emperor so readily associated with Frederick the Great, Queen Louise, and the glorious wars of 1864–1871—being used as a political weapon against him. He retaliated with energy and resourcefulness. In addition to allowing Bismarck to resort to the crude means of official chicanery and newspaper smears, the emperor ensured that his version of Frederick III's memory was communicated through public speeches, monuments, official architecture, and museums.

Important though it was, the management of his father's myth was not the chief concern of William II's politics of memory—the emperor cared even more about glorifying his much-adored grandfather. William I was to be celebrated as "William the Great," as a German worthy ranked alongside Luther and Goethe, and as the true embodiment of the nation.[5] William II would therefore hardly have relished the observation that several aspects of his own character and political style were noticeably unlike William I's somewhat dour Prussiandom. Rather, he owed much more to his father than is suggested by the claim that his accession marked a stark deviation from the path which Frederick III would have followed. It is ironic that the influence Emperor Frederick had on his eldest son was perhaps the most immediate and momentous way in which he impacted on the future government of Germany. There were several similarities between the two men on the level of personal foibles and habits. Both had a soft spot for uniforms and decorations. Both had relatively short attention spans and dealt with their low boredom thresholds by flitting from one activity to another. "He has no interests to which he devotes particular care," the Grand Duke of Baden observed about Crown Prince Frederick William in 1872. "His entire lifestyle essentially consists of a constant splintering of time." The crown prince's favourite means of escape from the tedium and restrictions of his daily life was frequent and increasingly restless travel. In 1886 a book on Berlin society described Frederick William as "more mobile than sedentary. The railway compartment is his second home." Within a few years, almost identical comments would be made about his son, who soon acquired popular epithets such as William the Impetuous and Travel-Emperor.[6]

The similarities between father and son went further than mere behavioural idiosyncrasies. William II shared Frederick III's deep concern with his own public image and in presenting the Hohenzollern dynasty as the embodiment of a continuous national mission. Following his father's lead, William II also appreciated the importance of the means by which these messages were communicated. He kept a close eye on his portrayal in the press and knew how to utilize other suitable media. William II's pompous and widely publicised journey to the Holy Land, for instance, was full of echoes of his father's trip in 1869. On 29 October 1898, William II entered Jerusalem on a white steed, wearing the splendid helmet and cuirass of the Garde du Corps. Two days later, he formally opened the Protestant Church of St. Saviour, built on the very strip of land that Crown Prince Frederick William had taken formal possession of on 7 November 1869. Like his father before him, William II was also at pains to emphasise how deeply he had been affected by the experience of standing atop the Mount of Olives. The continuity between the generations also manifested itself in William II's eager adoption of his father's projects to use architecture to exalt the Hohenzollern dynasty. Both the rebuilding of Wittenberg's Castle Church and the construction of Berlin's new cathedral were initiated by Frederick III and completed by his son. Our Fritz had clearly taught the "media monarch" William II a trick or two.[7]

Young William had picked up more from his father than an understanding of the media and a strong sense of dynastic continuity. As the emperor mentioned in his speech in Aachen in 1911, he and his father had often sat together and marvelled at colourful illustrations depicting the medieval splendour of the German Empire. The penchant for the romantic medievalism which the young prince acquired on these occasions would forever colour his imperial imagination and its artistic and cultural expression. When William II attended the formal commencement of the reconstruction of a Roman fortress in October 1900, he consecrated the foundation stone to the memory of his father. The late emperor not only deserved the credit for inspiring this project, William claimed, but also for the rebuilding of the headquarters of the Order of the Teutonic Knights, the Marienburg in West Prussia. Completed in 1910, the new imperial palace at Posen provided an even more conspicuous illustration of this continuity of taste and ideology. There was a strangely familiar look about the sculptures of the medieval emperors that adorned the façade: that of Frederick Barbarossa bore the countenance of Frederick III, while that of Charlemagne was graced with the face of William II.[8]

As had been the case with his father, William II's infatuation with the ancient glory and romantic majesty of the German Reich went hand in hand with rather overblown notions about the position of the modern German emperor and the way he should rule. William's attitude toward the other German princes, whom he viewed as vassals rather than allies, was utterly dismissive. He drew a clear line between the majesty of the Hohenzollerns' royal crown, based on military glory, and the lesser dignity of the kingdoms of Bavaria, Saxony, and Württemberg, whose kingly titles he regarded as nothing but Napoleonic gifts. When the emperor learned about the bad blood his stance was causing among the other ruling houses of Germany, his response was no less robust than his father's had been in 1870. There were eighteen Prussian army corps that could be employed against these obstinate southerners, he reminded Chancellor Hohenlohe-Schillingsfürst, a Bavarian nobleman, in 1897.[9]

Moreover, there were striking parallels between the concept of "Personal Rule" frequently associated with William II's reign and the plans the crown prince outlined for his own rule in 1885. Anticipating his father's imminent death, Frederick William had dreamt of restoring the monarch's power vis-à-vis the Reichstag and reducing the chancellor to a servant of the emperor. With the support of the armed forces and that of the nation as a whole, the monarch would be recognised as the only original source of political power and would personally conduct the affairs of the Reich. The extent to which William II ever succeeded in turning his boast that "the Reich ha[d] only one ruler and I am he" into reality, has remained hotly contested amongst historians. It seems clear, though, that he felt entitled to exercise this kind of authority and that his father's beliefs were at least one of the sources of this conviction. "To my notion in one point Papa's theory of the continuation of the Old Empire in the new one is right," William II wrote to his mother in September 1898, "he always [sic] maintained and so do I! for ever and ever, there is only one real Emperor in the world, and that is the German, regardless of his person and qualities, but by right of a thousand years tradition. And his Chancellor has to obey."[10]

Stressing these continuities between William II and his father touches on the counterfactual notion of how different Germany's history would have been if Emperor Frederick III had lived to a ripe old age. The observation that these two Hohenzollern monarchs were not entirely unlike is not, of course, tantamount to claiming that William II was a faithful executor of his father's political legacy. Since there were considerable differences in character and political outlook between these two men, Emperor Frederick's early death was unquestionably a crucial event. The argument that under him Germany would have pursued a different path from the one chosen by his son is most persuasively illustrated by considering the field of foreign policy. It appears almost inconceivable that Emperor Frederick and Empress Victoria would have adopted a policy of colonial and naval expansion understood to antagonize Britain. The removal—or postponement—of the unfortunate rhetorical contributions William II made to the Reich's diplomatic efforts would also very probably have had a positive effect on the country's international standing. The thrust of this counterfactual argument goes further, though, than merely proposing that a number of important mistakes would have been avoided had Emperor Frederick reigned for longer. In its strongest form, the argument imputes that Frederick's reign could have amounted to a liberal refounding of the Reich. In 1946 the historian Veit Valentin described Frederick as clinging "obstinately to parliamentary principles" and saw in his reign the imminent possibility of a "redirection of [Germany's] domestic and foreign policy toward western Europe."[11] Such statements do not stand up to closer scrutiny.

The counterfactual interpretation of 1888 as a fateful omission not only involves claims about the great depth of the changes that would have been wrought but also about the size of the group whose aspirations were quashed. The sense of loss caused by the purportedly grave consequences of Frederick III's death resonated down the decades because it was frequently perceived and portrayed as a collective calamity. The emperor's demise and the attendant collapse of hopes for liberal change did not merely affect the Noble Sufferer and the immediate circle of his family and confidants. Rather, it was argued that when power passed more or less directly from the nonagenarian William I to his twenty-nine-year-old grandson, a whole generation was robbed of its historical hour. This notion was already present in 1888, when the left-liberal weekly *Die Nation* contended that because of Frederick's death the ideas of his generation would not be realised. In 1899 the philosopher Theobald Ziegler came to a similar conclusion. In his widely read reflections on the forces that had shaped the nineteenth century, he argued that the "middle generation," which had been touched by the "old liberal ideas of unity and freedom like no other," had been omitted when "youth succeeded old age" in 1888. This had greatly impoverished the nation. Reflecting on the twenty-fifth anniversary of Frederick's death, the liberal *Frankfurter Zeitung* reiterated this point even more forcefully by insisting that the political influence of a whole generation had been more or less switched off when the emperor passed away.[12]

During the years of the Weimar Republic, this complaint surfaced with increased frequency. Robert Dohme's recollections of the late emperor, published in 1922, claimed that the generation in power after 1888 did not understand the "body of ideals of the older generation, whose formation had been influenced by 1848." Friedrich Curtius pursued the same argument four years later, and concluded that "along with Emperor Frederick an entire phase of Germany's constitutional development was omitted and [could] not be reinstated now."

According to Johannes Ziekursch's book of 1927, the tragedy of 1888 had deprived "the generation that had experienced the revolution of 1848 as adolescents and had fought through the Reich's founding decade as men" of the opportunity of "testing their ideals against reality." When reflecting on Frederick's centenary, even the *völkisch* (racist-nationalist) monthly *Der Türmer* commented on the damage done by the removal "of an entire generation from the calm, steady development of the new German Reich." Indeed, by the early 1930s, the argument that Emperor Frederick had embodied a political generation that was "skipped" in 1888 was so prominent that the young historian Gerhard Scholtz decided to make it the topic of a doctoral research project, which he completed at the University of Heidelberg in 1934.[13]

There are good reasons to be sceptical about claims of this magnitude. After a careful prosopographical analysis, Scholtz was able to show that this argument could not be sustained on the basis of a straightforward age-based concept. By the end of the 1880s, Frederick's age cohort (those born around 1831) were evidently occupying positions of power in the government, civil service, military, and parliament. They had been neither kept out by the older William I/ Bismarck group (1797–1815) nor supplanted by the generation of William II (1859). Applying the concept of a "political generation" does not produce any clear-cut results either. A "political generation" has been defined as those members of an age group who, confronted by certain key experiences, have arrived at a broadly similar attitude toward the key ideas and values of the political order in which they grew up. Frederick was too young to play an active role during the 1848–1849 revolutions, but his accounts of the events show that they constituted key experiences for him. Having to part with "our dear brave soldiers" and leaving the king at the mercy of Berlin's "faithless" citizenry brought tears to his eyes. Yet in spite of these reactions he developed a political outlook which encompassed substantial liberal and German-national components.[14]

Based on these criteria, Frederick's "political generation" can be said to encompass the group of liberal politicians with whom he maintained relations. All of them experienced 1848 as adolescents or young men. Older liberals—men like Forckenbeck (born in 1821), Virchow (1821), Bamberger (1823), Roggenbach (1825), and Lasker (1829)—played minor active parts in the revolutionary movement as fighters, local politicians, or junior functionaries. Others—like Bennigsen (1824), Bunsen (1824), Rickert (1833), Stauffenberg (1834), and Schrader (1834)—either chose not to become actively involved or were too young to do so. Apart from Virchow and Schrader, all these politicians actively cooperated with Bismarck at some point during the foundation and consolidation of the German Reich. As deputies of the National Liberal Party or the Liberal Imperial Party *(Liberale Reichspartei)* they supported the government during the so-called Liberal Era between 1867 and 1878. Bennigsen and Miquel, whose contributions to the Prussian Council of State found so much favour with the crown prince, continued their cooperation with the chancellor even after Bismarck's antiliberal turn of 1878–1879 and eventually helped to set up the conservative-liberal Kartell alliance of 1887. Just as Frederick William had planned in April 1884, Miquel eventually joined the government when he was appointed Prussian minister of finance in 1890. It can hardly be argued that the National Liberals experienced Frederick's death as a moment of collective disempowerment or that they had been denied the opportunity to "test their ideals against reality."

This leaves the left-liberal group around Forckenbeck, Bamberger, Stauffenberg, and Schrader, who turned away from the National Liberals in 1880. The claim that they, the so-called *Kronprinzenpartei* (Crown Prince Party), constituted a political generation who were denied their day when Frederick's death deprived them of a monarchical leader also lacks a credible foundation. On the one hand, the crown prince appears to have lost faith in his ability to spearhead change in German politics long before he was struck down by illness. In 1879, the forty-eight-year-old crown prince wrote to his wife about rumours that he might be passed over: his eighty-two-year-old father was going strong and his own son was acquitting himself well. Such amusing stories were just grist to his mill, he added wearily, "for I often ponder whether it would not be better not to attempt to govern with my generation." Throughout the 1880s, Frederick William continued to describe his own generation's political paradigm as increasingly irrelevant. "The liberal views, with which I have grown up and which I cannot renounce, have been pushed aside," Holstein recorded the crown prince as saying in November 1884. A few days later, Frederick William expressed similar feelings in a letter to Stosch: "My time lies behind me and the future belongs to the coming generation."[15]

At the beginning of the 1880s, the crown prince nevertheless appeared to be attracted by the prospect of a dominant left-liberal party that could provide him with political power independent of the chancellor. Their courtship proved all too brief, though. When the elections of 1884 deprived the Freisinn Party of its promised dowry of parliamentary clout, Frederick William lost interest and their relationship fizzled out. Instead, the crown prince turned to more moderate advisers such as Stosch and Roggenbach, who urged a continuation of Bismarck's chancellorship. That the differences and antipathies between Bismarck and the crown prince were not consistent or fierce enough to rule out a political modus vivendi was demonstrated by the speed and relative ease with which the chancellor's continuation in office was settled after 1884. Stosch, who doggedly advocated that the crown prince ought to cooperate with Miquel's National Liberals, had never been greatly perturbed by Frederick William's flirtation with the left-liberals anyway. "We know, after all," he observed a full six months before the left liberals' drubbing at the polls in October 1884, "that the gentleman's most inner nature is glaringly opposed to the Left."[16] Rather, the crown prince was enthralled by an exalted and politically controversial concept of the dignity and power that should be vested in the German emperor. His plans for government, which he confided to his diary in 1885, illustrate how far removed he was from wishing to make a reality of the Freisinn Party's dream of a parliamentary system. Thus, even a brief survey of Frederick III's own attitudes and beliefs and of his relationships with different political actors considerably weakens the claim that his early death disempowered a left-liberal group that would otherwise have shaped the country's destiny.

That the lament of a "skipped generation" enjoyed significant resonance and purchase in spite of its weak evidential basis points to the real origin of this notion. It is not primarily an argument derived from an analysis of what happened in and immediately after 1888, but belongs to the posthumous story of Frederick III. Gerhard Scholtz already sensed in 1934, a year after Hitler came to power, that the claim essentially concerned something rather intangible: "a specific manifestation of an ideological character publicly represented by the late monarch." The perceived generational loss encompassed the ideals of the mass of the liberal bourgeoisie, a certain experience of social relations, and the projection of social improvement and progress.[17] The realisation that the path taken after Frederick's death had led to war, defeat, and dictatorship caused the thwarting of the purported alternative in 1888 to be mourned more intensively and more widely. This wishful contention—that the tragic emperor could have given Germany an utterly different future and ultimately a preferable past—was the only aspect of the Frederick myth that actively survived until the emperor's latest marked anniversary in 1988.

Challenging the story of the liberal crown prince whose accession could have been a wonderful turning point that would have spared his country and the world untold misery does not strip Frederick III of his only claim on historical importance. Rather, it rescues the man from the dreamland of counterfactual fancy and restores him to a real place in German history. He was fully integrated into the society, culture, and politics of his age. In spite of the tensions and frustrations that cast a shadow over much of his political life, he was not a square peg bearing no resemblance whatsoever to the round hole in which he found himself. It is misleading to label Frederick a "not entirely Prussian" Hohenzollern, as Emil Ludwig did in 1926.[18]

Frederick was linked to his country, his family background, and his position by a multitude of continuities of outlook, preference, and conviction. His liberalism was not just influenced by the British predilections of his wife and father-in-law, but remained close to the moderate, constitutional German National Liberalism represented by Bennigsen and Miquel. He was also imprinted by the romantic nationalism that flourished across Germany in the first half of the nineteenth century. Frederick combined these impressions with stimuli derived from his own understanding of his family's history and mission, from the example of his father, and from a robust sense of Prussia's raison d'état. This variety of influences came with its own contradictions and could not be easily reconciled, but it enabled Frederick to play a part in the world he inhabited. Its politicians had to prepare themselves for a future under his reign. Its media were used by him and used him in return. He left his mark on his son, the next emperor; accelerated the internal unification of the Reich; and was loved by the public. The many who called him Our Fritz made a powerful point. For better, for worse, and with all his contradictions, Emperor Frederick belonged to them, to their time, to their culture, and to their country.

Abbreviations

AHH	Archive of the Hessische Hausstiftung, Fasanerie Palace
BArch	Bundesarchiv, Berlin-Lichterfelde
BPH	Brandenburg-Preussisches Hausarchiv (as part of GStA-PK)
BPK	Bildagentur für Kunst, Kultur und Geschichte (Preussischer Kulturbesitz)
GStA-PK	Geheimes Staatsarchiv Preussischer Kulturbesitz, Berlin-Dahlem
GW	Otto von Bismarck, *Die gesammelten Werke. Friedrichsruher Ausgabe*, 15 vols. (Berlin, 1924–1935)
RA	Royal Archives, Windsor Castle
SchP	Karl Schrader Papers, Niedersächsisches Staatsarchiv Wolfenbüttel
SP	Albrecht von Stosch Papers, Haus Stosch, Oestrich-Winkel
VIC	Victorian Archive (as part of RA)

Notes

Introduction

1. Richter, *Episoden*, 70–71.
2. Winkler, *Germany*, 232.
3. *Times* (London) (3 Oct. 1855).
4. *Hansard's Parliamentary Debates* (House of Commons, 18 June 1888), vol. 327, column 457.
5. Verba, *Comparative Political Culture*, 513; see also Rohe, "Kultur," 333, who defines "political culture" as the political code that steers and conditions the thought, action, and emotions of political agents.
6. Ullmann, *Politik*, 80–81; Steinbach, "Politische Kultur," 200; Jefferies, *Contesting*, 111; Anderson, *Practicing*, 400–437.
7. For an excellent introduction to the political culture of imperial Germany, see Kühne, "Das Deutsche Kaiserreich"; see also Biefang, *Zeremoniell*.
8. Winkler, *Germany*, 236–237, 252; Ullmann, *Politik*, 83, 89; Nipperdey, *Deutsche Geschichte*, 486–489; Kühne, "Jahrhundertwende."
9. Anderson, *Practicing*, 413; Kühne, "Political Culture," 182–183.
10. Blackbourn, "Discreet Charme"; Langewiesche, "Politikstile," 2–3; Nipperdey, *Deutsche Geschichte*, 892–893.

1. Shaping a Prince's Life

1. Schneider, *Hohenzollern*, 146; Ilsenmann, *Kaiser*, vol. 2, 243; Frederick William to Victoria, 12 Nov. 1883, Röhl, *Jugend*, 404.
2. Clark, *Kingdom*, 101–111.
3. Holstein, *Papiere*, vol. 2, 410.
4. Haym, *Leben*, 298.
5. Börner, *Wilhelm*, 45–50; Herre, *Kaiser*, 132–135.

6. Börner, *Wilhelm*, 75, 118–126.

7. Richter, *Episoden*, 20–21; Frederick William to William I, 24 March 1848 and 30 April 1848 (GStA-PK BPH, Rep. 52, Nrs. 149, 150).

8. Frederick William's letter (8 Jan. 1859), Curtius, "Kaiser," 393.

9. For Frederick William's support of military reforms, see Poschinger, *Kaiser*, vol. 1, 350, and Meisner, *Tagebücher*, 62 (11 Jan. 1860), 63 (9 March 1860), 64 (15 March 1860, 25 March 1860), 67 (5 May 1860), 68 (4 June 1860); Frederick William to Curtius, 3 Feb. 1861, Schuster, *Briefe*, 96–97.

10. Frederick William to Victoria, 22 Dec. 1857, Kollander, *Frederick III*, 3; Victoria to Queen Victoria, 30 April 1861, Fulford, *Dearest Child*, 327; Meisner, *Tagebücher*, 200 (11 June 1863).

11. Meisner, *Tagebücher*, 79 (18 Jan. 1861); Frederick William to Prince Albert, 27 April 1861 (RA VIC/I 35/66); Frederick William to William I, 4 Nov. 1861 (GStA-PK BPH, Rep. 52 J Preussen, Nr. 314).

12. Frederick William to Frederick of Baden, 15 Feb. 1862, Riehl, *"Tanz,"* 64; Frederick William to Victoria, 21 and 25 Feb. 1862 (AHH 7.1/1-BA5).

13. Frederick William to Victoria, 17 and 18 March 1862 (AHH 7.1/1-BA5).

14. Frederick William to Victoria, 20 March 1863 (AHH 7.1/1-BA5); Meisner, *Tagebücher*, 151 (10 July 1863).

15. Frederick William to Victoria, 19 Sept. 1862 (AHH 7.1/1-BA5), Meisner, *Tagebücher*, 159–161 (18–20 Sept. 1862).

16. Meiser, *Tagebücher*, 161 (23 Sept. 1863); Samwer to Freytag, 28 Feb. 1863, Wentzcke and Heyderhoff, *Liberalismus*, vol. 1, 133.

17. Meisner, *Kronprinz*, 10–11; Frederick William to William I, 31 May 1863, ibid., 65–66; Meisner, *Tagebücher*, 197 (31 May 1863).

18. William I to Frederick William, 1–2 June 1863; Frederick William to William I, 4 June 1863; Frederick William's Danzig speech; William I to Frederick William, 6 June 1863—all in Meisner, *Kronprinz*, 68, 70, 73–74; Meisner, *Tagebücher*, 198 (5 June 1863).

19. Meisner, *Kronprinz*, 17–22; Bismarck, *Auswahl*, vol. 8A, 248–249; Frederick William to William I, 7 June 1863; William I to Frederick William, 10 June 1863—both in Meisner, *Kronprinz*, 74–75, 78–79.

20. Müller, *Britain*, 191–192; Frederick William to Duncker, 14 July 1863, Poschinger, *Kaiser*, vol. 2, 28.

21. Meisner, *Tagebücher*, 208–209 (8–12 Aug. 1863), 213 (3 Sept. 1863), 515–522 (memorandum, 17 Sept. 1863); Frederick William to William I, 20 Nov. 1863, Schuster, *Briefe*, 125–126; Meisner, *Tagebücher*, 233 (11 Jan. 1864).

22. Poschinger, *Kaiser*, vol. 2, 242–243; Meisner, *Kriegstagebuch*, 337 (17 Jan. 1871).

23. Frederick of Baden to Gelzer, 6 April 1869, Oncken, *Großherzog*, vol. 2, 121; Königin von Preussen, *Bekenntnisse*, 292.

24. Hohenlohe-Schillingsfürst, *Denkwürdigkeiten*, vol. 2, 394–395 (5 Oct. 1886); Bismarck, *Staatssekretär*, 403 (9 Nov. 1886); Holstein, *Papiere*, vol. 2, 387 (17 May 1887); Eulenburg-Hertefeld, *Aus 50 Jahren*, 187–188; Meisner, *Tagebücher*, 388 (18 April 1864).

25. Besier, "Erinnerungen," 156; Frederick William to William I, 17 July 1864 (GStA-PK BPH, Rep. 52 J Preussen, Nr. 316, letter 32); see also Victoria to Queen Victoria, 9 March 1866, Fulford, *Your Dear Letter*, 59–60; Meisner, *Kriegstagebuch*, 417 (8 March 1871); Riehl, *"Tanz,"* 78 n. 81; Urbach, *Favourite Englishman*, 97; Holstein, *Papiere*, vol. 2, 178 (24 Oct. 1884); Hohenlohe-Schillingsfürst, *Denkwürdigkeiten*, vol. 2, 417 (29 March 1887).

26. Meisner, *Tagebücher*, 376 (8 Oct. 1864); Victoria to Queen Victoria, 15 Oct. 1870, Fulford, *Your Dear Letter*, 303; Frederick William to William I, 7 May 1873 (GStA-PK BPH, Rep. 52 J Preussen, Nr. 320, Bl. 60r); Victoria to Queen Victoria, 28 Nov. 1876, Fulford, *Darling Child*, 232; Frederick William to Victoria, 10 Nov. 1883 (AHH 7.1/1 XXIV).

27. Meisner, *Tagebücher*, 273–275 (27–28 Feb. 1864); Poschinger, *Kaiser*, vol. 2, 329; Schneider, *Aus dem Leben*, vol. 2, 164, vol. 3, 49; Meisner, *Kriegstagebuch*, 188 (29 Oct. 1870).

28. GStA-PK BPH, Rep. 52, FI7p (22 March 1876); Stosch to Freytag, 10 June 1877, Riehl, *"Tanz,"* 100; Frederick William to Victoria, 10 Sept. 1879 (AHH 7.1/1 XVII); Frederick William to Victoria, 8 Jan. 1880 (AHH 7.1/1 XIX); GStA-PK BPH, Rep. 52, FI7u (18 Oct. 1881); Frederick William to Victoria, 4 May 1886 (AHH 7.1/1 XXVII).

29. Frederick William to Victoria, 14 Nov. 1882 (AHH 7.1/1 XXIII); Frederick William to Victoria, 15 May 1883 (AHH 7.1/1 XXIV); Frederick William to Victoria, 14 Sept. 1886 (AHH 7.1/1 XXVII); Stosch to Freytag, 14 Aug. 1886 (SP); Lucius von Ballhausen, *Bismarck-Erinnerungen*, 390; Holstein, *Papiere*, vol. 2, 410 (13 Feb. 1888); Raschdau, *Unter Bismarck*, 20, 25.

30. GStA-PK BPH, Rep. 52, Nr. 3 (15 June 1888) and FI7u (18 Oct. 1881).

31. GStA-PK BPH, Rep. 52, Nr. 3 (25 Jan. 1888); Victoria to Queen Victoria, 21 June 1862, Fulford, *Dearest Mama*, 81; Meisner, *Tagebücher*, 379 (21 Nov. 1864); Frederick William to Victoria, 22 Jan. 1880 (AHH 7.1/1 XIX).

32. Schrader, "Viktoria," 451–453; Corti, *Wenn*, 15–63; Pakula, *Uncommon Woman*, 27–31, 43–57.

33. Queen Victoria to Leopold, 27 May 1851, Pakula, *Uncommon Woman*, 30; Frederick William to Prince Albert, n.d. [about 26 May 1851] (RA VIC/I 25/103); Müller, *Britain*, 160–163.

34. Queen Victoria to Frederick William, 15 Jan. 1855 (RA VIC/Y 125/1).

35. Ibid.; Frederick William to Augusta, 10 Sept. 1855, Meisner, *Tagebücher*, 38; Augusta to Prince Albert, 7 Sept. 1855 (RA VIC/Z 61/1); Pakula, *Uncommon Woman*, 43, 48–49; Corti, *Wenn*, 32–33.

36. Meisner, *Tagebücher*, 41–57 (14 Sept.–5 Oct. 1855); Frederick William to Queen Victoria, 1 Oct. 1855 (RA VIC/Z 71/2).

37. *Times* (London) (3 Oct. 1855).

38. Frederick William to Queen Victoria, 19 Oct. 1855 (RA VIC/Z 71/4); Bismarck to Gerlach, 19 March and 8 April 1856, Bismarck, *Auswahl*, vol. 2, 96–98.

39. *Kölnische Zeitung*, Epkenhans, "Victoria," 155.

40. *Times* (London) (26 Jan. 1858); Poschinger, *Kaiser,* vol. 1, 308–326; Bernhardi, *Aus dem Leben,* vol. 3, 5; Victoria to Prince Albert, 5 March 1858, Fulford, *Dearest Child,* 74.

41. Prince Albert to Victoria, 17 and 23 Feb. 1858, Corti, *Wenn,* 68–70.

42. Frederick William to Victoria, 30 Nov. 1879 (AHH 7.1/1 XVII); Frederick William to Victoria, 5 April 1880 (AHH 7.1/1 XX); Frederick William to Victoria, 29 Oct. 1884 (AHH 7.1/1 XXV); Frederick William to Victoria, 4 June 1860, Corti, *Wenn,* 101; Frederick William to Victoria, 20 Feb. 1879 (AHH 7.1/1 XVI); Frederick William to Victoria, 29 Aug. 1880 (AHH 7.1/1 XXI).

43. Victoria to Queen Victoria, 8 June 1863, Fulford, *Dearest Mama,* 227; Frederick William to Victoria, 22 Aug. and 28 Sept. 1885 (AHH 7.1/1 XXVI).

44. Frederick William to Victoria, 8 and 10 May 1879 (AHH 7.1/1 XVI); Frederick William to Victoria, 9 and 12 March 1864, Corti, *Wenn,* 201; Frederick William to Victoria, 20 Sept. 1879 (AHH 7.1/1 XVII); Frederick William to Victoria, 9 Nov. 1884 (AHH 7.1/1 XXV); Frederick William to Victoria, 31 Aug. 1886 (AHH 7.1/1 XXVII).

45. Frederick William to Augusta, 16 June 1886, Meisner, *Kronprinz,* 89; Frederick William to Victoria, 24 May 1879 (AHH 7.1/1 XVI); Frederick William to Victoria, 9 Nov. 1884 (AHH 7.1/1 XXV).

46. Victoria to Frederick William, 22 May 1879 (AHH 7/2 XIV); Victoria to Frederick William, 11 Jan. 1880 (AHH 7/2 XVII); Victoria to Frederick William, 7 Nov. 1884 (AHH 7/2 XXV).

47. Frederick William to Victoria, 27 May 1879 (AHH 7.1/1 XVI).

48. Victoria to Frederick William, 12 Sept. 1879 (AHH 7/2 XV); Frederick William to Victoria, 14 Sept. and 28 Nov. 1879 (AHH 7.1/1 XVII).

49. Frederick William to Victoria, 27 March 1880 (AHH 7.1/1 XX); Victoria to Frederick William, 24 March 1881 (AHH 7/2 XXI); Frederick William to Victoria, 27 March 1881 (AHH 7.1/1 XXII); Frederick William to Victoria, 14 Sept. 1885 (AHH 7.1/1 XXVI); Victoria to Frederick William, 15 Sept. 1886 (AHH 7/2 XXIX).

50. For Victoria's attitude toward breast-feeding, see Pakula, *Uncommon Woman,* 121, 220–221, 275, 302, 347, and Röhl, *Jugend,* 118–119; Victoria to Frederick William, 15 and 22 Sept. 1879 (AHH), Röhl, *Jugend,* 386–387, 886; Victoria to Frederick William, 18 Sept. 1879 (AHH 7/2 XV); Victoria to Prince William, 12 Aug. 1879, Röhl, *Jugend,* 386.

51. Röhl, *Jugend,* passim; Kohut, "Kaiser," 63–89; Cecil, *Wilhelm,* vol. 1, 30–87.

52. Frederick William to Victoria, 4, 15, and 25 Jan. 1880 (AHH), Röhl, *Jugend,* 397, 400.

53. Frederick William to Victoria, 3 Sept. 1880 (AHH), Röhl, *Jugend,* 402.

54. Röhl, *Jugend,* 432–434, 440–441. Frederick William to Victoria, 10 Nov. 1883 (AHH 7.1/1 XXIV).

55. Röhl, *Jugend,* 556–559.

56. Röhl, *Jugend,* 570–597; Clark, *Wilhelm,* 10–20 (quotation on 18); Frederick William to Victoria, 30 Aug. 1886 (AHH 7.1/1 XXVII).

57. Bigelow, *Memories*, 46; Putlitz to his wife, 7 July 1864, Poschinger, *Kaiser*, vol. 2, 114; see also Cecil, *Wilhelm*, vol. 1, 16–18, and Röhl, *Jugend*, 73–82, 87–94.

58. Frederick William to Victoria, 10 May 1879 (AHH 7.1/1 XVI).

59. Normann to Freytag, 20 Jan. 1882, Wentzcke and Heyderhoff, *Liberalismus*, vol. 2, 390; Stosch to Freytag, 25 Jan. 1882 (SP, memoirs/typescript, vol. 2, 225); Geffcken to Roggenbach, 6 March 1883, *Anklageschrift*, 30; Roggenbach to Stosch, 18 July 1885, Heyderhoff, *Ring*, 228; Stosch to Freytag, 6 Nov. 1883, Riehl, *"Tanz,"* 136 n. 40.

60. Wehrenpfennig to Heinrich von Treitschke, 21 Nov. 1868, Wentzcke and Heyderhoff, *Liberalismus*, vol. 1, 431; Holstein, *Papiere*, 74 (27 Jan. 1884); Stosch to Normann, 22 July 1885 (SP); Roggenbach's comment is quoted in Stosch to Normann, 26 April 1887 (SP, memoirs/typescript, vol. 3, 94); Bunsen, *Welt*, 183–184.

61. Cecil, *Wilhelm*, vol. 1, 3–5, 14 (quotations on 3, 14); Ponsonby, *Letters*, 16; Röhl, *Jugend*, 91; Bode, *Mein Leben*, 56.

62. William I to Pauline Scherff, 11 Oct. 1883, Riehl, *"Tanz,"* 79 n. 81.

63. Victoria to Prince Albert, 15 Dec. 1860 (RA), Cecil, *Wilhelm*, vol. 1, 6; Kollander, "Empress Frederick," 47–62; Kollander, "Constitutionalism," 187–201.

64. Pallat, *Schöne*, 212; Holstein, *Papiere*, vol. 2, 74 (27 Jan. 1884), 288 (3 Nov. 1885); Victoria to Queen Victoria, 30 Dec. 1884, Corti, *Wenn*, 372–373; for more examples of Victoria's continued attachment to all things British, see Riehl, *"Tanz,"* 67–75. As expressed in her will, Victoria was eventually buried in Potsdam's *Friedenskirche* next to her husband—in a coffin made in London.

65. Perthes to Albrecht von Roon, 27 March 1862, Roon, *Denkwürdigkeiten*, vol. 2, 74; Grand Duke Frederick to Gelzer, 1 Nov. 1868, Oncken, *Großherzog*, vol. 2, 117; Grand Duke Frederick to Gelzer, 21 March 1872, Fuchs, *Großherzog*, vol. 1, 55; *Der Sozialdemokrat* (2 Aug. 1883); Waldersee, *Denkwürdigkeiten*, 255 (diary entry, 6 April 1885); Holstein, *Papiere*, vol. 2, 211 (6 May 1885); Stosch to Freytag, 11 July 1885 (SP); Cecil, *Wilhelm*, vol. 1, 6.

66. Paget, *Embassies*, 104; on Frederick William's resolution of disagreements with his wife, see Kollander, "Empress Frederick," 50–52; see also Gelzer's diary entry of 5 June 1883, Fuchs, *Großherzog*, vol. 2, 207.

67. Frederick William to Victoria, 24 Oct. 1884 (AHH 7.1/1 XXV); Holstein, *Papiere*, 178 (24 Oct. 1884), 235 (11 July 1885).

68. Kollander, "Politics," 28–46; Holstein, *Papiere*, 165 (26 May 1884); Meisner, *Tagebücher*, 233 (11 Jan. 1864); Bismarck to Bernstorff, 17 March 1871, Urbach, *Favourite Englishman*, 75; Riehl, *"Tanz,"* 131–132; Herbert von Bismarck to William von Bismarck, 25 Aug. 1884, Bismarck, *Staatssekretär*, 253; Bismarck, *Auswahl*, vol. 7, 665. These concerns were not entirely without foundation. It is striking how many copies of highly sensitive documents concerning the relationship between Frederick William and his father are

deposited in the British Royal Archives. These include the crown prince's letters to King William of 4 November 1861 and 31 May 1863, in which he warned against dismissing the liberal ministry and breaches of the constitution, as well as Frederick William's letter of 3 June 1863, in which he accused Bismarck of unconstitutional acts. Moreover, the dramatic exchanges between King William and his son after the Danzig speech quickly found their way into the columns of the *Times* as a result of the detailed account Victoria sent to her mother on 8 June 1863, together with her wish that all this be made "known to your ministers and to all our friends in England." See RA VIC/I 37/71, 40/ 81, 40/82; Ponsonby, *Letters*, 41–42; Meisner, *Kronprinz*, 23–27; *Times* (London) (16 June 1863).

69. Frederick William to Stosch, 23 Oct. 1880 (SP); Cecil, *Wilhelm*, vol. 1, 109; Freund, *Drama*, 332.

70. Freytag, *Kronprinz*, 47.

71. Engelberg, *Urpreusse*, 525; Frederick William to Victoria, 19 Sept. 1863 (AHH 7.1/1-BA5).

72. Meisner, *Tagebücher*, 29 (22 March 1848), 64 (3 April 1860), 140 (17 May 1862), 161 (23 Sept. 1862), 179 (22 Dec. 1862); Poschinger, *Kaiser*, vol. 1, 58–59; Frederick William to Victoria, 15 July 1862 (AHH 7.1/1-BA5); Victoria to Queen Victoria, 19 July 1862, Fulford, *Dearest Mama*, 96; Frederick William to Bismarck, 28 Sept. 1862, Meisner, *Tagebücher*, 504; Frederick William to Bismarck, 30 June 1863, Schuster, *Briefe*, 113–114.

73. Morier to Earl Russell, 12 Nov. 1864, Morier, *Memoirs*, vol. 1 (London, 1911), 409; Moltke's minutes in Bismarck, *Auswahl*, vol. 2, 537; Frederick William to Ernest of Coburg, 26 March 1866, Schuster, *Briefe*, 148; Queen Victoria to Frederick William, 28 March 1866 (RA VIC/C 15/44); Frederick William to William I, 29 March 1866 (GStA-PK BPH, Rep. 52 J Preussen, Nr. 317, Bl. 71–72).

74. Bismarck to Frederick William, 13 and 29 Oct. 1862, Meisner, *Tagebücher*, 504–507; Bismarck, *Auswahl*, vol. 3, 255, 487, and vol. 8, 247–253; Bismarck did, however, vent his frustration during a visit to France in October 1865 with a furious tirade against the "liberalizing crown prince" (Radowitz, *Aufzeichnungen*, vol. 1, 81).

75. Meisner, *Tagebücher*, 469 (20 July 1866), 472–473 (24–25 July 1866), 478 (29 July 1866); Bismarck, *Auswahl*, vol. 8, 322–323; Poschinger, *Kaiser*, vol. 2, 242–243; on Frederick William's support of Bismarck in 1866 and Victoria's attempts to push for more radical aims, see Kollander, *Frederick III*, 80–84.

76. Abeken to his wife, 10 Aug. 1866, Poschinger, *Kaiser*, vol. 2, 250.

77. Forckenbeck's account of meeting with Frederick William (15 Aug. 1866) and minutes of meeting with liberal deputies (27 March 1867), Poschinger, *Kaiser*, vol. 2, 253, 273; Schweinitz, *Denkwürdigkeiten*, vol. 1, 256–257; Bismarck in conversation with Moritz Busch, 31 Aug. 1870, GW, vol. 7, 331–332.

78. Frederick William to William I, 13 July 1870 (GStA-PK BPH, Rep. 52 J Preussen, Nr. 319, Brief 5); Kollander, "Bismarck," 171–185; Meisner, *Kriegstagebuch*, 4 (15 July 1870).

79. Meisner, *Kriegstagebuch*, 6–7 (17–20 July 1870), 103 (3 Sept. 1870), 107 (4 Sept. 1870), 146–147 (30 Sept. 1879); Frederick William's memorandum on German unity, 14 Aug. 1870, Poschinger, *Kaiser*, vol. 3, 53–54; Abeken to his wife, 18 Oct. 1870, ibid., 79.

80. Frederick William to Victoria, 3 July 1868 (AHH); Kollander, *Frederick III*, 88; Meisner, *Kriegstagebuch*, 223–224 (16 Nov. 1870), 296–297 (29 Dec. 1870); Bamberger, *Spiel*, 223–225 (diary entry, 17 Nov. 1870); Oncken, *Großherzog*, vol. 2, 195 (Grand Duke Frederick's diary entry, 21 Nov. 1870); Hohenlohe-Schillingsfürst, *Denkwürdigkeiten*, vol. 2, 28 (diary entry, 28 Nov. 1870).

81. Waldersee, *Denkwürdigkeiten*, 116 (diary entry, 26 Dec. 1870); *GW*, vol. 6, 253–256; Bamberger, *Spiel*, 243–244 (diary entry, 5 Dec. 1870).

82. Meisner, *Kriegstagebuch*, 253 (3 Dec. 1870).

83. Meisner, *Kriegstagebuch*, 338–339, 343 (18 January 1871).

84. See Frederick of Baden to Gelzer, 20 March 1872, Fuchs, *Großherzog*, vol. 1, 54; Hübner, *Bismarck*, 128; file on Frederick William's attendance at ministerial meetings and circulation of cabinet papers (GStA-PK I. HA, Rep. 90A, Nr. 1949); Stosch to Frederick William, 2 May 1872 (SP, memoirs/typescript, vol. 2, 8).

85. Hohenlohe-Schillingsfürst, *Denkwürdigkeiten*, vol. 2, 105 (diary entry, 9 Sept. 1873); GStA-PK BPH, Rep. 52, FI7p (10 April 1876); Roggenbach's opinion recorded in Gelzer's diary, Fuchs, *Großherzog*, vol. 1, 257 (30 April 1877); Lady Odo Russell to Queen Victoria, 1 Sept. 1877 (RA VIC/Z 64/155).

86. Canis, "Bismarck," 137–154 (esp. 138, 145–146); Bamberger, *Spiel*, 243 (diary entry, 5 Dec. 1870).

87. Frederick William to Stosch, 8 May 1872 (SP, typescript/memoirs, vol. 2, 11), 28 Jan. 1873, 31 Oct. 1877 (SP); the confrontation in 1878 is recorded in Holstein, *Papiere*, vol. 2, 222–223.

88. GStA-PK BPH, Rep. 52 E III, Nr. 1a (Stellvertretung 1878), Mappe 3, f8; GStA-PK BPH, Rep. 52 FI7u (18 Jan. 1881); Holstein, *Papiere*, vol. 2, 194 (29 March 1885).

89. Frederick William to Victoria, 22 Feb., 16 May, and 25 May 1879 (AHH 7.1/1 XVI); Frederick William to Victoria, 15 Jan. 1880 (AHH 7.1/1 XIX); GStA-PK BPH, Rep. 52 FI7u (18 Oct. 1881).

90. Holstein, *Papiere*, vol. 2, 8 (22 Feb. 1882); Busch, *Tagebuchblätter*, vol. 2, 584–585 (12 April 1880), vol. 3, 94 (2 Oct. 1882); Bismarck to William I, 13 July 1879, *GW*, vol. 6c, 160; Poschinger, *Kaiser*, vol. 3, 321 (conversation with Cremer, March 1883); Bismarck, *Auswahl*, vol. 6, 468 (table talk, 17 Sept. 1880).

91. *GW*, vol. 8, 492 (love of approbation, 29 Nov. 1883); Bismarck, *Auswahl*, vol. 7, 60 (indolence, 9 Dec. 1883); Frederick William to Victoria, 6 May 1880 (AHH 7.1/1 XXI); Frederick William to Bismarck, 17 Aug. 1881, Bismarck, *Auswahl*, vol. 8A, 675; Holstein, *Papiere*, vol. 2, 21 (12 Dec. 1882).

92. Poschinger, *Kaiser*, vol. 3, 320 (conversation with Cremer, March 1883); Holstein, *Papiere*, vol. 2, 121–122 (14 April 1884), 131 (18 April 1884), 133 (21 April 1884); Lucius von Ballhausen, *Bismarck-Erinnerungen*, 298 (26

June 1884), 324 (6 Dec. 1885), 338 (14 March 1886); Frederick William to Stosch, 20 July 1884 (SP); Schrader to Stauffenberg, 21 Aug. 1884, Wentzcke and Heyderhoff, *Liberalismus*, vol. 2, 417–419.

93. Victoria to Friedberg, 1 July 1885, copy (Friedberg Papers, BArch N/2080: Nr. 50, Bl. 16r–20); Lucius von Ballhausen, *Bismarck-Erinnerungen*, 324 (6 Dec. 1885), 338 (14 March 1886), 395–396 (14 July 1887); see also Riehl, "*Tanz*," 733–737.

94. Poschinger, *Kaiser*, vol. 3, 321; Lucius von Ballhausen, *Bismarck-Erinnerungen*, 359–360 (13 Dec. 1886); Bismarck, *Auswahl*, vol. 8A, 529; Hohenlohe-Schillingsfürst, *Denkwürdigkeiten*, vol. 2, 462 (15 Dec. 1889). This suggests that Bismarck's noticeably warmer words for Frederick William after his dismissal [*GW*, vol. 9, 47 (8 June 1890), 248 (23 Aug. 1892); Bismarck, *Auswahl*, vol. 8A, 247, 529] had more to do with needling Emperor William II than with a reappraisal of his father.

95. Holstein, *Papiere*, 222–223 (18 June 1885); an edition of this manuscript (GStA-PK BPH, Rep. 52 FI7y, fol. 366–369) is appended to Kloosterhuis, "Victoria," 347–351; Schuster, *Briefe*, 340–341.

96. Bismarck, *Auswahl*, vol. 8A, 247 (italics in the original), 519; Delbrück, "Erinnerungen," 105.

2. Liberalism and Empire

1. Vierhaus, *Tagebuch*, 257; Perls, *Kaiser*, 3.
2. Taylor, *Course*, 71; Ludwig, "If the Emperor," 247–248; for Eyck, Valentin, and Holborn, see Kollander, *Frederick III*, xii; *Bonner General-Anzeiger* (26 Aug. 1989).
3. Waldau, *Max Waldau für Gottfried Kinkel*; Poschinger, *Kaiser*, vol. 1, 73 (Gerlach), 79 *(Deutsche Zeitung)*.
4. For Augusta's letter to Albrecht von Roon, see Wagner, *Prinzenerziehung*, 77.
5. Augusta to Prince Albert, 7 Sept. 1855 (RA VIC/Z 61/1); Queen Victoria to Victoria, 4 July 1868, Fulford, *Your Dear Letter*, 199.
6. Frederick William to Prince Albert, n.d. [about 26 May 1851] (RA VIC/I 25/103); Prince Albert to Frederick William, 2 June 1851, copy (RA VIC/I 26/3).
7. Frederick William to Prince Albert, 22 Oct. 1855 (RA VIC/I 29/86); Prince Albert to Frederick William, 6 Nov. 1855, copy (RA VIC/I 29/87); Prince Albert to Frederick William, 29 Nov. 1855, copy (RA VIC/I 29/90).
8. Frederick William to Prince Albert, 27 April 1861 (RA VIC/I 35/66); Prince Albert to Frederick William, 1 May 1861, copy (RA VIC/I 36/1).
9. Meisner, *Tagebücher*, 106; Jagow, *Letters*, 366.
10. Queen Victoria to Victoria, 5 April 1862, Fulford, *Dearest Mama*, 48; Queen Victoria to Frederick William, 14 Sept. 1863, copy (RA VIC/I 41/72); Frederick William to Victoria, 2 April 1863, Corti, *Wenn*, 202.
11. Schweinitz, *Denkwürdigkeiten*, 256; Meisner, *Kriegstagebuch*, 180 (24 Oct. 1870), 229 (18 Nov. 1870), 273 (14 Dec. 1870); Frederick William to Victoria, 26 Aug. 1882 (AHH 7.1/1 XXIII).

12. Fontane, *Briefe*, vol. 2 (Berlin, 1905), 169; *Berliner Zeitung* (14 March 1888); Studemund, *Rede*, 7; Dohme, "Erinnerungen," 121.

13. Stockmar to Prince Albert, 25 Oct. 1855, Pakula, *Uncommon Woman*, 58; Martin, *Life*, vol. 3, 388.

14. Prince Albert to Augusta, 9 March and 16 May 1858, Jagow, *Letters*, 296, 302.

15. Prince Albert to Victoria, 24 Nov. 1858 (AHH 7/02-BA 1), 13 Sept. 1859 (AHH 7/02-BA 2), 13 March 1861 (AHH 7/02-BA 5), 8 May 1861 (AHH 7/02-BA 5); Prince Albert to Ernst von Coburg, 12 July 1861, Bolitho, *Prince Consort*, 214.

16. Victoria to Frederick William, 13 March 1862, Kollander, *Frederick III*, 28; Victoria to Frederick William, 20 Sept. 1862, Pakula, *Uncommon Woman*, 168; Victoria to Queen Victoria, 8 June 1863, Fulford, *Dearest Mama*, 227; Victoria to Frederick William, 8 Dec. 1879 (AHH 7/2 XVI); Victoria to Frederick William, 7 Nov. 1884 (AHH 7/2 XXV).

17. Victoria to Queen Victoria, 16 June 1888, Ponsonby, *Letters*, 320.

18. See Droysen to Moritz Veit, 19 Oct. 1855, Hübner, *Droysen*, vol. 2, 362; Bernhardi, *Aus dem Leben*, vol. 3, 5 (28 Feb. 1858).

19. Meisner, *Tagebücher*, 184; *Die Grenzboten* 22 (3 July 1863), 36; the pamphlet "Der Kronprinz von Preußen und das Ministerium Bismarck" and related documents (Sept.–Oct. 1863) are located in GStA-PK I. HA, Rep. 90A, Nr. 1949.

20. Bismarck, *Auswahl*, vol. 4, 183; *National-Zeitung* (25 Jan. 1883); *Aus der Berliner Gesellschaft*, 7; *Berliner Tageblatt* (20 Oct. 1931).

21. Langewiesche, *Liberalism*, 1; Meisner, *Kriegstagebuch*, 415–416 (7 March 1871).

22. Frederick William to Bismarck, 30 June 1863, Schuster, *Briefe*, 114; Frederick William to Simson, 5 Dec. 1870, Meisner, *Kriegstagebuch*, 468; Frederick William to Victoria, 28 April 1880 (AHH 7.1/1 XX); proclamation "An den Reichskanzler" (12 March 1888), Schuster, *Briefe*, 341.

23. GStA-PK BPH, Rep. 52, FI7g f30.

24. GStA-PK BPH, Rep. 52, EIII, Nr. 1a (Mappe 6, f8); GStA-PK BPH, Rep. 52, FI7r (8 Aug. 1878); GStA-PK BPH, Rep. 52 J Preussen, Nr. 322, Bl. 122–122r; Stosch to his wife, 17 July 1878 (SP).

25. GStA-PK BPH, Rep. 52, FI7l (8 Nov. 1872); *Die Protokolle*, vol. 6/I, 289; Frederick William to William I, 11 Dec. 1872 (GStA-PK BPH, Rep. 52 J Preussen, Nr. 320, Bl. 96–96r); on the Kreisordnung issue, see Huber, *Verfassungsgeschichte*, vol. 4, 351–358.

26. Frederick William to Victoria, 31 Dec. 1879 (AHH 7.1/1 XVIII); Frederick William to Ernst von Stockmar, 18 Nov. 1880 (AHH 7.1/4); GStA-PK BPH, Rep. 52, FI7u (front flyleaves); Ernst von Stockmar to Frederick William, 23 Nov. 1880 (AHH 7.1/07-5); GStA-PK BPH, Rep. 52, FI7u (17 Jan. 1881). By then, Frederick William must have overcome the anti-Jewish feelings that can still be found in some of his earlier comments; see Meisner, *Tagebücher*, 67 (1 May 1860), 126 (4 Jan. 1862), 129 (26 Feb. 1862).

27. Prince Albert to Victoria, 18 Jan. 1860 (AHH 7/02-BA3); Victoria to Queen Victoria, 8 Nov. 1862, Fulford, *Dearest Mama*, 128.
28. Frederick William to Bismarck, 18 Nov. 1864, Kohl, *Bismarcks Briefwechsel*, vol. 2, 376–377; Frederick William to Victoria, 24 Oct. 1868, Kollander, *Frederick III*, 129; Meisner, *Kriegstagebuch*, 180 (24 Oct. 1870); Frederick William to Schweinitz, 22 Feb. 1875, Schweinitz, *Briefwechsel*, 102.
29. Werner, *Erlebnisse*, 139–141; Frederick William's diary (27 July 1883), Riehl, *"Tanz,"* 200; Bamberger, *Spiel*, 279–280.
30. Frederick William to Charles of Romania, 19 Oct. 1878, Poschinger, *Kaiser*, vol. 3, 255; Frederick William to Bismarck, 16 June 1878 (BArch), Schmid, *Der "Eiserne Kanzler,"* 114–115.
31. *Stenographische Berichte ... Reichstags, 4. Legislaturperiode, I. Session*, vol. 1 (Berlin, 1878), 169 (10 Oct. 1878).
32. Meisner, *Tagebücher*, 384 (9 Feb. 1865); Meisner, *Kriegstagebuch*, 180 (24 Oct. 1870); Frederick William to William I, 31 May 1878 (GStA-PK BPH, Rep. 52 J Preussen, Nr. 233, Bl. 115r); GStA-PK BPH, Rep. 52, EIII, Nr. 1a (Mappe 4, f29); Frederick William to Victoria, 20 April 1880 (AHH 7.1/1 XX); Frederick William to Wilhelm, 19 Oct. 1878 (GStA-PK BPH, Rep. 52 J Preussen, Nr. 322, Bl. 146–146r); GStA-PK BPH, Rep. 52, FI7x (30 Oct. 1884).
33. Frederick William to Victoria, 30 Oct. 1884 (AHH 7.1/1 XXV).
34. Frederick William to Victoria, 19 May 1879 (AHH 7.1 XVI); see also Frederick William to Victoria, 15 Feb. 1879 (ibid.); Victoria to Frederick William, 9 May 1879 (AHH 7/2 XIV); Frederick William to Victoria, 10 May 1879 (AHH 7.1/1 XVI); GStA-PK BPH, Rep. 52, FI7t (10 Sept. 1880).
35. Frederick William to Victoria, 6 Nov. 1884 (AHH 7.1/1 XXV); see also Frederick William's diary entry in GStA-PK BPH, Rep. 52, FI7x (4 Nov. 1884); Schuster, *Briefe*, 342; GStA-PK BPH, Rep. 52, FI7x (2 Nov. 1884) and FI7y (11 and 12 May 1885).
36. This passage is indebted to Hiery, "Der Kaiser," 155–166; Meisner, *Kriegstagebuch*, 275 (14 Dec. 1870); Zimmermann, *Geschichte*, 11, 42; Urbach, *Favourite Englishman*, 202; GStA-PK BPH Rep. 52, FII, 113 and 114.
37. GStA-PK BPH, Rep. 52, FI7t (27 April 1880); Frederick William to Victoria, 4 May 1880 (AHH 7.1/1 XXI); Pogge von Strandmann, "Consequences," 113; Urbach, *Favourite Englishman*, 202; Frederick William's memorandum (25 May 1884, RA VIC/O 22/39) was almost certainly based on his conversation with Hatzfeldt on 24 May [Hatzfeldt to Bismarck, 24 May 1884, *Die Grosse Politik*, vol. 4 (Berlin, 1922), 57–59]; Schuster, *Briefe*, 341; *Die Grenzboten* 47 (12 July 1888), 99.
38. *Economist* (23 June 1883).
39. Philippson, *Das Leben*, 80; Hinzpeter, *Der Kaiser Friedrich*, 1901 (GStA-PK BPH, Rep. 52, FIII, Nr. 3 f9).
40. Poschinger, *Kaiser*, vol. 1, 79; Augusta to Prince Albert, 7 Sept. 1855 (RA VIC/Z 61/1); Victoria to Queen Victoria, 30 April 1859, Fulford, *Dearest Child*, 190; Frederick William to Victoria, 4 June 1860, Corti, *Wenn*, 101; Meisner, *Tagebücher*, 383 (15 Jan. 1865).

41. Meisner, *Kriegstagebuch*, 318 (8 Jan. 1871); Frederick William to William I, 18 Jan. 1873 (GStA-PK BPH, Rep. 52J Preussen, Nr. 320, Bl. 44–46r); Schuster, *Briefe*, 341; *Der Reichsfreund* (7 April 1888); Richter, *Friedrich III*, 327–328.

42. Meisner, *Tagebücher*, 92 (28 May 1861); Normann to Freytag, 17 April 1874, Wentzcke and Heyderhoff, *Liberalismus*, vol. 2, 106; Delbrück, *Erinnerungen*, 107; see also Busch, *Tagebuchblätter*, vol. 2, 576.

43. Frederick William to Curtius, 26 July 1863, Schuster, *Briefe*, 118; Hintze, "Das Monarchische Prinzip," 381–412; on *Konstitutionalismus* and the British model, see Müller, "Parliamentary Impasse," 67–87; a convincing argument for doubting Frederick William's commitment to parliamentary government is made by Kollander, *Frederick III*, passim.

44. Meisner, *Tagebücher*, 160 (19 Sept. 1862); Frederick William to Victoria, 19 Sept. 1862 (AHH 7.1/1-BA5); see also Kollander, *Frederick III*, 33–34, and Nichols, *Year*, 8.

45. Frederick William to Grand Duchess Louise of Baden, 15 Oct. 1870, Schuster, *Briefe*, 207; Frederick William to Victoria, 16 May 1879 (AHH 7.1/1 XVI); Victoria to Frederick William, 8 Nov. 1884 (AHH 7/2 XXV).

46. Frederick William to Victoria, 22 May 1879 (AHH 7.1/1 XVI).

47. GStA-PK, Rep. 52, FI7t (21 Jan. 1880) and FI7w (16 June 1883); Holstein, *Papiere*, vol. 2, 185.

48. Frederick William to Victoria, 24 Dec. 1879 (AHH 7.1/1 XVIII); Lucius von Ballhausen, *Bismarck-Erinnerungen*, 338.

49. *Die Errichtung*, 19.

50. Dorpalen, "Frederick III," 15; Frederick William to Prince Albert, 7 June 1859 (RA VIC/Z 63/132); Frederick William to William I, 30 July 1861 (GStA-PK BPH, Rep. 52J Preussen, Nr. 314, Bl. 89ff); memorandum "Zur Situation, 22. Februar 1862," Meisner, *Tagebücher*, 493–494.

51. Frederick William to William I, 3 Jan. 1864 (GStA-PK BPH, Rep. 52J Preussen, Nr. 316, 1); *Die Protokolle*, vol. 5, 256.

52. Hohenlohe-Schillingsfürst, *Denkwürdigkeiten*, 303; Schweinitz, *Denkwürdigkeiten*, vol. 1, 245 (27 Sept. 1868).

53. Fehrenbach, *Wandlungen*, 52–64; Bismarck to Bernstorff, 17 Jan. 1870, Bismarck, *Auswahl*, vol. 4, 385.

54. On Bismarck's Kaiserplan of January 1870, see Fehrenbach, *Wandlungen*, 61–64; Huber, *Verfassungsgeschichte*, vol. 3, 703–708; Platzhoff, "England," 454–475; Frederick William's diary (7 Jan. and 25 April 1870), *GW*, vol. 6b, 212; Schweinitz, *Denkwürdigkeiten*, vol. 1, 257.

55. Freytag, *Kronprinz*, 23; Meisner, *Kriegstagebuch*, 133 (21 Sept. 1870), 147 (30 Sept. 1870).

56. Meisner, *Kriegstagebuch*, 260 (6 Dec. 1870), 470 (proclamation). See also ibid., 282–283 (18 Dec. 1870) and 338–339 (18 Jan. 1871); Bringmann, "Das neue Deutsche Reich," 799.

57. Schweinitz to Frederick William, 1 Feb. 1871, Meisner, *Kriegstagebuch*, 485; ibid., 394 (21 Feb. 1871); Victoria to Frederick William, 14 Jan. 1871, Krakau,

"Kaiserin Friedrich," 145–146. On Frederick William's attempt to obtain the imperial insignia, see Schieder, *Das Deutsche Kaiserreich*, 154–159.

58. Richter, *Im alten Reichstag*, vol. 1, 2; Richter's recollections were clearly guided by an article in which Freytag mocked the use of such "dignified junk" (Freytag, *Kronprinz*, 113–126); Dohme, "Erinnerungen," 3; GStA-PK BPH, Rep. 52, FI7q (19 Jan. 1877): "Der edlen Stämme sollen viel / In diesem Hause wohnen, / Bei Gottesdienst und Saitenspiel / Ein Herrscher in ihm thronen: / Der Herrlichste der ganzen Welt, / Ein Priester und ein Ritterheld, / Man heißt ihn: Deutscher Kaiser" (Max von Schenkendorf, "Brief in die Heimat").

59. Special report of the *Aachener Anzeiger-Politisches Tageblatt* (4 July 1885); Roggenbach to Stosch, 18 Aug. 1885, Heyderhoff, *Ring*, 229; Roggenbach's visit to San Remo is summarised in Stosch to Normann, 22 Dec. 1887 (SP, memoirs/typescript, vol. 3, 130); Lucius von Ballhausen, *Bismarck-Erinnerungen*, 423 (23 Feb. 1888).

60. Bismarck, *Auswahl*, vol. 5, 293; Oexle, "Canossa," 56–67; Vierhaus, *Tagebuch*, 134–135.

61. Sepp, "Das Resultat," 86–109.

62. Kaul, *Friedrich Barbarossa*; Vogel, "Herrscherideal," 213–230; Felix Dahn, "Heil dem Kaiser" (quoted from http://www.zeno.org, accessed 24 June 2009).

63. Bartmann, *Anton von Werner*, 318–329; Jefferies, *Imperial Culture*, 53–57; Arndt, *Kaiserpfalz*; Kaul, *Friedrich Barbarossa*, vol. 1, 529–531.

64. For a detailed discussion on the opposing views of Bismarck and Frederick William with regard to centralism versus federalism, see Riehl, "*Tanz*," 260–285.

65. Meisner, *Kriegstagebuch*, 351 (23 Jan. 1871).

66. Conversation with Theodor von Bernhardi (20 March 1860), Poschinger, *Kaiser*, vol. 1, 359; Meisner, *Tagebücher*, 465 (17 July 1866), 476 (27 July 1866); Meisner, *Kriegstagebuch*, 224 (16 Nov. 1870).

67. Frederick William to Stosch, 16 Feb. 1873 (SP); Holstein, *Papiere*, vol. 2, 43; Frederick William to Bismarck, 18 Aug. 1881, Bismarck, *Auswahl*, vol. 8A, 675; Waldersee, *Denkwürdigkeiten*, vol. 1, 211 (24 Jan. 1881).

68. GStA-PK BPH, Rep. 52, FI7l (12 Aug. 1872) and FI7o (25 May 1875); Hohenlohe-Schillingsfürst, *Denkwürdigkeiten*, vol. 2, 132 (22 Aug. 1874); see also Besier, "Erinnerungen," 140.

69. Hohenlohe-Schillingsfürst, *Denkwürdigkeiten*, vol. 2, 74 (30 Nov. 1871); Werner, *Erlebnisse*, 141.

70. Memorandum "Kurze Denkschrift für den Fall des Friedens" (14 Aug. 1870), Poschinger, *Kaiser*, vol. 3, 53–54; Frederick William to Louise of Baden, 15 Oct. 1870, Schuster, *Briefe*, 207; Meisner, *Kriegstagebuch*, 224 (16 Nov. 1870), 255 (4 Dec. 1870), 282–283 (18 Dec. 1870). On the different ideas pursued by Bismarck and the crown prince in 1870, see Fehrenbach, *Wandlungen*, 64–88.

71. Meisner, *Kriegstagebuch*, 271 (12 Dec. 1870), 300 (31 Dec. 1870), and 284 (19 Dec. 1870); Frederick William to Charles of Romania, 18 April 1872,

Schuster, *Briefe*, 224; Frederick William to Charles of Romania, 28 Oct. 1872, Poschinger, *Kaiser*, vol. 3, 169.

72. Frederick William to Stosch, 28 Jan. 1873 (SP); see also Frederick William to Stosch, 26 Oct. 1876 (SP), where the crown prince professed his "enthusiastic dedication to the issues of the Reich," combined with the conviction "that the intention must always be directed towards Germany and that there must be no special interests within her borders."

73. Frederick William to Schweinitz, 25 Jan. 1873, Schweinitz, *Briefwechsel*, 90; Frederick William to Stosch, 28 Jan. 1873 (SP). On the planned army bill, see also Frederick William to William I, 18 Jan. 1873 (GStA-PK BPH, Rep. 52 J Preussen, Nr. 320, Bl. 44–46r); the bill, eventually tabled in May 1873, was rejected by the Reichstag.

74. Frederick William to Stosch, 26 Aug. 1873 (SP); GStA-PK BPH, Rep. 52, FI7m (2 Oct. 1873); Frederick William to Schweinitz, 22 Feb. 1875, Schweinitz, *Briefwechsel*, 102; Frederick William to William I, 18 and 21 Sept. 1875 (GStA-PK BPH, Rep. 52, Nr. 231); Frederick William to Bismarck, 17 Dec. 1875, Schuster, *Briefe*, 241.

75. Meisner, *Kriegstagebuch*, 340 n. 3 (hunting invitations); Radziwill, *Empress Frederick*, 36–37 (queen or empress); Holstein, *Papiere*, vol. 2, 43 (27 March 1883); Frederick William to Queen Victoria, 1 Nov. 1884 (RA VIC/S 24/1).

76. Stosch to Normann, 8 Aug. 1885, Riehl, *"Tanz,"* 272; Prince William to Bismarck, 29 Nov. 1887, *GW*, vol. 15 (Berlin, 1932), 464.

77. GStA-PK BPH, Rep. 52, FI7u (18 Jan. 1881).

78. Bismarck in conversation with Christoph Cremer, Poschinger, *Kaiser*, vol. 3, 321; Bismarck, *Auswahl*, vol. 8A, 252–253.

79. Freytag, *Kronprinz*, 27; Besier, "Erinnerungen," 155; Dohme, "Erinnerungen," 128; Eulenburg, *Aus 50 Jahren*, 178.

80. Frederick William to William I, 5 July 1861, Schuster, *Briefe*, 100–101; Meisner, *Tagebücher*, 99 (6 July 1861); Frederick William to Stosch, 16 Feb. 1873 (SP); Holstein, *Papiere*, vol. 2, 40 (22 March 1883), 221 (6 June 1885).

81. Meisner, Tagebücher, 127 (31 Jan. 1862); Frederick William to Schweinitz, 30 Dec. 1869, Schweinitz, *Briefwechsel*, 66.

82. Poschinger, *Kaiser*, vol. 1, 101, 105; Meisner, *Tagebücher*, 293 (14 March 1864); Holstein, *Papiere*, vol. 2, 219 (1 June 1885); Queen Victoria to Victoria, 20 June 1885, Fulford, *Beloved Mama*, 191.

83. Riehl, *"Tanz,"* 274; Stosch to Freytag, 22 August 1885 (SP).

84. This manuscript (GStA-PK BPH, Rep. 52, FI7y, fols. 366–369) is edited in Kloosterhuis, "Victoria," 347–351 (emphasis/italics in the originals).

85. Kloosterhuis, "Victoria," 339.

86. Roggenbach to Stockmar, 29 Oct. 1885, Heyderhoff, *Ring*, 235.

87. See Frederick William to Victoria, 5 and 6 Nov. 1884 (AHH 7.1/1 XXV); GStA-PK BPH, Rep. 52, FI7y (11 May 1885); Holstein, *Papiere*, vol. 2, 194 (29 March 1885).

3. A National Treasure

1. Unidentified newspaper cutting, GStA-PK BPH, Rep. 52, FI7l (3 Sept. 1872); *Norddeutsche Allgemeine Zeitung* (18 Oct. 1881).
2. Geisthövel, "Den Monarchen im Blick," 59; see also Geisthövel, "Wilhelm I.," 163–185.
3. Plunkett, "Publicness," 12–13; Osta, "New Clothes," 182–183; Biefang, *Seite*, 277–279; *National-Zeitung* (25 Jan. 1883).
4. Geppert, *Pressekriege*, 47; Kohlrausch, *Monarch*, 48–53; Wehler, *Gesellschaftsgeschichte*, 1232; Retallack, "Obrigkeitsstaat," 130–134.
5. Nichols, *Year*, 164.
6. Meisner, *Tagebücher*, 406 (26 Dec. 1865), 478 (29 July 1866); Meisner, *Kriegstagebuch*, 10 (26 July 1870); Frederick William to Victoria, 30 Aug. 1880 (AHH 7.1/1 XXI); Waldersee, *Denkwürdigkeiten*, vol. 1, 243; Holstein, *Papiere*, vol. 2, 184–185 (3 March 1885).
7. A few examples will suffice: GStA-PK BPH, Rep. 52, FI7l (28 July and 14 Aug. 1872, correcting a factual mistake), FI7o (15 June 1875, with marginal comment: "Very true!"), FI7q (14 Dec. 1877, sampling English press), FI7y (9 June 1885, cuttings from several papers covering his trip to East Prussia), FI7z (8 Nov. 1886, with marginal comment: "Nonsense!"). See also Raschdau, *Unter Bismarck*, 25.
8. Meisner, *Kriegstagebuch*, 120–121 (12–14 Sept. 1870); Freytag to Normann, 18 July 1870, in *Vossische Zeitung* (14 Aug. 1927).
9. Frederick William to Victoria, 15 and 16 Sept. 1883 (AHH 7.1/1 XXIV); Frederick William to Friedberg, 11 Nov. 1886 (Friedberg Papers, BArch N/2080, Nr. 43, Bl. 97–99).
10. Meisner, *Kriegstagebuch*, 21 (2 Aug. 1870), 49 (9 Aug. 1870), 71 (23 Aug. 1870); *War Correspondence*, vol. 1, 22; *Times* (London) (15 and 19 Aug. 1870); see also the account of the happy conversation around the crown prince's table in Russell, *My Diary*, 76–78.
11. *Charakterzüge*, 77–78; see also Poschinger, *Kaiser*, vol. 3, 240; Dernburg, *Reise*, 7–10.
12. Meisner, *Tagebücher*, 297 (17 March 1864), 321 (5 April 1864); Meisner, *Kriegstagebuch*, 49 (9 Aug. 1870), 92 (1 Sept. 1870); Werner, *Erlebnisse*, 17.
13. Paret, *Art*, 165–180 (quotation on 169); Bartmann, *Anton von Werner*, 332–353; Meisner, *Kriegstagebuch*, 371 (7 Feb. 1871); Jefferies, *Imperial Culture*, 44–52.
14. Brunold, *Kaiser*, 64; Höcker, *Kaiser*, 128; Felseneck, *Friedrich*, 80; Müller-Bohn, *Kaiser*, 328; Ziemssen, *Friedrich*, 70.
15. Frederick William's diary (4–9 November 1869) in Poschinger, *Kaiser*, vol. 2, 358.
16. Rockel, *Wilhelm Gentz*, 122; see also Rhein, *Orientmalerei*, 105–108.
17. "Auf dem Ölberg" in Richter, *Kaiser*, 323; see also Ernst Fürste's poem "Crown Prince Frederick on the Mount of Olives," in which Frederick William connects his experiences in the Holy Land with premonitions of his own future suffering (Fürste, *Gedichte*).

18. Werner, *Erlebnisse*, 374; Jefferies, *Imperial Culture*, 52–53; Bracht, *Lebenserinnerungen*, 106–107.

19. Bartmann, *Anton von Werner*, 142–143, 370–372, 379–380, 389–390.

20. "Ein leuchtend Bildnis hängt an der Wand:/Sein Bildnis von Angelis Meisterhand, /Orangeband, Orden, Helmbuschzier, /Pasewalker Kürassier." In Fontane, *Gedichte*, 316.

21. Plunkett, *Queen Victoria*, 144–198; Giloi Bremner, *Ich kaufe*, 307–338; Windt, "Bilderflut," 67–77.

22. Windt, "Bilderflut," 67–72.

23. Schuster, *Briefe*, 287.

24. Dohme, *Erinnerungen*, 128; GStA-PK BPH, Rep. 52, Nr. 124 (9 June 1888).

25. Poschinger, *Kaiser*, vol. 3, 308; *Der Reichsfreund* (7 April 1883); the article was pasted into Frederick William's diary (GStA-PK BPH, Rep. 52, FI7w (11 April 1884).

26. *Der Reichsfreund* (31 March 1888); Poschinger, *Kaiser*, vol. 3, 399; GStA-PK BPH, Rep. 52, FI7y (9 June 1886, with several different cuttings); *Die Nation* (13 June 1885).

27. Richter, *Episoden*, 32, 48–50.

28. *Das Tagebuch*, 233–235 (swimming); Müller-Bohn, *Kaiser*, 424–425 (Bornstedt, Eiche).

29. GStA-PK BPH, Rep. 52, FI7l (14 Aug. 1872).

30. Dollinger, "Leitbild," 325–364 (esp. 329–333, 336–339, 345–346); Wienfort, *Monarchie*, 12.

31. Davidoff, *Family Fortunes*, 152; Hobhouse, "Monarchy," 58; Tyrrell, "God Bless," 120; Queen Victoria to King Leopold, 29 Oct. 1844, Benson, *Letters*, 27.

32. "Er ist Bürger auf dem Throne, /Und sein Stolz ist's, Mensch zu sein." In Stamm-Kuhlmann, "Friedrich Wilhelm III.," 442; Novalis in Lorenz, *Familienbild*, 184.

33. Schulte, "Aufstieg," 89–99; Giloi Bremner, *Ich kaufe*, 99–101.

34. Geisthövel, "Den Monarchen im Blick," 69–78; Biefang, *Seite*, 279–282; Hughes, "Demonstrations," 233–234.

35. Geisthövel, "Den Monarchen im Blick," 64; Geisthövel, "Wilhelm I.," 166.

36. See Bausinger, "Bürgerlichkeit," 122; on the evolution of "bürgerlich virtues," see Münch, *Ordnung*.

37. GStA-PK BPH, Rep. 52, FI7q (21 Nov. 1877); *Berliner Tageblatt* and *Vossische Zeitung* (18 Oct. 1881); GStA-PK BPH, Rep. 52, FI7w (24 April 1883) and FI7y (9 June 1885); *Deutschlands Trauer* (Stuttgart, 1888), 82.

38. Budde, *Blütezeit*, 25.

39. Petsch, *Unser Fritz*, 60–61; GStA-PK BPH, Rep. 52, FI7q (21 Nov. 1877); *Deutschlands Trauer*, 88; Perls, *Kaiser*, 3.

40. *Breslauer Zeitung* (25 Jan. 1883).

41. *Vossische Zeitung* (25 Jan. 1883); *Neue Preussische Zeitung* (26 Jan. 1883).

42. *Aus der Berliner Gesellschaft*, 338; Petsch, *Unser Fritz*, 107; Hengst, *Friedrich Wilhelm*, 182; Höcker, *Kaiser*, 182–183, 185.

43. Newspaper cutting enclosed with a letter by Frederick William to Victoria, 20 Aug. 1861 (AHH 7.1/1-BA3); Poschinger, *Kaiser*, vol. 2, 129.

44. Meisner, *Tagebücher*, 461 (12 July 1861); cutting in GStA-PK BPH, Rep. 52, FI7p (17 Feb. 1876); *Charakterzüge*, 20 (raffle tickets), 88 (ragman); Böhmert, *Kaiser*, 7–8.

45. *Vossische Zeitung* (25 Jan. 1883); on the couple's life at Bornstedt, see Müller-Bohn, *Kaiser*, 421–426.

46. Hengst, *Friedrich Wilhelm*, 196. For accounts of the crown prince's children's parties, see ibid., 196–199; Höcker, *Kaiser*, 192–195; Petsch, *Unser Fritz*, 212–216; and the unidentified newspaper cutting in GStA-PK BPH, Rep. 52, FI7m (24 July 1873).

47. Höcker, *Kaiser*, 192; Richter, *Episoden*, 54; for details of the allocation, see Poschinger, *Kaiser*, vol. 3, 317; the donation is also mentioned in Brunold, *Kaiser*, 92–93, and Höcker, *Kaiser*, 208–209.

48. Poschinger, *Kaiser*, vol. 3, 322–324.

49. *Pierer's Universal-Lexikon*, vol. 3, 474; Böhmert, *Kaiser*, 4; Müller-Bohn, *Kaiser*, 471–484; *Berliner Tageblatt* (18 Oct. 1881).

50. Kaschuba, "German *Bürgerlichkeit*," 407; *Das Tagebuch des Kronprinzen*, 167.

51. Poschinger, *Kaiser*, vol. 3, 238–239; on the scholarship foundation, see GStA-PK I HA, Rep. 89, Nr. 20482, 75; Müller-Bohn, *Kaiser*, 467–470; Suur, *Jahresbericht*, 12.

52. Frederick William to William I, 19 July 1871, GStA-PK BPH, Rep. 52 J Preussen, Nr. 319, Brief 14a; Frederick William to William 1, GStA-PK I HA, Rep. 89, Nr. 20482, 26–30; for Frederick William's future relationship with the museum, see ibid., 62–63, 126–128, 133–139; Müller-Bohn, *Kaiser*, 441–443.

53. Bode, *Mein Leben*, 50–51; Frederick William to Victoria, 6 Jan. 1880 (AHH 7.1/1 XIX); Pallat, *Richard Schöne*, 211–212; Knopp, "Der stumme Kaiser," 337–354; *Vossische Zeitung* (25 Jan. 1883); Schöne, "Rede," 203.

54. Baumgarten, *Zum Gedächtnis*, 5–6, 11; *Freisinnige Zeitung* (9 March 1888).

55. *Kölnische Zeitung* (15 June 1888); *Breslauer Zeitung* (25 Jan. 1883); Nipperdey, "Kommentar," 143–144.

56. Hardtwig, "Bürgertum," 284–285; Becker, "Strammstehen," 87–113; Klenke, "Der 'deutsche Mann,'" 60.

57. Rohrkrämer, *Militarismus*, 198–200; Hinzpeter, *Zum 25. Januar 1883*, 13.

58. Freytag, *Kronprinz*, 81–82; Barry, *Franco-Prussian War*, vol. 2, 90.

59. For a detailed list of Frederick William's military appointments, see *Kaiser Friedrich III.*, 161–162.

60. Richter, *Friedrich*, 104; Karl Anton von Hohenzollern-Sigmaringen to Max Duncker, 16 June 1866, Duncker, *Briefwechsel*, 379; see also Barry, *Road*, 172.

61. Showalter, *Wars*, 95, 250; Craig, *Battle*, 79–80; Wawro, *Franco-Prussian War*, 128; Meisner, *Kriegstagebuch*, 36; Howard, *Franco-Prussian War*, 207; Barry, *Franco-Prussian War*, vol. 2, 291, 350–355.

62. Craig (*Battle*, 127) sees no dilatoriness on the part of Frederick William or Blumenthal in moving their troops onto the battlefield. For the problem of the timing of Moltke's plan for enveloping the Austrian forces, see Wawro, *Austro-Prussian War*, 238–273; Ziemssen, *Friedrich*, 58; Höcker, *Kaiser*, 105.

63. Höcker, *Kaiser*, 135.

64. Hoffmeyer, *Friedrich*, 24.

65. Garlepp, *Kaiser*.

66. GStA-PK BPH, Rep. 52, FI7q (21 Nov. 1877); *Berliner Tageblatt* (18 Oct. 1881); *Die Post* (18 Oct. 1881); *Neue Preussische Zeitung* (20 Oct. 1881, 13 March 1888); *Breslauer Zeitung* and *Vossische Zeitung* (25 Jan. 1883).

67. Meisner, *Kriegstagebuch*, 8 (24 July 1870), 10–12 (26–28 July 1870), 217 (14 Nov. 1870); Poschinger, *Kaiser*, vol. 3, 38 (30 July 1870).

68. Meisner, *Kriegstagebuch*, XIX, 8 (24 July 1870), 73 (24 Aug. 1870), 114 (8 Sept. 1870); *Augsburger Allgemeine Zeitung* (17 July 1871); *Das Tagebuch*, 91–92.

69. Newspaper cuttings glued into GStA-PK BPH, Rep. 52, FI7w (24 April 1883) and FI7z (20 June 1886); *Neue Freie Presse* (15 June 1888); *Allgemeine Zeitung* (17 June 1888).

70. Meisner, *Tagebücher*, 69 (18 July 1860), 95 (12 June 1861), 143 (2 June 1862), 394 (24 July 1865); Rohkrämer, *Militarismus*, 138; Müller-Bohn, *Kaiser*, 353, 358; newspaper cutting in GStA-PK BPH, Rep. 52, FI7l (28 July 1872).

71. *National-Zeitung* (15 June 1888); *Der Reichsfreund* (12 July 1888).

72. Kugler, *Geschichte*, v–vii.

73. Hahn, *Friedrich der Grosse*, 1–66, esp. 20–21, 27; Kroll, "Friedrich der Grosse," 13–60.

74. Höfer quoted after Brunold, *Kaiser*, 46; Petsch in *Fürste*, *Gedichte*; Lang in Menge, *Trauer*, 93–94; Drobisch, *Der Alte Fritz*.

75. Maurenbrecher, *Hohenzollern-Legende*, 1–27; *Der Sozialdemokrat* (24 March 1888); Kroll, "Friedrich der Grosse," 624–628; *Norddeutsche Allgemeine Zeitung* (17 June 1888).

76. Paret, *Art*, 12–18; *Vossische Zeitung* (12 March 1888); *Berliner Zeitung* (14 March 1888).

77. Wülfing, Bruns, and Parr, *Historische Mythologie*, 68; *Neuer Görlitzer Anzeiger/Erste Beilage* (22 Oct. 1890).

78. Demandt, *Luisenkult*; Speth, "Königin Luise," 265–286; Wülfing, Bruns, and Parr, *Historische Mythologie*.

79. Kähler, *Zum Gedächtnis*, 16; Garlepp, *Kaiser*, 95–96; Demandt, *Luisenkult*, 436.

80. Königin von Preussen, *Bekenntnisse*, 175; Heinrich Lang quoted in Poschinger, *Kaiser*, vol. 3, 54; *Berliner Tageblatt* (18 Oct. 1881); *Freisinnige Zeitung* (9 March 1888); Treitschke, "Zwei Kaiser," 82; Perls, *Kaiser*, 1; Dohme, "Erinnerungen," 6; see also *Die Post* (16 June 1888), *Der Reichsbote* (16 June 1888); *Dresdner Nachrichten* (17 June 1888).

81. Freund, *Drama*, 156–157; Helmholtz (11 Nov. 1887) in Riehl, "Tanz," 57; Gerock, *Predigt*, 5; Forbes, "Diary," 610.

82. Meisner, *Tagebücher,* 63 (6 March 1860); Droysen to Heinrich von Sybel, 16 June 1861, in Hübner, *Droysen,* vol. 2, 759; Poschinger, *Kaiser,* vol. 3, 195–196; Dohme, "Erinnerungen," 1–2.

83. Meisner, *Tagebücher,* 70 (19 July 1860); Demandt, *Luisenkult,* 348, 431; GStA-PK BPH. Rep. 52 J Preussen, Nr. 322, Bl. 39; Frederick William's material on Queen Louise is available at GStA-PK BPH, Rep. 49 U I, Nr. 19–20; Ernst von Stockmar to Frederick William, 28 Feb. 1876 (AHH 7.1/07-5).

84. Dohme, *Unter fünf preussischen Königen,* 161; Giloi Bremner, *"Ich kaufe,"* 233–248, 269–278, 352–364, 394–408.

85. Dohme, *Unter fünf preussischen Königen,* 161–162; GStA-PK BPH, Rep. 52, FI7q (14 March 1877).

86. Kemper, *Monbijou,* 86–100; Luh, "Erbschaft," 200–207; *Berlin und die Berliner,* 199.

87. Adler, "Schlosskirche," 466–467.

88. Diary entry (30 April 1880), Gundermann, "Kronprinz Friedrich Wilhelm," 64, see also 68–70.

89. Steffens, "Wittenberger Schlosskirche," 114–116.

90. Nipperdey, "Nationalidee," 146; *Schümann, Der Berliner Dom,* 201–207; Delbrück, "Erinnerungen," 25–26.

91. Frederick William's voluminous collection of material for the crypt project is available at GStA-PK BPH, Rep. 52, FII, 105 (sarcophagi), 107 (for the 1876 memorandum and further material), 109 (mottos), 111 (historical material for inscriptions), 113–114 (Frederick William's own draft inscriptions), and 131 (various historians' comments on the inscriptions); Frederick William to Stockmar, 3 Feb. 1882 (AHH 7.1/4).

92. Dohme, "Erinnerungen," 79–80.

93. Röhl, *Aufbau,* 1016–1026.

94. Klingenburg, *Berliner Dom,* 163–164; Raschdorff, *Ein Entwurf;* communication slip glued into the emperor's diary—GStA-PK BPH, Rep. 52, Nr. 3 (30 March 1888).

95. Memorandum "Bau des Domes in Berlin," GStA-PK BPH, Rep. 52, FII, 107; Schümann, *Berliner Dom,* 217–219.

96. Becker, "Begriff," 138.

4. The Politics of Succession

1. Stosch to Normann, 7 May and 15 June 1886 (SP); Stosch to Freytag, 29 Dec. 1873 (SP); Stosch to Freytag, 6 Nov. 1883, Riehl, *"Tanz,"* 136 n. 40; Stosch to Normann, 29 Oct. 1887 (SP).

2. Frederick of Baden to Gelzer, 2 April 1866, Oncken, *Großherzog,* vol. 1, 498; Frederick of Baden to Gelzer, 21 March 1872, Fuchs, *Großherzog,* vol. 1, 55; Roggenbach to Stosch, 22 Oct. 1881, Heyderhoff, *Ring,* 214; Waldersee, *Denkwürdigkeiten,* vol. 1, 322 (1 April 1887); Freytag to Stosch, 8 Nov. 1883 and 13 May 1886, Freytag, *Briefe,* 145, 176.

3. *GW*, vol. 7, 331–332; Bamberger, *Spiel*, 243–244; Bismarck, *Auswahl*, vol. 8A, 252–253; Vierhaus, *Tagebuch*, 257; Eulenburg to Herbert von Bismarck, 5 Sept. 1883, Eulenburg-Hertefeld, *Korrespondenz*, vol. 1, 141; Herbert von Bismarck to Eulenburg, 7 Sept. 1883, Eulenburg, *Aus 50 Jahren*, 180; Holstein, *Papiere*, vol. 2, 166 (6 June 1884).

4. A letter he sent to Victoria is dated "Berlin cage, 23 Oct. 84" and begins: "My dear little wife, now I am sitting again in this horrid prison" (AHH 7.1/1 XXV); *Aus der Berliner Gesellschaft*, 3–4; Morier to Russell, 6 Sept. 1863 (Morier Papers, box 1, 1i).

5. Bode, *Mein Leben*, 89; Hohenlohe-Schillingsfürst, *Denkwürdigkeiten*, vol. 2, 260 (16 Nov. 1878); Frederick William to Stosch, 23 Oct. 1880 (SP).

6. Roggenbach to Stosch, 3 Feb. 1884, Heyderhoff, *Ring*, 225.

7. Bismarck in conversation with Deputy Christoph Cremer, March 1883, Poschinger, *Kaiser*, vol. 3, 320.

8. *Der Sozialdemokrat* (2 Aug. 1883).

9. Bismarck, *Auswahl*, vol. 8A, 252; Bennigsen to his wife, 2 Dec. 1867, Oncken, *Bennigsen*, vol. 2, 122; Forckenbeck to his wife, 7 Feb. 1872, Philippson, "Die Zeit," 146.

10. On the controversy surrounding the so-called Conservative Turn of 1878–1879, see Jefferies, *Contesting*, 61–69, and Ullmann, *Politik*, 77–79.

11. Declaration of the "Liberale Vereinigung" (30 Aug. 1880), Mommsen, *Parteiprogramme*, 157.

12. Sheehan, *Liberalism*, 186–215; Müller-Plantenberg, *Der Freisinn*, 33–38; Seeber, *Zwischen*, 110–128; Gall, *Bismarck*, vol. 2, 162–163.

13. Bismarck to William I, 3 July 1879, Bismarck, *Auswahl*, vol. 6, 320; Bismarck to William I, 1 July 1879, Riehl, *"Tanz,"* 88–89 n. 117; Lasker to unknown (perhaps Bennigsen or Miquel), 8 Nov. 1881, Wentzcke, *Liberalismus*, vol. 2, 386.

14. Hölder, *Das Tagebuch*, 145 (6 Nov. 1878); Széchényi to Kálnoky, 14 Jan. 1882, Riehl, *"Tanz,"* 108; GStA-PK I. HA, Rep. 90A, Nr. 1949.

15. Forckenbeck to his wife, 16 Aug. 1866, Poschinger, *Kaiser*, vol. 2, 251–253; Bamberger, *Spiel*, 278–281 (2 March 1884).

16. Schuster, *Briefe*, 186; Roggenbach to Stosch, 1 Feb. 1881, Heyderhoff, *Ring*, 212; *Aus der Berliner Gesellschaft* (Berlin, 1886), 39–40; Poschinger, *Kaiser*, vol. 3, 308; Bismarck, *Die politischen Reden*, vol. 8, 375; Bamberger, *Spiel*, 277 (2 March 1884); *Das Tagebuch*, 256 (23 Oct. 1884).

17. Frederick William to Victoria, 19 May 1879 (AHH 7.1/1 XVI); Bamberger, *Spiel*, 278 (2 March 1884); Sheehan, *Liberalism*, 192; Mommsen, *Parteiprogramme*, 157; Frederick William's diary entry, 27 June 1883, Riehl, *"Tanz,"* 200; Rachfahl, "Richter," 324; *Die Nation* (12 April 1884), 393.

18. GStA-PK BPH, Rep. 52, FI7s (18–21 May 1879); Victoria to Frederick William, 22 May 1879 (AHH 7/2 XIV); Frederick William to Victoria, 21, 22, 24 May 1879 (AHH 7.1/1 XVI), 8 Sept. 1879 (AHH 7.1/1 XVII).

19. GStA-PK BPH, Rep. 52, FI7s (27 Dec. 1879); Frederick William to Victoria, 28 Dec. 1879 (AHH 7.1/1 XVIII); Bamberger, *Spiel*, 331 (30 Dec. 1879);

GStA-PK BPH, Rep. 52, FI7t (10 Jan. 1880); Frederick William to Victoria, 11 Jan. 1880 (AHH 7.1/1 XIX).

20. Bamberger to Stauffenberg, 12 March 1880, and Forckenbeck to Stauffenberg, 14 March 1880, Wentzcke, *Liberalismus*, vol. 2, 300–301; Weber, *Bamberger*, 48; Seeber, *Zwischen*, 111; GStA-PK BPH, Rep. 52, FI7t (23 Aug. 1880); Philippson, *Forckenbeck*, 339.

21. Frederick William to Victoria, 25 Aug. 1880 (AHH 7.1/1 XXI); GStA-PK BPH, Rep. 52, FI7t (9–11 Sept. 1880).

22. GStA-PK BPH, Rep. 52, FI7u (8–11 Dec. 1881); GStA-PK BPH, Rep. 52, FI7v (15 June 1882).

23. Bunsen, "Liberal Party," 694, 713–714, 717 (italics in the original); *Germania* (25 Jan. 1883); Riehl, *"Tanz,"* 174.

24. *Die Tribüne* (13 Oct. 1882).

25. *Der Reichsfreund* (14 and 28 Oct. 1882, 7 April and 5 May 1883, 4 Jan. 1884); *Berliner Zeitung* (25 Jan. 1883); Riehl, *"Tanz,"* 174–176.

26. Seeber, *Zwischen*, 125–134; Bamberger to Lasker, 6 Sept. 1882, Wentzcke, *Liberalismus*, vol. 2, 391–392.

27. GStA-PK BPH, Rep. 52, FI7v (8 Aug. 1882); Rachfahl, "Richter," 323–333.

28. Programme of the "Deutsche Freisinnige Partei" (5 March 1884), Mommsen, *Parteiprogramme*, 158.

29. GStA-PK BPH, Rep. 52, FI7x (6 March 1884); *Die Nation* (8 March 1884), 321, (15 March 1884), 337, (12 April 1884), 393; *Berliner Zeitung* (16 March 1884).

30. Schrader to Stauffenberg, 21 Aug. 1884, Wentzcke, *Liberalismus*, vol. 2, 417–419.

31. Frederick William to Victoria, 5, 6, and 9 November 1884 (AHH 7.1/1 XXV); see also GStA-PK BPH, Rep. 52, FI7x (30 Oct. and 2 Nov. 1884); Holstein, *Papiere*, vol. 2, 180 (9 Nov. 1884); Schrader to his wife, 10 July 1885, Lyschinska, *Henriette Schrader-Breymann*, vol. 2, 297.

32. Seeber, *Zwischen*, 127; Rachfahl, "Richter," 321–322.

33. *Der Sozialdemokrat* (2 Aug. 1883).

34. Stosch to Freytag, 11 Feb. 1870, Stosch, *Denkwürdigkeiten*, 180.

35. Pflanze, *Bismarck*, vol. 2 (Princeton, 1990), 516–523; Engelberg, *Das Reich*, 320–337.

36. Gall, *Bismarck*, vol. 2, 160–163 (quotations on 160, 163).

37. Gall, *Bismarck*, vol. 2, 135; *GW*, vol. 8, 394; Lucius von Ballhausen, *Bismarck-Erinnerungen*, 193, 209 (diary entries, 25 Jan. and 12 June 1881); Bismarck to Puttkamer, 6 May 1822, *GW*, vol. 6/3, 254; Vierhaus, *Tagebuch*, 202.

38. Kollander, "Constitutionalism," 189–190.

39. Bismarck to Lucius, 5 Nov. 1879, *GW*, vol. 14/2, 910.

40. Pflanze, "Bismarck," vol. 3, 85–89; Riehl, *"Tanz,"* 183–186; Seeber, *Zwischen*, 122.

41. Kennedy, *Rise*, 162–165; Riehl, *"Tanz,"* 228–243; *Die Grenzboten* (22 May 1884), 411, 414.

42. Holstein, *Papiere*, vol. 2, 73–74 (27 Jan. 1884); GStA-PK BPH, Rep. 52, FI7x (6 and 28 Jan. 1884); Riehl, *"Tanz,"* 186–191; Bamberger, *Spiel,* 279.

43. Pflanze, "Bismarck," vol. 3, 111–112; Biefang, *Seite,* 273–277; *Stenographische Berichte* (Reichstag), *5. Legislaturperiode, IV. Session,* vol. 1 (Berlin, 1884), 28–34; Holstein to Herbert von Bismarck, 13 March 1884, Bismarck, *Staatssekretär,* 225.

44. Bamberger, *Gesammelte Schriften,* vol. 5, 62.

45. Oswald von Nostiz-Wallwitz to Alfred von Fabrice, 14 March 1884, Goldschmidt, *Das Reich,* 82, 301–302; Riehl, *"Tanz,"* 322–342 (quotation on 335); Fidel von Baur-Breitenfeld to Hermann von Mittnacht, 6 April 1884, Goldschmidt, *Das Reich,* 82; see also Lucius von Ballhausen, *Bismarck-Erinnerungen,* 290–291 (5 April 1884).

46. *Die Nation* (12 April 1884), 393; *Stenographische Berichte* (Reichstag), *5. Legislaturperiode, IV. Session,* vol. 1 (Berlin, 1884), 499–500.

47. GStA-PK BPH, Rep. 52, FI7x (16 March 1884); Riehl, *"Tanz,"* 204–207.

48. Riehl, *"Tanz,"* 209–214; Bamberger, *Spiel,* 290.

49. *Stenographische Berichte* (Reichstag), *5. Legislaturperiode, IV. Session,* vol. 1 (Berlin, 1884), 480, 483, 501.

50. Turner, "Imperialist Venture"; Pogge von Strandmann, "Origins"; Pogge von Strandmann, *Imperialismus;* Wehler, *Bismarck;* Smith, *Origins;* Riehl, *"Tanz";* Fitzpatrick, *Liberal Imperialism;* Holstein, *Papiere,* vol. 2, 174 (19 Sept. 1884).

51. All quotations after Wehler, *Bismarck,* 474–476.

52. Bismarck, *Auswahl,* vol. 7, 159–160 (23 June 1884); *Stenographische Berichte* (Reichstag), *5. Legislaturperiode, VI. Session,* vol. 2 (Berlin, 1884), 1074–1077.

53. Kollander, "Constitutionalism," 192; GStA-PK BPH, Rep. 52, FI7t (27 April 1880); Frederick William to Victoria, 4 May 1880 (AHH 7.1/1 XXI); Urbach, *Favourite Englishman,* 202; Holstein, *Papiere,* vol. 2, 167 (6 June 1884).

54. Hollyday, *Rival.*

55. Steinmetz, "Bismarck–Stosch," 703–713; *Stenographische Berichte* (Reichstag), *3. Legislaturperiode, I. Session,* vol. 1 (Berlin, 1877), 70.

56. Lucius von Ballhausen, *Bismarck-Erinnerungen,* 255 (18 March 1883); Frederick William to Friedberg, 31 March 1883 (Friedberg Papers, BArch N/2080: Nr. 43, Bl. 28–28r).

57. Holstein, *Papiere,* vol. 2, 50 (5 Jan. 1884), 82 (9 Feb. 1884); *Stenographische Berichte* (Reichstag), *5. Legislaturperiode, VI. Session,* vol. 2 (Berlin, 1884), 1077, 1079–1080, 1083.

58. *Norddeutsche Allgemeine Zeitung* (5 July 1884); Hollyday, *Bismarck,* 92–109.

59. Holstein, *Papiere,* 49 (5 Jan. 1884), 162 (22 May 1884); Rich, *Holstein,* vol. 1, 130–140; Kollander, *Frederick III,* 142–144; Riehl, *"Tanz,"* 520–527; Schröder, "Normann," 327–340.

60. Stosch to Freytag, 26 July 1883, Riehl, *"Tanz,"* 522; Holstein, *Papiere,* 158, 160–162 (17 and 21 May 1884); Kollander, *Frederick III,* 144–145; Schrader to Stauffenberg, 21 Aug. 1884, Wentzcke, *Liberalismus,* vol. 2, 417.

61. Windelband, *Berlin–Madrid–Rom*, 87–92, 110; Riehl, *"Tanz,"* 127–129.
62. Holstein, *Papiere*, vol. 2, 47 (3 Jan. 1884), 54, 56 (9 Jan. 1884); *GW*, vol. 8, 492.
63. Röhl, *Jugend*, 432–433; Riehl, *"Tanz,"* 132–136; Windelband, *Berlin–Madrid–Rom*, 117, 147–148, 172–177; Bismarck to Frederick William, 9 Aug. 1884, *GW*, vol. 6/III, 303.
64. GStA-PK BPH, Rep. 52, FI7x (12 April 1884); Riehl, *"Tanz,"* 364–383; Huber, *Verfassungsgeschichte*, vol. 4, 363–368.
65. Huber, *Verfassungsgeschichte*, vol. 4, 365; Podewils-Dürnitz to Crailsheim, 9 April 1884, Riehl, *"Tanz,"* 367; see also Bismarck's comments to Nostiz-Wallwitz, Riehl, *"Tanz,"* 371; Stosch to Normann, 26 April 1884 (SP, memoirs/typescript, vol. 3, 9).
66. Lucius von Ballhausen, *Bismarck-Erinnerungen*, 298 (26 June 1884); Holstein, *Papiere*, vol. 2, 178–179 (26 Oct. 1884).
67. Bismarck to Wilmowski, 28 Sept. 1884, Riehl, *"Tanz,"* 128.
68. Frederick William to Victoria, 31 Oct. and 1 Nov. 1884 (AHH 7.1/1 XXV); Holstein, *Papiere*, vol. 2, 131 (18 April 1884); Riehl, *"Tanz,"* 380–383; Philippson, *Friedrich III.*, 222.
69. Sheehan, *Liberalism*, 198–199.
70. Landrat von Bennigsen-Förder to Rudolf von Bennigsen, 23 Sept. 1880, Oncken, *Bennigsen*, vol. 2, 448; *Stenographische Berichte* (Reichstag), *4. Legislaturperiode, IV. Session*, vol. 2 (Berlin, 1881), 971–972.
71. *Stenographische Berichte* (Reichstag), *5. Legislaturperiode, IV. Session*, vol. 1 (Berlin, 1884), 31 (13 March 1884), 500 (9 May 1884); Holstein, *Papiere*, vol. 2, 36 (17 Feb. 1883).
72. Heidelberg Declaration of the National Liberal Party (23 March 1884), Mommsen, *Parteiprogramme*, 158–160; Sheehan, *Liberalism*, 199–201; H. Schulthess, *Schulthess' Europäischer Geschichtskalender 1884* (Nördlingen, 1885), 49–50.
73. Holstein, *Papiere*, vol. 2, 121–122 (14 April 1884), 125–126 (15 April 1884); see also ibid., 127 (16 April 1884).
74. Pogge von Strandmann, "Origins," 144–147; *Stenographische Berichte* (Reichstag), *6. Legislaturperiode, I. Session*, vol. 1 (Berlin, 1885), 142.
75. Nipperdey, *Deutsche Geschichte*, 329–330; Sheehan, *Liberalism*, 202, 343; Pflanze, *Bismarck*, vol. 3, 232–233.
76. Rachfahl, "Richter," 332.
77. GStA-PK BPH, Rep. 52, FI7x (11 June and 30 Oct. 1884); Frederick William to Victoria, 31 Oct. and 5 Nov. 1884 (AHH 7.1/1 XXV); Holstein, *Papiere*, 180 (9 Nov. 1884).
78. Bamberger to Stauffenberg, 25 Feb. 1887, Wentzcke, *Liberalismus*, vol. 2, 429; *New York Herald* (9 March 1887), Johnson, *False Dawn*, 138–140.
79. Pflanze, *Bismarck*, vol. 3, 228–234; Johnson, *False Dawn*, 1–114; Bennigsen to Friedrich Hammacher, 7 Dec. 1885, Wentzcke, *Liberalismus*, vol. 2, 423.
80. GStA-PK BPH, Rep. 52, FI7aa (14 and 26 Jan. and 4 Feb. 1887); *Kölnische Zeitung* (5 Feb. 1887); Busch, *Tagebuchblätter*, vol. 3, 217 (27 Jan. 1887); see also Hollyday, *Bismarck's Rival*, 226.

81. Stosch to Normann, 26 April 1884 (SP, memoirs/typescript, vol. 3, 9); Frederick William to Victoria, 7 May 1886 (AHH 7.1/1 XXVII); Stosch to Normann, 15 June 1886 and 4 April 1887 (SP); Stosch to Freytag, 3 March 1887 (SP); Hollyday, *Bismarck's Rival*, 225–228.

82. Wilhelm von Bismarck to Friedrich von Holstein, 31 May 1887, Holstein, *Papiere*, vol. 3, 192; Eulenburg, *Aus 50 Jahren*, 140 (11 June 87); Nichols, *Year*, 17–18, 22; Johnson (*False Dawn*, v) describes the "careful preparation for [Frederick William's] reign" as "one of the most brilliant and most promising of Bismarck's political manoeuvres."

5. Illness and Reign

1. Freund, *Drama*, 219–220, 384.

2. Neumann, *Friedrich*, 142–143; Stosch to Normann, 7 May 1886 (SP); Schweinitz, *Denkwürdigkeiten*, vol. 2, 318 (7 May 1886).

3. Neumann, *Friedrich*, 146–147; Werner, *Erlebnisse*, 139, 479; Röhl, *Jugend*, 643; Wolf, *Krankheit*, 1–2.

4. *Die Krankheit*, 1–8; Ponsonby, *Letters*, 225; Wolf, *Krankheit*, 2–12.

5. *Die Krankheit*, 17–18; Victoria to Queen Victoria, 17 May 1887, Corti, *Wenn*, 404.

6. *Die Krankheit*, 7; Bismarck to Victoria, 2 Dec. 1887, Corti, *Wenn*, 433; Victoria to Queen Victoria, 17, 20, and 22 May 1887, Ponsonby, *Letters*, 226, 232–233.

7. Freund, *Drama*, 69–70; Neumann, *Friedrich*, 169.

8. Wolf, *Krankheit*, 10–12, 99–101; Lucius von Ballhausen, *Bismarck-Erinnerungen*, 393; Victoria to Queen Victoria, 17, 19, and 24 May 1887, Ponsonby, *Letters*, 226, 231, 236.

9. Holstein, *Papiere*, vol. 2, 387 (20 May 1887); Neumann, *Friedrich*, 170–184; Lucius von Ballhausen, *Bismarck-Erinnerungen*, 391 (28 May 1887).

10. Wolf, *Krankheit*, 14–20; Röhl, *Jugend*, 650–652.

11. Holstein, *Papiere*, vol. 2, 387 (20 May 1887), 393 (28 Sept. 1887); Freund, *Drama*, 130–131; see also Lucius von Ballhausen, *Bismarck-Erinnerungen*, 399 (24 Oct. 1887).

12. Röhl, *Jugend*, 672–684.

13. *Daily News* (London)(22 June 1887); Freund, *Drama*, 155–159.

14. Neumann, *Friedrich*, 185–199; Freund, *Drama*, 169; Mackenzie, *Illness*, 51–52; Röhl, *Jugend*, 657.

15. Queen Victoria to Victoria, 29 Aug. 1887, Ramm, *Beloved*, 55; Mackenzie, *Illness*, 55–58; *Die Krankheit*, 29–37.

16. Stosch to Freytag, 2 Feb. 1880 (SP); Mackenzie, *Illness*, 62.

17. Mackenzie, *Illness*, 63, 65; Wolf, *Krankheit*, 22–25; Freund, *Drama*, 219–233; Neumann, *Friedrich*, 204–213.

18. Wolf, *Krankheit*, 26–31; *Die Krankheit*, 55–62; Count Radolin to Holstein, 12 Feb. 1888, Holstein, *Papiere*, vol. 3, 231–232.

19. Wolf, *Krankheit*, 31–34; Freund, *Drama*, 310–330; *Die Krankheit*, 80–81.

20. Ponsonby, *Letters*, 249.
21. *Die Krankheit*, 81; Wolf, *Krankheit*, 104–112; Ponsonby, *Letters*, 259.
22. *Die Krankheit*, 109; Neumann, *Friedrich*, 213; *Der Reichsfreund* (7, 14, 28 Jan., 25 Feb., 10 March 1888); Holstein, *Papiere*, vol. 2, 403 (14 Nov. 1887); Eulenburg, *Aus 50 Jahren*, 155 (27 Dec. 1887).
23. Röhl, *Jugend*, 688–692, 701–710; Holstein, *Papiere*, vol. 2, 392 (28 June 1887); Radolinski to Holstein, 10 and 21 Nov. 1887; Holstein, *Papiere*, vol. 3, 205–208.
24. Radolinki to Holstein, 4 July 1887, Holstein, *Papiere*, vol. 3, 193; Röhl, *Jugend*, 707, 778–782.
25. Holstein, *Papiere*, vol. 2, 388–389 (20 May 1887), 390 (1 June 1887), 397 (28 Sept. 1887); Röhl, *Jugend*, 701; Lucius von Ballhausen, *Bismarck-Erinnerungen*, 425 (8 March 1888).
26. Wolf, *Krankheit*, 90–95; Röhl, *Jugend*, 699.
27. Röhl, *Jugend*, 701–703; Lucius von Ballhausen, *Bismarck-Erinnerungen*, 423 (23 Feb. 1888).
28. GStA-PK BPH, Rep. 52, Nr. 3 (9 March 1888); Nichols, *Year*, 164–169.
29. *The Standard* (31 March 1888); Freund, *Drama*, 368; Ziemssen, *Friedrich*, 150; *Freisinnige Zeitung* (9 March 1888); *Neue Preussische Zeitung* (13 March 1888).
30. *Die Grenzboten*, 47 (1888), 144 (12 April 1888); *Neue Preussische Zeitung* (10 April 1888).
31. Turk, "Battenberg," 241; *Freisinnige Zeitung* (11 March 1888); *Vossische Zeitung* (12 March 1888); *Der Reichsfreund*, 99–100 (31 March 1888), 180 (7 June 1888).
32. *Vossische Zeitung* (13 March 1888); *Berliner Zeitung* (14 March 1888); *Frankfurter Zeitung* quoted after *Freisinnige Zeitung* (15 March 1888); Perls, *Kaiser*, 36; *National-Zeitung* (13 March 1888).
33. *Neue Preussische Zeitung* quoted after *Germania* (14 March 1888); *Konservative Korrespondenz* quoted after *Norddeutsche Allgemeine Zeitung* (14 March 1888).
34. Stosch to Frau von Rosenstiel, 17 May 1888 (SP, memoirs/typescript, vol. 3, 159).
35. *Berliner Zeitung* (16 March 1888); *Der Reichsfreund* (17 March 1888), 82; *Vossische Zeitung* (5 June 1888); *Die Volkszeitung* (25 March 1888).
36. *Die Grenzboten*, 47 (1888), 164 (19 April 1888); Nichols, *Year*, 197–198; Hohenlohe-Schillingsfürst, *Denkwürdigkeiten*, vol. 2, 430; Lucius von Ballhausen, *Bismarck-Erinnerungen*, 437–438, 461; Windelband, *Briefe*, 73; Röhl, *Jugend*, 816–817.
37. Beyerhaus, "Krise," 1, 9.
38. Lyschinska, *Henriette Schrader-Breymann*, vol. 2, 400–414; Schrader to Bamberger, 26 March 1888 (Bamberger Papers, BArch N/2008, Nr. 188).
39. Bamberger, *Spiel*, 341–406; Nichols, *Year*, 259–268.
40. Bamberger, *Spiel*, 354, 363–368.
41. Nichols, *Year*, 305–334; Bamberger, *Spiel*, 391.

42. Lucius von Ballhausen, *Bismarck-Erinnerungen,* 461–462; Lyschinska, *Henriette Schrader-Breymann,* vol. 2, 401; Bamberger, *Spiel,* 344; Vierhaus, *Tagebuch,* 247; Stosch to Normann, 17 March 1888 (SP); Holstein, *Papiere,* vol. 2, 424.

43. Waldersee, *Denkwürdigkeiten,* vol. 1, 402 (30 May 1888); Vierhaus, *Tagebuch,* 252.

44. Coburg, *Mitregenten,* 25, 27.

45. Bamberger, *Spiel,* 345.

46. On the Battenberg affair, see Corti, *Wenn,* 344–394; Riehl, *"Tanz,"* 141–152, 419–426, 449–484, 538–542, 641–658; Kollander, "Politics"; Kollander, "Auswirkungen."

47. Röhl, *Jugend,* 518–546, 797; Holstein, *Papiere,* vol. 2, 224 (18 June 1885); Bamberger, *Spiel,* 349–350; Victoria to Frederick William, 25 Aug. 1883 (AHH 7/2 XXIII).

48. Riehl, *"Tanz,"* 150, 426, 477, 653; Holstein, *Papiere,* vol. 2, 155; Röhl, *Jugend,* 536, 546; Kollander, "Auswirkungen," 187.

49. Nichols, *Year,* 206–207; Pakula, *Uncommon Woman,* 520–521; Herbert von Bismarck to Wilhelm von Bismarck, 28 March 1888, Bismarck, *Staatssekretär,* 511; Holstein, *Papiere,* vol. 2, 413 (31 March 1888), vol. 1, 140.

50. Bamberger, *Spiel,* 389–390.

51. Nichols, *Year,* 175; Bismarck, *Auswahl,* vol. 7, 628; Klemm, *Was,* 438; Ponsonby, *Letters,* 293; Bamberger, *Spiel,* 358; Corti, *Wenn,* 531; Lucius, *Bismarck-Erinnerungen,* 464

52. Wolf, *Krankheit,* 34–35; Lucius von Ballhausen, *Bismarck-Erinnerungen,* 462; Ponsonby, *Letters,* 304; Corti, *Wenn,* 498; Nichols, *Year,* 192–194.

53. Ponsonby, *Letters,* 309; Bamberger, *Spiel,* 361–367; Corti, *Wenn,* 531; Röhl, *Jugend,* 790; Lucius von Ballhausen, *Bismarck-Erinnerungen,* 425.

54. Holstein, *Papiere,* vol. 2, 417 (11 April 1888).

55. Ibid., vol. 2, 414–415 (11 April 1888); Nichols, *Year,* 207–210; *Die Grosse Politik,* vol. 6 (Berlin, 1922), 282–289; Turk, "Battenberg."

56. Nichols, *Year,* 211–213, 227–228; Holstein, *Papiere,* vol. 2, 415–416 (11 April 1888); Ponsonby, *Letters,* 294–296.

57. Ponsonby, *Letters,* 296; *Kölnische Zeitung* (9 April 1888), Turk, *Battenberg,* 240–241; Nichols, *Year,* 219; *Die Grenzboten* 47 (1888), 147 (12 April 1888), 160 (19 April 1888).

58. Nichols, *Year,* 214, 217–218; Turk, "Battenberg," 238; *Der Reichsfreund,* 115 (14 April 1888); Richter's speech (26 May 1888), Schulthess, *Schulthess' Europäischer 1888,* 88.

59. Bismarck, *Auswahl,* vol. 7, 634; Röhl, *Jugend,* 800–801; Nichols, *Year,* 227–228.

60. Nichols, *Year,* 228; *Die Grosse Politik,* vol. 6, 289–292; Turk, "Battenberg," 246–247; Holstein, *Papiere,* vol. 2, 414; Ponsonby, *Letters,* 298.

61. Nichols, *Year,* 232–233; Holstein, *Papiere,* vol. 2, 415–417; Lucius von Ballhausen, *Bismarck-Erinnerungen,* 447.

62. Bamberger, *Spiel,* 343; Vierhaus, *Tagebuch,* 249.

63. For this and the preceding paragraph, see Nichols, *Year,* 96, 141–143, 214–219, 222–223, 231.

64. Pflanze, *Bismarck,* vol. 3, 287–301; Röhl, *Jugend,* 599–627, 712–768, 800; Nichols, *Year,* 215–216; Holstein, *Papiere,* vol. 2, 414, 416, 418; Turk, "Battenberg," 247–249.

65. Holstein, *Papiere,* vol. 2, 413 (31 March 1888); Nichols, *Year,* 176, 212–213.

66. Röhl, *Jugend,* 795–796; Nichols, *Year,* 216–217; Holstein, *Papiere,* vol. 2, 416, 418; Cecil, *Wilhelm II,* vol. 1, 111; Ponsonby, *Letters,* 293, 310–311.

67. Lucius von Ballhausen, *Bismarck-Erinnerungen,* 437–438.

68. Pflanze, *Bismarck,* vol. 3, 281–282; Huber, *Verfassungsgeschichte,* vol. 4, 169–170, 176; Corti, *Wenn,* 492.

69. Richter, *Friedrich III,* 325–326; Nichols, *Year,* 254–258; Lucius von Ballhausen, *Bismarck-Erinnerungen,* 453–454.

70. Lucius von Ballhausen, *Bismarck-Erinnerungen,* 440, 445; Holstein, *Papiere,* vol. 2, 424; Corti, *Wenn,* 492–493.

71. Lucius von Ballhausen, *Bismarck-Erinnerungen,* 455–460.

72. Ibid., 460–461; Müller, "Puttkamer," 373; Nichols, *Year,* 327–330.

73. Lucius von Ballhausen, *Bismarck-Erinnerungen,* 462.

74. Freund, *Drama,* 389; Ponsonby, *Letters,* 314–315.

6. Contested Memory

1. *Times* (London) (16 June 1888); Nichols, *Year,* 339; Dohme, "Erinnerungen," 80–82.

2. Röhl, *Jugend,* 677, 820–821; Röhl, *Aufbau,* 83–86; Bulle, *Gedächtnis,* 20–21.

3. *Der Sozialdemokrat* (2 Aug. 1883).

4. Schrader to Bamberger, 26 March 1888 (Bamberger Papers, BArch N/2008, Nr. 188); Lyschinska, *Henriette Schrader-Breymann,* vol. 2, 423.

5. Schrader to Stauffenberg, 21 June 1888, Wentzcke, *Liberalismus,* vol. 2, 443–444; Victoria to Henriette Schrader, 8 Aug. 1888 (AHH 7/15-1).

6. Schrader to Stauffenberg, 11 Aug. 1888, Wentzcke, *Liberalismus,* vol. 2, 446.

7. *Vossische Zeitung* (15 and 16 June 1888); *Volkszeitung* (16 June 1888); *Die Nation* (16 June 1888); *Freisinnige Zeitung* (17 June 1888); *Der Reichsfreund* (21 June 1888).

8. *Berliner Zeitung* (21 Sept. 1888); *Vossische Zeitung* (21 Sept. 1888); *Freisinnige Zeitung* (22 Sept. 1888); *Volkszeitung* (23 Sept. 1888); *Der Reichsfreund* (27 Sept. 1888); *Berliner Tageblatt* (18 Oct. 1888).

9. Perls, *Kaiser,* 2, 5, 47; Kleyst, *Kaiser,* 5–6, 9; Böhmert, *Kaiser,* 4; Ziemssen, *Friedrich,* 152.

10. *Berliner Zeitung* (15 June 1889)—"Was Du erstrebt in diesem Erdenthale / Wir halten fest an Deinem Ideale"; *Freisinnige Zeitung* (15 June 1889); *Volkszeitung* (15 June 1889); *Berliner Tageblatt* (15 June 1889); *Vossische Zeitung* (15 June 1889); *Die Nation* (15 June 1889).

11. Vorlagen für die Stadtverordneten-Versammlung von Berlin (No. 568; 27 Sept. 1888), one copy in SchP (N240, Gr V, Nr. 6); GStA-PK I. HA, Rep. 89, Nr. 20934, 3a; Ramm, *Beloved*, 79.
12. Marschall to Turban, 3 Nov. 1888, Fuchs, *Großherzog*, vol. 2, 580; GStA-PK I. HA, Rep. 89, Nr. 20939, Bl. 3r–6r, 142a–r.
13. *Die Nation* (20 Oct. 1888); Bulle, *Gedächtnis; Gothaisches Tageblatt* (19 Oct. 1888); SchP (N 240, GrV, Nr. 8).
14. SchP, Nr. 1/V and Nr. 8 (invitations, speech 1889); *Neuer Görlitzer Anzeiger* (*Erste Beilage zu No. 247*, 22 Oct. 1890).
15. Quidde, *Kaiser's Double*, 3; Kohlrausch, *Monarch*, 118–154.
16. *Berliner Tageblatt* (14 June 1898); *Volkszeitung* (15 June 1898); *Vossische Zeitung* (15 June 1898); *Berliner Zeitung* (15 June 1898).
17. *Berliner Tageblatt* (10 and 13 June 1913); *Neue Preussische Zeitung* (14 June 1913); *Vossische Zeitung* (15 June 1913); *Die Hilfe* (12 June 1913), 372–373; *Frankfurter Zeitung* (14 June 1913); *Vossische Zeitung* (15 June 1913).
18. Mackenzie, *Illness*, 179–181; *Die Krankheit*.
19. Röhl, *Aufbau*, 76, 575; Treitschke, "Kaiser," 83; Pakula, *Uncommon Woman*, 549–674.
20. *Deutsches Wochenblatt* (27 June 1888), 158; *Die Grenzboten* (12 July 1888), 107–108; *Neue Preussische Zeitung* (29 Sept. 1888); *Der Reichsbote* (19 Oct. 1888); Coburg, *Programm*, 3–11, 33–34.
21. Röhl, *Aufbau*, 161–163; Schulthess, *Schulthess' Europäischer, 1888*, 156–158.
22. Marschall to Turban, 3 Nov. 1888, Fuchs, *Großherzog*, vol. 2, 579–580; *Volkszeitung* (31 Oct. 1888). The example mentioned was the decision of certain Freisinn papers to criticise William's recent praise for the aristocracy by referring to Frederick's statement that all the citizens were equally dear to him; *Die Nation* (3 Nov. 1888), 62.
23. Busch, *Tagebuchblätter*, vol. 3, 268 (10 Feb. 1889); Gründler, *Bismarck*.
24. The *Börsen-Courier* cited after Schulthess, *Schulthess' Europäischer, 1888*, 133–134; Marschall to Turban, 21 Sept. 1888, Fuchs, *Großherzog*, vol. 2, 574; Hohenlohe-Schillingsfürst, *Denkwürdigkeiten*, vol. 2, 450; Beyerhaus, "Bismarck," 315, 320.
25. Röhl, *Aufbau*, 86–88; Bismarck to Schelling, 5 Oct. 1888, copy (Bamberger Papers, BArch N/2008, Bl. 155); Gründler, *Bismarck*, 70; *Anklageschrift*, 23; Bunsen to Morier, 20 Dec. 1888 (Morier Papers, Box 27, 2).
26. Grelling, *Kaiser;* Gründler, *Bismarck*, 70.
27. *Anklageschrift*, 26–44; *Stenographische Berichte der Verhandlungen des Deutschen Reichstags, 7. Legislaturperiode, IV. Session*, vol. 2 (Berlin, 1889), 813 (5 Feb. 1889); *Die Grenzboten* (21 Feb. 1889), 346; Roggenbach to Grand Duke Frederick, 10 Nov. 1888, Fuchs, *Großherzog*, vol. 2, 584.
28. Ponsonby, *Letters*, 357; Bismarck, *Auswahl*, vol. 7, 665–668.
29. Pflanze, *Bismarck*, vol. 3, 304–305; Loë to Morier, 23 Jan. 1889 (Morier Papers, Box 27, 2).

30. *Die Grenzboten* (27 Sept. 1888), 1; various attacks against Emperor Frederick quoted after *Die Nation* (6 Oct. 1888), 1.
31. *Deutsches Wochenblatt* (4 Oct. 1888), 325; Gründler, *Bismarck*, 18; Engelberg, *Reich*, 527; Robolsky, *Drei Jahre*, 20; the conversation between Roggenbach and Grand Duke Frederick is summarized in Stosch to Freytag, 20 Dec. 1888 (SP, memoirs/typescript, vol. 3, 190); Gall, *Bismarck*, vol. 2, 199–200.
32. Freytag, *Kronprinz*; Röhl, *Aufbau*, 575; Robolsky, *Drei Jahre*, 13.
33. *Die Post* (16 June 1888); *Norddeutsche Allgemeine Zeitung* (17 June 1888); *Der Reichsbote* (19 Oct. 1888).
34. *Der Reichsbote* (15 June 1898); *Neue Preussische Zeitung* (15 June 1898, 16 June 1913); *Norddeutsche Allgemeine Zeitung* (15 June 1913).
35. Klaußmann, *Kaiserreden*, 378; Penzler, *Reden*, pt. 2, 22; William II's speech in 1904 in GStA-PK BPH I. HA, Rep. 89, Nr. 20939, Bl. 142a–r; *Die Errichtung*, 19; William II, *Life*, 3.
36. Alings, *Monument*; Hardtwig, *Geschichtskultur*, 264–301; GStA-PK I. HA, Rep. 89, Nr. 20934, 2; Csallner, *Kaiserdenkmäler*, Nr. 129.
37. Wentzcke, *Liberalismus*, vol. 2, 447.
38. Schröter, *Denkmäler*, 3; Bismarck's submission (30 Aug. 1889), GStA-PK I.HA, Rep. 77, Tit. 151, Nr. 106, Bd. 1, 247–248.
39. GStA-PK I. HA, Rep. 77, Tit. 151, Nr. 106, Bd. 11, 205–205r; Rep. 89, Nr. 20935, 180–183r; Rep. 89, Nr. 20937, 122–125; Rep. 89, Nr. 20936, 202; Rep. 89, Nr. 20938, 165.
40. Schröter, *Denkmäler*, 16–19, 51, 57–63; Alings, *Monument*, 82–85; GStA-PK I. HA, 89, Nr. 20936, 202.
41. Lucius von Ballhausen, *Bismarck-Erinnerungen*, 472–473; GStA-PK I. HA, Rep. 93, Nr. 2530; Schümann, *Dom*, 245–255.
42. GStA-PK I. HA, Rep. 93 B, Nr. 2530, Bl. 5–27, 79–97; *Schwäbischer Merkur* (3 Sept. 1889); Röhl, *Aufbau*, 998–1002; *Neueste Mittheilungen* (19 June 1894), accessed at http://amtspresse.staatsbibliothek-berlin.de (7 Dec. 2009).
43. Giloi Bremner, *"Ich kaufe*," 394–395.
44. GStA-PK I. HA, Rep. 89, Nr. 20934, 108–111; Hardtwig, *Geschichtskultur*, 271–273.
45. Adami, *Büchlein*; Höcker, *Kaiser*; Hottinger, *Kaiser*; Brunold, *Kaiser*; Hiltl, *Fritz*; Felseneck, *Friedrich*; Seidel, *Friedrich III*; Hoffmeyer, *Friedrich III*; Garlepp, *Kaiser*; Epstein, *Kaiser*; Müller-Bohn, *Kaiser*, 539–540.
46. Hutton, *History*, 78–81; Baberowski, *Sinn*, 164–173; Hein, "Mythosforschung," 1–13; Gerwarth, *Bismarck Myth*, 3–6; Münkler, *Mythen*, 18.
47. Sheehan, *Liberalism*, 221–257; Thompson, *Left Liberals*.
48. *Der Sozialdemokrat* (24 March and 23 June 1888); *Stenographische Berichte* (Reichstag), *9. Legislaturperiode, V. Session*, vol. 3 (Berlin, 1897–1898), 1844 (28 March 1898).
49. *Stenographische Berichte* (Reichstag), *9. Legislaturperiode, V. Session*, vol. 3 (Berlin, 1897–1898), 1844 (28 March 1898) and *Anlagenband* No. 3 (Ber-

lin, 1898), 1805; GStA-PK I. HA, Rep. 89, Nr. 20939, Bl. 27–142r; Schröter, *Denkmäler*, 28–33; Csallner, *Kaiserdenkmäler*, Nr. 7.

50. Engel, *Tagebuch*, 7–8, 72–74; Dohme, "Erinnerungen."
51. Meisner, *Kriegstagebuch*, xxv–xxvi, *Tagebücher*, and *Kronprinz*.
52. Freytag, *Kronprinz*, 21–23, 28, 47, 81–82; Stosch to Roggenbach, 29 Nov. 1889 (SP, memoirs/typescript, vol. 3, 204); *Breslauer Zeitung* (27 Oct. 1889); *Die Nation* (2 Nov. 1889), 62–65; Delbrück, "Freytag."
53. Philippson, *Friedrich III*; SchP (N240, Gr V, Nr. 9); Philippson to Baumgarten, 12 May 1891 (Baumgarten Papers, BArch N/2013, Nr. 19); Stosch to Freytag, 26 Feb. 1893 (SP, memoirs/typescript, vol. 3, 289).
54. Kaufmann, "Philippson"; Kaufmann, "Müller-Bohn"; Poschinger, *Kaiser*, vols. 1–3.
55. Pflanze, "Bismarck's Gedanken," 54–56; Curtius, "Kaiser," 386–388, 401, 403, 407; Ziekursch, *Geschichte*, 415–421.
56. Wolbe, *Kaiser*, puff on dust jacket and 294; Richter, *Friedrich III*, 353.
57. Ludwig, *Wilhelm*, 21–24; Curtius, "Kaiser," 385; Ludwig, "Kaiser"; Raumer, "Kaiser," 150; Rothfels, "Kriegstagebuch," 293–295.
58. *Der Tag* (17 and 18 Oct. 1931).
59. Ibid. (18 Oct. 1931); *Potsdamer Tageszeitung* (19 Oct. 1931); Vogel, *Ansprache*, 2, 4–7.
60. *Berliner Morgenpost* (18 Oct. 1931); *Berliner Tageblatt* (20 Oct. 1931).
61. Münkler, *Mythen*, 9; Knopp, "Erinnerung," 9.
62. WDR *Hörfunksendung "Forum West" zur Ausstellung "Friedrich III." in Bonn, 26 Aug. 1989* (GStA-PK Dienstregistratur, G2–18); *Das Parlament* (22 Sept. 1989); *Bonner Rundschau* (25 Aug. 1989); *Rhein-Zeitung* (28 Aug. 1989).

Conclusion

1. Bruch, "Nachwort," 367.
2. *GW*, vol. 8, 492.
3. *Allgemeine Zeitung* (17 June 1888); Geisthövel, "Tote Monarchen"; Blessing, *Staat*, 180; Weichlein, *Nation*, 349–350, 363.
4. Cecil, *Wilhelm II*, vol. 1, 298.
5. Kohut, *Wilhelm II*, 134, 138, 156.
6. Frederick of Baden to Gelzer, 21 March 1872, Fuchs, *Großherzog*, vol. 1, 55; *Aus der Berliner Gesellschaft*, 3–4; Röhl, *The Kaiser and His Court*, 9–27; König, *Wilhelm II.*, 195–198.
7. Clark, *Wilhelm II*, 218–255; Fröhlich, *Imperialismus*, 11–16; Röhl, *Aufbau*, 1058–1060.
8. *Die Errichtung*, 19; Röhl, *Aufbau*, 985–989; Kaul, *Friedrich Barbarossa*, vol. 1, 529–531.
9. Cecil, *Wilhelm II*, vol. 2, 11–15.
10. William II to Victoria, 25 September 1898, Röhl, *Personal Monarchy*, 873; on the issue of "Personal Rule," see also Jefferies, *Contesting*, 84–89; Hull,

"Persönliches Regiment," 3–23; Röhl, *Kaiser,* 107–130; Eley, "View"; Huber, *Verfassungsgeschichte,* vol. 4, 329–347.

11. Valentin, *People,* 502.
12. *Die Nation* (29 Dec. 1888), 188; Ziegler, *Strömungen,* 528–529; *Frankfurter Zeitung* (14 June 1913).
13. Dohme, "Erinnerungen," 8; Curtius, "Kaiser," 401–402; Ziekursch, *Geschichte,* 421; Roth, "Tragik," 46; Scholtz, *Generation.*
14. Scholtz, *Generation,* 22, 41, 43; Fogt, *Generationen,* 21; Mannheim, "Problem"; Meisner, *Tagebücher,* 21.
15. Frederick William to Victoria, 5 Dec. 1879 (AHH 7.1/1 XVIII); Holstein, *Papiere,* vol. 2, 180 (9 Nov. 1884); Frederick William to Stosch, 30 Nov. 1884 (SP).
16. Stosch to Normann, 26 March 1884 (SP, memoirs/typescript, vol. 3, 9).
17. Scholtz, *Generation,* 42.
18. Ludwig, *Wilhelm,* 22.

Sources and Works Cited

Archival Sources

ARCHIVE OF THE HESSISCHE HAUSSTIFTUNG
(SCHLOSS FASANERIE, EICHENZELL BEI FULDA)
  Papers of the Empress Frederick (Victoria)

ARCHIVE OF THE VON STOSCH FAMILY (OESTRICH-WINKEL)
  Papers of Albrecht von Stosch

BALLIOL COLLEGE (OXFORD)
  The Diplomatic, Personal, and Family Correspondence of Sir Robert B. D.
  Morier (1826–1893)

BUNDESARCHIV (BERLIN-LICHTERFELDE)
  Papers of Ludwig Bamberger (N/2008)
  Papers of Hermann Baumgarten (N/2013)
  Papers of Heinrich Friedberg (N/2080)
  Papers of Franz Schenk von Stauffenberg (N/2292)

GEHEIMES STAATSARCHIV PREUSSISCHER KULTURBESITZ (BERLIN-DAHLEM)
  Files of the Civilkabinett (I. HA, Rep. 89)
  Files of the Innenministerium (I. HA, Rep. 77, tit. 151)
  Files of the Ministerium der öffentlichen Arbeiten (I. HA, Rep. 93B)
  Files of the Staatsministerium (I. HA, Rep. 90A)
  Papers of Emperor and King Frederick III (BPH, Rep. 52)
  Papers of Maximilian von Forckenbeck (VI. HA, NL Forckenbeck)
  Papers of Queen Louise (BPH, Rep. 49)

NIEDERSÄCHSISCHES STAATSARCHIV WOLFENBÜTTEL
Papers of Karl Schrader (240 N)

ROYAL ARCHIVES (WINDSOR)
Victorian Archive (RA VIC)
Victorian Additional Archive (RA VIC/Add)

Newspapers and Periodicals

Aachener Anzeiger, Allgemeine Zeitung (Munich), *Augsburger Allgemeine Zeitung, Berliner Illustrierte Zeitung, Berliner Morgenpost, Berliner Tageblatt, Berliner Zeitung, Bonner General-Anzeiger, Bonner Rundschau, Breslauer Zeitung, The Daily News* (London), *Deutsche Zeitung* (Heidelberg), *Deutsches Wochenblatt, Dresdner Nachrichten, The Economist* (London), *Frankfurter Zeitung, Die Freisinnige Zeitung, Germania, Gothaisches Tageblatt, Die Grenzboten, Die Hilfe, Kölnische Zeitung, Die Nation, National-Zeitung* (Berlin), *Neue Freie Presse* (Vienna), *Neuer Görlitzer Anzeiger, Neue Preussische Zeitung* (Berlin), *The New York Herald, Norddeutsche Allgemeine Zeitung, Das Parlament, Die Post* (Berlin), *Potsdamer Tageszeitung, Der Reichsbote, Der Reichsfreund, Rhein-Zeitung, Schwäbischer Merkur, Der Sozialdemokrat, The Standard* (London), *Der Tag* (Berlin), *The Times* (London), *Die Tribüne* (Berlin), *Der Türmer, Die Volkszeitung, Vorwärts, Vossische Zeitung, Wilhelmshavener Zeitung und Anzeiger.*

Other Printed Primary Sources and Secondary Literature

Adami, Paul. *Das Büchlein vom Kaiser Friedrich. Ein Lebensbild dem deutschen Volke und Heere geschildert* (Berlin, 1888).

Adler, Friedrich. "Die Schlosskirche in Wittenberg." *Zeitschrift für Bauwesen* 45 (1895): 466–479.

Alings, Reinhard. *Monument und Nation. Das Bild vom Nationalstaat im Medium Denkmal—zum Verhältnis von Nation und Staat im deutschen Kaiserreich* (Berlin/New York, 1996).

Anderson, Margaret Lavinia. *Practicing Democracy: Elections and Political Culture in Imperial Germany* (Princeton, 2000).

Anklageschrift gegen den Geheimen Justizrath, Professor a. D. Dr. jur. Friedrich Heinrich Geffcken, in *Drucksachen zu den Verhandlungen des Bundesraths des Deutschen Reichs,* vol. 1 (Berlin, 1889), 6–45.

Arndt, Monika. *Die Goslarer Kaiserpfalz als Nationaldenkmal. Eine ikonographische Untersuchung* (Hildesheim, 1976).

Aus der Berliner Gesellschaft, 2nd ed. (Berlin, 1886).

Baberowski, Jörg. *Der Sinn der Geschichte. Geschichtstheorien von Hegel bis Foucault* (Munich, 2005).

Bamberger, Ludwig. *Bismarcks grosses Spiel. Die geheimen Tagebücher Ludwig Bambergers,* ed. Ernst Feder, 2nd ed. (Frankfurt am Main, 1933).

———. *Gesammelte Schriften,* vol. 5 (Berlin, 1897).

Barry, Quintin. *The Franco-Prussian War, 1870–1871,* 2 vols. (Solihull, 2007).

———. *The Road to Königgrätz: Helmuth von Moltke and the Austro-Prussian War 1866* (Solihull, 2010).

Bartmann, Dominik (ed.). *Anton von Werner. Geschichte in Bildern* (Munich, 1993).

Baumgarten, Hermann. *Zum Gedächtnis Kaiser Friedrichs. Rede bei der Gedenkfeier der Kaiser-Wilhelms-Universität am 30. Juni 1888* (Strassburg, 1888).

Bausinger, Hermann. "Bürgerlichkeit und Kultur." In Jürgen Kocka (ed.), *Bürger und Bürgerlichkeit im 19. Jahrhundert* (Göttingen, 1987), 121–142.

Becker, Frank. "Begriff und Bedeutung des politischen Mythos." In Barbara Stollberg-Rilinger (ed.), *Was heißt Kulturgeschichte des Politischen?* (Berlin, 2005), 129–148.

———. *Bilder von Krieg und Nation. Die Einigungskriege in der bürgerlichen Öffentlichkeit Deutschlands 1864–1913* (Munich, 2001).

———. "Strammstehen vor der Obrigkeit? Bürgerliche Wahrnehmung der Einigungskriege und Militarismus im Deutschen Kaiserreich." *Historische Zeitschrift* 277 (2003): 87–113.

Benson, Arthur C., and Viscount Esher (eds.). *The Letters of Queen Victoria*, vol. 2 (London, 1908).

Berlin und die Berliner. Leute, Dinge, Sitten, Winke (Karlsruhe, 1905).

Bernhardi, Theodor von. *Aus dem Leben Theodor von Bernhardis*, vol. 3 (Leipzig, 1894).

Besier, Gerhard. "Die Persönlichen Erinnerungen des Chefs des Geheimen Zivilkabinetts Karl von Wilmowski (1817–1893)." *Jahrbuch für Berlin-Brandenburgische Kirchengeschichte* 50 (1977): 131–182.

Beyerhaus, Gisbert. "Bismarck und Kaiser Friedrichs Tagebuch. Ein Beitrag zur Geschichte des deutschen Liberalismus." In *Historische Aufsätze. Aloys Schulte zum 70. Geburtstag gewidmet von Schülern und Freunden* (Düsseldorf, 1927), 314–327.

———. "Die Krise des deutschen Liberalismus und das Problem der 99 Tage." *Preussische Jahrbücher* 239 (1935): 1–19.

Biefang, Andreas, Michael Epkenhans, and Klaus Tenfelde. *Die andere Seite der Macht. Reichstag und Öffentlichkeit im "System Bismarck" 1871–1890* (Düsseldorf, 2009).

——— (eds.). *Das politische Zeremoniell im Deutschen Kaiserreich 1871–1918* (Düsseldorf, 2008).

Bigelow, Poultney. *Prussian Memories 1864–1914* (New York/London, 1916).

Bismarck, Herbert von. *Staatssekretär Herbert von Bismarck. Aus seiner politischen Privatkorrespondenz*, ed. Walter Bussmann with Klaus-Peter Hoepke (Göttingen, 1964).

Bismarck, Otto von. *Die gesammelten Werke*, 15 vols. (Berlin, 1924–1935).

———. *Die politischen Reden des Fürsten Bismarck*, ed. Horst Kohl, vol. 8 (Stuttgart, 1893).

———. *Werke in Auswahl*, 8 vols. (Darmstadt, 1962).

Blackbourn, David. "The Discreet Charm of the Bourgeoisie: Reappraising German History in the Nineteenth Century." In David Blackbourn and Geoff

Eley, *The Peculiarities of Germany History. Bourgeois Society and Politics in Nineteenth-Century Germany* (Oxford, 1984), 159–292.

Blessing, Werner K. *Staat und Kirche in der Gesellschaft. Institutionelle Autorität und mentaler Wandel in Bayern während des 19. Jahrhunderts* (Göttingen, 1982).

Bode, Wilhelm von. *Mein Leben,* ed. Thomas W. Gaethgens and Barbara Paul, 2 vols. (Berlin, 1997).

Böhmert, Victor (ed.). *Kaiser Friedrich als Freund des Volkes* (Leipzig, 1888).

Bolitho, Hector (ed.). *The Prince Consort and His Brother. Two Hundred New Letters* (London, 1933).

Börner, Karl-Heinz. *Wilhelm I.* (Berlin, 1984).

Bracht, Eugen. *Die Lebenserinnerungen von Eugen Bracht,* ed. Rudolf Theilmann (Karlsruhe, 1973).

Bringmann, Michael. "Das neue Deutsche Reich und die Kaiserkrone—Realität und Mythos." In Mario Kramp (ed.), *Krönungen. Könige in Aachen—Geschichte und Mythos,* vol. 1 (Mainz, 2000), 795–808.

Bruch, Rüdiger vom. "Nachwort." In Werner Richter, *Friedrich III. Leben und Tragik des zweiten Hohenzollern-Kaisers* (Munich, 1981), 367–377.

Brunold, F. [i.e., August Ferdinand Meyer]. *Kaiser Friedrich III. von Deutschland. Ein Lebensbild für jung und alt* (Reutlingen, 1889).

Bruyn, Günter de. *Preussens Luise. Von Entstehen und Vergehen einer Legende* (Berlin, 2001).

Budde, Gunilla. *Blütezeit des Bürgertums. Bürgerlichkeit im 19. Jahrhundert* (Darmstadt, 2009).

[Bulle, Constantin.] *Zum Gedächtnis Kaiser Friedrichs des Dritten. Versammlung im Casino zu Bremen veranstaltet von dem Verein der Deutschen freisinnigen Partei in Bremen am 18. Oktober 1888.—Vortrag des Reichstagsabgeordneten Prof. Dr. Bulle* (Bremen, 1888).

Bunsen, Georg von. "The Liberal Party in Germany." *Fortnightly Review* 38 (1882): 693–717.

Bunsen, Marie von. *Georg von Bunsen. Ein Charakterbild aus dem Lager der Besiegten* (Berlin, 1900).

———. Bunsen, Marie von. *Die Welt, in der ich lebte. Erinnerungen aus glücklichen Jahren 1860–1912* (Leipzig, 1920).

Busch, Moritz. *Tagebuchblätter,* 3 vols. (Berlin, 1899).

Canis, Konrad. "Bismarck und die Monarchen." In Lothar Gall (ed.), *Otto von Bismarck und die Parteien* (Paderborn, 2001), 137–154.

Cecil, Lamar. *Wilhelm II: Prince and Emperor, 1859–1900,* vol. 1; *Emperor and Exile, 1900–1941,* vol. 2 (Chapel Hill / London, 1989, 1996).

Charakterzüge aus dem Leben des deutschen Kaisers und Königs von Preussen Friedrich. Für Schule und Haus sowie allen Vaterlandsfreunden und Verehrern des unvergesslichen Kaisers Friedrich dargeboten (Langensalza, 1890).

Clark, Christopher. *Iron Kingdom: The Rise and Downfall of Prussia, 1600–1947* (London, 2006).

———. *Kaiser Wilhelm II: A Life in Power* (London, 2009).

[Coburg, Ernst von.] *Auch ein Programm aus den 99 Tagen* (Berlin, 1888).

[————.] *Mitregenten und fremde Hände in Deutschland* (Zürich, 1886).

Corti, Egon Caesar Conte. *Wenn . . . Sendung und Schicksal einer Kaiserin* (Graz/Vienna/Cologne, 1954).

Craig, Gordon A. *The Battle of Königgrätz* (London, 1965).

Csallner, Heinz. *Deutsche Kaiserdenkmäler in alten Ansichten* (Zaltbommel, Netherlands, 1994).

Curtius, Friedrich. "Kaiser Friedrich und das deutsche Volk." *Hochland* 23, no. 10 (1926): 385–407.

Davidoff, Leonore, and Catherine Hall. *Family Fortunes: Men and Women of the English Middle Class, 1780–1850* (London, 1987).

Delbrück, Hans. "Gustav Freytag über Kaiser Friedrich." *Preussische Jahrbücher* 64 (1889): 587–595.

————. "Persönliche Erinnerungen an Kaiser Friedrich und sein Haus." *Preussische Jahrbücher* 62 (1888): 97–116.

Demandt, Philip. *Luisenkult. Die Unsterblichkeit der Königin von Preussen* (Cologne, 2001).

Dernburg, Friedrich. *Des deutschen Kronprinzen Reise nach Spanien und Rom. Journalistische Reiseskizzen* (Berlin, 1884).

Deutschlands Trauer, Des Reiches Hoffnung. Die ersten drei Kaiser des Deutschen Reiches. Wilhelms I. und Friedrichs III. Leben, Tod und Bestattung. Wilhelms II. Regierungsantritt (Stuttgart, 1888).

Dohme, Robert. "Erinnerungen an Kaiser Friedrich." *Deutsche Revue* 47, no. 1 (1922): 1–14, 117–131, 264–257; and *Deutsche Revue* 47, no. 2 (1922): 73–84.

————. *Unter fünf preussischen Königen. Lebenserinnerungen,* ed. Paul Lindenberg (Berlin, 1901).

Dollinger, Heinz. "Das Leitbild des Bürgerkönigs in der europäischen Monarchie des 19. Jahrhunderts." In K. F. Werner (ed.), *Hof, Kultur und Politik im 19. Jahrhundert* (Bonn, 1985), 325–364.

Dorenwell, Karl. *Unser Kaiser Friedrich als Kronprinz. Charakterzüge aus seinem Leben. Für jung und alt* (Minden, 1888).

Dorpalen, Andreas. "Frederick III and the German Liberal Movement." *American Historical Review* 54 (1948): 1–31.

Drobisch, Theodor. *Der Alte Fritz und Unser Fritz. Ein Buch für die Jugend* (Dresden, 1875).

Duncker, Max. *Politischer Briefwechsel aus seinem Nachlaß,* ed. Johannes Schultze (Stuttgart/Berlin, 1923).

Eley, Geoff. "The View from the Throne: The Personal Rule of Kaiser Wilhelm II." *Historical Journal* 28 (1985): 469–485.

Engel, Eduard. *Kaiser Friedrichs Tagebuch* (Halle, 1919).

Engelberg, Ernst. *Bismarck. Das Reich in der Mitte Europas* (Berlin, 1990).

————. *Bismarck. Urpreusse und Reichsgründer* (Berlin, 1985).

Epkenhans, Michael. "Victoria und Bismarck." In Rainer von Hessen (ed.), *Victoria Kaiserin Friedrich (1840–1901). Mission und Schicksal einer englischen Prinzessin in Deutschland* (Frankfurt am Main/New York, 2002), 151–178.

Epstein, Ludwig. *Kaiser Friedrich III. Ein Lebensbild für jung und alt* (Torgau, 1913).

Die Errichtung des Denkmals Kaiser Friedrichs III. in Aachen und seine Enthüllung am 18.X.1911 (Aachen, 1911).

Eulenburg-Hertefeld, Philipp zu. *Aus 50 Jahren. Erinnerungen, Tagebücher und Briefe aus dem Nachlass des Fürsten*, ed. Johannes Haller (Berlin, 1923).

———. *Philipp Eulenburgs politische Korrespondenz*, ed. John C. G. Röhl, 3 vols. (Boppard am Rhein, 1976–1983).

Fehrenbach, Elisabeth. *Wandlungen des deutschen Kaisergedankens 1871–1918* (Munich/Vienna, 1969).

Felseneck, Marie von [i.e., Maria Mancke]. *Friedrich III. Deutscher Kaiser und König von Preussen. Ein Lebensbild* (Berlin [1899]).

Ferdinand, M. *Friedrich—Deutscher Kaiser und König von Preussen. Ein Lebensbild für das deutsche Volk* (Berlin, 1888).

Fischer, Karl August. *Kaiser Friedrich III. als Vorbild eines Fürsten in Krieg und Frieden dem deutschen Volke gewidmet* (Stuttgart [1888]).

Fitzpatrick, Matthew. *Liberal Imperialism in Germany: Expansionism and Nationalism, 1848–1884* (New York, 2008).

Fogt, Helmut. *Politische Generationen. Empirische Bedeutung und theoretisches Modell* (Opladen, 1982).

Fontane, Theodor. *Briefe an seine Familie*, vol. 2 (Berlin, 1905).

———. *Gedichte* (Stuttgart, 1905).

Forbes, Archibald. "The Emperor Frederick's Diary." *Contemporary Review* 54 (1888): 609–622.

Freund, Michael. *Das Drama der 99 Tage. Krankheit und Tod Friedrichs III.* (Cologne, 1966).

Freytag, Gustav. *Gustav Freytags Briefe an Albrecht von Stosch*, ed. Hans F. Helmholt (Stuttgart/Berlin, 1913).

———. *Der Kronprinz und die deutsche Kaiserkrone. Erinnerungsblätter* (Leipzig, 1889).

Fröhlich, Michael. *Imperialismus. Deutsche Welt- und Kolonialpolitik 1880–1914* (Munich, 1994).

Fuchs, Walther Peter (ed.). *Großherzog Friedrich I. von Baden und die Reichspolitik 1871–1907*, 4 vols. (Stuttgart, 1968, 1975, 1980).

Fulford, Roger (ed.). *Beloved Mama: Private Correspondence of Queen Victoria and the German Crown Princess, 1878–1885* (London, 1981).

——— (ed.). *Darling Child: Private Correspondence of Queen Victoria and the German Crown Princess, 1871–1878* (London, 1976).

——— (ed.). *Dearest Child: The Private Correspondence of Queen Victoria and the Princess Royal, 1858–1861* (London, 1964).

——— (ed.). *Dearest Mama: Letters between Queen Victoria and the Crown Princess of Prussia, 1861–1864* (London, 1968).

——— (ed.). *Your Dear Letter: Private Correspondence of Queen Victoria and the German Crown Princess, 1865–1871* (London, 1971).

Fürste, Ernst. *Gedichte zum Gedächtnis unserer in Gott ruhenden Kaiser Wilhelm I. und Friedrich III.* (Magdeburg, 1889).

Gall, Lothar. *Bismarck. Der weisse Revolutionär* (Frankfurt am Main, 1980).

Garlepp, Bruno. *Friedrich Wilhelm IV und Kaiser Wilhelm der Große (II. Teil), Kaiser Friedrich III. und Kaiser Wilhelm II. als Thronfolger* (Breslau, 1911).

Geisthövel, Alexa. "Den Monarchen im Blick. Wilhelm I. in der illustrierten Familienpresse." In Habbo Knoch and Daniel Morat (eds.), *Kommunikation als Beobachtung. Medienwandel und Gesellschaftsbilder 1880–1960* (Munich, 2003), 59–80.

———. "Tote Monarchen. Die Beisetzungsfeierlichkeiten für Wilhelm I. und Friedrich III." In Andreas Biefang, Michael Epkenhans, and Klaus Tenfelde (eds.), *Das politische Zeremoniell im Deutschen Kaiserreich 1871–1918* (Düsseldorf, 2008), 139–161.

———. "Wilhelm I. am 'historischen Eckfenster.' Zur Sichtbarkeit des Monarchen in der zweiten Hälfte des 19. Jahrhunderts." In Jan Andres, Alexa Geisthövel, and Matthias Schwengelbeck (eds.), *Die Sinnlichkeit der Macht. Herrschaft und Repräsentation seit der Frühen Neuzeit* (Frankfurt am Main, 2005), 163–185.

Geppert, Dominik. *Pressekriege. Öffentlichkeit und Diplomatie in den deutsch-britischen Beziehungen 1896–1912* (Munich, 2007).

Gerock, Karl. *Predigt zum Trauergottesdienst für seine Majestät weiland den deutschen Kaiser Friedrich am 18. Juni 1888 gehalten in der k. Schlosskapelle zu Stuttgart* (Stuttgart, 1888).

Gerwarth, Robert. *The Bismarck Myth: Weimar Germany and the Legacy of the Iron Chancellor* (Oxford, 2005).

Giloi Bremner, Eva. *"Ich kaufe mir den Kaiser": Royal Relics and the Culture of Display in 19th Century Prussia* (PhD dissertation, Princeton University, 2000).

Goldschmidt, Hans. *Das Reich und Preussen im Kampf um die Führung. Von Bismarck bis 1918* (Berlin, 1931).

Grelling, Richard. *Kaiser Friedrichs Tagebuch und der Prozess Geffcken* (Berlin, 1889).

Die Grosse Politik der Europäischen Kabinette 1871–1914. Reihe 1, vols. 1–6: Die Bismarckzeit (Berlin, 1922).

Gründler, Gerhard E. *Bismarck auf Treibjagd. Die missglückte Strafaktion gegen Geffcken und die Deutsche Rundschau* (Hamburg, 2009).

Gundermann, Iselin. "Kronprinz Friedrich Wilhelm von Preussen und die Schlosskirche in Wittenberg." In Martin Steffens and Insa Christiane Hennen (eds.), *Die Wittenberger Schlosskirche* (Wittenberg, 1998), 63–73.

Hahn, Peter-Michael. *Friedrich der Grosse und die deutsche Nation* (Stuttgart, 2007).

Hansard's Parliamentary Debates (London, 1888), vol. 327.

Hardtwig, Wolfgang. "Bürgertum, Staatssymbolik und Staatsbewusstsein im Deutschen Kaiserreich 1871–1914." *Geschichte und Gesellschaft* 16 (1990): 284–285.

———. *Geschichtskultur und Wissenschaft* (Munich, 1990).

Haym, Rudolf. *Ausgewählter Briefwechsel Rudolf Hayms,* ed. Hans Rosenberg (Berlin/Leipzig, 1930).

———. *Das Leben Max Dunckers* (Berlin, 1891).

Hein, Heidi. "Historische Mythosforschung." In *Virtuelle Fachbibliothek Osteuropa* (http://epub.ub.uni-muenchen.de/639/1/hein-mythosforschung.pdf), accessed 16 Febuary 2009.

Hengst, Hermann. *Friedrich Wilhelm, Kronprinz des Deutschen Reiches und von Preussen* (Berlin, 1883).

Herre, Franz. *Kaiser Wilhelm I. Der letzte Preusse* (Cologne, 1980).

Heyderhoff, Julius (ed.). *Im Ring der Gegner Bismarcks. Denkschriften und politischer Briefwechsel Franz von Roggenbachs mit Kaiserin Augusta und Albrecht von Stosch 1865–1896* (Leipzig, 1943).

Hiery, Hermann. "Der Kaiser, das Reich und der Kolonialismus. Anmerkungen zur Entstehung des deutschen Imperialismus im 19. Jahrhundert." In Franz Bosbach and Hermann Hiery (eds.), *Imperium-Empire-Reich. Ein Konzept politischer Herrschaft im deutsch-britischen Vergleich* (Munich, 1999), 155–166.

Hiltl, Georg. *Unser Fritz. Deutscher Kaiser und König von Preussen,* amended and completed by Hermann Müller-Bohn, 4th ed. (Berlin, 1889).

Hintze, Otto. "Das monarchische Prinzip und die konstitutionelle Verfassung." *Preussische Jahrbücher* 144 (1911): 381–412.

Hinzpeter, Georg. "Der Kaiser Friedrich—die poetische Gestalt unter den Hohenzollern." Unpublished manuscript (Dec. 1901), GStA-PK BPH Rep. 52, F III, Nr. 3.

———. *Zum 25. Januar 1883. Eine Unterhaltung am häuslichen Herd für den Tag der silbernen Hochzeit des Kronprinzlichen Paares* (Bielefeld/Leipzig, 1883).

Hobhouse, Hermione. "The Monarchy and the Middle Classes: The Role of Prince Albert." In Adolf M. Birke and Lothar Kettenacker (eds.), *Bürgertum, Adel und Monarchie. Wandel der Lebensformen im Zeitalter des bürgerlichen Nationalismus* (Munich/London/New York/Paris, 1989), 53–69.

Höcker, Oskar. *Kaiser Friedrich als Prinz, Feldherr und Herrscher. Ein vaterländisches Lebensbild der deutschen Jugend und dem deutschen Volke gewidmet* (Berlin, 1888).

Hoffmeyer, Ludwig. *Friedrich III. Deutscher Kaiser und König von Preussen. Ein Fürstenbild der Schule und dem Hause gewidmet* (Breslau, 1901).

Hohenlohe-Schillingsfürst, Chlodwig zu. *Denkwürdigkeiten des Fürsten Chlodwig zu Hohenlohe-Schillingsfürst,* ed. Friedrich Curtius, 2 vols. (Stuttgart/Leipzig, 1907).

Hölder, Julius. *Das Tagebuch des Julius Hölder 1877–1880,* ed. Dieter Langewiesche (Stuttgart, 1977).

Hollyday, Frederic B. "Bismarck and the Legend of the 'Gladstone Ministry.'" In Lillian P. Wallace and William C. Askew (eds.), *Power, Public Opinion, and Diplomacy* (Durham, NC, 1959), 92–109.

———. *Bismarck's Rival: A Political Biography of General and Admiral Albrecht von Stosch* (Durham, NC, 1960).

Holstein, Friedrich von. *Die Geheimen Papiere Friedrich von Holsteins*, ed. Norman Rich and M. H. Fisher, German edition by Werner Frauendienst, 4 vols. (Göttingen, 1958–1963).

Hottinger, Christlieb Gotthold. *Kaiser Wilhelm I.—Kaiser Friedrich III.—Kaiser Wilhelm II. Wort und Bild* (Strassburg, 1888).

Howard, Michael. *The Franco-Prussian War: The German Invasion of France 1870–1871* (London, 1961).

Huber, Ernst Rudolf. *Deutsche Verfassungsgeschichte seit 1789*, vol. 4 (Stuttgart, 1969).

Hübner, Joachim. *Bismarck und Kaiser Friedrich III.* (PhD dissertation, University of Kiel, 1953).

Hübner, Rudolf (ed.). *Johann Gustav Droysen. Briefwechsel*, vol. 2 (Berlin/Leipzig, 1929).

Hughes, Michael L. "Splendid Demonstrations: The Political Funerals of Kaiser Wilhelm I and Wilhelm Liebknecht." *Central European History* 41 (2008): 229–253.

Hull, Isabel V. "Persönliches Regiment." In John C. G. Röhl (ed.), *Der Ort Kaiser Wilhelms II. in der deutschen Geschichte* (Munich, 1991), 3–23.

Hutton, Patrick H. *History as an Art of Memory* (Hanover/London, 1993).

Ilsenmann, Sigurd von (ed.). *Der Kaiser in Holland. Aufzeichnungen des letzten Flügeladjutanten Kaiser Wilhelms II*, 2 vols. (Munich, 1967–1968).

Jagow, Kurt (ed.). *Letters of the Prince Consort, 1831–1861* (London, 1938).

Jansen, Christian. "Bismarck und die Linksliberalen." In Lothar Gall (ed.), *Otto von Bismarck und die Parteien* (Paderborn, 2001), 91–110.

Jefferies, Matthew. *Contesting the German Empire, 1871–1918* (Oxford, 2008).

———. *Imperial Culture in Germany, 1871–1918* (Basingstoke, 2003).

Johnson, John J., Jr. *False Dawn, Bismarck, the Cartel, and the Crown Prince, November 1886 to June 1887* (PhD dissertation, University of Illinois at Urbana-Champaign, 1972).

Kähler, Martin. *Zum Gedächtnis Friedrich III., Deutschen Kaisers und Königs von Preussen. Rede gehalten am 30. Juni 1888* (Halle, 1888).

Kaiser Friedrich III. (1831–1888). Ausstellung des Geheimen Staatsarchivs Preussischer Kulturbesitz anlässlich der 100. Wiederkehr des Dreikaiserjahres 1888—catalogue (Berlin, 1988).

Kaschuba, Wolfgang. "German *Bürgerlichkeit* after 1800: Culture as Symbolic Practice." In Jürgen Kocka and Allan Mitchell (eds.), *Bourgeois Society in Nineteenth-Century Europe* (Oxford, 1993), 392–422.

Kaufmann, Georg. [Review of] "Hermann Müller-Bohn, Kaiser Friedrich der Gütige. Vaterländisches Ehrenbuch (Berlin, 1900)." *Historische Zeitschrift* 87 (1901): 121–122.

———. [Review of] "Martin Philippson, Das Leben Kaiser Friedrichs III. (Wiesbaden, 1900)." *Historische Zeitschrift* 87 (1901): 117–121.

Kaul, Camilla G. *Friedrich Barbarossa im Kyffhäuser. Bilder eines nationalen Mythos im 19. Jahrhundert*, 2 vols. (Cologne, 2007).

Kemper, Thomas. *Schloss Monbijou. Von der königlichen Residenz zum Hohenzollern-Museum* (Berlin, 2005).

Kennedy, Paul. *The Rise of the Anglo-German Antagonism, 1860–1914* (London, 1980).

Klaußmann, Anton Oskar (ed.). *Kaiserreden. Reden und Erlasse, Briefe und Telegramme Kaiser Wilhelms II.* (Leipzig, 1902).

Klemm, Max. *Was sagt Bismarck dazu? Ein Wegweiser durch Bismarcks Geistes- und Gedankenwelt*, vol. 1 (Berlin, 1924).

Klenke, Dietmar. "War der 'deutsche Mann' im 19. Jahrhundert 'bürgerlich' oder 'feudal'?" *WerkstattGeschichte* 12 (1995): 56–64.

Kleyst, J. L. *Kaiser Friedrich der edle Dulder, seine Ärzte und das Buch Mackenzie's* (Berlin, 1888).

Klingenburg, Karl-Heinz. *Der Berliner Dom. Bauten, Ideen und Projekte vom 15. Jahrhundert bis zur Gegenwart* (Berlin/Leipzig, 1987).

Kloosterhuis, Jürgen. "Victoria im Preussenjahr." *Jahrbuch Preussischer Kulturbesitz* 38 (2002): 323–352.

Knopp, Werner. "Erinnerung an Friedrich III. (1831–1888)." In *Kaiser Friedrich III (1831–1888). Ausstellung des Geheimen Staatsarchivs Preussischer Kulturbesitz anlässlich der 100. Wiederkehr des Dreikaiserjahres 1888* (Berlin, 1988), 9–14.

———. "Der stumme Kaiser. Erinnerung an Kaiser Friedrich III. (1831–1888). *Jahrbuch Preussischer Kulturbesitz* 18 (1981), 337–351.

Kohl, Horst (ed.). *Aus Bismarcks Briefwechsel. Anhang zu den Gedanken und Erinnerungen von Otto Fürst von Bismarck*, vol. 2 (Stuttgart, 1901).

Kohlrausch, Martin. *Der Monarch im Skandal, Die Logik der Massenmedien und die Transformation der wilhelminischen Monarchie* (Berlin, 2005).

Kohut, Thomas A. "Kaiser Wilhelm II and His Parents: An Inquiry into the Psychological Roots of German Policy towards England before the First World War." In John C. G. Röhl and Nicolaus Sombart (eds.), *Kaiser Wilhelm II: New Interpretations* (Cambridge, 1982), 63–89.

———. *Wilhelm II and the Germans: A Study in Leadership* (New York/Oxford, 1991).

Kollander, Patricia. "Bismarck, Crown Prince Frederick William, and the Hohenzollern Candidacy Revisited." *European Review of History* 3 (1996): 171–185.

———. "Constitutionalism or Staatsstreich? Bismarck, Crown Prince Frederick William, Crown Princess Victoria and the Succession Crisis of 1880–1885." *European Review of History* 8 (2001): 187–201.

———. "Empress Frederick: The Last Hope for a Liberal Germany?" *Historian* 62 (1999): 47–62.

———. *Frederick III: Germany's Liberal Emperor* (Westport, CT, 1995).

———. "Politics for the Defence? Bismarck, Battenberg and the Origins of the Cartel of 1887." *German History* 13 (1995): 28–46.

———. "Die politischen Auswirkungen der 'Battenberg Affäre.'" In Rainer von Hessen (ed.), *Victoria Kaiserin Friedrich (1840–1901). Mission und Schicksal einer englischen Prinzessin in Deutschland* (Frankfurt am Main/New York, 2002), 179–195.

König, Wolfgang. *Wilhelm II. und die Moderne. Der Kaiser und die technisch-industrielle Welt* (Paderborn, 2007).

Königin von Preussen, Augusta. *Bekenntnisse an eine Freundin. Aufzeichnungen aus ihrer Freundschaft mit Jenny von Gustedt* (Dresden, 1935).

Krakau, Wiltrud-Irene. "Kaiserin Friedrich, ein Leben im Widersteit zwischen politischen Idealen und preussisch-deutscher Realität." In Karoline Müller and Friedrich Rothe (eds.), *Victoria von Preussen 1840–1901 in Berlin 2001* (Berlin, 2001), 94–202.

Die Krankheit Kaiser Friedrich des Dritten dargestellt nach amtlichen Quellen (Berlin, 1888).

Kraus, Hans-Christof. "Militärreform oder Verfassungswandel? Kronprinz Friedrich von Preussen und die 'deutschen Whigs' in der Krise von 1862/63." In Heinz Reif (ed.), *Adel und Bürgertum in Deutschland I, Entwicklungslinien und Wendepunkte im 19. Jahrhudert* (Berlin, 2000), 207–232.

Kroll, Frank-Lothar. "Friedrich der Grosse." In Etienne François and Hagen Schulze (eds.), *Deutsche Erinnerungsorte*, vol. 3 (Munich, 2001), 620–635.

Kugler, Franz. *Geschichte Friedrichs des Grossen*, new ed. (Leipzig, 1856).

Kühne, Thomas. "Das Deutsche Kaiserreich 1871–1918 und seine politische Kultur: Demokratisierung, Segmentierung, Militarisierung." *Neue Politische Literatur* 43 (1998): 206–263.

———. "Die Jahrhundertwende, die 'lange' Bismarckzeit und die Demokratisierung der politischen Kultur." In Lothar Gall (ed.), *Otto von Bismarck und Wilhelm II. Repräsentanten eines Epochenwechsels* (Paderborn, 2001), 85–118.

———. "Political Culture and Democratization." In James Retallack (ed.), *Imperial Germany, 1871–1918* (Oxford, 2008), 174–195.

Langewiesche, Dieter. *Liberalism in Germany* (Basingstoke, 2000).

———. "Politikstile im Kaiserreich. Zum Wandel von Politik und Öffentlichkeit im Zeitalter des 'politischen Massenmarktes.'" In Lothar Gall (ed.), *Regierung, Parlament und Öffentlichkeit im Zeitalter Bismarcks. Politikstile im Wandel* (Paderbron, 2003), 1–21.

Liehner, Leo. *Vaterländische Schulfeier. Ansprachen, Lieder und Gedichte zu Schulfeierlichkeiten* (Langensalza, 1893).

Lorenz, Angelika. *Das deutsche Familienbild in der Malerei des 19. Jahrhunderts* (Darmstadt, 1985).

Lucius von Ballhausen, Robert Freiherr. *Bismarck-Erinnerungen des Staatsministers Freiherr Lucius von Ballhausen*, 4th ed. (Stuttgart/Berlin, 1921).

Ludwig, Emil. "If the Emperor Frederick Had Not Had Cancer." In J. C. Squire (ed.), *If It Had Happened Otherwise* (London, 1972 [1st ed., 1932]), 223–248.

———. "Kaiser Friedrichs Liberalismus." *Vossische Zeitung* (28 Sept. 1926).

———. *Wilhelm der Zweite* (Berlin, 1926).

Luh, Jürgen. "Eine Erbschaft der Monarchie: Das Hohenzollern Museum." In Thomas Biskup and Martin Kohlrausch (eds.), *Das Erbe der Monarchie.*

Nachwirkungen einer deutschen Institution seit 1918 (Frankfurt am Main, 2008), 200–216.

Lyschinska, Mary I. *Henriette Schrader-Breymann. Ihr Leben aus Briefen und Tagebüchern zusammengestellt und erläutert,* 2 vols. (Berlin/Leipzig, 1922).

Mackenzie, Sir Morell. *The Fatal Illness of Frederick the Noble* (London, 1888).

Mannheim, Karl. "The Problem of Generations." In Karl Mannheim, *Essays on the Sociology of Knowledge* (London, 1952), 276–320.

Martin, Sir Theodore. *The Life of His Royal Highness the Prince Consort,* vol. 3 (London, 1877).

Maurenbrecher, Max. *Die Hohenzollern-Legende. Kulturbilder aus der preussischen Geschichte vom 12. bis zum 20. Jahrhundert,* 2 vols. (Berlin, about 1910).

Meisner, Heinrich O. (ed.). *Friedrich III., Das Kriegstagebuch von 1870/71* (Berlin/Leipzig, 1926).

———. (ed.). *Friedrich III., Tagebücher von 1848–1866* (Leipzig, 1929).

———. *Der preussische Kronprinz im Verfassungskampf 1863* (Berlin, 1931).

Menge, Karl. *Trauer und Treue. Gedichte zur Feier der Geburts und Sterbetage der deutschen Kaiser weiland Wilhelm I. und Friedrich III. sowie des Geburtstages Sr. Majestät des deutschen Kaisers und Königs von Preussen Wilhelm I.* (Leipzig, 1890).

Mommsen, Wilhelm (ed.). *Deutsche Parteiprogramme* (Munich, 1964).

Morier, Sir Robert. *Memoirs and Letters of the Right Hon. Sir Robert Morier, G.C.B. from 1826 to 1876,* 2 vols. (London, 1911).

Müller, Frank Lorenz. *Britain and the German Question: Perceptions of Nationalism and Political Reform 1830–1863* (Basingstoke, 2002).

———. "Perhaps Also Useful for Our Election Campaign: The Parliamentary Impasse of the Late Wilhelmine State and the British Constitutional Crisis, 1909–1911." In Dominik Geppert and Robert Gerwarth (eds.), *Wilhelmine Germany and Edwardian Britain: Essays on Cultural Affinity* (Oxford, 2008), 67–87.

Müller, Harald. "Robert von Puttkamer. Der Polizeiminister Bismarcks." In Gustav Seeber (ed.), *Gestalten der Bismarckzeit,* vol. 1 (Berlin, 1986), 355–377.

Müller-Bohn, Hermann. *Kaiser Friedrich der Gütige. Vaterländisches Ehrenbuch* (Berlin, 1900).

Müller-Plantenberg, Urs. *Der Freisinn nach Bismarcks Sturz. Ein Versuch über die Schwierigkeit des liberalen Bürgertums, im wilhelminischen Deutschland zu Macht und zu politischem Einfluss zu gelangen* (Phil. dissertation, Freie Universität Berlin, 1970).

Münch, Paul (ed.). *Ordnung, Fleiss und Sparsamkeit. Texte und Dokumente zur Entstehung der "bürgerlichen Tugenden"* (Munich, 1984).

Münkler, Herfried. *Die Deutschen und ihre Mythen* (Berlin, 2009).

Murray, Scott W. *Liberal Diplomacy and German Unification: The Early Career of Robert Morier* (Westport, CT, 2000).

Neumann, Hans-Joachim. *Friedrich III. Der 99-Tage-Kaiser* (Berlin, 2006).

Nichols, J. Alden. *The Year of the Three Kaisers: Bismarck and the German Succession 1887–1888* (Urbana/Chicago, 1987).

Nipperdey, Thomas. *Deutsche Geschichte 1866–1918. Machtstaat vor der Demokratie*, vol. 2 (Munich, 1992).

———. "Kommentar: 'Bürgerlich' als Kultur." In Jürgen Kocka (ed.), *Bürger und Bürgerlichkeit im 19. Jahrhundert* (Göttingen, 1987), 143–148.

———. "Nationalidee und Nationaldenkmal in Deutschland im 19. Jahrhundert." In Thomas Nipperdey, *Gesellschaft, Kultur, Theorie. Gesammelte Aufsätze zur neueren Geschichte* (Göttingen, 1976), 133–173.

Oexle, Otto Gerhard. "Canossa." In Etienne François and Hagen Schulze (eds.), *Deutsche Erinnerungsorte*, vol. 1 (Munich, 2001), 56–67.

Oncken, Herman (ed.). *Großherzog Friedrich I. von Baden und die deutsche Politik von 1854–1871. Briefwechsel, Denkschriften, Tagebücher*, 2 vols. (Stuttgart, 1927).

———. *Rudolf von Bennigsen. Ein deutscher liberaler Politiker. Nach seinen Reden und hinterlassenen Papieren*, 2 vols. (Stuttgart/Leipzig, 1910).

Osta, Jaap van. "The Emperor's New Clothes: The Reappearance of the Performing Monarchy in Europe, c. 1870–1914." In Jeroen Deploige and Gita Deneckere (eds.), *Mystifying the Monarch: Studies on Discourse, Power, and History* (Amsterdam, 2006), 181–192.

Paget, Walburga Lady. *Embassies of Other Days*, 2 vols. (London, 1923).

Pakula, Hannah. *An Uncommon Woman: The Empress Frederick, Daughter of Queen Victoria, Wife of the Crown Prince of Prussia, Mother of Kaiser Wilhelm* (New York, 1995).

Pallat, Ludwig. *Richard Schöne. Generaldirektor der Königlichen Museen zu Berlin. Ein Beitrag zur Geschichte der preussischen Kunstverwaltung 1872–1905* (Berlin, 1959).

Paret, Peter. *Art as History: Episodes in the Culture and Politics of Nineteenth-Century Germany* (Princeton, 1988).

Penzler, Johannes (ed.). *Die Reden Kaiser Wilhelms II. in den Jahren 1896–1900, Zweiter Teil* (Leipzig, 1904).

Perls, Arnold. *Kaiser Friedrich und seine hunderttätige Regierung. Ein Büchlein der Erinnerung allen freidenkenden Deutschen gewidmet* (München, 1888).

Petsch, Wilhelm. *Unser Fritz. Kronprinz Friedrich Wilhelms, Generalfeldmarschalls des deutschen Reichs, Leben und Thaten. Der deutschen Jugend erzählt* (Bielefeld/Leipzig, 1873).

Pflanze, Otto. *Bismarck and the Development of Germany*, 3 vols. (Princeton, 1990).

———. "Bismarck's Gedanken und Erinnerungen." In George Egerton (ed.), *Political Memoir: Essays on the Politics of Memory* (London, 1994), 28–61.

Philippson, Martin. *Friedrich III. als Kronprinz und Kaiser* (Berlin, 1893).

———. *Das Leben Kaiser Friedrichs III.*, 2nd ed. (Wiesbaden, 1908).

———. *Max von Forckenbeck. Ein Lebensbild* (Dresden/Leipzig, 1898).

———. "Die Zeit um 1870 in parlamentarischer Beleuchtung. Aus Forckenbecks Briefen an seine Gemahlin." *Deutsche Revue* 24 (1899): 129–146.

Pierer's Universal-Lexikon, vol. 3 (Leipzig, 1857), http://www.zeno.org/Pierer-1857, accessed 10 Aug. 2009.

Platzhoff, Walter. "England und der Kaiserplan vom Frühjahr 1870. Mit Benutzung unveröffentlichten Materials." *Historische Zeitschrift* 127 (1923): 454–475.

Plunkett, John. "Civic Publicness: The Creation of Queen Victoria's Royal Role 1837–61." In Laurel Brake and Julie F. Codell (eds.), *Encounters in the Victorian Press: Editors, Authors, Readers* (Basingstoke, 2005), 11–28.

———. *Queen Victoria: First Media Monarch* (Oxford, 2003).

Pogge von Strandmann, Hartmut. "Consequences of the Foundation of the German Empire: Colonial Expansion and the Process of Political-Economic Rationalization." In Stig Förster, Wolfgang J. Mommsen, and Ronald Robinson (eds.), *Bismarck, Europe, and Africa* (Oxford, 1988), 105–120.

———. "Domestic Origins of Germany's Colonial Expansion under Bismarck." *Past and Present* 42 (1969): 140–159.

———. *Imperialismus vom Grünen Tisch. Deutsche Kolonialpolitik zwischen wirtschaftlicher Ausbeutung und "zivilisatorischen" Bemühungen* (Berlin, 2009).

Ponsonby, Frederick (ed.). *Letters of the Empress Frederick* (London, 1928).

Poschinger, Margaretha von. *Kaiser Friedrich. In neuer quellenmässiger Darstellung,* 3 vols. (Berlin, 1899–1900).

Die Protokolle des Preussischen Staatsministeriums 1817–1934/38, ed. Berlin-Brandenburgische Akademie der Wissenschaften, vols. 5, 6/I, 6/II, and 7 [i.e., Acta Borussica, Neue Folge, Erste Reihe] (Hildesheim/Zürich/New York, 1999, 2001, 2004).

Quidde, Ludwig. *The Kaiser's Double: Being a Translation by Claud Field of the Celebrated Pamphlet by Prof. Ludwig Quidde entitled "Caligula: A Study in Imperial Insanity"* (London, 1915).

Rachfahl, Felix. "Eugen Richter und der Linksliberalismus im neuen Reiche." *Zeitschrift für Politik* 5 (1912): 261–374.

Radowitz, Joseph Maria von. *Aufzeichnungen und Erinnerungen aus dem Leben des Botschafters Joseph Maria von Radowitz,* vol. 1 (Berlin/Leipzig, 1925).

Radziwill, Princess Catherine. *The Empress Frederick* (London, 1934).

Ramm, Agatha (ed.). *Beloved and Darling Child: Last Letters between Queen Victoria and Her Eldest Daughter, 1886–1901* (Stroud, 1990).

Raschdau, Ludwig. *Unter Bismarck und Caprivi. Erinnerungen eines deutschen Diplomaten aus den Jahren 1885–1894* (Berlin, 1939).

Raschdorff, Julius Carl. *Ein Entwurf seiner Majestät des Kaisers und Königs Friedrich III. zum Neubau des Domes und zur Vollendung des Königlichen Schlosses in Berlin* (Berlin 1888).

Raumer, Kurt von. [Review of] "Kaiser Friedrich III. Das Kriegstagebuch von 1870/71. Herausgegeben von Heinrich Otto Meisner (Leipzig, 1926)." *Historische Zeitschrift* 140 (1929): 149–151.

Retallack, James. "Obrigkeitsstaat und politischer Massenmarkt." In Sven Oliver Müller and Cornelius Torp (eds.), *Das Deutsche Kaiserreich in der Kontroverse* (Göttingen, 2009), 121–135.

Rethwitsch, Ernst. *Culturfragen. Heft 4: Kaiser Friedrich und Bismarck* (Berlin, 1888).

Rhein, Karin. *Deutsche Orientmalerei in der zweiten Hälfte des Neunzehnten Jahrhunderts. Entwicklung und Chrakteristika* (Berlin, 2004).

Rich, Norman. *Friedrich von Holstein: Politics and Diplomacy in the Era of Bismarck and Wilhelm II,* vol. 1 (Cambridge, 1965).

Richter, B. *Kleine Episoden und Charakterzüge aus dem Leben unseres Kaisers Friedrich III.* (Reudnitz/Leizig, 1888).

Richter, Eugen. *Im alten Reichstag. Erinnerungen,* 2 vols. (Berlin, 1894, 1896).

Richter, Julius. *Kaiser Friedrich III.,* 12th ed. (Berlin, undated).

Richter, Werner. *Friedrich III. Leben und Tragik des zweiten Hohenzollern-Kaisers* (Munich, 1981 [1st ed., 1938]).

Riehl, Axel T. G. *Der "Tanz um den Äquator." Bismarcks antienglische Kolonialpolitik und die Erwartung des Thronwechsels in Deutschland 1883–1885* (Berlin, 1993).

Robolsky, Hermann. *Drei Jahre auf dem Thron 1888–1891* (Leipzig, 1891).

Rockel, Irina. *Wilhelm Gentz* (Berlin, 1997).

Rogge, Bernhard. *Friedrich der Dritte. Deutscher Kaiser und König von Preussen. Ein Lebensbild,* 3rd ed. (Leipzig, 1895).

Rohe, Karl. "Politische Kultur und ihre Analyse. Probleme und Perspektiven der politischen Kulturforschung." *Historische Zeitschrift* 250 (1990): 321–346.

Rohkrämer, Thomas. *Der Militarismus der "kleinen Leute." Die Kriegervereine im Deutschen Kaiserreich 1871–1914* (Munich, 1990).

Röhl, John C. G. *The Kaiser and His Court: Wilhelm II and the Government of Germany* (Cambridge, 1994).

———. *Wilhelm II. Der Aufbau der Persönlichen Monarchie 1888–1900* (Munich, 2001).

———. *Wilhelm II. Die Jugend des Kaisers 1859–1888* (Munich, 1993).

———. *Wilhelm II: The Kaiser's Personal Monarchy, 1888–1900* (Cambridge, 2004).

Roon, Albrecht von. *Denkwürdigkeiten aus dem Leben des Generalfeldmarschalls Kriegsministers Grafen von Roon,* vol. 2, 5th ed. (Berlin, 1905).

Roth, Ludwig. "Die Tragik im Leben Kaiser Friedrichs III." *Der Türmer* (Oct. 1931): 46–48.

Rothfels, Hans. "Das Kriegstagebuch Kaiser Friedrichs." *Preussische Jahrbücher* 203 (1926): 292–296.

Russell, William H. *My Diary during the Last Great War* (London, 1874).

Schieder, Theodor. *Das Deutsche Kaiserreich von 1871 als Nationalstaat* (Cologne/Opladen, 1961).

Schmid, Michael. *Der "Eiserne Kanzler" und die Generäle. Deutsche Rüstungspolitik in der Ära Bismarck, 1871–1890* (Paderborn, 2003).

Schneider, Louis. *Aus dem Leben Kaiser Wilhelms 1849–1873,* vol. 2 (Berlin, 1888).

Schneider, Reinhold. *Die Hohenzollern* (Cologne, 1958 [1st ed., 1933]).

Scholtz, Gerhard. *Übersprungene Generation 1888* (PhD dissertation, University of Heidelberg, 1934).

Schöne, Richard. "Rede bei der Trauerfeier der K. Museen zum Gedächtnis Seiner Majestät des in Gott ruhenden Kaisers und Königs Friedrich III." *Jahrbuch der Königlich Preussischen Kunstsammlungen* 9 (1888): 201–208.

Schrader, Karl. "Viktoria, verwitwete Kaiserin und Königin Friedrich." In Anton Bettelheim (ed.), *Biographisches Handbuch und deutscher Nekrolog* 7 (Berlin, 1905), 451–465.

Schröder, Ernst. "Karl von Normann (1827–1888)." In Adolf Hofmeister and Wilhelm Braun (eds.), *Pommersche Lebensbilder. Vol. 3, Pommern des 18., 19. und 20. Jahrhunderts* (Stettin, 1939), 327–340.

Schröter, Barbara. *Die Denkmäler Kaiser Friedrichs III.* (MA dissertation, Freie Universität Berlin, 1989).

Schulte, Regina. "Der Aufstieg der konstitutionellen Monarchie und das Gedächtnis der Königin." *Historische Anthropologie* 6 (1998): 76–104.

Schulthess, Heinrich. *Schulthess' Europäischer Geschichtskalender 1883, 1887, 1888, 1889* (Nördlingen, 1884, 1888, 1889; Munich, 1890).

Schümann, Carl Wolfgang. *Der Berliner Dom im 19. Jahrhundert* (Berlin, 1980).

Schuster, Georg (ed.). *Briefe, Reden und Erlasse des Kaisers und Königs Friedrichs III* (Berlin 1907).

Schweinitz, Lothar von. *Briefwechsel des Botschafters General v. Schweinitz* (Berlin, 1928).

———. *Denkwürdigkeiten des Botschafters General v. Schweinitz*, 2 vols. (Berlin, 1927).

Seeber, Gustav. *Zwischen Bebel und Bismarck. Zur Geschichte des Linksliberalismus in Deutschland 1871–1893* (Berlin, 1965).

Seidel, L. E. *Friedrich III. Kaiser von Deutschland und König von Preussen. Ein Lebensbild für Schule und Haus*, 2nd ed. (Langensalza, 1890).

Sepp, Johannes and Bernhard Sepp. "Das Resultat der deutschen Ausgrabunden in Tyrus." *Historische Zeitschrift* 44 (1880): 86–109.

Sheehan, James J. *German Liberalism in the Nineteenth Century* (Chicago/London, 1978).

Showalter, Dennis. *The Wars of German Unification* (London, 2004).

Smith, Woodruff. *The Ideological Origins of Nazi Imperialism* (Oxford, 1986).

Speth, Rudolf. "Königin Luise von Preussen—deutscher Nationalmythos im 19. Jahrhundert." In Sabine Berghahn and Sirgrid Koch-Baumgarten (eds.), *Mythos Diana—von der Princess of Wales zur Queen of Hearts* (Giessen, 1999), 265–286.

Stamm-Kuhlmann, Thomas. "War Friedrich Wilhelm III. ein 'Bürgerkönig'?" *Zeitschrift für historische Forschung* 16 (1989): 441–460.

Steffens, Martin and Gunnar Hermann. "Die Wittenberger Schlosskirche als Denkmalsbau." In Martin Steffens and Insa Christiane Hennen (eds.), *Von der Kapelle zum Nationaldenkmal. Die Wittenberger Schlosskirche* (Wittenberg, 1998), 105–122.

Steinbach, Peter. "Politische Kultur. Politische Wertvorstellungen zwischen ständischer Gesellschaft und Moderne." In Dieter Langewiesche (ed.), *Ploetz. Das deutsche Kaiserreich 1867/71–1918*. *Bilanz einer Epoche* (Freiburg/Würzburg, 1984), 197–214.

Steinmetz, Hans-Otto. "Noch einmal, Bismarck–Stosch." *Wehrwissenschaftliche Rundschau* 19 (1969): 703–713.

Stenographische Berichte über die Verhandlungen der beiden Häuser des Landtages. Haus der Abgeordneten, vol. 1 (Berlin, 1884).

Stenographische Berichte über die Verhandlungen des Reichstags (Berlin, 1871–).

Stosch, Albrecht von. *Denkwürdigkeiten des Generals und Admirals Albrecht von Stosch*, ed. Ulrich von Stosch (Stuttgart, 1904).

Studemund, Wilhelm. *Rede zum Gedächtniss Sr. Majestät des hochseligen Kaisers und Königs Friedrich III. in der Aula Leopoldia der kgl. Universität Breslau am 25. Juni 1888 gehalten* (Breslau, 1888).

Suur, Hemmo. *Erster Jahresbericht der Kaiser-Friedrichs-Schule zu Emdem* (Emden, 1889).

Das Tagebuch des Kronprinzen. Aussprüche, Briefe und andere Kundgebungen (Berlin, 1886).

Taylor, Alan J. P. *The Course of German History: A Survey of the Development of German History since 1815* (London/New York, 2001).

Thompson, Alastair. *Left Liberals, the State and Popular Politics in Wilhelmine Germany* (Oxford, 2000).

Treitschke, Heinrich von. "Zwei Kaiser." *Preussische Jahrbücher* 62 (1888): 77–86.

Turk, Eleanor L. "The Batttenberg Affair: Chancellor Crisis or 'Media Event'?" *German Studies Review* 5 (1982): 233–255.

Turner, Henry A. "Bismarck's Imperialist Venture: Anti-British in Origin?" In Prosser Gifford and William R. Louis (eds.), *Britain and Germany in Africa: Imperial Rivalry and Colonial Rule* (New Haven, CT, 1967), 47–82.

Tyrrell, Alex, and Yvonne Ward. "'God Bless Her Little Majesty': The Popularising of Monarchy in the 1840s." *National Identities* 2 (2000): 109–125.

Ullmann, Hans-Peter. *Politik im deutschen Kaiserreich 1871–1918* (Munich, 1999).

Unser Fritz. Patriotische Erzählung aus unsern Tagen (Dresden, 1888).

Urbach, Karina. *Bismarck's Favourite Englishman. Lord Odo Russell's Mission to Berlin* (London, 1999).

Valentin, Veit. *The German People: Their History and Civilization from the Holy Roman Empire to the Third Reich* (New York, 1946).

Verba, Sidney. "Comparative Political Culture." In Lucian Pye and Sidney Verba (eds.), *Political Culture and Political Development* (Princeton, 1969), 512–560.

Vierhaus, Rudolf (ed.). *Das Tagebuch der Baronin Spitzemberg. Aufzeichnungen aus der Hofgesellschaft des Hohenzollernreiches* (Göttingen, 1960).

Vogel, Jakob. "Zwischen protestantischem Herrscherideal und Mittelaltermystik. Wilhelm I. und die 'Mythosmotorik' des Deutschen Kaiserreichs." In Gerd

Krumeich and Hartmut Lehmann (eds.), *Gott mit uns! Nation, Religion und Gewalt im 19. und frühen 20. Jahrhundert* (Göttingen, 2000), 213–230.

Vogel, Johannes. *Ansprache bei der Gedenkfeier an den 100jährigen Geburtstag weiland Sr. Majestät Kaiser Friedrich III. gehalten in der Friedenskirche zu Sanssouci am 18. Oktober 1931* (Potsdam, 1931).

Wagner, Yvonne. *Prinzenerziehung in der 2. Hälfte des 19. Jahrhunderts. Zum Bildungsverhalten des preussisch-deutschen Hofes im gesellschaftlichen Wandel* (Frankfurt am Main, 1995).

Waldau, Max. *Max Waldau für Gottfried Kinkel. An den Prinzen Friedrich Wilhelm von Preussen* (Ratibor, 1850).

Waldersee, Alfred Graf von. *Aus dem Briefwechsel des Generalfeldmarschalls Alfred Grafen von Waldersee. Vol. 1, Die Berliner Jahre 1886–1891*, ed. Heinrich Otto Meisner (Berlin/Leipzig, 1928).

———. *Denkwürdigkeiten des General-Feldmarschalls Alfred Grafen von Waldersee*, ed. Heinrich Otto Meisner, 3 vols. (Stuttgart/Berlin, 1922, 1923).

War Correspondence of the Daily News 1870, 2 vols. (London, 1871).

Wawro, Geoffrey. *The Austro-Prussian War: Austria's War with Prussia and Italy in 1866* (Cambridge, 1996).

———. *The Franco-Prussian War: The German Conquest of France in 1870–1871* (Cambridge, 2003).

Weber, Marie-Lise. *Ludwig Bamberger. Ideologie statt Realpolitik* (Stuttgart, 1987).

Wehler, Hans-Ulrich. *Bismarck und der Imperialismus* (Cologne, 1969).

———. *Deutsche Gesellschaftsgeschichte*, vol. 3: 1849–1914 (Munich, 1995).

Weichlein, Siegfried. *Nation und Region. Integrationsprozesse im Bismarckreich* (Düsseldorf, 2004).

Wentzcke, Paul, and Julius Heyderhoff (eds.). *Deutscher Liberalismus im Zeitalter Bismarcks. Eine politische Briefsammlung*, 2 vols. (Bonn/Leipzig, 1925, 1926).

Werner, Anton von. *Erlebnisse und Eindrücke 1870–1890* (Berlin, 1913).

———. *Jugenderinnerungen, 1843–1870*, ed. Dominik Bartmann (Berlin, 1994).

Wienfort, Monika. *Monarchie in der bürgerlichen Gesellschaft. Deutschland und England von 1640 bis 1848* (Göttingen, 1993).

William II. *My Early Life* (London, 1926).

Windelband, Wolfgang. *Berlin-Madrid-Rom. Bismarck und die Reise des Deutschen Kronprinzen 1883* (Essen, 1939).

——— (ed.). *Johanna von Bismarcks Briefe* (Berlin, 1924).

Windt, Franziska. "Majestätische Bilderflut. Die Kaiser in der Photographie." In *Die Kaiser und die Macht der Medien*, ed. Generaldirektion der Stiftung Preußische Schlösser und Gärten Berlin-Brandenburg (Berlin, 2005), 67–77.

Winkler, Heinrich August. *Germany: The Long Road West, Vol. 1: 1789–1933* (Oxford, 2006).

Wippermann, Karl. *Deutscher Geschichtskalender für 1888*, vol. 2 (Leipzig, 1889); *Deutscher Geschichtskalender für 1889*, vol. 1 (Leipzig, 1889).

Wolbe, Eugen. *Kaiser Friedrich. Die Tragödie des Übergangenen* (Hellerau bei Dresden, 1931).

Wolf, Hans-Joachim. *Die Krankheit Friedrichs III. und ihre Wirkung auf die deutsche und englische Öffentlichkeit* (Berlin, 1958).

Wülfing, Wulf, Karin Bruns, and Rolf Parr. *Historische Mythologie der Deutschen 1798–1918* (Munich, 1991).

Ziegler, Theobald. *Die geistigen and sozialen Strömungen des neunzehnten Jahrhunderts* (Berlin, 1911 [1st ed., 1899]).

Ziekursch, Johannes. *Politische Geschichte des neuen deutschen Kaiserreiches. Vol. 2: Das Zeitalter Bismarck, 1871–1890* (Frankfurt am Main, 1927).

Ziemssen, Ludwig. *Friedrich. Deutscher Kaiser und König von Preussen. Ein Lebensbild* (Berlin, 1888).

Zimmermann, Alfred. *Geschichte der deutschen Kolonialpolitik* (Berlin, 1914).

Acknowledgments

Writing can sometimes feel like a solitary occupation. It is therefore a real pleasure to look back and realise how many people have come to my aid at every step of the way. Numerous institutions and individuals provided crucial support for the completion of this book and I am glad to record my gratitude to them.

My research attracted generous funding from the Arts and Humanities Research Council, the Royal Society of Edinburgh/Caledonian Research Foundation, the Carnegie Trust for the Universities of Scotland, and the School of History at St. Andrews University, which also granted me two semesters of leave. Besides, I am greatly indebted to the staff of the Geheimes Staatsarchiv Preußischer Kulturbesitz, the Hessische Hausstiftung at Fasanerie Palace (where Ms. Christine Klössel spent weeks patiently dealing with my requests), the Royal Archives in Windsor Castle, the Bundesarchiv, the Niedersächsisches Staatsarchiv in Wolfenbüttel, the archive of Balliol College Oxford, the Staatsbibliothek Preußischer Kulturbesitz, and St. Andrews University Library for their expert assistance. The Wehrgeschichtliches Museum (Rastatt), the archive of the Bonner General-Anzeiger, and the city archives in Aachen, Augsburg, Wilhelmshaven, Wittenberg, and Wuppertal promptly answered my queries. For help with the illustrations, I am grateful to the Bildagentur für Kunst, Kultur und Geschichte (Preußischer Kulturbesitz), the Hessische Hausstiftung, and the Stiftung Preußische Schlösser und Gärten Berlin-Brandenburg. Finally, I would like to acknowledge the kind permissions of Her Majesty Queen Elizabeth II and of the Hessische Hausstiftung to make use of material I examined in the Royal Archives and at Fasanerie Palace.

Over the last few years, several colleagues and friends have supported my work on this book in a variety of kind ways. I received tremendous advice from Michael Bentley, Konrad Canis, Chris Clark, Jerry DeGroot, Michael Gratzke, the late Iselin Gundermann, Jürgen Luh, Jan Rüger, Martin Steffens, and Miles Taylor. Andy Eccles cheerfully came to my rescue every time my computer skills proved inadequate.

Manfred von Stosch could not have been more charming when he invited me into his family home to examine the Stosch Papers. I owe a particular debt of gratitude to Riccardo Bavaj, Susan Chesters, Hartmut Pogge von Strandmann, Bernhard Struck, the two readers commissioned by Harvard University Press, and especially to Rona Johnston Gordon, who all commented on the manuscript. Their eagle eyes, linguistic skill, historical expertise, and sound judgement vastly improved the final product. As ever, Dominik Geppert not only read the entire text but has also helped me with numerous queries. His counsel and friendship continue to be a delight. I am grateful to my friends and colleagues at St. Andrews, whose patience, wit, and good cheer make the School of History such an excellent place to work; to Kathleen McDermott at Harvard University Press and to Barbara Goodhouse and Frances Lyon at Westchester Book Group for their friendly professionalism; and to my parents for being such great friends and marvellous hosts during my many trips "home" to Berlin.

I would like to end by thanking my wonderful wife, Celia, whose unwavering support enabled me to concentrate happily on *Our Fritz*. Our sons, Hugo and Nicholas, never fully approved of my leaving the house in the morning "to write my book," but they still welcomed me back enthusiastically every evening. It is for this generosity of spirit—and with much love—that I dedicate it to them.

Index